QUERENCIA

QUERENCIAS SERIES

Miguel A. Gandert and Enrique R. Lamadrid | SERIES EDITORS

Querencia is a popular term in the Spanish-speaking world that is used to express a deeply rooted love of place and people. This series promotes a transnational, humanistic, and creative vision of the US-Mexico borderlands based on all aspects of expressive culture, both material and intangible.

Also available in the Querencias Series:

Nación Genízara: Ethnogenesis, Place, and Identity in New Mexico
  edited by Moises Gonzales and Enrique R. Lamadrid
El Camino Real de California: From Ancient Pathways to Modern Byways
  by Joseph P. Sánchez
Imagine a City That Remembers: The Albuquerque Rephotography Project
  by Anthony Anella and Mark C. Childs
The Latino Christ in Art, Literature, and Liberation Theology
  by Michael R. Candelaria
Sisters in Blue/Hermanas de azul: Sor María de Ágreda Comes to New Mexico/
  Sor María de Aztlán: Essays on the Chicano Homeland, Revised and
  Expanded Edition edited by Francisco A. Lomelí, Rudolfo Anaya
  and Enrique R. Lamadrid
Río: A Photographic Journey down the Old Río Grande edited by
  Melissa Savage
Coyota in the Kitchen: A Memoir of New and Old Mexico by Anita Rodríguez
Chasing Dichos through Chimayó by Don J. Unser
Enduring Acequias: Wisdom of the Land, Knowledge of the Water
  by Juan Estevan Arellano
Hotel Mariachi: Urban Space and Cultural Heritage in Los Angeles
  by Catherine L. Kurland and Enrique R. Lamadrid
Sagrado: A Photopoetics across the Chicano Homeland by Spencer R. Herrera
  and Levi Romero

For additional titles in the Querencias Series, please visit unmpress.com.

Querencia

REFLECTIONS ON THE
NEW MEXICO HOMELAND

Edited by Vanessa Fonseca-Chávez, Levi Romero,
and Spencer R. Herrera ❉ *Foreword by Rudolfo Anaya*

University of New Mexico Press Albuquerque

ISBN 978-0-8263-6160-8 (paper)
ISBN 978-0-8263-6161-5 (e-book)

Library of Congress Cataloging-in-Publication data is on file
with the Library of Congress.

*Support for indexing was generously provided by the University of New Mexico
Center for Regional Studies (A. Gabriel Meléndez) and the University of
New Mexico Southwest Hispanic Research Institute (Irene Vásquez).*

DEDICACIÓN

Dedicamos esta obra a Juan Estevan Arellano, quien sus reflexiones y amor a la querencia dieron nacimiento a una continuación de búsqueda y afirmación de nuestro sentido sobre nuestras querencias y lo perteneciente.

We dedicate this work to Juan Estevan Arellano, whose reflections and love of *la querencia* gave birth to a continued search and affirmation for our own sense of home and belonging.

CONTENTS

ILLUSTRATIONS

Querencia, Mi patria chica

RUDOLFO ANAYA

One of the fondest and most impressionable memories of my childhood was when my father bought two solares on which to construct our home. This was in Santa Rosa, New Mexico, in the early 1940s. The solares were across the river from the town. On that lomita, my father, my three older brothers, friends, and neighbors slowly raised our casita de adobes, built a two-sitter escusa'o, dug a cisterna, used dynamite to dig a well, constructed a windmill, and built a corral for the cow and a hutch where I raised rabbits and chickens.

This all took time; we didn't have the money to raise the house all at once. One morning, the men gathered, drove stakes in the ground, tied a yellow string to mark the foundation, and started digging. We had no architect. Still, poco a poco, the house, a labor of love, rose to the sky on that lomita. I grew up in that humilde casita that, each day, rose to the sky to greet the sun. With my dog, Sporty, I explored the llano. I was king of tall yucca, junipers, mesquites, jackrabbits, lizards, chipmunks, gavilanes, mockingbirds, owls, and an occasional coyote. Down the gentle slope of the lomita lay the Pecos River, where I spent my summers playing with neighborhood kids. Across the river rose the town.

A solar has a different connotation than a lote. The name implies it is a place blessed by the sun. Solar is the beginning of home, where the sun shines, where family lives and thrives. The sun blessed our casita, giving birth to resolana.

Resolana: the bright morning sun that warms the east-facing adobe wall. For me, resolana implies the reasoning/planning part of the day, the brain activated for work. The men helping my father would take time to sit on bancos against the warm wall before starting to work. Tools were readied, plans for the day's labor were discussed and perhaps a vecino would drop by to help. Or just to shoot the bull.

"Buenos días le dé Dios. ¿Cómo va la casa?" So began la plática, discussing the day's work, talking, sharing experiences—"Cuando yo levanté mi casa . . ."—on and on, telling stories, cuentos—the oral tradition expanding from centuries past to the present, the wisdom of the ancestors alive, and I listening.

My uncle Pedro con sus adivinanzas: "Una mujer vieja con un diente, que llama a toda la gente. ¿Qué es?"

"¡La campana de la iglesia! ¡La campana!"

"Toma un nicle. Curre, cómprate un dulce."

I gave the nickel to my sisters, Angie and Edwina, and they ran to the gas station by the bridge to buy candy.

Other concerns rose in la plática: "Pues, mis niños need shoes. Clothes for school."

"Mi vieja keeps asking when I'm going to buy her a sewing machine. No hay dinero."

"We have to teach the chamacos respeto, the correct way to greet tíos, tías, abuelos, older people. 'Ora hablan puro inglés."

Then there was Don José, who drove in from town just to watch the progress and gossip. "Agarra la pala, José," my father said, "vamos hacer adobes."

"No, no tengo tiempo. Voy pal post office por mi cheque." As he drove away, the men chuckled. Don José only liked to supervise.

I remember my brothers mixing the mud, the zoquete they poured into forms, two—sometimes four—adobes to each form. My job was to wash the inside of the form before the mud was poured. If it was nice and wet, the adobes would slide right off, leaving perfect adobes in place. After the top dried, I went down the row turning each adobe over, so the bottom side would dry. The hot New Mexico sun was at work, so our casita was made of mud and sun energy.

My mother didn't have the luxury of a true resolana. Her work was constant—preparing meals, always piles of tortillas on the table, a pot of beans bubbling on the stove, the aroma of home, watching over us kids, dishes, washing clothes, ironing. She worked as hard as any man. Resolana belonged to the men; my mother's work was continuous and hard. Her resolana was the prayers she offered to La Virgen to take care of her family.

After a hard day's work, my father and his friends would sit in la sombra where resolana had now turned into shade. Tired and immensely proud of what they had accomplished that day, they gave thanks. "Gracias a Dios." One of the men had brought home-brewed beer, which had cooled in the well all day. That and roll-your-own cigarettes were a treat at the end of the day. There is nothing tastier and more robust than home-brewed beer. I know: my father let me taste it.

Sombra is the sister of resolana. She sneaks in late in the afternoon. Both men and animals seek the shade on a hot New Mexico afternoon. My mother would arrive to look over the work done that day. She was especially interested in the kitchen, the sacristy of the home. Now she, too, rested and gave thanks. Time to let the working part of the brain rest.

For me, sombra is the intuitive part of the day, that in-between time that leads to supper, then sleep. A welcomed quietness would come over our lomita, with only the sounds of us kids playing hide-and-seek or kick-the-can well into darkness.

Querencia is love of home, love of place. That is the love I felt for our humble home. Querencia are those prayers I still hear echoing in our sala where, nightly, my mother led us in rosaries and prayers for her family. When World War II started, my three brothers enlisted. Gone to foreign places far from home. My mother's prayers grew in length and intensity.

El soldado razo went not only to defend his country: he went to defend his querencia. His querida patria included family and neighbors. La querida patria is our querencia. We live in a big country, but we also live in the smaller patria chica that contains the villages of the vicinity, los vecinos. Every village or town is a city-state, a patria chica. Love for our querencia spreads out to the larger country. Our love is strong because it has its center at home, in our casita, en los solares, our neighbors, the land, the river, and the llano.

El maestro Cleofes Vigil from San Cristobal called the villages of northern New Mexico "las naciones de las montañas de la Sangre de Cristo." Each village is a nation-state, like the city-states of ancient Greece. He taught us the history of la patria chica, which included all the Hispano villages and the Indian pueblos. La patria chica includes all the vecinos. What an honor and joy it was to hear him singing in that booming voice he possessed, playing his mandolin. He taught querencia to generations of New Mexicans. He taught us wisdom and heritage. I miss the maestro.

I remember once, at his home, he intoned in his deep voice, "When the españoles came from Mexico, they didn't bring many women. They found the beautiful inditas." With that simple statement, he described our Indo-Hispano heritage and history. For him, our love of querencia had led back to the Pueblos, our Native American vecinos. Their love of querencia is centuries old. From them, we learned a deep, enduring love for the sacredness of the earth, for the unity of life, for a harmony that brings peace and happiness. Querencia means vecinos.

Our villages and towns throughout the state, from the mountains of el norte to the southern desert, are the web of our querida patria, united in language, culture, and history. Our first love and loyalty are to our parents, la casa, el solar, but also to our neighbors. From the intimate rincones of home, love spreads out to encompass vecinos, villages, the state, the nation. Each village is a city-state, a querencia embodying the wisdom that our ancestors passed down to us. The history they created is our querencia, and we must know it and honor it.

Querer is to love, querencia is love. For me, it is more than sense of place: it is a special relationship to la madre tierra that produces our food. I learned about this relationship from the love we had for our solar, our casa, the extended family. I also learned from my abuelo and tíos who farmed in Puerto de Luna.

Acequias came into my life when, as a child, I visited my abuelo and saw how the village men diverted water from the river and passed it down the acequia madre to each parciante. They endured the hard work of survival in the summer sun, the loss of flowering trees to late spring freezes, grasshoppers, working through dust storms knee-deep in zoquete. This, too, is my querencia.

La tierra is inseminated by el Abuelo Sol, he who grants us solar, he who creates green, the energy of life. We greet the morning light, el amanecer, and give thanks to a Greater Power. Long ago, I heard a Native woman sing this song to the morning sun: "Grandfather, a song I am sending, a song I am sending. Come bless all of life, warm the earth so our crops will blossom, bless our home and family, our neighbors, bless the children and our old people, bless all forms of life, fish and fowl, the two-legged and the four-legged. Grandfather, a song of blessing I am sending you, warm Mother Earth, bring us rain, for el agua es vida." This song still resonates with me and, so, each morning I give thanks for the amanecer, the first light of dawn. I ask a blessing from Dios Grande and all of my mother's santitos. I ask Grandfather Sun to bless the earth and all life within and upon it.

What happens when two cultures meet, each with its own sensibility of querencia? Such was the case in 1598 when the españoles came from Mexico to settle in the Pueblo world of northern New Mexico. El norte. The

Indigenous Pueblos long ago had established their sovereign knowledge and their identities, which included religion and oral tradition. In short, each Pueblo enjoyed a deep, abiding sense of querencia.

I believe the Pueblos influenced, in very meaningful ways, how the españoles came to view their new home in el norte. Two different worlds but each tied to a sense of place, la madre tierra, the water, farming techniques, chile and corn. The Pueblos assisted the españoles and, at the same time, they had to resist the power of colonial oppression. They had to resist part of the foreigner's knowledge that was harmful to their own. Thus, we have 1680. My point is this: to understand querencia from our viewpoint today, we have to understand the history of querencia. If querencia is anything, it is respect for vecinos, love for the sacred earth, knowing that el agua es vida. Querencia love permeates our history.

Cleofes Vigil understood how much the Pueblos had shared with the españoles. They helped them survive those years after 1598. The Pueblo love of querencia was shared with the españoles through hard work, stories, songs, ceremonies, fiestas. I think it is fair to say that the Pueblo World's subliminal knowledge of querencia became part of our birthright. In 1680, the love between vecinos broke down. The Pueblos resisted. After that revolution, querencia had to be reestablished and la querida patria made to thrive again. The lesson learned: all world views must be respected. This is part of our querencia, and we must teach it to the young.

Mi abuelo Liborio Mares and his sons took water from the Pecos River and farmed the Puerto de Luna Valley. The first bite of one of their apples always burst sweet in my mouth, spraying juices made in heaven. They harvested the best and most picante chile verde in the state. By October, dozens of ristras hung against houses and barns. People came from everywhere to buy ristras, apples, sweet corn, pumpkins, and other vegetables.

As a child visiting my tíos y tías, I first learned the knowledge of acequias. Now, I am a parciante on the West Side acequia in Jemez Springs. For the past thirty years, I have turned the water from the acequia to my arboleda de manzanas. I have become a green man. With a pala in hand, I turn the water to the trees to quench their New Mexico thirst.

Ay Dios, time caught up with me. I can no longer farm, cannot turn the water down to the trees. I am forever grateful to my vecino Melvin Maestas who makes sure the trees are getting irrigated. I am there in memory. The apples ripen in September, boxes of fruit for family, friends, vecinos. The apples from Puerto de Luna and Jemez Springs awaken querencia. I dream of empapá Liborio. I give thanks.

I learned how acequia culture developed and became a village that included the parciantes who built the compuerta at the river, dug the ditch a pura pala, elected mayordomos and commissioners to set rules, designated the days when each parciante could irrigate, called each parciante in the spring to clean the acequia on el Día de San Juan. With this water, they baptized. All these endeavors formed a village. Acequia culture is a village that has its own government, a patria chica. The vecinos take care of each other. All this is querencia, and it has a history.

If there is an acequia culture, I have come to believe there is also a pala culture, the culture of the shovel, a tool the españoles brought. Working la madre tierra is a spiritual endeavor; it is also hard work. To create a village is hard work but, in the end, the water flows down the rows and creates the magic of green. El agua es vida. Every querencia needs the spiritual water of life that sustains the soul. Ánima is querencia.

I asked my grandfather, "How did you dig this acequia?"

"A pura pala," he answered. With shovel in hand.

A pura pala is a nuevomexicano chant, a mantra, a song sung on the way to work. Hard work. Miles of ditch dug with only shovels in hand.

A student asked me, "How did you write all those books?"

I answered, "A pura pala."

These anecdotes I have shared describe what querencia means to me, starting with our casita in Santa Rosa. Although one moves from place to place, the querencia of childhood cannot be erased from memory. There were five houses in our neighborhood then, but many years later when I went back our lomita was dotted with homes. Someone else's home now sits on our solar. The well is dry, the windmill only a memory. Todo se acabó. Sólo la memoria queda.

I have fond memories of our home in Alburquerque, a querencia in the barrio. Then, years later, my wife Patricia and I built a beautiful adobe home dedicated to peace and harmony on the West Mesa. The round room contains the sipapu. My journey as a Nuevomexicano Chicano has come full circle.

I share some of my personal journey with you fully realizing that each one of you has a different history of home and querencia, which leads me to believe that one can make querencia wherever one lives. Whether you live in a house or apartment in the city, an army tent in Iraq or a bunk in an aircraft carrier on the Sea of Japan, or in the loneliest of places—prison—love can make querencia. Your spiritual quest can make querencia.

Over the years I have received letters from prisoners serving time. I have files full of these letters and, recently, I read through them. The prisoners have one thing in common—the desire to reconnect with their culture and history. In other words, forced by discrimination and all its gross ramifications, these men have been separated from the teachings of our ancestors. One man wrote that he found a few answers in some of my books that had found their way into his hands. We need to send more of our literature into prisons. Books as teachers.

These men realize that la cultura cura, but where can they find the cultura they've lost? Where is their querencia and how can they recover it? Mario, a young man from Los Angeles, has written a play and many stories. Can his writings become his querencia? Some pintos have come out of prison with excellent, self-taught mastery in writing. Their stories are our querencia.

Carlos read my essay on Aztlán and that has become his focus and sanity while in prison. He calls me the Gran Aztlanero. Being Aztlaneros connects us. It connects him not only to the outside world, but also to the central concept of Chicanismo. Aztlán is querencia, and Carlos has made it his home. He promised to look me up when he got out. I hope one day he comes knocking at my door.

The terrible "three strikes, you're out" California law sentenced Bruce to a very long time in prison. That law is incarcerating mostly Blacks and Chicanos. Bruce didn't join the Chicano prison gangs, so he found himself isolated. And he certainly didn't fit in with the skinheads. But while doing time, he attended a sweat lodge ceremony and found a family there. He found his Native American roots. Today, he is head drummer at ceremonies. The lodge and the drumming have become his querencia. He still writes me and always sends a blessing from the Great Spirit.

Just days ago, I received a request from a young man doing time at the Bernalillo County Metropolitan Detention Center here in town: "Send me books about Chicanos. Who are we? I feel lost." There someone was again, seeking roots, seeking querencia.

Where do we go from here if we know there are so many without a home? Or who are in prisons, hospitals, nursing homes, suffering from abuse? Where can they find a home, a center that will sustain them? I am thankful that during my childhood I enjoyed the center of family and home, but what can

I do now for others not so fortunate? What can *we* do, we who have enjoyed the love of querencia? I think we have to expand the meaning of querencia. This is what pintos searching for their roots have taught me. In their deepest memories, they know la cultura cura. Our culture cures. They know querencia can be that spiritual center that will sustain them.

There is an old nuevomexicano song, an indita, that is part of our folklore. Enrique Lamadrid turned me on to "Marcelina, la cautiva." I have listened many times to this song, the saddest song ever composed in New Mexico. Quite often, I find myself singing verses from this indita, be it aloud or in my mind.

It goes like this. Many, many years ago a gang of Natives attacked the village where Marcelina lived with her family and neighbors. The Natives killed some and took others captive, including Marcelina. As she is being dragged away, Marcelina turns and, one by one, she tells the story of those who were killed.

Her heart is heavy with grief, her song plaintive. At the end of each verse, she says she will never love again. To have loved those who now lie dead is a great sorrow. She understands that to love is to feel pain when loss occurs. Each verse ends with a mournful cry, "Por eso ya en este mundo no quiero más amar. De mi quierida patria, me van a retirar."

Even her children lie dead, those she loved the most. That is why she will never love again. She is overcome with the most tragic pain there is "en este mundo." As she is being torn away from her home, her village, and her querencia, she sings, "de mi querida patria me van a retirar." She will never see her patria chica again. This song expresses the greatest love for querencia I know.

If we pinpoint all our querencias on a map of New Mexico, they form a grid—millions of querencias connected to each other. This grid is our patria chica, our community, our village. This querencia grid identifies and describes our knowledge and cultura, and it is a great source of power. La cultura cura. This poetic grid contains the stories, songs, poetry, alabados, fiestas, the joy and suffering of our ancestors. The grid is the source and inspiration for the stories, songs, and poetry we write today.

Our poetic grid is infused with the creative spirit that fills our soul. This spirit is the duende, our New Mexico Cucui (Kookooee) that is part of our inheritance, our DNA. The flamenco dancer who reaches ecstatic moments in her dance and the guitarist suddenly hitting heavenly notes are filled with duende. In the movie *Fiddler on the Roof*, the old man fiddling on the roof is filled with duende. When Zorba dances in the movie *Zorba the Greek*, he, too, is filled with duende.

We call duende "locura," the maddening creative spirit that takes hold of us when we sing, dance, recite poetry, or are filled with love for querencia. Faith in family and vecinos, a centuries-old faith that is the fé of our ancestors, moves us. It connects the entire patria chica and, when immersed in locura, we are connected to the profoundist depths of soul. Locura does not mean crazy or insane. Locura is being filled with the power and energy of our cultura. During those ecstatic moments when we are truly happy and filled with faith is when we give the world a view into our creative spirit.

I am writing a children's story in which the grandma goes in search of her children who are in trouble. One is abusing alcohol, another meth, the third opioids and heroin. No amount of chastising or threatening is going to help the children break their habits. Instead, she leads the three to the plaza in front of the church, El Santuario de Chimayó. There, the Matachines are dancing. The music moves the dancers and la Malinche and el Monarca step lively to the guitar and violin melody. The dance drama is complete. The audience is filled with an exuberant feeling of completeness. The plaza where the dance takes place is our querencia. Faith is restored.

The grandma does not lecture her children: all she has done is to take them to the dance. The dance, the people, the music, and the sky overhead unite the people. The children understand, la cultura cura. They have become separated from their roots and history, forgotten the culture of their ancestors. Leading the children back to the dance allows them to participate in cultura. The healing way begins.

I understand problems in our society are not so easily solved. I am no Pollyanna. I do know that those prisoners who write me and want books about their cultura want to get back to the healing way, the way of querencia and roots. We know the problem: it's all around us. Too many have become separated from the querencia of family and ancestors. The joy locura brings to the heart is no longer there. El duende has lost its way in a technological culture that separates us from querencia. The center is missing. Can we help our brothers and sisters who are suffering by doing something as simple as exposing them to the culture they left behind? Can we say that con el corazón abierto, la cultura cura?

We treasure our community, but communities are not supposed to remain isolated. We do not build walls around our village, we open doors. Throughout our history, the cultures of New Mexico have shared their mythopoetic core with one another. Languages and histories thrive and will continue to thrive as long as we respect the unique character of each group. We move in and out of different cultures, aware there is always a larger, accepting querencia that includes us all.

DEDICATED TO MY FATHER, MARTÍN ANAYA,
AND MY MOTHER, RAFAELITA MARES ANAYA.

AGRADECIMIENTOS Y RECONOCIMIENTOS

The editors would like to thank the contributors for their work in this anthology and for creating new and emerging scholarship on the topic of querencia. We would also like to acknowledge them for the collective process that helped shape and forge these *ensayos*. We are hopeful readers will find the essays enlightening, inspiring, and thought-provoking, and that the writings will lead them toward their own contemplations on querencia. The compilations and editing were done through the spirit of *comunidad* and in the honoring of *nuestros antepasados*, whose lives aimed to create places of home and belonging. We remember our ancestors as we, too, embark on our own quests for querencia, for ourselves and for our loved ones. We are especially grateful to Enrique Lamadrid, whose *maestría* and mentorship guided the anthology through its various incarnations. We express our heartfelt gratitude and appreciation to Rudolfo Anaya for his kindness and spirit of generosity. And finally, we recognize the many Indigenous homelands of New Mexico and the Indigenous tribes and communities who have taught us much about how to cultivate a love and sense of place.

The editors gratefully acknowledge the assistance of A. Gabriel Meléndez from the UNM Center for Regional Studies and Irene Vásquez from the Southwest Hispanic Research Institute for making the indexing of this book possible.

The contributors would like to extend their gratitude to the scholars, community members, and families who have inspired and shaped us all and deepened our sense of querencia in our own work. In no particular order, we thank Tey Diana Rebolledo; A. Gabriel Meléndez; Denise Chávez; María Dolores Gonzales; Eric Romero; José T. Valenzuela and Jeronima Pulido de Valenzuela; Elisabeth, Mercedes, Maribel, and Lucy Valenzuela; Matthew, Andrea, and Rita Padilla; Doña Juliana Molina; Luisa "Luisita" Durán; Fernando Carrillo; Greg Bowes; Gail B. Fox; Michelle Trujillo; Cruzita Chávez; Pedro Trujillo; Edward Desantis; Hector Torres; the Tularosa Downwinders Consoritum; the Multicultural Alliance for a Safe Environment; and Concerned Citizens for Nuclear Safety. We also would like to thank Kallie Johnson, who worked as a research assistant during the early stages of the book.

QUERENCIA

Mi Querencia

A Connection between Place and Identity

LEVI ROMERO

—*Dime dónde te creastes y te diré quién eres.*
—Tell me where you were raised and I'll tell you who you are.

What is the connection between place and identity? The story of human existence is one of movement and settlement. And people have pondered for millennia how these ways of being in the world influence who we are and who we might become. Origin stories the world over feature accounts of where a people came *from* as a way of telling how they came to *be*. Northern New Mexico cultural envoy Juan Estevan Arellano used the traditional northern New Mexico concept of *querencia* to define the relationship between place and identity. Querencia, he wrote, "is that which gives us a sense of place, that which anchors us to the land, that which makes us a unique people" (Arellano 2007, 50).

Although I grew up hearing the term used, it had no particular relevance for me beyond what I understood querencia to be: the place where one is born and raised. And then I began teaching my course *Querencia: Place and Identity* at the University of New Mexico. Through the classroom discussions and students' papers, it became evident that a person's sense of querencia is unique to them and that their experiences might differ from my and Arellano's definition. One young woman ran away from home at fifteen years of age and found her nurturing and sense of belonging in all-night diners and homeless shelters. Many others' meaning of querencia might express aspects of nurturing and belonging but lack a connection to the ideals of family, community, and place. It startles me when I encounter people who have no sense of querencia, no sense of home.

My worldview has been shaped by the place of my upbringing. Querencia, as Arellano wrote, is "a place where one feels safe, a place from which one's strength of character is drawn, where one feels at home" (2007, 50). In my contemplations regarding the theme for this anthology, I began to consider where that place is for me. I speak of querencia from an experience embedded in an upbringing among close-knit relations. For me, querencia is not only personal; it is communal and deeply connected to the people and place where I was raised, *mi gente, mi pueblito* (my people, my hometown). *¿Quién soy? Soy yo. Yo soy. Y soy como soy porque soy de aquí, y no me parezco a nadien.* (Who am I? I am myself. I am how I am because I am from here, unique and unlike anyone else).

I come from a unique people, the *manito* (Hispanic New Mexican) culture of northern New Mexico. *Soy de esta querencia—mi querencia* (I am from this querencia—my querencia). But more specifically, *soy de El Puesto del Embudo de San Antonio,* a small village nestled in the juniper-dotted foothills and ter-raced mesas along the Río Grande between Española and Taos, settled in 1725. As fate would have it, the town's name was changed to Dixon after Col-lins Dixon—a resident school teacher and postmaster. I have been told that people would say *"llévenle este correo a Dixon"* and the "take this mail to Dixon" phrase stuck and his name was thus appropriated for the village. Although I have lived most of my adult life in Albuquerque, a two-hour drive away, *Dixon, El Dique, the Little Dipper, Dixon-13, D-Town, El Barrio de Los Mal-ditos* is still the place I call home. The instant I get out of the car to open the gate, it is at that moment when I feel I am at home. The place that nurtures me, where I feel I belong, the place I retreat to like the bull in the bullring when he is wounded. Where I am understood by those who know me without explanations or footnotes for what I say, think, or feel. This is the land of my upbringing, mi querencia.

In Gabriel García Márquez's novel *One Hundred Years of Solitude,* José Arcadio Buendía argues with his wife about wanting to move from their hometown of Macondo. José wishes to leave but Ursula insists on staying. "A person does not belong to a place until there is someone dead under the ground," retorts José (García Márquez 1967, 13). When I visit or drive by the various *camposantos* (cemeteries) around the Embudo Valley, I contemplate the people whose names are scripted on the crosses and headstones. Many were friends and relatives I knew intimately—the warm cackle of their laugh-ter, the heavy paleness of their sorrow. Other names belong to people I never met except through the stories I've heard relaying their idiosyncrasies, ad-venturous spirits, gifts and talents, kindness and generosity. If an account of a deceased person leans toward a negative portrayal, it is done with respect. No ill is spoken of the dead. *Que en paz descansen*, may they rest in peace. It is a form of conduct we should learn to apply to the living as well. For no one is truly dead until their name is no longer spoken or remembered. *Mis familiares, amistades, y vecinos* (My relatives, friends, and neighbors) are buried in these camposantos.

"When can I say that I am from here?" is a question that was posed to me at a book-signing I was doing at the local community library several years ago by an Anglo gentleman who had moved there at least thirty years before. Without much pause, I pointed toward the cemeteries in the *cañada* (narrow valley) behind the community library. "When the camposantos' crosses are filled with the names of your loved ones, you can say you're from here," I replied. The audience applauded. While that may not be the definitive answer for when a person can claim a place as home, it is certainly one that emphasizes a binding connection to place and people. And even that, as Ursula argued, might not be enough to keep us from leaving. But it is something that can draw us back for periodic visits to the places where we were born and raised, our querencias. For some, it is also the location they choose as their final resting place, whether they've been gone for fifty years or never left. *Cuando me muera, aquí es donde quiero que me entierren.* Bury me here, this place that cradles the bones and memories of my *antepasados* (ancestors).

When I was younger, I yearned to see the world, but now that I have more opportunities to travel than ever before, I look forward most to the times I can go back to my grandmother Anita's house, where she raised my sister and me during our summer breaks from school. Although the house was vacant for a good number of years after she passed away, whenever I walked inside, each room had a distinct smell that defies description, for I have never smelled anything else like it. It was not quite lavender, jasmine, rose, old wood, moist earth, or the geraniums growing in a coffee can on the window shelf. It smelled like no other place on earth. It smelled like Grandma's house. It smelled like home.

In the evenings, we would gather out on the porch while she played harmonica and told stories. We would sit transfixed on the low-set windowsills or the porch edge hearing Mama Ane tell of a not-so-long-ago way of life while hummingbirds came to suckle on Las Varas de San José flowers growing between the heirloom grapevines along the portal. She recalled the Fiestas de Santa Rosa that converged on August 28th with out-of-town guests who came annually for the feast day celebrations and reacquaint with *paren-tela*, family, friends, and vecinos. People's homes filled with good cheer and commotion as their visitors' buckboards sat parked under the orchard trees through the several days of the town's festivities. The bleating sounds of the feast lambs and goats could be heard across the village.

The *salas* (gathering halls) were bustling with music and dancing. La Sala Filantrópica, la sala de mana Jacinta, la sala Mutua, la sala aca Gimez Durán, Las Tres Palomas, la sala de La Plaza de los Rendones, and la sala de Georgito Rendón served as community centers where people gathered for various types of occasions such as wedding receptions. Some were informal community gathering places where people congregated to dance and celebrate the simple bounties of their daily lives. At La Sala Filantrópica, people gathered to watch the traveling acrobatic circuses held by the *turcos*, also known as *los maromeros*, traveling Turkish gypsies who performed throughout northern New Mexico's towns and villages. In addition to being warned about *La Llorona* when we were kids, we were also told to keep away from the river at night because the turcos who camped under the bridge would abduct wandering children. By the time I was growing up, the turcos, like the festive sala events, were a thing of *recuerdos* (memories), but the stories and memories of a waning way of life were carried on not too far removed from the recent past. In the village of my upbringing, once-upon-a-very-long-time-ago stories are told as if they might have happened only yesterday morning. I was raised hearing about people who were deceased long before I was born. *En mi Embudo todo cambia pero nada muere*—everything changes but nothing dies.

"*Curre, mi 'jito, trae agua*" (go, my son, get water), my grandmother would instruct me, handing me the pail. I always looked forward to drawing water from the well. The splashing and banging of the pail against the river-rock-lined *noria* was as soothing and nourishing as the sweet water it contained. Her house was void of modern conveniences. No electricity, indoor plumbing, or propane heating. The scent of kerosene still conjures up memories of lantern-lit evenings as the wick's flames danced mesmerizingly on the pastel pink, rose-patterned wallpaper. When I hear the San Antonio de Padua church bells ringing in the village, I remember the Sunday morning picnics we'd have in the hills behind her house. Grandma would pack a bag of whatever foods she had at hand—Beanee Weenees, Vienna sausages, sardines, tortillas, oranges, and a few other nonperishables—and off we'd go to gather under the shade of a juniper and listen for the tolling of the church bells.

Occasionally, a cousin or two would accompany my sister and me on our summer stays at grandma's. "*Shhh! ¡Ya callen!*" Grandma would yell to us—"Quiet, already"—after the lantern had been extinguished and we continued with our muffled, giggling racket in the darkness of the small bedroom where we all slept crammed into two beds.

We entertained ourselves trading schoolyard gossip of kids with interesting nicknames like *la Pimpora* and *el Sapo*, or embellishing stories of our encounters with local village personalities such as El Mary Jane and Gonito, or tales of Lalito riding through town on a Schwinn Panther bicycle with an American flag and bugle horn mounted on the handle bars and his transistor radio tuned to the local Spanish radio station. "*¡Pita, Lalito, pita!*," we'd plead for him to honk his bike horn as he rode past the elementary-school grounds. Showing off the scabs on our knees or boasting of our daily escapades was always fodder for bedtime reflections. The landscape of northern New Mexico is adorned with abandoned houses that seem to be frozen in a muted utterance of untold stories and histories. These dilapidated structures, whose interiors evoke recuerdos of a once-thriving home life, sit abandoned in ruin. If these walls could talk, I ponder the old cliché, imagine what stories they would tell.

"*¿Qué se mira pa' Alcalde?*" I once asked a cousin who lived in a neighboring town. He replied, "*No sé. Yo no soy de Alcalde, soy de La Villita*," annoyed because I mistakenly asked how things were in Alcalde, when he actually lived in the subcommunity of La Villita. A person's sense of allegiance and territorial affection toward their community will be quickly noted as a reminder in the event of a mistake made in identifying where a person is from. "*Este es mi querencia, aquí, en la plaza donde nací y me creé. Tu querencia es allá 'bajo en el Arroyo de La Mina, donde te creastes tú*," my eighty-seven-year-old *primo* remarked to me recently. Even though in general terms we are both from the same village, share the same querencia, he distinguished between the area of town where I was raised, known as El Arroyo de La Mina, from the place of his upbringing, La Plaza del Embudo. In the same manner that my younger primo had corrected me, my elder primo also reminded me that my querencia and his were different even though we were from the same village.

Someone who is not from my pueblito might refer to it by one name—Dixon. But for those of us who grew up in the Embudo Valley, we are known and characterized among our vecinos by the various areas of the valley where we were raised—La Nasa, El Embudo, La Ciénega, La Bolsa, La Rinconcada,

La Apodaca, El Cañoncito, El Montecito, El Bosque, La Plaza, La Otra Banda. There are also homes along the various arroyos where people reside— Arroyo de la Mina, Arroyo del Pino, Arroyo de la Baca, Arroyo de Lorenzo, Arroyo del Oso, Arroyo de los Pinos Reales, Arroyo Corcobado, Arroyo del Capulín, Arroyo de los Angeles, Arroyo del Plomo, Arroyo de la Apodaca. The arroyos are not named after an individual or family, but an animal, tree, fruit variety, or distinguishing feature in the topography. It can even be said that people are prone to exhibit certain traits and behavioral characteristics based on which part of town they are from. For everyone, as my primo pointed out, carries the DNA of their own querencia.

As a young girl, my mother learned to speak the Northern Tiwa language while working in her father's gardens alongside a family from Picurís Pueblo who came annually to help harvest my grandfather's crops in exchange for produce. My maternal grandfather, Silviares Durán, was one of the valley's most successful fruit growers. He had a trade route that extended north from Embudo to Cimarrón, Dawson, and Ratón. Delivering his products on a horse-drawn wagon, he was known among his clientele as "*El Verdulero*." My Tío Celestino, who left in the early 1950s for employment opportunities in California's San José Valley, fondly recalls his travels with my grandfather into those towns to sell or barter fruit and vegetables. One of my uncle's duties was to walk up to houses, knock on the door, and inquire if they would like to purchase something. "*Mamá*," the young person at the door would inform their mother, "*andan vendiendo fruta*" (they are selling fruit). The usual reply from the kitchen would be, "*Si es el Verdulero, sí queremos*" (If it's the vegetable vendor, we want some). People's familiarity with the quality of his produce and the cultivation and nurturing of friendships over the years ensured he would have a successful trip. Whenever I drive by the *ojito* (spring) in the box canyon at Pilar where he stopped for a respite and to water the horses, I am reminded of the difficult trek my grandfather must have endured to sustain his family's well-being. In addition, he must have felt an obligation to provide for the needs of the people who depended on him to deliver produce of such quality that the woman of the house preferred his fruit and vegetables to those of other vendors. My querencia is more than a cornucopia of memories. It has a geographical imprint with stories etched across its landscape.

Years ago, someone spray-painted a message on a boulder along the main highway in the Embudo Canyon that read, "*NO VENDER LA TIERRA*." It was a plea reminding the local Hispano community to refrain from selling their lands—lands that had been in their families for centuries. By the early 1970s, many properties sat abandoned. Old adobe houses and farms were on the real estate market, placed on the county's tax delinquent accounts list, or in such a state of neglect that almost any offered purchase price seemed a guaranteed sale. The local youths were beginning to move away and the *ancianos* (elders) could no longer tend to their farms. Agrarian traditions were being replaced by a western cultural lifestyle made more possible through employment at the Los Alamos National Labs, state and local government jobs, or other work-places that lured people away from home.

With this evolving new form of self-reliance and financial independence, the pathways between people's houses began to disappear. Gate openings in the fence lines were wired shut. Interactions and bartering between neighbors began to decline. The Bureau of Land Management (BLM) and the United States Forest Service closed off roads to areas that had once been communal lands and deprived people of access to natural resources they had relied on for centuries to sustain their querencias. "No Trespassing" signs began to appear, and the phrase *cuando llegó el alambre, llegó el hambre* (when the fences arrived, hunger arrived) became a reality. What might have once been a grandma's, tía's, tío's, vecino's, or pariente's residence now belonged to an outsider, *un de porfuera*.

Juxtaposed against the ever-growing arrival of *extranjeros* (foreigners) were land rights activist groups and cultural preservationists such as Reies López Tijerina's Alianza Federal de Mercedes and La Academia de La Nueva Raza. La Academia was a land-based organization dedicated to the preservation of cultural traditions through fully engaged community activism and the col-lecting of oral histories. It was spearheaded by a collective of young Chicano organic intellectuals, including Embudo *nativos* Tomás Atencio and Juan Estevan Arellano. The Academia's headquarters had been established in my great-grandmother's house in the old Plaza del Embudo. The group called for the maintenance of traditional ways of living nurtured by acts of *mutualismo* (mutualism) and an appreciation for *familia, comunidad, y tradiciones* (family, community, and traditions).

During my childhood, words like "sustainability" and "resiliency" were not part of the lexicon. Yet people lived in accordance with traditions that sustained their livelihood as they had been accustomed to do for centuries. The shelves of my grandmother Juanita's *suterrano* (storm cellar) were always lined with a colorful array of jars filled with preserves of various fruits and vegetables. From the storm cellar's *vigas* hung *ristras* of *cueritos* (porkskins) and *carne seca* (beef jerky). And from the rafters in the *sotella*, strings with strips of dried green chili and red chile ristras dangled in the attic dust. Sometimes I would accompany her out to the fields to look for a specific grass that she used to make her brooms. Although she had a cold-water hookup for the kitchen sink, she preferred to draw water for drinking from the ojito in the *veguita* (marsh), where footpaths along the Río Embudo extended from one end of the village to the other. This pastoral and idyllic life greeted the counterculture refugees fleeing the social turbulence of the 1960s. When a new pet has been introduced into a household, the fear that its first inclination is to leave or wander off is always imminent. After a short period during which it becomes accustomed to its surroundings, it is said, *"ya no se va, ya se aquerenció"* (He won't leave, he feels at home). It is during this time when it begins to recognize its new settings as home and the potential for it to stray is diminished. The same was said of the counterculture "new settlers" after their arrival in the villages throughout northern New Mexico became a common occurrence. *"Ya se aquerenciaron"* was a phrase used to describe their acclimatization to what, for many of them, would become their querencia.

To leave or not to leave one's querencia is the ultimate dilemma. *El que se va se va suspirando, y él que se queda se queda llorando* (He who leaves does so sighing, and he who stays, mourns). Sometimes the conflict between staying or leaving gives birth to an equal regret. When I was still quite young, I saw the phrase *Sal si puedes* (Leave if you can) brushed on the wall of a dilapidated building in a neighboring town. For many people, moving away was not by choice. The pursuit of employment or education, enlistment in the military, or a desire for a better quality of life were some of the most common reasons people left their villages. As time went on, people's desire to leave was replaced by a yearning to stay. *Quédate si puedes* (Stay if you can) became the overriding cultural mantra. One evening, my cousin and I were sitting on the bridge of one of the village's lower roads reflecting on the changes that had occurred since he was in his teens and living in an area of Dixon known as La Otra Banda before his family relocated to Albuquerque in the mid-1960s. It seemed that every person who went by was a nonnative resident. "What do you think about all the changes that have happened since you lived here?" I asked. "They can change Dixon all they want," he said, moving his hand over his heart, *"pero, aquí, en mi corazón nunca lo van a cambiar"* (but here, in my heart, they will never change it). As I drive through the village, I notice that many yards along the highway have been enclosed with high walls or coyote fences. Many people who move here bring with them the lifestyles they are seeking to get away from. "The first thing that goes up," said another primo to me once, "is the wall." The wave of 'mano Ignacio sitting under his porch and the smile from 'mana Rufina tending her flower beds have been replaced by walls that prevent people from greeting each other. *Buenos días* (Good morning) has been replaced with *no me molestes* (Don't bother me!). That is not querencia. That is a life lived in isolation among one's neighbors.

Years ago, as a young man, I was hitchhiking out of town. I recognized the car approaching me and quickly decided as an act of respect that I would not extend my hand and gesture for a ride. For the person driving the car was elderly and known to never pick up hitchhikers. As the car approached, I waved but kept my gaze on the road for the next oncoming vehicle. A few seconds passed, and I heard the honk of a car. I turned, and the elderly gentleman had pulled over. I ran toward the car and peered in. Inside were the gentleman, his mother, and an elderly woman sitting in the back seat. "*¡Súbete!*" (Get in!), said the driver, and motioned toward the back. As we began to drive away, he turned back toward me and said, "*¿Romero, qué no?*" "*Sí, hijo de Elías y Carolina,*" I replied. He smiled, adjusted his fedora, and said, "*Pues, te conocimos. Sabemos quien es tu familia.*" The gentleman who was known to never offer a ride to anyone had pulled over for me because his family knew mine. My family's name, going back generations and generations, was honorable and reputable. When they saw me standing on the side of the road, who they observed was not me, but my parents, grandparents, mi familia, mis antepasados. As a child, I wondered why people who were no relation to the family referred to my grandmother as Tía Juanita. She was everyone's aunt because she was also every mother's sister, *'mana Juanita.* That is also querencia.

With the inevitable changes that come with time, as my primo said at the bridge, what we knew lives on in our hearts. *Lo que nos llevamos al pozo cuando muremos es nada más que un puño de tierra. Pero lo que dejamos son recuerdos e historias de quien fuimos y como caminamos entre la gente. Por feos, bonitos, ricos, pobres, buenos o malos, inteligentes, medio zafa'os, generosos o cuscos, si no van a decir "tan bueno que fue" o "pobrecita, tan buen corazón que tenía," pues tan siquiera que digan, "tanto que peleó por su pueblo, aunque nada se llevó."* (All we take to the grave when we die is a handful of dirt. But what we leave behind are memories and histories of who we were and how we walked among people. Whether we are ugly, pretty, rich, poor, nice or mean, intelligent, kind of slow, generous or greedy, if they are not going to say "he was such a good person" or "poor thing, she had such a big heart," well, at least they should say, "he fought so hard for his community, although he took nothing with him").

In 1957 my father, a *comisionado* (commissioner) on the Acequia de la Plaza, along with the *mayordomo* (ditch boss) and the other comisionados on the acequia's governing body, were successful in registering the *parciantes'* (ditch members') water rights. At that time, few people were concerned with matters pertaining to acequias outside of their seasonal and daily operations. The maps, oral history testimonials, and carbon copies of my father's original typed letters I found at the state engineer's office are a startling record and reminder of the contributions made by a group of men whose efforts have never been recognized nor celebrated. *Unos cargan la lana y otros ganan la fama* (some carry the wool, others gain the fame).

Other letters I have found are from an ongoing correspondence by my father, representing a group of cattlemen from the Embudo Valley, who aimed to reacquire the grazing rights to what were once *ejidos* (communal lands) that had been claimed by the Bureau of Land Management. Upon my father's untimely passing in 1977, these efforts came to a halt. But I remember one of the gentlemen from the group years later telling me, "*Con la ayuda de tu papá, fuéramos agarrando los ejidos pa 'tras.*" I also believe that, had my father not passed away, they would have been successful in reacquiring the grazing rights. It would be inconceivable for me to write about my querencia and not remember my father, who was an educator by profession, but whose real passion was as a Notary Public and helping people with their property deeds and land titles.

In the early 1970s, the BLM filed suit against people in the valley who had constructed homes on what had once been recognized as *herencia* (heritage) or communal lands but that had become BLM lands after the government resurveyed its holding claims. It was my father who helped them acquire their land titles from the government. He also helped many of the men from the villages who had worked as sheepherders, in agriculture, or on the railroad to acquire the pensions they had been denied. My childhood years were spent at the courthouses in Tierra Amarilla, Santa Fe, and Taos while my father researched property deeds on behalf of his clients' interests, most often doing it doing it pro bono. In the early '60s, after he had grown frustrated with seeing the arroyos, back roads, and hillsides littered with trash, through his efforts the BLM dedicated a portion of property to be used as a landfill site.

Community adoration for my father in his lifetime did not come with the dedication of a building in his name, nor was he given an award for his service. But on the funeral procession to the Veterans Memorial Cemetery in Santa Fe, where he was interred, I looked back from the top of the hill and the line of cars was several miles long. Many men and women who dedicated their lives to the well-being of their querencia have gone unrecognized for their unselfish servitude or any measure of recognition by which we have come to honor some of our *maestros y maestras* (teachers) in more recent times. Or the *madrecitas* (mothers) who raised families and maintained the querencia while our *abuelos* (grandfathers) were on the manito trail working away from home *en la borrega, el betabel, el fierro carril, las minas, o las pizcas* (in sheepherding, the sugar-beet field, the railroad, the mines, or the fields) throughout the southwest. *Las mujeres, ellas también merecen reconocimiento* (The women, they also deserve recognition). So do the young local men who toil in the acequias during the annual spring cleanings to ensure that parciantes will have water for irrigating. Those same men, uncelebrated stewards of the land, neither acknowledged nor recognized for sustaining traditions that enable others to live an agrarian lifestyle, are instead viewed suspiciously when they enter the local *tiendita* (general store).

Are people obligated to participate in the maintenance of their querencia? Sometimes when I am driving into the village, I will notice a tall, older Anglo man alongside the road picking up the trash that people toss out of their cars. And I wonder if he loves this querencia more than those whose ancestors labored with undying determination to clear the virgin fields of rocks, trees, and shrubs. What would nuestros antepasados think if they saw what has become of their querencia? We owe our gratitude to the men and women who toiled unceremoniously to level the land for agriculture and constructed *acequias* with mules and burros and crude wooden implements, and who *con la pala y la mano* (with a shovel and their bare hands) built a home for their families and their descendants. It is not enough to speak of one's love for querencia without participating in the maintenance that ensures its health and well-being. *La querencia es de él quien la mantiene* (the homeland belongs to those who care for it).

No matter where I find myself, the arrow of my internal compass always points toward my ancestral home, where my cultural and spiritual point of reference originates. My strengths and weaknesses, my biggest insecurities and strongest self-assurances were shaped and formed there. Essentially, it shaped my *locura*, my worldview. Where a person is raised can tell a lot about who they are. *Dime dónde te creastes y te diré quién eres*. As was stated earlier, origin stories the world over feature accounts of where a people came *from* as a way of telling how they came to *be*. Who I am, like a tightly woven *trenza*, is braided to the landscape, the people, the culture, the place where I was raised.

Recently, I met a woman who considers her querencia to be a small town in northern New Mexico where her family lived before moving to another state. Although she was born and raised in Wyoming, she considers the family's home origins as her querencia. Some may ask, "Can I have more than one querencia?" Others may emphatically proclaim, "I don't feel like I have a querencia." Within the pages of this anthology are stories that tell, ask, ponder, and examine querencia in its various manifestations. Ultimately, the goal is to inspire the reader to embark on a journey toward his or her own querencia. *¿Dónde está tu querencia?* (Where is your querencia?).

WORKS CITED

Arellano, Juan Estevan. 2007. *Taos: Where Two Cultures Met Four Hundred Years Ago.* Seattle: Grantmakers in the Arts.
García Márquez, Gabriel. 1967. *One Hundred Years of Solitude.* New York: Harper.

In *Community Querencias*, readers are asked to reflect on the claiming of querencia through contestatory communal practices related to identity formation within different geographic spaces. The three chapters contained in this section illuminate the need for storytelling and active listening as a necessary process for agency and claiming homespace. Specifically, the authors demonstrate that community legacies—what we inherit and what we choose to pass on—are an important aspect of the ever-evolving nature of querencia for new generations of Indigenous tribes and Nuevomexicanos.

In chapter one, "The Long, Wondrous Life of Ventura Chávez, 1926–2013," Simón Ventura Trujillo engages in questions of land-grant tenure and dispossession through the eulogy of his grandfather, Ventura Chávez, also referred to as El Viejo. For Trujillo, El Viejo's life connects the individual to the communal through an extensive network of Indigenous memory. The military veteran returned to his homeland in northern New Mexico and became active in La Alianza Federal de Mercedes in the late 1960s. Trujillo reflects on the wisdom of his grandfather as a social critic and an important storyteller not only in his family, but for the rest of the Indo-Hispano pueblo. Trujillo's commitment to El Viejo's stories came through an active listening process, coupled with his own research on Reies López Tijerina, a land-grant activist. Tijerina's decolonial desire for land, as Trujillo states, merged what seemed like two dissimilar paths of knowledge into one that left him reckoning with the forms of settler forgetting that animate US policies in New Mexico and the broken promises of the Treaty of Guadalupe Hidalgo. Unfortunately, as many of us have experienced, our desire to see grandparents as keepers of subjugated knowledge often comes late. In 2011, El Viejo was diagnosed with dementia and lost the ability to hear and tell stories. In this context, Trujillo uncovers El Viejo's written journals and reveals the decolonial emotion and passion still evident in the last two years of his life. He ends his chapter by reinforcing El Viejo's claim to an Indo-Hispano identity under the Treaty of Guadalupe Hidalgo—"an occupied territory under alien landlords." For Trujillo, El Viejo embodies the querencia for a homeland as an "ongoing and active formation of rebellious storytelling." Stories are integral to sustaining a holistic sense of self, as they connect us to our querencias and to the people with whom we share our love for the land. Through the eulogy form, Trujillo activates storytelling through the land. The land gives us our stories and the stories sustain our place in the land.

In chapter two, "Remapping Patriotic Practices: The Case of the Las Vegas 4th of July Fiestas," Lillian Gorman analyzes cultural materials during a three-year period of the 4th of July Fiestas in Las Vegas, New Mexico, as a way to examine how self-identified Hispanics from this area contribute to larger conversations on nationhood. She looks at the Plaza de Las Vegas and affirms it as a home space for locals and for *parientes* (relatives) who make an annual pilgrimage to the fiestas to reunite with *familia* and see old friends. Many "Diasporic Hispanos" from Las Vegas and surrounding communities who were forced by economic conditions to move elsewhere return each year, reacquaint themselves with their culture and traditions, and partake in the celebrations around food, music, the parade, and the crowning of *la reina* (the queen). This notion of homecoming, writes Gorman, "is key to understanding the ways in which returning for fiestas contests dominant narratives around the 4th of July and re-semantifies the celebration." While these fiestas are celebrated during a patriotic national holiday, cultural markers associated with the 4th of July are often not present. Gorman shows how, instead, New Mexican Hispanics engage in a transposition of local stories as a way to demonstrate how tradition works as a contestatory practice. For her, this site embodies both grounded and disrupted querencia: it sparks memory and remembering for Hispanic New Mexicans who reside in Las Vegas, allowing them to gather as longstanding communities and to participate in storytelling, while people who have left and returned must go through the painful process of collapsing past memories with present traditions. Nonetheless, as Gorman argues, Las Vegas serves as a homespace that resists patriotic memory and instead celebrates the ways in which Nuevomexicanos reinsert querencia and local histories into larger national narratives.

Chapter three, "Critical Conversations on Chicanx and Indigenous Scholarship and Activism," is organized around four central questions prompted by Vanessa Fonseca-Chávez. The discussants, Kevin Brown, Tey Marianna Nunn, Irene Vásquez, and Myla Vicenti Carpio, begin by situating the conversation in relation to their own senses of place across New Mexico and the southwest United States. By doing so, they recognize where they are coming from and how this has informed their social and political commitments in New Mexico and elsewhere. Each participant reflects on the practices of commemoration, memory, and placemaking and, more specifically, how Chicanx and Indigenous communities can work together to build bridges and solidarity for decolonization. For Nunn, it is not enough to say we are working with community: we must always look beyond the façade of words and think about how we enact and embody community in our work. Vicenti Carpio and Vásquez highlight responsibility and obligation as necessary mechanisms to work with the community through an understanding of Indigenous methodologies and Chicana and Chicano studies critical frameworks. Brown emphasizes the need to speak out against colonial representations such as the Three Peoples mural at the University of New Mexico. In doing so, he notes that student organizations like the UNM's Kiva Club have been pivotal to breaking down boundaries and creating community on college campuses. Each of the participants looks with a critical eye at claiming space and is cognizant of the need for Chicanx and Indigenous communities to work together to tell stories that transcend colonial narratives. They end their conversation by offering suggestions on how to heal from colonial trauma.

As each of these authors demonstrates, active engagement with the community is necessary to define querencia through contestatory practices. As we encounter dominant systems of erasure and attempts to limit New Mexico Indigenous, Hispanic, Indo-Hispano, and borderlands agency, we do so with a heightened awareness of our querencia. *La comunidad aquerenciada* (the querencia community) resists the imposition of identity and history and, instead, elevates local voices and stories and considers homeplace as an important site of resistance and identity formation.

CHAPTER ONE

The Long, Wondrous Life of Ventura Chávez, 1926–2013

SIMÓN VENTURA TRUJILLO

Corncobs and husks, the rinds and stalks of animal bones were not regarded by the ancient people as filth or garbage. The remains were merely resting at a midpoint in their journey back to dust. Human remains are not so different.

LESLIE MARMON SILKO | "Interior and Exterior Landscapes: The Pueblo Migration Stories"

Makers pose a danger to those who fear. Because revolutions begin with love. Campesino wars begin with love. Art begins with love. Love is inspired by art. We makers have nothing to lose and nothing to hide. We are fearless, fearless. We are born, we love, we die, and there is not much more that really matters in the end. And so we pass the rope, not thinking about what will happen to us once we collide with the earth, force the ash to rise. And trust you can withstand the fire in your hands.

HELENA MARÍA VIRAMONTES | "The Writes Ofrenda"

Family, friends, and all of our relatives.[1]

Hello, *bienvenidos* (welcome), and good evening.

Thank you for meeting here to read this eulogy on the life and work of my grandfather, Ventura Chávez.

I used to call him El Viejo.

At the age of eighty-six, after a three-year struggle with Alzheimer's disease, El Viejo returned to the land at his home in Albuquerque, surrounded by family, on March 11, 2013.

The *Oxford English Dictionary* defines a eulogy as "a set oration in honour of a deceased person." As this is an oration dedicated to El Viejo's long and wondrous life, however, I want to put the eulogy form to a different kind of use to explore connections between genealogies of land-grant tenure and dispossession, the colonial legacies of racialized and gendered labor, and the politics of land and organic radicalism in New Mexico. This means violating

certain narrative precepts of the eulogy form. Rather than stressing the excep-
tional trajectory of El Viejo's life in individual terms, I'm telling his story to
constellate a broader network of Indigenous memory and endurance within
occupied New Mexico. Rather than equating his death with finitude, this
eulogy is about coming to terms with the fact that the dead never stay still—
that, as Raymond Williams (2009) writes, "the dead may be reduced to fixed
forms, though their surviving records are against it" (129).

As some of you may know, in the 1960s and early 1970s El Viejo and my
grandmother, Cruzita Chávez, were active members of the New Mexican
land-grant movement *La Alianza Federal de Mercedes* (The Federal Alliance
of Land Grants). For the past decade, I have been researching and writing
about La Alianza's cultural politics as a way of rethinking the questions of
land, race, and indigeneity in the formation and dispossession of Spanish and
Mexican land grants in the Americas. El Viejo's eulogy, then, is also a story
of how I came to this work. Or rather, it is a story of how this work came
to me—how I came to inherit this work from my grandparents, and what it
means to remake it in our present moment.

In addition to being a grandfather, parent, husband, son, and brother, El
Viejo was one of the sharpest social critics I've ever met. For someone who
only attended school until the age of thirteen, he possessed a wisdom that
came from way before his time. He found lifelong inspiration from the stories
of our Indigenous and settler ancestors. Despite his limited formal schooling,
he was an avid reader of New Mexican history and culture. His personal
library, in a single bookcase in his room, was an eclectic mix of Spanish and
Mexican land-grant historiography, Chicana/o borderland history, Native
American philosophy, Christian mystical literature, and Western fiction. Titles such as David Weber's *Foreigners in Their Native Land* and Vine Deloria
Jr.'s *Behind the Trail of Broken Treaties* sat next to a vast collection of Louis
L'Amour novels. Frank Waters' *Book of the Hopi*, Fabiola Cabeza de Baca's
We Fed Them Cactus, and Fray Angélico Chávez's *My Penitente Land* resided
alongside works on prophecy and interplanetary influence by Edgar Cayce.
As an organic radical intellectual, his embrace of the power of storytelling
upended the social and disciplinary boundaries among myth, history, and fiction. He knew that stories are the way we make this life meaningful in the
face of death. He knew that without our stories, we have nothing. In short,
among being a cowboy, a railroad worker, a sailor, an aircraft painter, and a
radical civil rights activist, El Viejo was a storyteller.

Here is a story about the storyteller.

El Viejo was born on October 30, 1926 on a small ranch a few miles outside of Cuervo, New Mexico—a small village east of Santa Rosa that was reduced to a virtual ghost town by the construction of Interstate 40 in the middle of the twentieth century. He was the youngest of thirteen children born to Mariana Maestas and Manuel Chávez. Mariana was the granddaughter of a woman of Cherokee descent who was adopted to be a servant for the Lucero family in New Mexico.[2] Manuel was a sheepherder who worked for the Bond and Weist Company on land that was formerly the Anton Chico and Pablo Montoya Land Grants, which itself was terrain that hosted a complex network of Kiowa, Comanche, and Apache tribes before that.

With instruction from his father, *tíos* (uncles), and older siblings, El Viejo learned how to ride horses, herd sheep, and work as a cowboy. When he was thirteen, his father froze to death after getting caught in a blizzard while returning home one night from Anton Chico. Three years later, El Viejo lied about his age and joined the Navy. After training in San Diego, he was stationed in Okinawa, Japan, and served as a gunner on a battleship during World War II. While in the Navy, he met a professional fighter from New Orleans named Earhardt who taught him how to box, a skill that would serve him well in subsequent years.

After the war, El Viejo returned to New Mexico for a while, picked up work as a cowboy, and helped at a gas station that he and his brother, Procopio, had built. Later, with assistance from the GI Bill, he moved to Kansas City, Missouri and attended a trade school for paint and body work on cars and airplanes. When he completed school, he returned to New Mexico and met Cruzita Baros, or, as her grandchildren call her, Nana. They married in 1957, and together had five children.

Sometime in the early 1960s, El Viejo attended a meeting of a newly formed organization in New Mexico called La Alianza Federal de Mercedes. While there, he met its president, Reies López Tijerina. For a long time, the United States government and the media told Native and mestiza/o peoples who were poor and landless that their poverty came from being culturally backward, from not being able to speak English, from not knowing how to "develop" the land properly, and from being a degenerate mixture of American Indian and Spanish. Many people continue to believe that story to this day. Yet with members like Nana and El Viejo, La Alianza provided a way of speaking back to the lies and misrepresentations proffered by the US government and our national culture. The group challenged the idea that being mixed American Indian and Spanish was a marker of shame. They challenged the idea that the poverty endured by Pueblo and Indohispano peoples was a result of our so-called backward nature. Rather, they linked poverty to centuries of land theft by the US government, the US Forest Service, and a number of cattle, mining, and timber corporations.

As a descendant of American Indian servants living on land-grant land that would ultimately be taken from his family, El Viejo had a memory that resonated with La Alianza's work in a powerful way. He was part of a pivotal generation of people of Mexican, Indigenous, and mestiza/o descent who went abroad to fight for the United States, only to return and discover ongoing exclusion from the basic rights and protections of US citizenship.

This realization would prompt his participation in one of the most renowned events in New Mexican history: the armed raid of the Tierra Amarilla courthouse on June 5, 1967. Along with twenty other Aliancistas, El Viejo attempted to place then–New Mexico District Attorney Alfonso Sánchez under citizen's arrest for violating La Alianza's right to peaceful assembly. The courthouse raid was one of El Viejo's favorite and most guarded stories.

> *We were scouring the place*
> *looking for Sánchez and anyone else*
> *who was hiding out.*
> *When we got upstairs, we found a door that was closed*
> *locked from the inside.*
> *I knocked once and*
> *gunshots tore through the door.*
> *They just barely missed my head.*
> *Now that pissed me off.*
> *Reies and I were carrying machine guns.*
> *Together we blasted the door open.*
> *The jailer just stood there*
> *holding his gun, looking scared.*
> *He dropped it right away.*

> *I walked over to him*
> *punched him right in the face*
> *split his cheek open.*

I was lucky enough to know El Viejo not only as a grandparent, but as a father figure who worked to feed, shelter, care for, and educate me and my sister, Michelle. Indeed, the memories I have of El Viejo as a storyteller are coupled with memories of him picking us up from school, of him taking me to buy toys when I was little, of sharing meals, of road trips, of him working in his garden, of him cleaning beans for supper. His courthouse raid story was tied to a bundle of other stories, jokes, and observations he would tell over the years that existed atmospherically in our Albuquerque home. Because they were El Viejo's stories, they surrounded everything. Yet I knew nothing about from where they came, nor even what it could mean to listen.

One evening El Viejo is chopping onions for dinner. He stops and looks at me.

Our People, the Indohispano,
need to become educated
because an education is
the one thing
they cannot take away from you.

El Viejo pulls his hand back quickly.
I nicked my finger
he says.
Blood trickles down his hand.
He gets up to wash his hands.
Over the sound of running water
he jokes
There goes the Iberian part of me.

In 2002, a worker from the US Census Bureau visited our home on the west side of Albuquerque. I was twenty-two and completing my last year of undergraduate study at the University of New Mexico. The census worker began his interview with El Viejo by asking questions about his work and recent retirement. He then asked about El Viejo's racial status.

Are you Hispanic, sir?
Hispanic?

El Viejo laughed as if
he was hearing
the punchline of a joke.
No.
We are Indohispanos.
We are mixed
Half Native American and half Iberian
mostly Jewish.
We are not Hispanic.

The census worker smiled
with confusion
and looked at me.
He didn't know what to do.
Neither did I.
El Viejo did not relent.

Our people are Indohispano.
We are not "Spanish."
"Spain" was not a sovereign country when Columbus came here.
And we are not only Iberian.
My great-great grandmother was half Apache and half Cherokee.
She became a slave to the Spaniards
and was named Dolores Lucero.
We are mixed.

The census worker sits up,
adjusts his glasses, and says,
Sir, that is fascinating.
Under race, you may want to fill in
the "other" box.

I had heard this narrative many times before without knowing where it came from. I did not know how to listen to his stories. I was always called "Hispanic" in school. I heard it everywhere on the news. I had seen it on applications for schools and on doctor's forms. I had even heard of "Chicano" from some faculty and Movimiento Estudiantil Chicano de Aztlán programs in high school. But Indohispano? I had only heard El Viejo talk that way. No other member of my immediate or distant family had ever really talked that way. Without an ear for his stories, I took the encounter as yet another example of his "eccentric" historical worldview. But nothing more.

I moved to Seattle in 2005 to begin the PhD program in the Department of English at the University of Washington (UW). During my second year, I became interested in Black cultural politics and the ways in which Black radical intellectuals critiqued the racist underpinnings of liberal forms of emancipation and capitalist modes of production. In graduate seminars and reading groups, I encountered work by W. E. B. DuBois, Cedric Robinson, Robin Kelly, Angela Davis, and C. L. R. James. Together, they taught me that contemporary iterations of capitalism, nationalism, state power, and citizenship—i.e., the hallmarks of Euroamerican modernity—were not self-originating and self-perfecting concepts and political structures born out of the grandeur of European civilization. Rather, I learned how the political, cultural, and economic structures of modernity remain financed and organized through antiblackness and the captivity of black life in forms that ranged from chattel slavery to segregation and into our contemporary nightmare of mass incarceration.

DuBois's *Darkwater* (1920) importantly connects the US racial doctrines of White patriarchal supremacy to a global structure of European capitalist imperialism: "The World War," he writes, "was primarily the jealous and avaricious struggle for the largest share in exploiting darker races" (29). Cedric Robinson's *Black Marxism* and his theory of racial capitalism in particular exposed how antiblack racism structures capitalist and nationalist social formations, yet remains irreducible to Marxist conceptions of class struggle. Reading Robinson showed me the powerful and perennially challenged role that the Black Radical tradition played in formulating a materialist theory of race that enabled "opposition to the alienation of labor and the ordering of social life according to the dictates of private property" (Robinson 1983, 45). By virtue of these critiques, I was starting to consider the ways that Black writers and cultural workers manifested acts of what Fred Moten and Stefano Harney call "fugitive enlightenment"—that is, a "ruptural and enraptured disclosure of the commons" enacted by "the life stolen by enlightenment and stolen back" (Robinson 1983, 28).

This is the path that led me back to El Viejo's stories. One evening in the summer of 2007, I was browsing the Black Studies section in Magus Books, a small independent bookstore close to the UW. While scanning the titles, I came across a book edited by Angela Davis titled *If They Come in the Morning: Voices of Resistance*. The book is a collection of writings by and about imprisoned radical intellectuals during the freedom and decolonization struggles of the 1960s and 1970s. I pulled it off the shelf and opened it at random, thinking I was going to find something written by George Jackson, James Baldwin, or any of the other authors listed on the back cover whom I wanted to read.

Instead, I encountered an entry on "Reies Tijerina."

Reies Tijerina?

That name struck an uncanny chord with me. I had heard it before but couldn't place it at the moment. I read the beginning of the entry: "Since the Treaty of Guadalupe Hidalgo between Mexico and the United States in 1848, Mexican Americans have lost over 4,000,000 acres of land-grant territory in the Southwest. The Chicano demand for lands illegally wrested from their ancestors received militant expression as early as 1963 in the *Alianza Federal de Mercedes*. This mass movement, deeply rooted in the rural population in northern New Mexico, was headed by Reies Tijerina. In 1966, it was estimated that the organization had a membership of over 14,000 families" (Davis, 96). El Viejo's stories of the courthouse raid slowly resurfaced. I kept reading:

> The day before the *Alianza's* national conference was scheduled to take place in June 1967, it was arbitrarily pronounced an unlawful assembly by the local District Attorney, who threated to arrest all the participants. That same day he rounded up 18 *Alianzans* on charges which were clearly fabricated. The District Attorney's actions, undisguised violations of the *Alianzans'* constitutional rights, prompted other members to plan a citizen's arrest. Twenty armed men, deputized by the People's Republic of San Joaquin, descended upon Tierra Amarrilo [*sic*] courthouse and seeking the District Attorney, whom they never located, held it for 90 minutes. In the course of the raid, a policeman went for his gun and he and the local jailer were wounded. An undersheriff and a reporter were escorted away from the scene, but later released. Ten *Alianzans* were brought up on charges (96–97).

I read the entire entry over and over in the middle of the bookstore. I was stunned, disoriented. A set of people, events, and keywords pivotal to the history of New Mexico and the Chicana/o movement began to find their connective threads to stories that I had grown up with, yet somehow and some way never really thought carefully about: Reies López Tijerina, the courthouse raid, the People's Republic of San Joaquín, the Treaty of Guadalupe Hidalgo, and the land grants.

I called him the next morning.

Hey Viejo
I have a question for you.
Were you a member of La Alianza?
Did you know Reies López Tijerina?
Were you a part of the Courthouse Raid?

There was a pause on his end of the line.

What the hell
do you think
I've been telling you?

The stun redoubled. The ground shifted beneath my feet. A disassembled puzzle that had apparently always surrounded my life began to take shape. Only now was I beginning to recognize it as a puzzle and discern the shape of its pieces and the depths of its logic.

That moment sparked an itinerant quest to learn everything I could. I flew home in between terms at school to record El Viejo's long monologues about the land grants, La Alianza, Tijerina, and the Indohispano. I researched accounts of the movement in Chicana/o, Latina/o, and Native American and Indigenous studies. I pursued narratives of land-grant formation and dispossession in the sociology, history, and anthropology of the US–Mexico borderlands. I sought examples of decolonial intellectual labor from work on subaltern movements and Indigenous racialization in Latin American Studies. And I began to research the surviving records of La Alianza that are housed in numerous archives in New Mexico.

Because of the courthouse raid and other instances of direct action protest against the settler politics of the US state, La Alianza was an organization that produced indelible militant imagery and critical terminology central to Chicana/o historical consciousness. Indeed, it gave a public language and a historical narrative to what the proletarianized, increasingly urbanized, and unevenly assimilated New Mexican land-grant heirs have been experiencing over the course of generations since the Mexican-American War: the systemic plunder of land, water, and other natural resources by the US state. Roughly thirty-five million acres of the land annexed to the United States after the Mexican-American War in 1848 was in the form of Spanish or Mexican land grants. By 1910, despite promises that land-grant rights would be honored under the Treaty of Guadalupe Hidalgo, 70 percent of that land would be lost through a series of legal obfuscations, US property tax impositions, political maneuverings, mistranslations, and outright thieveries within the land-grant adjudication process.[3] By connecting the politics of land dispossession to the ascendance of a number of cultural, political, economic, and military institutions in the US state, La Alianza triggered a public, academic, and governmental reexamination of Spanish and Mexican land-grant dispossession that continues to this day.

Prior to the US invasion, land grants were the dominant form of usurping Pueblo and Plains Indian land and administering the violence of territorial rights under Spanish and Mexican rule. As a concession to the Pueblo Revolt of 1680 that lasted into Mexican independence, the land grants became places where detribalized Indigenous captives and slaves known as *genízara* and *genízaro* Indians were forcibly resettled into large common-property tracts in the borderlands between the colonial interior and the territories dominated by the Utes, Navajos, Comanches, and Apaches.[4]

In the process of learning about the overlaid colonization of New Mexico, I began to see how the political economy of Spanish and Mexican land dispossession offered a distinct, yet complementary genealogy of slavery, property, nationalism, patriarchy, race, and revolution that Cedric Robinson and other Black radical thinkers traced in the reverberations of the modern transatlantic slave trade. That is, while Black radical intellectuals attuned me to the theft of Black life and labor that sustained legal and cultural logics of private property, I began to see how La Alianza connected the freedom of individual and corporate ownership of land as alienable property to a massive racialized and gendered process of land dispossession under US sovereignty that dismantled the land-grant communities' subsistent and communal mode of occupancy. The racialized effect of this dispossession reframed generations of Mexican and genízaro land-grant subjects—that is, La Alianza's constituency—with a "Spanish American" identity that excised the mestiza/o and Indigenous pasts of the land grants from public knowledge. Thus, the formation and doctrine of La Alianza shattered the nationalist fantasy of New Mexico as an enclosed and alienable land of triracial harmony among Anglos, Pueblo Indians, and Spanish Americans. The movement importantly opened up a decolonial language for understanding the historic and contemporary violence of land-grant dispossession in US politics and public culture.

It was this decolonial desire for land that stoked El Viejo's stories about La Alianza. As I began to listen actively to his stories, it became clear that he was less interested in telling me how it really was as an Aliancista. He was telling me how the land was stolen, how he tried to take it back, and he wanted to know why my work mattered for such a labor. El Viejo's demand for the land compounded the urgency and oddity of my research. It put my politics of reading La Alianza's writing and listening to his stories into crisis. Why would I desire simultaneously to recover the organization's history, yet presume the question of the land grants was settled? What politics of knowledge would sanction a study on La Alianza while also sanctioning the impossibility of land reclamation? What modes of violence are brought to La Alianza's archive by a reading practice that presumes US sovereignty as a settled state? These questions reframed the movement and the land-grant political economy as a landscape inhabited with multiple scales of violence, erasure, silence, mystery, and absence. I began to see how these resonated in my inability to listen to El Viejo's stories. Although this found expression in the everyday dynamics of my family, I was beginning to see its reflection in a systematic politics of opacity and motivated amnesia of Native and Mexican land usurpation that attended the imposition of colonial modernity in the Americas.

This discovery came hand in hand with a rather terrible loss. In the spring of 2011, El Viejo began to show the first signs of what would become a long and painful descent into dementia. For the following two years, until his death, my family cared for him in our house in Albuquerque. While his loyal, selfless, and feisty emotional core remained intact, we witnessed the slow, yet unpredictable loss of El Viejo's memories of his family and friends; the loss of his sense of place and time; the loss of his sense of continuity between the days and nights; the loss of his ability to hear and tell stories. It remains an irony of astonishing cruelty to witness the last years of a life dedicated to challenging the systemic forgetting of settler colonialism succumb to the physiological disintegration of memory.

In a remarkable stroke of foresight and resistance before his diagnosis, El Viejo began to write his life story. That spring and into the early summer, he handwrote memories from his childhood, his service in the Navy during World War II, and his work as a cowboy in eastern New Mexico in two spiral notebooks. On the inside cover, he wrote:

Ventura Chávez.
Life Story
I live under the Treaty of Guadalupe Hidalgo

El Viejo does not state that he lives under the United States. Rather, by living under the "Treaty of Guadalupe Hidalgo," he is insisting that he lives in occupied territory under alien landlords. Written in the eclipse of memory, the notebooks articulate his life story as a prism for a set of critical ruminations on the racial politics of New Mexican land-grant tenure and US sovereignty. I share them in a rewoven form not merely to illuminate the intersecting concerns of land, storytelling, memory, and insurgency that animated El Viejo's life; I also share them to affirm the endurance of his memory as an ongoing and active formation of rebellious storytelling in the present moment. I share them as the pathway to recognizing a more diffuse account of life and stories that can equip us to dismantle the global dictatorship of private property and activate a future attuned to the instructions of the land and its first peoples.

The last word belongs to El Viejo.

In August 15,
Kearny stood in the plaza in Las Vegas
to tell those he had just conquered
that he was among them for their benefit,
not their injury.
"We come as your friends
to better your condition.
I am your governor, look to me for protection.
We are your friends."

Seems to me that our friends are not our friends.
We have fought in all wars—
the Civil War, World War I and II.
And we'll fight in every war that comes
always the orphans in this land
to support the good USA.

Then a man came from Texas
and started to teach about the Treaty of Guadalupe Hidalgo.
We are here under their treaty.
We belonged to two grants: Anton Chico and Pablo Montoya.
My grandmother was born in the Pablo Montoya Grant.
My great-grandmother is buried in that grant.
My great-grandmother helped the Whites control the Pablo Montoya Grant
because she was half Apache, half Cherokee.
They married her with a White man named Barney Gare.
Her name was Dolores Lucero.
The Luceros adopted her.
My great-grandma had three daughters.
Juanita, Chonita, and Asención.
The Apache and Comanche liked to hunt buffalo there
and they left the land grant because
I guess she had pull with the Indians.
But they got pushed off the Pablo Montoya Grant.
Because now it is Anglo law.

The land that was our father's, grandfather's, and great grandfather's was stolen.
Anybody who tried to help us was branded a bandit.
We were second hand.
With World War II, they started calling on our people
and then we were suddenly
Americans.
But our land grants are not ours.
They were given to white people.
But we had nothing. Our people fight in all wars.
Our people have to defend this land
but we have no land grants.

We are the Indohispanos of this country.
We were raised in New Mexico.
Since we are 85% Indian,
I feel bad.
I miss what I feel they went through.
I belong to the Anton Chico Grant but I can't be there.

My dad would tell me
how he loved his ancestors.
They had other bosses and
heard a different language.

I was in World War II.
Seems now like we are prisoners of war.
We are free but can't speak our own tongues.
And then it hit me
We are being used here.
They are only in charge of this land.
They don't own it.
The white people are under order of
the government of the USA.
The white people are only holding the land
for the brown and red people.
They can never own it.
I am 84 years old. I haven't gotten my land grant back.
What is the United States?
We need to tell the people some stories
like the ones we've heard
a long time ago.
Give it all back
Take it all back.

NOTES

1. This chapter is based on a eulogy I delivered at my grandfather's memorial service in Albuquerque, New Mexico on March 17, 2013.

2. Her name was Dolores Lucero. As a detribalized indigenous servant for the Lucero family, Dolores would have been racialized as a *genízara*. For an extended account of La Alianza's relationship to the vexed genealogies of *genízara/o* racialization in New Mexico, see Trujillo 2016.

3. Several subsequent studies confirm and extend La Alianza's land-grant historiography. See Correia 2013, Dunbar-Ortiz, 2007, and Ebright 1994.

4. See Reséndez 2016.

WORKS CITED

Cabeza de Baca, Fabiola. 1954. *We Fed Them Cactus*. Albuquerque: University of New Mexico Press.

Chávez, Fray Angélico. 1974. *My Penitente Land: Reflections on Spanish New Mexico*. Santa Fe: Museum of New Mexico Press.

Corriea, David. 2013. *Properties of Violence: Law and Land Grant Struggle in Northern New Mexico*. Athens: University of Georgia Press.

Deloria, Vine Jr. 1985. *Behind the Trail of Broken Treaties: An Indian Declaration of Independence*. Austin: University of Texas Press.

DuBois, W. E. B. 1920 [1999]. *Darkwater: Voices from within the Veil*. Mineola, NY: Dover Publications.

Dunbar-Ortíz, Roxanne. 2007. *Roots of Resistance: A History of Land Tenure in New Mexico*. Norman: University of Oklahoma Press.

Ebright, Malcolm. 1994. *Land Grants and Lawsuits in Northern New Mexico*. New Mexico Land Grant Series. 1st ed. Albuquerque: University of New Mexico Press.

Harney, Stefano, and Fred Moten. 2013. *Undercommons: Fugitive Planning and Black Study*. Wivenhoe, UK: Autonomedia.

Reséndez, Andrés. 2016. *The Other Slavery: The Uncovered Story of Indian Enslavement in America*. New York: Houghton Mifflin Harcourt.

Robinson, Cedric. 1983. *Black Marxism: The Making of the Black Radical Tradition*. Chapel Hill: University of North Carolina Press.

Silko, Leslie Marmon. 1996. "Interior and Exterior Landscapes: The Pueblo Migration Stories." In *Yellow Woman and a Beauty of the Spirit: Essays on Native American Life Today*, 25–47. New York: Simon and Schuster.

Trujillo, Simón Ventura. 2016. "'USA Is Trespassing in New Mexico': La Alianza Federal de Mercedes and the Subaltern Historiography of Indo-Hispano Mestizaje." In *The Chicano Studies Reader: An Anthology of Aztlán, 1970–2015*, 2nd ed., edited by Chon A. Noriega, Eric Avila, Karen Mary Davalos, Chela Sandoval, and Rafael Pérez-Torres, 402–27. Los Angeles: UCLA Chicano Studies Research Center Press.

Viramontes, Helena María. 1997. "The Writes Ofrenda." In *Máscaras*, edited by Lucha Corpi, 124–31. Berkeley, CA: Third Woman Press.

Waters, Frank. 1963. *Book of the Hopi*. New York: Penguin Books.

Weber, David J., ed. 1973. *Foreigners in Their Native Land: Historical Roots of the Mexican Americans*. Albuquerque: University of New Mexico Press.

Williams, Raymond. 2009. *Marxism and Literature*. Oxford: Oxford University Press.

CHAPTER TWO

Remapping Patriotic Practices
The Case of the Las Vegas 4th of July Fiestas

LILLIAN GORMAN

On June 11, 2013, before Game 3 of the NBA finals in San Antonio, eleven-year-old Sebastien De La Cruz stepped up to the microphone to sing the National Anthem. Clad in a black-and-silver *charro* suit, a typical mariachi outfit, De La Cruz belted out a pitch-perfect rendition. Despite the crowd's roaring applause and the boy's spot-on vocal ability, the backlash on social media was swift and severe.[1] Not unlike the negative responses to the Spanish-language version of the National Anthem released in 2006 (Cepeda 2010) entitled *"Nuestro Himno"* (Our Anthem) and the multilingual singing of "America the Beautiful" in Coca-Cola's 2014 Super Bowl commercial, De La Cruz's performance was criticized as unpatriotic and un-American. The boy spoke with reporters the following day, emphasizing that Mexican heritage did not disqualify him from being an American. As quoted in a *New York Daily News* article, he explained, "My father was actually in the [US] Navy for a really long time . . . People don't know; they just assume that I'm just Mexican. But I'm not from Mexico. I'm from San Antonio, born and raised, a true San Antonio Spurs fan" (Knowles 2013). Presumably reacting to a visual and sonic merging of traditionally "American" markers of patriotism with cultural and linguistic markers of *Mexicanidad*,[2] viewers' social media responses revealed an exclusionary ideology regarding who was allowed to claim "Americanness" and how American patriotism should look, sound, and be performed. Additionally, they completely negated De La Cruz's deep connection to the place of San Antonio.

This nationally situated social-media backlash ignored the intimate, consistent, and continuous long-term relationships that many local Mexican American and Latina/o/x identifying communities have had with US markers of patriotism and US places. As De La Cruz notes, being American and Mexican are not mutually exclusive. In fact, his Mexican-style dress in the place of San Antonio, the cause of such controversy, actually made visible a unique sense of belonging. Estevan Arellano's 2014 work on the notion of *querencia* complements this idea of belonging. He theorizes querencia as a multilayered and complex "sense of place" (19), "knowledge of place" (142), and "love of place" (17) framed through discourse revolving around land and water in New Mexico. Yet the notion provides a useful framework for theorizing home (24) and connecting distinct US Latina/o/x experiences with place both within and outside of New Mexico. In this way, De La Cruz's relationship to San Antonio and the sonic cases of belonging of "Nuestro Himno" and "America the Beautiful" illustrate multiple dimensions of querencia.

Similarly, Margaret Dorsey and Miguel Díaz-Barraga (2011) explain the relationship between expressing belonging to the US and Mexican American cultural forms through the notion of "cultural citizenship," which

> can be thought of as a broad range of activities of everyday life through which Latinos and other groups claim space in society and eventually claim rights. Although it involves difference, it is not as if Latinos seek out such difference. Rather, the motivation is simply to create space where the people feel "safe" and "at home," where they feel a sense of belonging and membership. Typically, claimed space is not perceived by Latinos as "different." The difference is perceived by the dominant society, which finds such space "foreign" and even threatening (222).

Surely the sonic space of the two anthems and the visual marker of the charro suit in De La Cruz's performance unsettled artificially dichotomous notions of nation, patriotism, and identity that ultimately rendered these manifestations of cultural citizenship as threatening and foreign. Yet many celebrations that claim this type of belonging and querencia such as the George Washington parade in the majority Mexican-origin community in Laredo, Texas (Cantú 1995), the "El Veterano" *conjunto* festival in South Texas (Dorsey and Díaz-Barraga 2011), and even the more recent 4th of July festival in the border town of San Luis, Arizona,[3] seamlessly and routinely merge patriotic "American" symbols with daily lived experiences of being Mexican American and/or Latina/o/x in different Latina/o/x home spaces.

Held every year since 1888, the 4th of July Fiestas[4] in Las Vegas, New Mexico, represent one of the oldest articulations of such cultural citizenship and denote an active embodiment of querencia. These events in this 81 percent Hispanic[5] town represent much more than a simple commemoration of the

United States' Independence Day. Consider the poster hanging on the wall adjacent to the cash register in Johnny's Mexican Kitchen. This particular example, by George Lucero, commemorates the 2002 Las Vegas Fiestas. It shows the figures of a man and a woman (presumably New Mexican Hispanics) in the middle of a dance. The woman's arms extend above her head in what looks like a fifth-position ballet or flamenco pose. The man is to her side with his arm behind his back, looking intently into her eyes. The woman's dress suggests that of a flamenco dancer with its tight, leotard-like top and flared skirt. The man's distinctive hat recalls a traditional *huasteco* ensemble from Mexico's state of Tamaulipas. However, the colors and patterns of the clothing are the most salient features in the poster. The woman's top is blue with white stars and she wears a red skirt with a white ruffle. The man's shirt is white, adorned with a red-and-white-striped bandana. The dancers together represent a living, breathing, and dancing American flag. The 2002 fiesta theme is printed on the poster: "Fidelidad—A Una Nación, Una Comunidad, y Las Fiestas Bajo De Dios." The loyalty to nation, community, and the fiestas is presented together—as one inextricably linked package.

In what follows, I would like to tease out more closely the ways in which the 4th of July Fiestas in Las Vegas reveal the complex relationship between nation, community, and place in this majority Hispanic community. Taking as points of departure Mérida Rúa's (2012) notion of "grounded identidad" and Arredondo's (2008) theory of "lived regionalities," I argue that the fiestas represent a transculturative and contestatory practice against historical marginalization through what I term a "grounded regionality." I explore this practice of grounded regionality through a close analysis of the discourse produced within the annual fiesta guides during a three-year period (2006–2009), as well as recent interviews with Las Vegas natives. Ultimately, my reading of the Las Vegas Fiestas serves to complicate the essentialist notions of citizenship that critique national displays of Latina/o/x patriotism because, in reality, these displays exist as complex local everyday practices outside of the national spotlight. The case of the 4th of July Fiestas in Las Vegas also serves to expand the notion of querencia and works as a productive tool to connect distinct US Latina/o/x homes.

SOME NOTES ON TERMINOLOGY

I would like to clarify my use of the terms "Latina/o/x," "Hispanic," and "Mexican American" throughout this chapter. The literature I cite uses distinct terms in each of its studies based on its theoretical approach and the specific Latina/o/x community in which it is based. All of these studies center around Mexican American or, more broadly defined, Latina/o/x communities. Yet New Mexicans who trace their family roots to New Mexico for more than a century have clear inclinations toward certain terms of ethnic identity that are generally distinct from the terms "Mexican American" and "Latina/o/x." Those who identify as part of this population do not have a recent immigration history and do not identify as Mexican (Nieto-Phillips 2004). New Mexico is their families' homeland. My previous study (Gorman 2015) demonstrates the term "Hispanic" to be a term of preference and the term "Latino" to be used rarely or not at all among Hispanic New Mexicans. In fact, for many of them, rather than a pan-ethnic identifier, "Hispanic" references a place-based northern New Mexico identity.

It is not my wish to impose the use of the term "Latino" on communities that clearly do not use it. However, I do think it is useful, in the spirit of Frances Aparicio (2009), not to erase historical and cultural specificities between national-origin groups but, rather, to "tease out the power differentials and the historical, social and cultural dilemmas that these terms evoke as we identify the interactions between and among peoples of various Latin American national identities" (625). For this reason, when I highlight the power dynamics or knowledge that is produced between the groups, as well as the theoretical framework of Latinidad itself (Aparicio 2003; Rúa and García 2007), I will use the term strategically. Otherwise, I will use the identifiers of "Hispanic," "Hispano," or "Hispanic New Mexicans" when referring to the community members in Las Vegas, in accordance with how these communities choose to identify themselves.

LAS VEGAS AND NEW MEXICO HISPANIC FIESTAS

Founded in 1835 as part of the San Miguel del Bado Land Grant, and the last major Hispanic town to be established in northern New Mexico (Mares 1985), the subject of this study took on the patron saint of Our Lady of Sorrows and became known as *La Villa de Nuestra Señora de los Dolores de Las Vegas Grandes*. On August 15, 1846, General Stephen Watts Kearny entered the Las Vegas Plaza and claimed the town and the entire territory known as Nuevo México in the name of the United States. I suggest that this historical moment cannot avoid leaving its traces on the celebration of the 4th of July Fiestas in Las Vegas. The plaza serves as the common site for both events. In fact, the many food booths and folding chairs that populate the Las Vegas Plaza Park during the fiestas surround the plaque commemorating Kearny's words to the citizens of Las Vegas. On that August morning, from a rooftop overlooking the plaza, Kearny stated: "I have come amongst you by the orders of my government, to take possession of your country, and extend over it the laws of the United States. We consider it, and have done for some time, a part of the territory of the United States . . . Henceforth, I absolve you from all allegiance to the Mexican government . . . There goes my army—you see but a small portion of it; there are many more behind—resistance is useless" (quoted in Weber 1973, 161–62). Commemorating the moment of union with the United States, August 15, 1846, serves as the birthday of an American national identity for not only Las Vegas residents, but all inhabitants of New Mexico at the time.

However, this date also served as a catalyst for contradictory feelings and ambivalence toward this new union. Though Kearny urged New Mexicans to avoid any forms of resistance, not all of them accepted their precarious territorial status and many were skeptical of Kearny's pledges of protection. For the next sixty years, Las Vegas served as a site from which New Mexican Hispanics resisted this shift in national identity and the broken promises flowing from it. The 1890s, in particular, represented a time in which residents fought for protection of their land from its illegal seizure by Anglo settlers, sometimes manifesting their resistance to Anglo encroachment in uprisings and fence-cutting (Weber 1972, 234). It also represented a particularly productive time in literary and cultural production (Meléndez 1997). Las Vegas existed as an intellectual powerhouse for northern New Mexico and was a site from which Hispanic New Mexicans publicly debated, rallied, and professed a loyalty to the Spanish language and cultural rights amid a reconfiguration of national allegiances. Eusebio Chacón's 1901 "A Protest Rally" and Aurora Lucero-White's award-winning early-twentieth-century essay "Plea for the Spanish Language" are but two representations of this cultural production.

Despite the city's rich historical and cultural legacy, the Las Vegas Fiestas are a consistently overlooked area within New Mexico cultural studies. Scholarship regarding the study of Hispanic fiestas in New Mexico extends back to Aurelio Espinosa's 1926 work on the region's Spanish folk life. Yet Espinosa's research and the two most comprehensive bodies of work regarding Hispanic culture in New Mexico (Arthur Campa's 1979 volume *Hispanic Culture in the Southwest* and Mary Montaño's 2001 compilation *Tradiciones Nuevomexicanas: Hispano Arts and Culture of New Mexico*) make no explicit mention of the Las Vegas celebration. Lucero-White alludes to them in her 1953 study *Literary Folklore of the Hispanic Southwest* when she explains that a few New Mexico villages observe national holidays, such as the Fourth of July, through fiestas (223). Typically, New Mexican Hispanic town fiestas center around the patron saint of the town. Jeffrey Smith's 2004 analysis of the Las Vegas Plaza as a Hispanic space briefly mentions the Las Vegas Fiestas, yet his work does not engage in any detailed analysis of the celebration. Sylvia Rodríguez's (2002) reference to the Taos fiestas does not directly mention the Las Vegas celebration, yet her study highlights the cultural processes of resistance and (re)appropriation of space that have occurred in Taos.

This notion of (re)appropriation is relevant to the study of the Las Vegas Fiestas. In the present study, I explore the (re)appropriation of historical and national narratives to contest marginalization. Within a larger context of US Latina/o/x festivals, Mérida Rúa and Lorena García (2007) provide a helpful framework for understanding the complex cultural work of festive forms. As they explain, "Participants and spectators use public events to debate, challenge, and mediate representation imbuing the events with their life experiences. Festive forms thus can be understood as locations of social action where notions of identity and community are rethought and negotiated with transformative potential" (321). In the analysis that follows, I trace the ways that Las Vegans articulate their own theorizations regarding identity, community, and place.

According to Lucero's 2002 fiesta poster, the Las Vegas Fiestas recognize loyalty to the nation, the community, and the fiestas themselves. A note in the 2009 fiesta guide reads, "Patriotism and Culture: Fiestas de Las Vegas is all about the culture of northern New Mexico, but it's also a patriotic celebration because it's during the Fourth of July weekend" (25). Interestingly, despite the visual image from the 2002 poster, both the textual representations for the 4th of July Fiestas in the fiesta guides and the visual markers at the actual fiestas over the three-year period lack a real presence of traditional "American" patriotic symbols. US flags and red, white, and blue colors do not have a major presence within the multiday celebration. The quote from the 2009 guide mentions patriotism, but almost as an afterthought to the real purpose of the festive form: the celebration of northern New Mexico culture.

Unlike other Hispanic town fiestas, Las Vegas's does not honor its patron saint. The feast day of Our Lady of Sorrows is September 15. During my three years of living, working, and researching in Las Vegas, it seemed curious to me that, after asking numerous longtime local residents if they knew of any date for the celebration of the Fiestas de Las Vegas other than the 4th of July, given that Las Vegas was founded in 1835 (a full thirteen years before becoming part of the United States), not a single resident seemed to carry any historical or collective memory of their being held on an alternate date. Yet the fiestas do not commemorate any history related directly to the events of US independence in 1776. And, unlike the more "historical" fiestas of Santa Fe and Española, there is no reenactment of a historical event related to Spanish history and conquest in New Mexico. If not a historical celebration commemorating a particular event or a religious celebration in honor of a patron saint, what, then, do the 4th of July Fiestas in Las Vegas celebrate?

In words similar to the 2009 fiesta guide, Las Vegas native Michaelann Cavazos states that "The Fiestas in Las Vegas, New Mexico is a celebration of Independence but to someone growing up in this small town, it is much more. It is a walk back in time to culture and tradition. Where generations of families unite and where new friends are always welcome. New Mexican Food at its best!! And of course the music . . . the mariachis and the local artists display the music that [has] deep roots in Northern New Mexico."[6] Again, the recognition of the 4th of July and Independence Day are subordinated to the "so much more." This phrase references the specific local histories, "deep roots," and interactions of Las Vegas Hispanics. I propose that it indexes a transposition of local Hispanic New Mexican histories and experiences onto the 4th of July holiday, embodying a continuous process of transculturation that recalls the "transformative potential" of festive forms described by Rúa and García (2007). Diana Taylor's (1991) conceptualization of transculturation provides a useful framework for this idea. She explains that transculturation "allows the 'minor' culture (in the sense of positionally marginalized) an impact on the dominant one, although the interactions are not, strictly speaking, 'dialogic' or 'dialectical.' Transculturation suggests a shifting or circulating pattern of cultural transference" (93). In Las Vegas, it seems that the 4th of July is transculturated and transformed into a day in which daily, lived, grounded cultural practices are celebrated and activated. This re-semantification of the holiday contests a larger historical marginalization of Hispanics in New Mexico. The discursive deployment of the concept of "tradition" plays a key role in this process.

UNPACKING TRADITION: WRITTEN AND VISUAL DISCOURSE ABOUT THE FIESTAS

Every year, the local newspaper *The Las Vegas Optic* or the City of Las Vegas produces an official guide and schedule booklet for the Las Vegas Fiestas. This provides a breakdown of the entertainment and the times and locations of the fiesta mass, the crowning of the fiesta queen, the fiesta parade, the veterans' celebration, and other events. The booklet is also filled with advertisements, short articles, and statements of good wishes from the Las Vegas Fiesta Council members and city government officials. For my purposes, the booklets provide an excellent sampling of the discourse that surrounds the event as articulated by the residents themselves. The 2008 edition contains an article with a concise description of the weekend of Las Vegas Fiestas. It is worth reproducing this text in its entirety here, not only because it will inform the reader regarding the general structure of the Las Vegas Fiestas, but also because it underscores several important themes that connect to identity, community, and place. The article explains:

> During the first week of July, thousands make their way to Plaza Park for the annual Fiestas de Las Vegas. It's the biggest, brightest and most anticipated event in the Meadow City . . . The vendors surround Plaza Park and line up on Bridge Street, providing visitors with *traditional* eats such as Navajo tacos, roasted corn on the cob, fajitas, beans, hamburgers and much more that can all be, of course, ordered with that New Mexico staple, chile . . . The aroma of the food fills the park as locals and visitors alike gather to hear *traditional* music live. The gazebo serves as a bandstand—and a dance area for those who like to get their boots moving. The fiesta is a *traditional* celebration, preserving the area's language and *tradition* for both young and old. (4, emphases mine)

The notion of "tradition" is prevalent throughout this description. Indeed, the very motto for the 2009 fiestas, "Nuestras tradiciones, nuestros tesoros" (Our traditions, our treasures) clearly emphasizes that the concept of tradition, expressed in Spanish, defines the Fiestas of Las Vegas. Additionally, fiesta historian and longtime master of ceremonies Cipriano Aguilar explains, the annual fiestas are "where people enjoy our *heritage, culture, traditions*, foods and family fun" (19, emphasis mine). Clearly, the notion of tradition circulates consistently throughout the discourse around the 4th of July Fiestas. Additionally, the short narratives in the guides speak of not only the importance of remembering traditions, but also about engaging in traditional activities such as gathering in the Plaza Park, the consumption of certain foods, music, dancing, and speaking Spanish. These ideas signify traditions as an active process. Walter Mignolo (2003) illuminates this notion of tradition as process, explaining that

> my insistence in understanding the past and speaking the present invites an understanding of "traditions" not as *something* that is there to be remembered, but the process of remembering and forgetting itself . . . "Traditions" would be, in this sense, a multiplexed and filtered ensemble of acts of saying, remembering, and forgetting. In such enactments "traditions" are the loci where people are bonded in communities by languages, eating habits, emotions, ways of

dressing, and organizing and conceiving themselves in a given space (country or border) by constructing an image of both the self and the other (xv–xvi).

Traditions thus represent the process of remembering a certain past from a location in the present. If the 4th of July Las Vegas Fiestas embody a simultaneous process of remembering and a daily living out of certain traditions, then the holiday is also defined by these very same traditions. The day of US independence does not allude to some vague "American" set of traditions that exist outside of New Mexico Hispanic points of reference. The active process of traditions discursively constructed within the fiesta guides reorients the 4th of July patriotic practices toward Las Vegas Hispanic traditions. The good wishes from the City of Las Vegas in the 2008 fiesta guide read, "Congratulations on *keeping* 120 years of Tradition! Qué vivan las fiestas!" (30, emphasis mine). The idea of "keeping" tradition, again, denotes tradition as a process. In the words of the city, this process engages both past and present. Hispanics in Las Vegas are to be congratulated for the accomplishment of "remembering" and "theorizing the past in the present" (Mignolo 2003, xv).

One fascinating example of this active process of problematizing past and present through the notion of tradition is the case of food. Recall the fiesta guide's list of festive foods. Rather than mentioning foods that are commonly thought to be traditional to the area or indigenous to the Americas, such as what Luz Calvo and Catriona Rueda Esquibel (2015) refer to as the heritage crops of corn, beans, squash, greens, herbs, and seeds, the fiesta guide includes fajitas, hamburgers, and Navajo tacos alongside chile, beans, and corn. It is not my intent to label certain foods as more traditional than others, but instead to call attention to the active process of tradition at work here. Through a lens of what Vivian Nun Halloran (2016) terms "gastronomic nostalgia" in the New South, we see a manifestation of the "interactions between change and tradition" (67). She includes the Southwest in her conceptualization of this region and describes it as "full of contradictions: it simultaneously invites culinary innovation while preserving its multiple and storied cooking traditions" (86). This interplay between change and tradition allows for innovations such as fajitas, hamburgers, and Navajo tacos to be incorporated and then embraced as traditional foods within the 4th of July Fiestas. This process blurs lines between past and present traditions and continues to disrupt any notion of static traditions.

In her theorizations of diasporic celebrations of Central American fiestas in the United States, Martiza Cárdenas (2017) highlights the transformative power that these festive forms have in Los Angeles. She states that for the diaspora, these celebrations "become the critical terrain where Central Americans can contest their marginalization from U.S. American and Latina/o imaginaries" (128). The 4th of July Fiestas in Las Vegas offer a similar opportunity. The discourses of Hispanic Las Vegans around the fiestas engage with a notion of not only revisiting traditions, but actively living them out as a practice that creates visibility. In the 2008 fiesta guide, Aguilar states, "Our past fiestas should be studied and read about by everyone, especially our younger generation, as a way to learn more of the history de Fiestas that our *forefathers* enjoyed for many years" (19, emphasis mine). The term "forefathers" often evokes an image of the founding fathers of the United States.

On a day like the 4th of July, this is certainly a common image within popular discourse and cultural production throughout the nation. Yet the intense emphasis on tradition and the "localness" of the Las Vegas Fiestas suggest that Aguilar's words refer to a different set of "forefathers." He states, "The Las Vegas Fiestas . . . really belong to you and your families" (19). Fiesta Council member Rosita Ellis echoes this idea in the 2008 guide when she exclaims, "You, the community, make this wonderful event enjoyable" (6). The "forefathers" of Las Vegas represent the living, breathing community currently celebrating the fiestas. This is a radical move. Rather than using figures from another time and place in US history, the city inserts its people and community into a grounded understanding of the 4th of July with the reference points rotating around Hispanic Las Vegas. This is precisely the critical terrain that contests marginalization to which Cárdenas refers.

In the 2008 fiesta guide, Aguilar notes that "the Fiestas bring the past, the present, and the future together" (19). The multigenerational participation and the influx of Las Vegas natives who return for the 4th of July play a part in this contestatory practice of transforming and transculturating the holiday. The words of 2008 Las Vegas Fiesta parade marshals Lina and Chemo Valdez effectively communicate this grounding in the guide: "¡Qué vivan las fiestas del cuatro de julio. Ay nos vemos en Las Vegas para el cuatro!" The couple index Las Vegas as a meeting place, a gathering place in which one expects to see the return of old friends and reunite with family.

In the 2007 *Fiestas de Las Vegas Official Fiesta Guide*, Mayor Henry Sánchez states, "The Fiestas de Nuestra Señora de Los Dolores de Las Vegas Grandes bring everyone together from places far and near to share family values and to remind us of our heritage" (4). Sánchez's words underscore the power of the celebration to reunite families through space and time. A 2009 statement from Fiesta Council member Rosita Ellis says, "The Fiestas are a time to visit with people who live locally and those that have traveled" (6). The emphasis on the return of family highlights the notion that the events create a space for Las Vegas locals. Indeed, attendees express similar sentiments. Las Vegas native Michaelann Cavazos points out that the fiestas are "where generations of families unite."[7] Another longtime Las Vegas resident notes, "The fiestas is a time where the entire community comes together."[8] A former Las Vegas Fiesta queen and committee member explains, "A lot of family reunions happen around 4th of July. Or class reunions. But I think a lot of people just kind of build visiting their family around the 4th of July because it's just kind of like a homecoming. A Las Vegas homecoming. Everybody knows well, 'are you coming for fiestas?' That's usually the first question that people ask."[9] This notion of homecoming is key to understanding the ways in which returning for fiestas contests dominant narratives around the 4th of July and re-semantifies the celebration.

The Las Vegas accounts of reunions and returning are similar to Sarah Bronwen Horton's (2010) work documenting the Santa Fe Fiestas and what she terms "diasporic Hispanos." She explains that "Diasporic Hispanos who return for the Fiesta may be said to be making a pilgrimage" (193) and highlights the fact that the "fiesta serves as a kind of homecoming for a significant constituent of Fiesta organizers and participants—those who return annually for the event even though economic conditions have forced them to move elsewhere" (183). Indeed, primarily due to economic conditions in New Mexico during and after World War II, many New Mexican Hispanos sought work opportunities in other western states, particularly California, Colorado, and Wyoming.

Vanessa Fonseca (2017) has engaged in extensive research documenting the experiences of New Mexican Hispanos who moved to Wyoming in her work on the state's "Manito Trail." Las Vegas homecomings during fiestas serve as contestatory acts in and of themselves. Horton (2010) elaborates on the notion that diasporic Hispanos "involve themselves in the fiesta not only out of nostalgia . . . but also out of a commitment to ensuring the Hispano presence in northern New Mexico" (191). Similarly, she states, "During Fiesta weekend, the gathering of returning New Mexicans and native Santa Feans on the Plaza symbolically reconstitutes a dispersed Hispano community" (196). With this in mind, the 4th of July Fiestas serve to affirm a majority Hispano presence in Las Vegas while also transforming the holiday itself into a space in which the dominant presence is that of local Hispanics. A local educator and lifelong Las Vegan echoes this point: "It's a community block party, all day, everyday with more of a cultural aspect, but it's not for tourists, strictly locals and for people who moved away."[10] This last utterance referring to "strictly locals" establishes the "safe space" theorized by Dorsey and Díaz-Barraga (2011). In this way, notions of return and a strict sense of locality ground the 4th of July Fiestas within a framework of coming home to one's querencia.

Yet it is important to note that querencia is not necessarily fixed. Consider what Horton (2010) terms "failed returns" in her work on the Santa Fe fiestas (196). She documents the disappointment of diasporic Hispanos upon returning for fiestas as one laments, "Now it's just Zozobra and tourists" (198). She explains, "In returning for the Fiesta, diasporic Hispanos . . . seek the experience of an unchanged relationship to a homeland site . . . Instead, many returning New Mexicans find that the city's material transformation disrupts the illusion of temporal reversal, deferring their hopes of homecoming" (199). These deferred homecomings illustrate a "querencia disrupted" and a sense of loss. This disruption is similarly expressed by former fiesta queen Sarah Flores. She explains, "Back then the fiesta queen pageant was a big deal . . . but now that tradition is kind of dying it's kind of sad. I think this year there was only two girls who ran for fiesta queen . . . there's not so much culture and tradition anymore. And I think my generation hasn't really brought that in . . . a lot of people aren't bringing that culture back and showing how important it is."[11] Flores's words communicate a sense of loss toward the very elements that Las Vegans use to define the 4th of July Fiestas: traditions and culture. Thus, one's relationship to querencia is not necessarily static and can, indeed, at times be a struggle. This fluidity is apparent through the fact that querencia may feel both disrupted and grounded at the same time.

Rúa's (2012) theorization of a "grounded identidad" provides a productive lens through which to view both the grounded and dynamic elements of querencia within the 4th of July Fiestas. She explains, "Identidad, complex and fluid, needs to be recognized and explored as 'grounded,' as rooted in both time and place, and as manifest in everyday exchanges" (xv). The 4th of July

Fiestas provide this site through which New Mexico Hispanics ground themselves in a querencia that embodies their multiple encounters and reunions with family and community members. Through the fiestas, they live out their attachment to the multiple terrains within the place of Las Vegas and the familiar site of the festivities. Arredondo (2008) discusses the notion of "lived regionalities" in relation to the experiences of Mexican women in the Midwest during the post-WWII era. She coins the term "in an attempt to capture tangible and intangible terrains as they were actually experienced by women themselves" (96). The discourse around the Las Vegas Fiestas also captures the tangible and intangible terrains that make up the (re)telling of past, present, and future Las Vegas Hispanic stories. By combining the concepts of grounded identidad and lived regionalities into grounded regionalities, we can contemplate the meaning-making processes taking place within the fiestas, particularly through the act of returning, and understand these active and living traditions as a space in which historical marginalization is contested.

In order to better understand this marginalization, I'd like to revisit the words regarding the fiestas being "strictly for locals." Even in a place like Las Vegas with a rich history of Hispanic political participation and a demographic reality of a majority of Hispanic residents whose families can claim a Las Vegas heritage for more than a century, it is still important to think about *who* is telling the city's story. Historical accounts of Las Vegas told and circulated by Las Vegas Hispanic residents are few and far between: Nasario García's collection of oral histories (2005), Anselmo Arellano and Julian Josue Vigil's 1985 locally published history, and, perhaps, A. Gabriel Meléndez's accounts of local Spanish-language newspaper history (1997, 2005). Yet the story of Las Vegas in Las Vegas is widely told by history professors at the local university (who are from elsewhere) and the largely Anglo Citizens' Committee on Historic Preservation. Therefore, in a town where its own local Hispanic story is largely marginalized or told through nonlocal Anglo mediators, the lived, grounded regionalities embodied in the 4th of July Fiestas do the work of contesting erasure. The Las Vegas Fiestas position Las Vegas Hispanics to tell their stories in an environment that is "strictly for locals."

A letter by Las Vegas Fiesta Council President Mathew Martínez in the 2007 fiesta guide provides an additional dimension to this contestatory practice. He writes, "Bienvenidos! The 119th Fiestas de Nuestra Señora de los Dolores de Las Vegas Grandes truly brings everyone together to share this great tradition and our culture. Es un tiempo de recordarnos de la importancia de nuestras familias, cultura, tradiciones, amor, amistad y como que no . . . la música, comida, y los gran bailes" (5). Martínez centers the importance of the Las Vegas Fiestas around family, tradition, and culture; his codeswitching between English and Spanish marks these traditions within a linguistic framework that claims both languages. He actually switches to Spanish when he describes the components of the fiestas. It is clear that this is not due to any semantic gaps or linguistic deficiency. Ana Celia Zentella (1997) and Shana Poplack (1980) are the authors of just two of the many linguistic studies that affirm this. He is able to communicate in both languages. But the switch from an English-dominant discourse to Spanish at that particular point in his utterance seems to suggest that the phrase in Spanish holds more meaning for him, and the community, if it is communicated in the heritage language of Las Vegas.

Documenting Spanish-language practices, repression, and maintenance in Las Vegas is a book project in and of itself. I will leave the discussion of these important linguistic experiences for future research. I would, instead, like to highlight how Martínez's words situate linguistic practices as part of the "safe space" that is "strictly for locals." Robert Tinajero (2016) denotes a "multi-consciousness" as a way of "existing within a multiplicity of linguistic and cultural borders" (22). Martinez's discourse localizes and grounds this practice of existing within multiple cultural and linguistic practices as part of a linguistic querencia in Las Vegas. Alistair Pennycook (2001) describes one of the key concerns of critical applied linguistics as finding "ways of thinking about the micro-contexts of everyday language use and macro concerns of society, culture, politics, and power" (172). The micro-context of language use within the 4th of July Fiestas addresses a larger power differential in which local Hispanics continuously engage in a linguistic and cultural insertion of their experiences into the larger storytelling of Las Vegas. This insertion creates a counternarrative regarding the larger meaning of the 4th of July.

CONCLUDING THOUGHTS

Alberto Lopez's poster appears on the cover of the official 2007 fiesta guide. It displays nine figures standing side by side that seem to be welcoming the community to the Las Vegas Fiestas: a modern-looking middle-aged New Mexico Hispanic man dressed in a white *guayabera*; a Pancho Villa–like figure reminiscent of the Mexican Revolution; a modern-looking Native American

FIGURE 2.2 Alberto López, Las Vegas Fiesta Guide cover, 2007. Photo courtesy of Lillian Gorman.

woman clad in a pink dress, white shawl, moccasins, and silver-and-turquoise jewelry; a young Hispano boy playing the guitar; a male Aztec dancer and a young girl dancing a step from a ballet *folklórico* routine; a Spanish conquistador in armor and boots; a pachuco in a purple zoot suit; and a Hispanic World War II veteran. The figures are standing on Bridge Street, the street that leads west into the Plaza Park. Alberto López's poster visually inserts all of these figures into the story of the 4th of July Fiestas, the story of Las Vegas, and ultimately the larger narrative of US history.

This contestatory practice of grounded regionalities opens a conversation that validates multiple figures of New Mexico history. Michael L. Trujillo (2009) underscores the importance of this remapping of history. He states, "When we go to school, we are told that our ancestors came from the East. Well, I don't know of many Martínezes, Arellanos, or Archuletas who had any ancestors who landed at Plymouth Rock . . . In this way, the dominant American iconography of the frontier, pioneers, and westward expansion represses the reality of Chicano/Hispanic claims to the Southwest" (38). Each of the figures in López's poster engages in a process of not only reclaiming the historical narratives of the Southwest, but also reconfiguring the picture of us citizenship, both cultural and national.

In Olivia Cadaval's (1998) study of the Latino Festival in Washington, DC, she underscores a key role that festival celebrations play for Latina/o/x immigrants there. She explains that through the festival "we are confronted with the need to seek and establish an identity, and to define 'American' for ourselves" (8). The Las Vegas Hispanic community does not necessarily represent an immigrant community;[12] however, the process of establishing a distinct way of being "American" within this locality and through these fiestas emerges through the discursive articulation surrounding the notion of tradition and the grounded lived realities that these traditions embody. The 4th of July Fiestas in Las Vegas remap the terrain of national narratives and American history by elevating New Mexico Hispanic traditions and cultural innovations as just as "authentically" American and patriotic as stars and stripes and red, white, and blue. Thus, with every celebration of the 4th of July Las Vegas Fiestas, New Mexico Hispanics effectively (re)insert themselves, their history, culture, community, traditions, and querencia into the larger narrative of American history.

In closing, I would like to revisit the dynamic nature of querencia and underscore that new querencias can also emerge. Just a few weeks before the 2017 4th of July Fiestas, I was teaching a course in Las Vegas for educators from different parts of the state. A Las Vegas educator was explaining the fiestas to students who were not from the area. One educator from Hatch, New Mexico, whose family has lived in southern New Mexico for centuries, exclaimed, "I'm so jealous of you guys up here. You have so much heritage, so much culture. It's so rich. In Hatch, I feel like we've lost that over the years. I feel so at home up here."[13] This educator felt an immediate deep sense of connection to Las Vegas and, through this connection, a new querencia.

This is not unlike the way in which Las Vegas emerged as one of my own querencias. My Chicana roots reside in Albuquerque's South Valley, Belen, Santa Fe, and Taos, yet living and working in Las Vegas ignited a new querencia for me as well. One afternoon, after speaking on KNMX 540 AM's Friday afternoon radio program about Spanish-language revitalization and maintenance in northern New Mexico, a caller contacted the studio and insisted on speaking with me. The DJ put the call through on an off-air line. The female voice on the other end asked me, "¿Eres pariente de Magdalena Gorman?" I responded that Magdalena was my great-grandmother from Santa Fe. She

then joyfully exclaimed, "¡Mi prima Magdalena! Tú y yo somos parientes."
The caller was Dolores "Lola" Alire, a ninety-eight-year-old lifelong resident
of Las Vegas. She was part of a local family I did not know I had. Over the
next two years, we would visit on a near-daily basis.

I am not suggesting that one needs to find distant cousins in new places
in order to establish a querencia. I'm simply sharing my story to illustrate the
many levels of querencia on which Las Vegas functions and the ways in which
new querencias may emerge dynamically. Understanding querencia as multiple, dynamic, and complex serves as an additional framework to complicate
considerations of home, citizenship, and patriotism. Considering these concepts together reveals the active ways in which US Latina/o/x homeplaces like
Sebastien De La Cruz's San Antonio and Las Vegas, New Mexico, emerge
and connect.[14] Querencia productively illuminates the grounded regionalities
within the 4th of July Fiestas and throughout other US Latina/o/x homeplaces and provides a productive site for expanding the notion, reading its
distinct dimensions, and creating a contestatory practice.

NOTES

1. See Knowles' *New York Daily News* article from two days after the performance
and its documentation of the negative reactions at http://www.nydailynews.com
/news/national/mexican-american-boy-national-anthem-performance-sparks
-racist-backlash-article-1.1371990.

2. I invoke the notion of "Mexicanidad" (or Mexicanness), taking as a point of
departure the works of Menchaca (1995), Ochoa (2004), and Vila (2006). These three
works present a continuum of Mexicanidad and highlight the multiple ways of being
Mexican in the United States.

3. Nathalie González, personal interview, March 7, 2017.

4. In this chapter, I generally capitalize the term "fiesta" when it appears as part of
the phrase "Las Vegas Fiestas," "4th of July Fiestas," or "Fiestas de Las Vegas" in order to be consistent with the conventions most commonly adhered to by Las Vegans
writing about the event. Otherwise, I adhere to Spanish-language conventions for
leaving the term in lower-case.

5. According to the 2010 US Census (https://www.census.gov/quickfacts/map
/IPE120213/3539940/accessible), 15 percent of Las Vegas's population identifies as
White, non-Hispanic/Latino, 2 percent as Native American, and 2 percent as more
than one race.

6. Facebook direct message to author, March 13, 2017.

7. Facebook direct message to author, March 13, 2017.

8. Leah Wolff, Facebook direct message to author, March 15, 2017.

9. Sarah Flores, personal interview, July 5, 2017.

10. Martina Tapia, personal interview, April 11, 2017.

11. Sarah Flores, personal interview, July 5, 2017.

12. The ways that first-generation Mexican immigrants figure into this contestatory grounded regionality are most definitely the subject of a future study.

13. This individual wishes to remain anonymous.

14. I use "homeplaces" here in the spirit of Bell Hooks's (1990) theories regarding it as a site of resistance.

WORKS CITED

Aparicio, Frances. 2003. "Jennifer as Selena: Rethinking Latinidad in Media and Popular Culture." *Latino Studies* 1: 90–105.

———. 2009. "Cultural Twins and National Others: Allegories of Intralatino Subjectivities in U.S. Latino/a Literature." *Identities: Global Studies in Culture and Power* 16: 622–64.

Arellano, Anselmo, and Julian Josue Vigil. 1985. *Las Vegas Grandes on the Gallinas 1834–1985*. Las Vegas, NM: Editorial Teleraña.

Arellano, Estevan. 2014. *Enduring Acequias: Wisdom of the Land, Knowledge of the Water*. Albuquerque: University of New Mexico Press.

Arredondo, Gabriela. 2008. "Lived Regionalities: Mujeridad in Chicago, 1920–1940." In *Memories and Migrations: Mapping Boricua and Chicano Histories*, edited by Vicki Ruíz, 93–120. Urbana: University of Illinois Press.

Cadaval, Olivia. 1998. *Creating a Latino Identity in the Nation's Capital: The Latino Festival*. New York: Garland Publishing.

Calvo, Luz, and Catriona Rueda Esquibel. 2015. *Decolonize Your Diet: Plant-Based Mexican-American Recipes for Health and Healing*. Vancouver, BC: Arsenal Pulp Press.

Campa, Arthur. 1979. *Hispanic Culture in the Southwest*. Norman: University of Oklahoma Press.

Cantú, Norma. 1995. *Canícula: Snapshots of a Girlhood en la Frontera*. Albuquerque: University of New Mexico Press.

Cárdenas, Martiza. 2017. "Performing Centralaméricanismo: Isthmian Identities at the COFECA Independence Day Parade." In *U.S. Central Americans: Reconstructing Memories, Struggles, and Communities of Resistance*, edited by Karina Alvarado, Alicia Ivonne Estrada, and Ester Hernández, 127–43. Tucson: University of Arizona Press.

Cepeda, María Elena. 2010. "Singing the 'Star Spanglish Banner': The Politics and Patholization of Bilingualism in U.S. Popular Media." In *Beyond El Barrio:*

Everyday Life in Latina/o America, edited by Gina Pérez, Frank Guridy, and Adrian Burgos, 27–43. New York: New York University Press.

Chacón, Eusebio. 2002. "A Protest Rally." In *Herencia: The Anthology of Hispanic Literature of the United States*, edited by Nicolás Kanellos, 130–35. New York: Oxford University Press.

Dorsey, Margaret, and Miguel Díaz-Barraga. 2011. "Patriotic Citizenship, the Border Wall, and the 'El Veterano' Conjunto Festival." In *Transnational Encounters: Music and Performance at the U.S.–Mexico Border*, edited by Alejandro Madrid, 207–27. New York: Oxford University Press.

Espinosa, Aurelio. 1926. "Spanish Folklore in New Mexico." *The New Mexico Historical Review* 1, no. 2: 135–55.

Fonseca, Vanessa. 2017. "'Donde mi amor se ha quedado': Narratives of Sheepherding and *Querencia* along the Wyoming Manito Trail." *Annals of Wyoming* 89, no. 2–3 (Spring–Summer): 6–12.

García, Nasario. 2005. *Old Las Vegas: Hispanic Memories from the New Mexico Meadowlands*. Lubbock: Texas Tech University Press.

Halloran, Vivian Nun. 2016. *The Immigrant Kitchen: Food, Ethnicity, and Diaspora*. Columbus: Ohio State University Press.

Hooks, Bell. 1990. *Yearning: Race, Gender, and Cultural Politics*. Boston: South End Press.

Horton, Sarah Bronwen. 2010. *The Santa Fe Fiesta, Reinvented: Staking Ethno-Nationalist Claims to a Disappearing Homeland*. Santa Fe: SAR Press.

Knowles, David. 2017. "Mexican-American Boy, Sebastien de la Cruz, Sings Encore Performance of National Anthem at NBA Finals in Response to Bigoted Comments." *New York Daily News*, June 14, 2013. http://www.nydailynews.com/news/national/mexican-american-boy-national-anthem-performance-sparks-racist-backlash-article-1.1371990/.

Lucero-White, Aurora. 1953. *Literary Folklore of the Hispanic Southwest*. San Antonio: The Naylor Company.

———. 2002. "Plea for the Spanish Language." In *Herencia: The Anthology of Hispanic Literature of the United States*, edited by Nicolás Kanellos, 135–39. New York: Oxford University Press.

Mares, E. A. 1985. *Las Vegas, New Mexico: A Portrait*. Albuquerque: University of New Mexico Press.

Meléndez, A. Gabriel. 1997. *So All Is Not Lost: The Poetics of Print in Nuevomexicano Communities, 1834–1958*. Albuquerque: University of New Mexico Press.

———. 2005. *Spanish Language Newspapers in New Mexico, 1834–1958*. Tucson: University of Arizona Press.

Menchaca, Martha. 1995. *The Mexican Outsiders: A Community History of Marginalization and Discrimination in California*. Austin: University of Texas Press.

Mignolo, Walter. 2003. *The Darker Side of the Renaissance: Literacy, Territoriality, and Colonization*. Ann Arbor: University of Michigan Press.

Montaño, Mary. 2001. *Tradiciones Nuevomexicanas: Hispano Arts and Culture of New Mexico*. Albuquerque: University of New Mexico Press.

Nieto-Phillips, John. 2004. *The Language of Blood: The Making of Spanish-American Identity in New Mexico, 1880s–1930s*. Albuquerque: University of New Mexico Press.

Ochoa, Gilda. 2004. *Becoming Neighbors in a Mexican American Community: Power, Conflict, and Solidarity*. Austin: University of Texas Press.

Pennycook, Alistair. 2001. *Critical Applied Linguistics: A Critical Introduction*. Mahwah, NJ: Lawrence Erlbaum Associates.

Poplack, Shana. 1980. "Sometimes I'll start a sentence in Spanish Y TERMINO EN ESPAÑOL: Toward a Typology of Codeswitching." *Linguistics* 18: 581–616.

Rodríguez, Sylvia. 2002. "The Taos Fiesta: Invented Tradition and the Infrapolitics of Symbolic Reclamation." In *Nuevomexicano Cultural Legacy: Forms, Agencies, and Discourse*, edited by Francisco A. Lomelí, Victor A. Sorell, and Genaro M. Padilla, 185–202. Albuquerque: University of New Mexico Press.

Rúa, Mérida. 2012. *A Grounded Identidad: Making New Lives in Chicago's Puerto Rican Neighborhoods*. Oxford: Oxford University Press.

Rúa, Mérida, and Lorena García. 2007. "Processing Latinidad: Mapping Latino Urban Landscapes through Chicago Ethnic Festivals." *Latino Studies* 5: 317–39.

Smith, Jeffrey. 2004. "The Plaza in Las Vegas, New Mexico: A Community Gathering Place." In *Hispanic Places, Latino Spaces: Community and Cultural Diversity in Contemporary America*, edited by Daniel D. Arreola, 39–54. Austin: University of Texas Press.

Taylor, Diana. 1991. "Transculturating Transculturation." *Performing Arts Journal* 13. 90–104.

Tinajero, Robert. 2016. "Borderland Hip-Hop Rhetoric: Identity and Counterhegemony." In *La Verdad: An International Dialogue on Hip Hop Latinidades*, edited by Melissa Castillo-Garsow and Jason Nichols, 17–40. Columbus: Ohio State University Press.

Trujillo, Michael. 2009. *Land of Disenchantment: Latino/a Identities and Transformations in Northern New Mexico*. Albuquerque: University of New Mexico Press.

2007 Fiestas de Las Vegas Official Fiesta Guide [Brochure]. 2007. Las Vegas, NM: Las Vegas Fiesta Council, Tidbits of Las Vegas and Mora, and Las Vegas Times.

2008 Fiestas de Las Vegas Fiesta Guide [Brochure]. 2008. Las Vegas, NM: Las Vegas Optic.

2009 Fiestas de Las Vegas Fiesta Guide [Brochure]. 2009. Las Vegas, NM: Las Vegas Optic.

Vila, Pablo. 2006. "The Polysemy of the Label 'Mexican' on the Border." In *Ethnography at the Border*, edited by Pablo Vila, 105–39. Minneapolis: University of Minnesota Press.

Weber, David, ed. 1973. *Foreigners in Their Own Land: Historical Roots of the Mexican Americans*. Albuquerque: University of New Mexico Press.

Zentella, Ana Celia. 1997. *Growing Up Bilingual*. Oxford: Blackwell.

CHAPTER THREE

Critical Reflections on Chicanx and Indigenous Scholarship and Activism

KEVIN BROWN, VANESSA FONSECA-CHÁVEZ,
TEY MARIANNA NUNN, IRENE VÁSQUEZ,
AND MYLA VICENTI CARPIO

The conversation that follows centers New Mexico as a critical site of com-memoration, particularly because of its unique spatial and cultural ties to discussions of race, identity, and ethnic heritage. New Mexico is the ances-tral homeland of nineteen Indigenous Pueblo communities, three Apache tribal nations, the Navajo Nation, and various Genízaro communities. While national controversies have arisen in recent years about Confederate monu-ments and colonial memorials, longstanding debate about the implications of commemoration in New Mexico continue to influence public memory. Com-memorations offer a roadmap to a complicated ethnic history that necessarily calls us to untangle the colonial frameworks that have shaped the state since the sixteenth century, when Spanish explorers and conquerors claimed this space for the Spanish Crown. The territory later became part of Mexico as an independent republic. In 1848, at the conclusion of the Mexican-American War, the US emerged as a new colonial power in the territory. As a result of the layered colonial histories in New Mexico and the Southwest more generally, myriad groups have engaged in discussions about how to recognize their contributions and histories within these spaces. New Mexicans often manifest the legacies of these colonial periods in public commemorations of statues, pageantry, and other forms of memorialization that seek to privilege one history over another. In doing so, they fail to recognize the complex racial histories of Indigenous and Chicanx communities throughout the state.

The discussants consider the strategies that Chicanx and Indigenous schol-ars with ties to New Mexico utilize to engage in discussions of commemora-tion and placemaking. Indigenous communities have called this space home for thousands of years. Chicanx, as products of a Spanish colonial period and as a colonized population under the US, continue to wrestle with the state's colonial past while simultaneously, and alongside Indigenous communities, calling for a more nuanced retelling of New Mexico's cultural history. If New Mexico is "home" to multiple ethnic groups, what are the responsibilities of non-Indigenous individuals in creating dialogue that recognizes Indigenous nations as the original inhabitants of this land and in exposing the tensions of colonial endeavors?

As their responses show, the participants feel a need to critique modes of oppression that are manifested via commemorative endeavors. These are not new conversations in New Mexico and thus require sustained energy to overcome continued patterns of erasure through the recognition and disavowal of a long history of colonialism. Each of our discussants, in his or her own work, has demonstrated an investment in placemaking and the creation of spaces that honor multiple histories. We hope that this discussion aids in readers' understanding of how to work with the community and promotes scholarship that advances policies and knowledge that value all visions of home.

VANESSA: *We begin this conversation by asking you all to situate and reflect upon your sense of place. In the past several years, Chicanx and Indigenous communities in New Mexico have been active in critical conversations about history, space, and belonging. What personal investments do you have in New Mexico, and how does that positionality pertain to or impact the work that you do at a time when our histories and sense of belonging are being disrupted and challenged?*

TEY: As a native Nuevomexicana, and as the Director and Chief Curator of the National Hispanic Cultural Center Art Museum, I am personally involved, on a constant basis, in place- and space-making, especially for artists, colleagues, and interns whose inclusion is underrepresented (practically invisible, really) in our state's cultural institutions. My work, scholarship, and advocacy focus on Hispana/o and Latinx cultural producers who, because of their ethnicity, have their visual work valued differently (both aesthetically and monetarily). In short, their artistry is not treated in the same manner as that of "other" visual artists. In this day and age, community involvement and voice need to be authentic and meaningful (nothing at the table about us—without us). Many say they are "working with the community" without doing any work. It is a falsehood and, frankly, insulting to state one is doing this type of community engagement, yet it persists and shapes perspectives all the time.

KEVIN: I was born in the northwest corner of New Mexico in Shiprock, New Mexico. To us Diné, Shiprock is a place of historical memory, as one of our cherished twin saviors dispatched a giant eagle and the eagle's blood formed the wings of the rock outline. This place forever named *Tsé Bit'a'í* (Rock That Has Wings) is where I was born, but where I call home is Chinle, Arizona. The place of my people is forever entwined with memory and stories, and the maps of today overlay our rich stories and traditions with Anglo words, boundaries, and labels.

New Mexico, as it is called in English, is part of an already-established epistemological network of Indigenous language, history, and memory. This resonance cannot be overstated, because connection to place is extremely important for the continuation of Indigenous existence. For me, this connection is a literal connection. After my birth, my mother saved the umbilical [cord] and buried it at her mother's residence in Chinle, near the sheep corral. This act permanently connects myself to land and me to the duties of my being. I can recollect thinking that there are thousands, if not millions of umbilical cords buried across New Mexico, tethering life to land, and many Nuevomexicano or Anglo people do not even recognize the significance of this act. This act is a continuation of my ancestor's claim to not just land, but the potential of a successful life and existence.

This perspective has informed me, as I am program administrator of the Indigenous Nations Library Program at the University of New Mexico. I oversee a physical space for Indigenous students, faculty, and scholarly resources on campus. This Indigenous space at times is the refuge for Indigenous students at UNM because the current built environment is at times hostile to Indigenous students. . . . My program is the only library program dedicated to the support of Indigenous people at a research university. Outside of tribal colleges, this program is truly the first to indigenize higher-education spaces by simply offering a different Indigenous approach to learning that is not competitive but, rather, collaborative and cooperative. We also support a critical approach to customary privileged western academic disciplines by including nontraditional forms of Indigenous scholarship into the academic canon. These scholarship resources present an alternative source of knowledge such as information coming from nontextual and deeply philosophical sources.

IRENE: Somewhere deep down inside I feel like I belong to the Greater Southwest, yet I cannot stake a claim to one community or site. I have been shaped by its history and molded through its social economic patterns. I've been a part of generations of migrant families on both sides. My mother was born in Coahuila, Mexico, and my father was born in Bellbrook, Ohio. I was born in El Paso, Texas, but moved as an infant with my family to Rosemead, California. This theme of moving from place to place has impacted how my family raised me and how I have lived my life as an educator. My uncles and mom worked in Deming, New Mexico as laborers in the fields and in private homes. My mother had my brother in Santa Fe, New Mexico, and he is now a recognized member of the Chihene Nde Nation of New Mexico. This multiethnic, multilingual, and migrant background of my families provides me with a critical view of the world and the academy.

In my role as Chair of Chicana and Chicano Studies (CCS) and as Director of the Southwest Hispanic Research Institute (SHRI), I find that our faculty are increasingly interested in the interactive thematic of *history, space, and placemaking*. As academics, we tend to imagine place and space as human-centric, i.e., we define and give meaning to spatial geographies and landscapes. Chicanas and Chicanos have an important historical connection to North America; this is evident in our stories and in the written record. Increasingly in the field of Chicana and Chicano Studies we have had to reexamine our understanding of the relationship between land and people and think critically about what it means to claim land and define space in Indigenous lands and multispecies environments. When we claim land and space, who are we dispossessing and how does that relate to struggles for decolonization and emancipation? Do our claims liberate us and others? Chicana and Chicano scholars have informed the understanding of decolonization going back to the 1960s and even prior to then. Mexican people's efforts at liberation were informed by numerous Indigenous, ethnic/racial groups', women's, immigrants', and national movements that were deeply involved in critiquing colonization. Yet the theories and concepts were still bound to oppressive ideologies, including racism, sexism, ableism, and homophobia. Discussions of decolonization have been greatly advanced by our Indigenous scholars and activists and Chicanas and Chicanos and Latinos generally are influenced by these critical perspectives. When I teach about space- and placemaking, I underscore that our conceptions are meaningful, but they are also subjective and relational and for that reason we have to be self-critical.

MYLA: As a citizen of the Jicarilla Apache nation and of Laguna and Isleta heritage, New Mexico is home. My ancestors have been in this place and space from our origins. When I reflect upon place, this is what I always come back to—the place where I am from and the space that intercon- nects my spiritual, historical, and political relationships to the place of my ancestors. Therefore, I have personal investment in the lands and the people which impacts my writing and teaching. In my book *Indigenous Albuquerque*, I argue that Albuquerque *is* Indigenous space. While Albu- querque constitutes a complicated landscape with multiple colonizations, complex racial formations, and layered histories, it is important to recon- textualize why this place is Indigenous. Indigenous peoples have had to create or demand spaces for critical conversations about history, space, and placemaking. Indigenous scholars and communities have created such spaces through tribal museums, conferences, writings, and activ- ism. The need for critical conversations or interventions around history/ memory are important because of the ways in which Indigenous histories have been erased or imagined. Thanksgiving is one clear way Indigenous history has been imagined and erased. Presented by settler society as a peaceful gathering of Pilgrims and Indians sharing their bounty, this holiday erases the contempt the colonists had toward Indians as well as the genocide of Indigenous peoples. This erases the history of genocide in which American society was founded. Without critical conversations or interventions in history/memory, master narratives that negate or erase Indigenous histories have legitimized settler claims to Indigenous space and place. Settler histories have justified the dispossession of and reloca- tion of Indigenous communities from our lands, have taught an incom- plete and erroneous story about our cultures to our children in schools, and have limited and denied Indigenous rightful claims and access to political, spiritual, and cultural spaces.

When we look at New Mexico from an Indigenous perspective, it means we first look at the land not in geopolitical terms or boundar- ies, but as Indigenous space. The landscape is not property or a place of residence. Rather, as the place of our origins, it constitutes a place with religious, cultural, and spiritual significance from time immemorial. These views are not just from the past but remain into the present. Through my pedagogy, I try to emphasize theory to praxis. I work with my students to critically focus on issues facing Indigenous peoples and to identify and develop solutions to those issues in ways that honor Indigenous ways of knowing and being. In my classes we ask how to reassert Indigenous histories and persistence so that Indigenous peoples might reclaim connections to places, humanity, and each other. Colonization has fragmented our societies and we urgently need to reconnect with our knowledge systems and reclaim our humanity. I teach a class called Actualizing Decolonization where all of us in the class, Indigenous or not, examine the impacts of colonization on ourselves, our environments, and our communities; we work to imagine and develop new (and old) ways of healing and living by exploring what constitutes our worldviews.

RESPONSE

TEY: Many organizations and institutions say they are "working with the community" without doing any work. "Collaborators" must realize that working with the community means more and deeper work. It does not mean asking for a mailing list of contacts in order to justify that one is engaging the community. Besides, there are communities within a so-called community. To engage and work with these many groups one has to understand nuances and stereotypes.

MYLA: I agree, but I wish you would elaborate. What are the ways that one can work *with* the community? As an academic, I look at this in terms of research methodologies, specifically Indigenous methodologies that push . . . for a relationship that . . . is community-driven, where relationship is center. The development of relationships with the community becomes important and the relationship engenders responsibility and obligations.[1] Our communities need to expect these types of relationships from whoever wants to work with them. Then our communities would be initiating critical conversations instead of having to always respond to events after the fact. This relates back to what Kevin at the Indigenous Nations Library at UNM commented. As an intellectual space and physical space it could create relationships between scholars and community.

IRENE: In academia, we often talk about making university research and education more accessible to historically underrepresented communities and individuals. This does, in fact, require us to develop authentic relationships with communities. Although the definition of communities varies by context, Chicana and Chicano Studies as a discipline identified working-class communities as an important site of engagement and empowerment. One can refer to the university as a community, a school, a neighborhood, an organization, or even a more loosely configured congregation of people. In CCS and SHRI, our definitions of communities are based in and cross through these affiliations. I agree with Myla that working with community engenders responsibility and obligations.

For example, in CCS we now have Chicana and Chicano Studies dual-enrollment courses being taught in four public high schools. We see this as a way of working with communities, many . . . educationally and institutionally disenfranchised. Someone else may not see this work as a form of community engagement and that's OK. Yet today, social and economic conditions increasingly require us to draw bigger circles and ovals. Our current situation with loss of species, environmental degradation, and limited life and educational opportunities for humans is requiring us to think in different ways regarding space- and placemaking. We can bridge space by working with youth, elders, artists, and teachers in the communities that do not have access to higher-learning educational institutions. We have to do better here because youth learn their attitudes and values in interaction with their peers. If we teach Ethnic Studies in K–12, we can start the conversations about shared histories, reconciliations, and solidarity much earlier than at the college level.

MYLA: I agree, and as I read your reflection, Irene, it makes clear that as we examine and reexamine critically our relationships, claims, and colonizations, common themes provide specific entrances for critical conversations.

KEVIN: I hear what everyone is saying, and it feels like it is a value difference from people with long generational ties to a place versus the recent arrival of people in the region. This tension between cultural values is truly telling in what counts as knowledge. The critical conversations appear to be talking across each other rather than to each other. It may be the system of academic conversations that enables competition and racing for publications rather than collaboration. I truly value this format of this discussion because it allows myself and the other colleagues in this manuscript to converse with each other.

IRENE: I agree with Kevin that it is incredibly important to engage in critical conversations that address the tensions around points of arrival. When we look out across the New Mexico landscape, we have to acknowledge the people who have ancestral ties to the land that go back millennia. Populations that arrived later lived off the land, labor, and resources of the original Indigenous people and, as a result, minimized their life chances, and this still happens today through tourism, real estate, and economic development. My feeling is that if we start with that basic acknowledgment of the region's history and present and then support the efforts of Indigenous people's claims to place, land, and economic resources, we will be in a better position to value difference. This type of work starts with dialogue.

VANESSA: *What do Indigenous and Chicanx communities have at stake in controversies in New Mexico over historical commemoration (statues, monuments, celebrations)? There have been several recent examples in New Mexico, relating to fiestas, murals, and statues. What do those controversies say about the state of race relations in the region?*

TEY: Indigenous and Latinx communities have everything at stake in these controversies. Perceptions and perpetuation of stereotypes, among other things, make some think that there can be only one story told about a given historical event is to ignore all of the other stories. Who is telling the story and who are the gatekeepers who let the stories in are crucial to issues of race and ethnicity as well as place- and space-making. Whoever tells the story has the power and that power is unbalanced without including all communities involved. In addition, the community often is comprised of multiple communities. Controversies happen when some members feel ignored, invisible, and silenced. Controversies also happen when thinking about the past, present, and future.

KEVIN: The obvious stake in New Mexico is having a voice and participating in discussions that have excluded or glossed over another people's history. New Mexico has a strong and deep Indigenous history that outweighs settler colonial history. It is those colonial narratives that are often commemorated and celebrated. For instance, at the University of New Mexico, where the Indigenous Nations Library Program is housed, there is an infamous mural titled *The Three Peoples*.[2] It was commissioned using Carnegie Foundation funds in the 1930s by then UNM President James Zimmerman. This mural was designed to be the signature mural installed in four niches in the university's signature building, the library (later renamed Zimmerman Library). The murals are broken up into four distinct sections highlighting stereotypical and common thinking of a group of people in those times. The first is of Indigenous people making pottery, basketry, and weaving. The second is of Hispanic people laboring in agriculture and construction. The third mural is of Anglo people as scientists studying. Finally, the fourth mural is all three peoples engaging in a symbolic handshake with the Anglo person in the middle in a messiah pose with full facial features (eyes and a mouth). The Hispanic and Indigenous man on the other side of him are indistinguishable—just two Brown men.

The artist, Kenneth Adams, was given specific instructions as to what was to be painted, by Zimmerman himself, and this depiction of Indigenous and Hispanic people by the latest settler (Anglo people) is quite telling. It is the theory of cultural evolution in artistic form. Each mural depicts people in specific sociocultural stages of progress with Anglo people as the one with specific scientific knowledge. It minimizes the distinct cultural knowledge, language, and science of the independent sovereign Indigenous Pueblo, Apache, and Navajo Nations. In addition, it positions Hispanic people only as laborers and the working class and the Anglo people as the thinkers. Furthermore, as an educational institution of New Mexico, it is possible that this university may have biased its recruitment and outreach to Native and Hispanic communities. It is plausible because at the time of this mural commission, there was not a single Indigenous person enrolled at UNM and only a handful of Hispanic students enrolled.

The murals were defaced twice, as green paint was thrown at the face of the Anglo man in the fourth mural. A rally to remove the mural was held in 1993, and just recently, twenty-one library faculty and staff (including myself) wrote a letter requesting to the Dean of the college to remove the murals and store them in a museum. We were inspired by the activism and advocacy of the Kiva Club student organization who, at the same time, were requesting the UNM President and Board of Regents to abolish the official seal of UNM, which depicts a Spanish conquistador and a frontiersman.[3] We state in the letter that we "object to the Adams mural's embodiment of racial and gender inequality, its promotion of cultural appropriation, its overriding perspective of Anglo and male superiority and its failure to portray the diverse contributions of the region's Indigenous Native American and Hispanic/Mexicano/Mestizo/Chicana (o) groups." This specific example is currently unfolding, and I don't know the ultimate resolution to this yet, but I feel this effort was possible due to the engagement of students at UNM, to create an inclusive learning environment on campus. It has been decided in the short term by the UNM President to cover the murals with curtains until a permanent solution is decided and acted upon.

IRENE: In the past few years, there has been a resurgence in advocacy against symbols and monuments that glorify the symbolic, structural, and physical violence rooted in European colonialism and its associated policies and practices, including the genocide and enslavement of Indigenous, African, Asian, and racially mixed peoples. Controversies such as those that have occurred in New Mexico over the past decades involving public monuments and celebrations tend to be seen as short-term aberrations that can be resolved on an institutional level or on a short-term basis. However, the issues and conflicts at stake cannot be easily addressed because they are the product of colonization, a process that dispossessed Indigenous peoples and subjected Mexican peoples and made their full lives an impossibility. For some, not being from New Mexico disqualifies my perspectives on conflicts and tensions over place, space, and meaning. And yet, in some of these cases, Indigenous activists in New Mexico have looked to Hispanos, Chicanx, and Latinx peoples for support in their advocacy against monuments and festivities that gloss over and celebrate the elimination of Indigenous peoples. The UNM seal used from the early 1900s on diplomas and on public backgrounds centers the (male) symbolic of the conquistador and Anglo frontiersman. Native American students and community activists have questioned its use for decades. In 2015, the Kiva Club and The Red Nation launched another public campaign against the UNM seal. In May 2016, I wrote a letter to the editor of the *Albuquerque Journal* titled "Relic has no place in our future" that advocated for the termination of the UNM seal. In it, I stated:

RELICS HAVE NO place in our future. I don't mean old objects that people collect and put in their homes or museums. When I say relics, I am talking about the outdated symbolic representations of the past. UNM has an eyesore of one called the university seal. Hundreds of students, faculty and staff oppose it. If we polled the community outside the university, we might have a landslide of opposition. UNM should take the voices of criticism so far expressed as a looming sign of the future. Symbols that uphold the brutal actions and bloody outlines of the past should very quickly be eliminated. Recognizing the valid concerns of students and community members is actually a step toward the future.

When I wrote the above letter to the editor against the UNM official seal, a few leaders of New Mexico Latino civic organizations berated me on Facebook and made threats of action against me. I wasn't naïve and I understood when I submitted the letter that my professional qualifications and personal life would be the subject of public scrutiny. However, I have been motivated by students and activists to use my position as a platform to address tensions and issues and push back on discourse that minimizes the historical and contemporary depredations against People of Color and the language, imagery, and practices that uphold injustice. Young people in our state are open to dialogue. I learn so much from them. Some people may want to characterize Nuevomexicanos in one certain way, as being deeply committed to Spain and its legacy of colonialism. I have found an impressive diversity of opinions and experiences about the past and its repercussions on the present.

MYLA: This is where master narratives are institutionalized over Indigenous histories and spaces. Commemorations focus on a particular person or event that creates a strategic memory that entrenches a particular version of history with specific goals. In New Mexico, those commemorations, statues, and monuments work toward creating a settler narrative that negates or refashions Indigenous claims to lands and space. When place meaning attached to a specific space, such as a particular place that is imbued with a particular cultural/political/spiritual relationship, is erased or misrepresented, Indigenous claims to place are weakened or forgotten. This allows for others to assert their history at the expense of other, equally valid historical experiences. A great example is Tiguex Park in Albuquerque. Prior to the Tiguex Park issue, the controversy of the Oñate statue emerged. Juan de Oñate, the Spanish conquistador who established

New Mexico as a colony for Spain, is remembered by Indian nations in New Mexico as a brutal colonizer who was convicted in Spain of cruelty against Indigenous people. When a statue of Oñate was erected in the Spanish town of Alcalde over the protests of the local Pueblo people, the statue's left foot was sawed off to memorialize his order that males in Acoma Pueblo have their left foot amputated as punishment for their role in the death of his nephew. Despite the Oñate statue controversy at Alcalde, the Albuquerque Arts Board and the Albuquerque Cuarto Centenario Committee commissioned a statue of Oñate to be placed in Tiguex Park, a park dedicated to Indians. (The city council approved the project, and then-Mayor Jim Baca vetoed it.) This blatant disregard for Indians' experiences of colonization shows how memorials are contested sites about what we choose to remember and honor and what we choose to ignore or forget.

Commemorations also help to present a more palatable history of settler society. I remember learning about the "bloodless reconquest" of New Mexico by the Spanish in 1692 after the Pueblo Revolt. The annual commemoration of that event is reenacted as the Santa Fe Fiestas Entrada, celebrating a "peaceful" reconquest of the Spanish over the Pueblos and other Indigenous peoples. The celebration does not acknowledge the violence of colonialism, imagining this reconquest as "peaceful" while ignoring the murder, torture, and rape of Indigenous men, women, and children.

That Indigenous people and groups . . . have to protest to be heard indicates that settler society does not want to hear Indigenous views or acknowledge divergent Indigenous histories that challenge their settler narrative. It speaks volumes about race relations when it takes a foot being cut off an Oñate statue or young people getting arrested protesting the Santa Fe Fiesta Entrada (in 2018) to force critical dialogues to take place about the contested meanings behind such statues and commemorations.

We also need to remember that these contestations are not only or even primarily about race relations. Many Native people in the US are citizens of their Indigenous sovereign nations. We maintain a political status as sovereign nations. Framing these controversies only as race relations further obscures the ongoing relations between Indigenous sovereign nations and the United States.

MYLA: We are all talking about the creation and control of certain narratives. How might some of these narratives or histories look if we create them together? What might they look like if we engaged with the tensions and worked together to discuss and embrace these critical conversations, not only in opposition, but in a space where a complex narrative can begin to address some of the concerns we see here? What might be the ground rules to start such conversations?

KEVIN: Myla, I would first state the obvious, that the ground rules have to come from a mutual respect for each other's perspectives and histories. There is no erasing the traumatic history of colonization among Indigenous people, but there has to be an agreement that the act of colonization is deeply hurtful and traumatic. The acknowledgment of the colonization process is the start of a true discourse of the underlying structures of power dynamics. Also, colonization is an ongoing process and all of my colleagues have provided excellent examples of it in action. In addition, academia has played a pivotal role in reinforcing colonial ideology, especially in the early foundational scholarship of historical and cultural studies. These foundational works reinforced settler notions of Eurocentric ideas of hierarchy, patriarchy, and white supremacy.

IRENE: In reference to Myla's and Kevin's suggestions about engaging in conversations to address the imposition of settler colonialism and its repercussions on relations between Indigenous peoples and Latinos generally, I think admission and acknowledgment are important expressions of positionality. I see so much more willingness on the part of younger generations to see themselves as complicit in what Kevin refers to "underlying structures of power dynamics." They are taking responsibility and assuming collective forms of leadership to a degree that we haven't seen in decades. It is inspiring. Mexican and Latino populations have to admit how their families, communities, or societies have "perpetuated Eurocentric ideas of hierarchy, patriarchy, and white supremacy." At the same time, Mexicans and Latinos and their ancestors going back centuries have faced US and global forms of imperialism that have dispossessed them and turned large numbers into perpetual migrants that lack claims to civil and human rights. The space they live in strips them of their humanity in such a way that they can be detained in cages and deported to countries where they face extermination. This is a crisis that also needs to be better understood among all people. Migration in the Western Hemisphere is a result of settler colonialism and is a strategy to destabilize and dehumanize peoples that goes back to colonialism.

VANESSA: *What progress (if any) has been made to raise awareness about these issues, and what more can be done to address issues of commemoration? In what ways might our communities move toward an ethics of solidarity and mutual respect?*

TEY: I can't stress this enough, but there needs to be multiple voices and multiple stories—always. Being safe and fearing other perspectives is not going to solve the problems of commemoration. The resentment will continue when we fear a perspective different from what we believe. We need to be better and create meaningful and safe spaces for authentic community participation in cultural debates and controversies. To not do so means we are sweeping it away rather than dealing directly. We need safe spaces for all opinions and perspectives. Yet even within these spaces in the so-called community, there are different opinions and points of view. A controversy can be fueled by emotions and different experiences. Today, even within the Hispanic "community" in New Mexico, there are those that identify as Spanish and those who identify as Chicana/o or Latinx.

KEVIN: The fact that the *Three Peoples* mural at UNM has been contested through defacement, rallies, and opposition letters and *is still up* is testament to the privilege and authority colonial narratives have over the local community. It is also a testament to the differing value systems between historical accuracy and historic preservation. The current argument and support for the mural is rooted in arguments for its historic qualities. This position has been supported, for instance, by the Editorial Board of the *Albuquerque Journal.* In an editorial on this topic, they state; "Judging the murals by today's standards, there's no question they give greater emphasis to Anglo culture, placing Hispanic and Native American cultures as subservient. But we shouldn't lose sight of the fact that Adams—and his artwork—were products of their time. There is no evidence he was denigrating Native Americans or Hispanics, and neither he nor his work should be vilified or erased from UNM's rich history. On the contrary, this New Deal artwork should be studied and its shortcomings explored so today's UNM students can learn from it."[4] Furthermore, they claim this call for the cover and removal of the murals is "political correctness run amok" and "Trying to rid UNM of artwork or things too 'controversial' is the antithesis of higher education and unworthy of our state's flagship institution."

My counter to this argument is we are trying to include diverse experiences and lived realities of people of color in the discourse. The intentions of this mural are to rewrite the narrative of the lived experiences of the so-called three peoples in New Mexico into easier-to-consume pieces of a complicated and rich history into the Anglo-American experience. New Mexico is unlike any place in the country because of the deep, rich history of Indigenous people that precedes European exploration by thousands upon thousands of years. Every person coming into this land has settled onto previous settlements and that evidence cannot be ignored. The only people who had a chance to paint the narrative is the Anglo and it excluded the realities of the Indigenous and Nuevomexicano people. I reject this on the principle of historical inaccuracy. I also reject the murals for their racial and gender inequality representations. As a place of learning, the murals do not contribute to the spirit of learning and disrupt . . . the nature of higher education. Since the murals are in a public place, UNM also has to think of its responsibility to its public audience. It is the responsibility of the institution to publicly display items that are agreeable to the public. It has been demonstrated that some in the public do not support or enjoy this mural.

IRENE: The heightened and tense public dialogue and discourse around commemorations is an essential part of reckoning with colonialism. In order to create possibilities for an ethics of responsibility and mutual solidarities, our communities need to acknowledge the ravages of colonialism for all. Mexican-descent people and their ancestors faced extreme exploitation at the hands of the Spanish, Mexican, and US governments. The ideologies and practices of these authoritarian governments have been shrouded in imagery, architecture, visual arts and symbols, and ceremonial practices of authority. If we accept this idea as Mexican people, then we need to apply this same critical perspective in the US for Indigenous communities. With acceptance, we then have to resolve to remove the relics of colonialism. Belief without action is meaningless. Our public tax-supported educational institutions need to be leaders in Indigenous and Chicana and Chicano Studies programs so we can work together with our communities to build an ethics of respect and mutual solidarity.

MYLA: Around the country in states such as Georgia, Florida, California, North Carolina, Alabama, New York, and others, we have seen how numerous controversies and protests regarding Confederate memorials and statues have led to their removal or the name changes of spaces. These have been important articulations highlighting racism in specific narratives or commemorations. Taking down these statues [has] given voice about and against racism based in slavery in the US. These protests provide a space for discussions about racism, especially in the South. However, those conversations usually remain in the context of Black/White race relations. In different areas of the nation, especially the Southwest, discussions that derive from similar controversies or protests highlight different regional contexts. When we bring Indigenous views into the discussions, the contexts change from racism to colonialism and settler colonialism. While it is important to see all the protests as antiracist, antisexist, or anti-LGBT, looking at the controversies in more regional contexts shows intricacies and layers of oppression.

I have seen numerous ways awareness about Indigenous issues has been raised around the country. The tremendous push of Idle No More helped to invigorate Indigenous activism. This is not to say there was no activism taking place prior, but this movement involved more youth in learning about issues, participating in protests, and in planning protests. Water is Life also is a great example of how awareness has been raised not only on an Indigenous level, but also for settlers.[5]

Another important area of progress has been the work on [the] public school curriculum in New Mexico. The Public Education Department's Indian Education Division has an initiative to create [a] Native-driven curriculum for grades 7–12. They have brought in educators and elders from all the tribes in New Mexico to develop and write [a] curriculum for educators in the state of New Mexico. This follows the Indian Pueblo Cultural Center's development of [a] Pueblo-based K–12 curriculum based on its exhibit about the century of impact of federal and state policy on Pueblo nations.

On a personal level, I participated in a conference that gave me a sense of hope. In 2012, Northern New Mexico College (NNMC) held an academic and community conference called Historias de Nuevo Mexico/

New Mexico Histories. The conference was organized by Drs. Patricia Trujillo and Mathew Martínez and supported by then-president of NNMC Dr. Rusty Barceló. They featured critical conversations about contestations over New Mexico history. The panels mixed perspectives and encouraged conversation and questions between the audience and presenters. On my panel, I met Paula García, Executive Director of the New Mexico Acequia Association, who described the work to protect and maintain the acequias in northern New Mexico. She spoke of *querencia*, which literally refers to a sense of place and rootedness, belonging, in relation to the lands and waters of the region. I felt discomfort, perceiving this discussion as making claims over Indigenous lands, including the traditional lands of the Jicarilla Apache (from where I am a citizen). When the conversation addressed these overlapping claims to the same place, I was surprised to learn that they had reached out to Jicarilla elders and travelled with them to learn the cultural and epistemological meanings they invested in that shared space. At that point, I felt that our shared respect and love of that place allowed us to take steps toward solidarity and mutual respect to protect that place. It was not about who owned or occupied the land, but about protecting the land. It took an abundance of work, conversation, negotiation, and patience for the organizers to create a space of mutual respect and dialogue at the conference. For various communities to get to that place, individuals must understand their own history, positionality, and privilege.

RESPONSE

MYLA: In all our responses, I see a need not just to address the implications of colonialism on our communities, but the need to unpack the complex dynamics within our own communities.

KEVIN: Unpacking has to be done in a controlled manner. Opening up these historical and intergenerational wounds can cause harm in unpredictable ways. There needs to be a way to close the wound, so it doesn't affect or impact other people in the process.

IRENE: In order for deeper and more meaningful understanding and conversations to occur, as Myla states, our communities should work toward unpacking complex social and historical dynamics within our own communities. Despite colonization, Indigenous and Latino peoples still constitute themselves through making community, putting forward claims to identity and homelands. These processes are dynamic and complex and often contested by societal institutions. Within Latino communities, our mothers and fathers have replicated patriarchal and heteronormative beliefs and practices that limit our understanding of other people's fullest expression of dignity and sovereignty. This incapacitates individuals' understanding of difference and relatedness and creates blinders that stifle solidarity with other oppressed peoples.

VANESSA: *From your own disciplinary perspective, what is one useful tool you can offer to the conversation about how communities heal from colonial trauma?*

TEY: I'm not sure we ever "heal" from colonial trauma. The only useful tool I can offer is to not be afraid of other opinions and perspectives. They are just as valid as one's own. Multiple stories contribute to vibrant cultural communities and we need to allow that more so that divisions and myths of tricultural harmonies (as in the case of NM) are unraveled. My comments are coming from numerous recent and fatiguing experiences with inauthentic diversity, equity, and inclusion rhetoric. When different points of view are not equally valued, there can't be meaningful and long-lasting change. Too many institutions aren't walking the walk when it comes to true community engagement before, during, and after controversies. We need to be fearless in this work.

KEVIN: Conversationally, healing from trauma is a topic often encountered on social media and from my experiences on Twitter following the hashtag #NativeTwitter. I have encountered many memes and tweets about healing. Some tweet for healing in the wake of another case of a murdered and missing Indigenous woman, others tweet for prayers and support in dealing with domestic violence or sexual assault, some tweet about finding healing in culture and community, others tweet about healing as a form of resistance. For Indigenous people, it is a form of strategy to exist, to be hopeful for the future, or to look at healing perhaps as a last resort. In the trajectory of Indigenous history, this period is perhaps the time for resurgence of Indigenous people on a global scale.

In academic settings, I have seen the role of Critical Indigenous Studies as a theory and praxis rise among scholars and students. This intellectual movement is seen in the increased number of publications using

Indigenous theory and methodology or other decolonial frameworks. This momentum is mirrored in hashtag frequencies of Indigenous movements such as #NoDAPL, #MMIW, #NativeTwitter, and other hashtags. This movement is also seen in other communities of color also such as #BLM or #BlackLivesMatter, #NoJusticeNoPeace, #NoBanNoWall, #StopSeparatingFamilies, and #OpenBorders.

These movements are not a recognition of the power of social media, but the power of a collective voice to promote justice for their own community and to recognize that their collective power is a form of healing. Organizing among themselves can change the outcome of their communities to enact a real-world change for their community. These specific hashtags are bringing awareness to a real-world problem and finding a collective solution . . . Through each other, healing is realized.

IRENE: Healing is an aspirational process. There is hope in critical and collective praxis. Healing is not an end point, but rather the recognition of historical and contemporary afflictions and continuous efforts to mediate our well-being. We cannot access a fixed point of injury. Our traumas are embedded in layers and layers of injury. Women and Queer of Color theorists and activists have unpacked these oppressive overlays and have advocated for critical praxis as a tool for understanding and dismantling of structural forms of violence. Healing involves a resolution to overturn what is oppressive and to reconstruct a more dignified life for all within a bountiful multispecies future. We cannot heal in isolation. People of Color have generational trauma that is experienced differently at an individual and group level. Yet we do share a collective series of afflictions and experiences of patriarchal colonialism, racialized capitalism, and gendered and sexualized imperialism. Dealing with pain or trauma is a deep and ongoing process.

MYLA: One tool that American Indian Studies (AIS) offers that directly addresses colonial trauma is decolonization. While decolonization means different things to people, decolonization in the AIS context means having a critical understanding of the impact that colonization has had on Indigenous lives. As we begin to understand how our lives and cultures have been disrupted, we also can begin to imagine and develop new (old) ways of living and reclaiming our histories. If we can reconceptualize such things as health, sovereignty, politics, environment, food, and education though a critical cultural framework that reflects our specific histories, experiences, and knowledge, we can develop solutions that support our relationships to our political, cultural, and spiritual spaces and strengthen our positions as sovereign nations.

NOTES

1. See Margaret Kovach, *Indigenous Methodologies: Characteristics, Conversations and Contexts* (Toronto: University of Toronto Press, 2009) and Shawn Wilson, *Research Is Ceremony: Indigenous Research Methods* (Halifax, NS: Fernwood, 2009).

2. https://library.unm.edu/zimmerman75/art.php.

3. https://news.unm.edu/news/university-seal-remains-the-same.

4. https://www.abqjournal.com/1232609/pull-back-the-curtains-on-mural-discourse-at-unm.html.

5. "Settler" (in the broadest definition) is from the concept of settler colonialism, usually meaning a non-Indigenous person who lives, claims, and/or benefits from the displacement of Indigenous peoples and their occupied or unoccupied lands. For a more detailed discussion, see Corey Snelgrove, Rita Kaur Dhamoon, and Jeff Corntassel, "Unsettling Settler Colonialism: The Discourse and Politics of Settlers, and Solidarity with Indigenous Nations," *Decolonization: Indigeneity, Education & Society* 3, no. 2 (2014): 1–32.

WORKS CITED

Botts, Carroll. "Celebrating Zimmerman @ 75: Zimmerman Library Artwork." https://library.unm.edu/zimmerman75/art.php.

"Editorial: Pull Back the Curtains on Mural Discourse at UNM." 2018. *Albuquerque Journal Online.* https://www.abqjournal.com/1232609/pullback-the-curtains-on -mural-discourse-at-unm.html.

Vásquez, Irene. 2016. "Relics Have No Place in Our Future." *Albuquerque Journal Online.* https://www.abqjournal.com/779539/letters-150.html.

The idea of nation and nationhood, although in existence since biblical times, was strongly developed during the early period of the printing press, when books could help define a people and a place. It was through the written word, at least for the reading public, that imagined communities could be created and sustained. The advent of film, however, helped disseminate the notion of imagined communities even further, as the viewing public was and is much larger than the reading public. Those with access to movie theaters could now see these imagined communities and view themselves as part of them. But the power of film goes beyond that. Filmmakers learned early on that their work had the ability to influence minds by serving as political propaganda. Films about New Mexico are no exception. In this section, with Vanessa Fonseca-Chávez's commentary on the documentary film *The Last Conquistador* (2008), Karen R. Roybal's analysis of the blacklisted film *Salt of the Earth* (1954), and Spencer R. Herrera's critique of the US government propaganda film *And Now, Miguel* (1953) and the New Mexico tourism campaign "New Mexico True," the authors show the influence and power of film and media and how they can help forge *una querencia nuevomexicana*.

Vanessa Fonseca-Chávez's chapter "Contested Querencia in *The Last Conquistador* (2008) by John J. Valadez and Cristina Ibarra" focuses on a well-versed theme within New Mexico cultural and historical studies: Juan de Oñate and the colonization of New Mexico. Fonseca-Chávez contends, and many scholars would agree, that there is still much to be discussed and uncovered regarding this period of New Mexico's colonial history. Fonseca-Chávez grew up in Grants, New Mexico, forty-three miles east of El Morro National Monument, where Oñate carved the phrase "pasó por aquí" into the rock formation on April 16, 1605. Yet despite the proximity to such an important historical landmark, she and her classmates did not learn in the public schools about the controversy surrounding Oñate and the massacre at Acoma. It was not until she was a first-year doctoral student at Arizona State University that she had the opportunity to engage in an academic discussion about this particular historical trauma after watching a screening of the documentary film *The Last Conquistador* (2008) by John J. Valadez and Cristina Ibarra. The film details the controversy surrounding a thirty-six-foot-high bronze statue in El Paso that honors Juan de Oñate as a founding father of the region. The statue was renamed "The Equestrian" to limit the negative press the city was receiving for what some saw as honoring a perpetrator of war crimes. With the screening of the film, and the wounds freshly reopened, Fonseca-Chávez knew that there was still dialogue to be had between various Hispanic and Pueblo communities of the state. She leaves us with an important concluding task—"to reaffirm our commitment to querencia, while also honoring the querencia that others share in this contested space." Until we can learn to do this, there is still work to be done.

Karen R. Roybal's chapter "Deep Roots in Community: Querencia and *Salt of the Earth*" examines the idea of defending one's querencia, as portrayed in the blacklisted film *Salt of the Earth* (1954), which depicts the 1951 mine strike in Bayard, New Mexico. The film centers on a group of Nuevomexicano miners and their families, who live in a small mountain community in southwestern New Mexico. Subjected to dangerous working conditions, less pay than their Anglo counterparts, and other discriminatory practices, the miners, with the help of their wives, engage in a strike against their employer, Delaware Zinc, the pseudonym for the Empire Zinc Mining Company. The film was progressive for its time, drawing attention to the efforts made by both Nuevomexicanos and Nuevomexicanas in fighting for dignity and respect from the local authorities and the Empire Zinc representatives. The progressive nature of the film is evident even more so for the women, led by Esperanza Quintero, the wife of the main strike organizer, as they were also fighting to gain a sense of acknowledgment and respect for their work in the home from their own husbands, thus dealing with discrimination on two levels. Although the strike and fight for equality play a central role in the film's narrative, Roybal is quick to point out that the idea of querencia is imbued throughout the film. In fact, the people's connection to the land is brought to light at the beginning, when we hear Esperanza in a narrative voiceover state: "Our roots go deep in this place, deeper than the pines, deeper than the mine shaft." Roybal's analysis in her aptly titled chapter defends Esperanza's claim: the roots certainly do go deep in this place.

Spencer R. Herrera's chapter "New Mexico Triptych: Querencia Etched in Wood, in Media, and in Our Memory" compares the US government film *And Now, Miguel* (1953), the State of New Mexico's Department of Tourism marketing campaign "New Mexico True," and Levi Romero's Spanish-language poem "Molino abandonado." The triptych represents three different panels and how each reflects the idea of querencia. *And Now, Miguel* is a documentary-style film that shows in detail the pastoral lifestyle of a Hispanic sheepherding family in Los Cordovas, New Mexico, in the Sangre de Cristo Mountains region, during the early 1950s. The film focuses mostly on the hard work and family and community unity, but toward the end it quickly transitions into a Cold War political propaganda message about protecting freedom from those whose ideologies threaten the "American" way of life. In another form of propaganda, but for economic purposes, the New Mexico True tourism campaign uses billboards, magazine ads, and digital media to draw visitors to the state through a clever marketing campaign that focuses on natural wonders and cultural treasures. The campaign is directed at an audience who seek an adventurous and "true" experience, but at the expense of telling a more complete story of the different truths about New Mexico. "Molino abandonado" takes a more critical look at what is happening to the sense of community within the villages of New Mexico. Romero's poem forces us to think about how we can recover that sense of a united community, or resign ourselves to its fading and disappearance. Herrera's analysis reminds us that what was lost can be found, if we are willing to put in the hard work of cultural recovery and maintenance.

The three chapters in this section teach us about the influence that film and media can have in developing a cultural identity and querencia in the New Mexico homeland. Although the histories that they cover have existed for some time, they are still relevant and resonate with a contemporary viewing public. Some people argue that we should move on from the past. But you don't have to travel far within the state to see that New Mexico's history is an ongoing dialogue. Fortunately, film and other media genres help bring history to life for new audiences, which ensures that our stories continue to be told.

CHAPTER FOUR

Contested Querencia in *The Last Conquistador* (2008) by John J. Valadez and Cristina Ibarra

VANESSA FONSECA-CHÁVEZ

INTRODUCTION

Spanish colonizer Juan de Oñate's expedition into present-day New Mexico is documented in the 1610 epic poem *Historia de la Nueva México* by Gaspar Pérez de Villagrá. In the last twenty years or so, the poem has received significant critical literary attention through numerous reproductions, the most recent in 2010 by the University of Alcalá, Madrid, Spain, to commemorate the four hundredth anniversary of its original publication.[1] The poem illustrates the military violence exacted upon Pueblo communities, specifically Acoma Pueblo. Four hundred years after the arrival of Oñate to the Southwest and the subsequent military and religious colonization of the native people, the memory of this event remains. John Kessell (2008) declares: "Regrettably, the atrocities of Acoma and Santa Fe, 1599 and 1680, live on in bitter memory. Certain descendants of Pueblos and Spaniards today, along with their respective sympathizers, remember conflict not coexistence" (186). The reasons for this are vast, and in no small way are attributed to the ways in which Oñate jumps off the pages of the sixteenth-century literary text to occupy more contemporary spaces of cultural performance, such as reenactments and statues that glorify and revere the Spanish conquistador, while simultaneously provoking debates about his legacy in New Mexico and throughout the southwest United States.

This chapter concentrates on the contemporary controversies surrounding Oñate, more commonly known as the last Spanish conquistador, whose sixteenth-century expedition is the emphasis of Villagrá's epic poem. In this work, I focus on the 2008 documentary *The Last Conquistador* by John J. Valadez and Cristina Ibarra and read it as a way to highlight the ever-present cultural conflict among Hispanics, Hispanophiles, and the Indigenous community of Acoma Pueblo.[2] Perhaps the most lingering debate concerning New Mexico's colonial history is the way in which these legacies endure in a contemporary context and how discordant groups respond to these disputes. More importantly, the discussion opens up important questions about what it means to live within and negotiate a space of contested *querencia*.

CONTESTED QUERENCIA

While 2010 was a landmark year to celebrate the literary legacy of Villagrá's epic poem, 1998 represented, for many people, a pivotal historical moment for celebrating the four hundredth anniversary of the arrival of Oñate and the subsequent founding of the first Spanish settlement, San Juan de los Caballeros. Cultural celebrations arose in the form of statues, new bodies of literature, and reenactments—all of which exposed deep sociopolitical and historical wounds concerning the perceived benefits of colonization. Sarah Bronwen Horton (2002) asserts that many New Mexicans look for a historical continuity anchored in this conquest. Regarding the celebration that took place in Albuquerque,[3] Horton states, "All in all, the ceremony seemed to suggest not merely a *re-encuentro* (or reencounter) of Spaniard and Hispanos but a *return*, a reinvigoration of Spanish-ness that aimed to collapse the gap between the conquistador past and a less glorious present" (49). This notion is affirmed by Joan Ramon Resina's (2005) observations on the desired longevity of Hispanism as a colonizing project, including the present symbolic dominance of the former Spanish empire. As a necessary element of negotiating colonial relationships, the continued desire to replicate former Spanish glory has been met, historically, with opposition from those whose querencia was established long before the arrival of Spanish explorers, as well as those who have rejected colonialism in all its manifestations outright.

Juan Estevan Arellano (2014) notes that Oñate's characterization of querencia stems from the description of the landscape as he claimed space in la Nueva México in the late sixteenth century. He writes, "In his Act of Taking Possession of April 30, 1598 . . . Oñate defined querencia as 'from the leaves of the trees in the forests to the stones and sands of the river, and from the stones of the sands of the river to the leaves in the forest'" (19). Because the Spanish Crown was concerned about the possession of land as a way to exploit natural resources and to expand empire, Oñate staked his claim through these boundaries. This was when querencia first became a contested term. If Indigenous communities use natural boundaries and landscape as a way to demark sacred spaces—ones that are not akin to spaces of ownership—how, then, did

Oñate recognize querencia as it existed before his arrival? Querencia is not simply a recognition of landscape, but rather a profound knowledge of the roots of the landscape and how we interact with the ecosystem that surrounds us. Oñate's querencia was shortsighted, as he looked to the land primarily as an economic venture in line with Spanish imperialism and did not consider how that vision contrasted with existing systems of knowledge. The claiming of land as part of colonial expansion negated querencias held by existing communities, those who *did* and *do* possess a deep knowledge of the land.

Native communities developed important relationships with the landscape that Oñate failed to consider as an integral part of querencia. In regard to Indigenous querencia, C. Maurus Chino, an Acoma artist and activist, remarks that "the brutal occupation of our beloved lands has become so engrained into the psyche of Hispanics and non-Hispanic Hispanophiles that they don't even recognize the racism and, if they do, it says something for this land" ("Let's Talk," 2017). Chino's conceptualization of New Mexico as beloved lands demonstrates a form of querencia that predates Oñate's view of it as a financial endeavor. The word "beloved" connotes a deep, abiding love for land that is synonymous with respect and reverence, concepts that are central to Indigenous worldviews. Furthermore, Chino's Acoma ancestors were prepared to fight for their land and their querencia in 1599 when it came under threat by Oñate and his men.[4] And they have been doing so ever since as a mode of survivance and resistance against colonial ideologies.

CONFRONTING COLONIAL LEGACIES

In the late 1990s, in celebration of the four hundredth anniversary of Oñate's arrival, a statue of Oñate was placed in front of the Oñate Monument Resource and Visitors Center near Española, New Mexico.[5] In response to this, an anonymous group cut off the left foot of the statue, just as Oñate and his men did as an infernal punishment to the Acoma men in 1599.[6] This action was accompanied by a letter titled "We Have Oñate's Foot," in which the group expressed its lack of interest in glorifying a man who was accused of crimes against humanity. The letter established the group's political ideology: "We have no quarrel with our Hispanic brothers and sisters. There is neither racial motivation nor any attempt to disrupt any of our communities. This land was ours before the Conquistadors, Mexicans or Anglos came here. We know the history of this place before their time, and we have not forgotten it since their arrival. We see no glory in celebrating Oñate's fourth centennial, and we do not want our faces rubbed in it. If you must speak of his expedition, speak the truth in all its entirety" ("We Have" 1998, 2). While the author(s) of the letter are not identified, these actions demonstrate the complexities of historical memory attached to Spanish conquest and speak to the importance of protecting spaces that are under threat, a pivotal defense mechanism attached to one's querencia. While the Indigenous pueblos lament the violent history of the Spanish colonizers and advocate for a more balanced view of history, those who support Spanish colonial ideologies look to Oñate as a hero of his time and fully support a continued celebration of his supposed merits. This argument is in no way dissimilar to the controversy surrounding the documentary *The Last Conquistador* (2008), though the events are separated by ten years.

WHERE I STAND

Before analyzing *The Last Conquistador*, I first want to situate myself in relation to its theme. In 2008, I left New Mexico for the first time to begin a PhD program at Arizona State University (ASU). As a new doctoral student in the Spanish program studying Chicano/a literature, I was primarily interested in how colonial legacies manifested within contemporary cultural and literary spaces. Despite being told by others that this topic was overdone, I maintained an interest in these questions. I walked into a large and crowded lecture hall at ASU where the documentary was being screened. John J. Valadez, one of the two filmmakers, had been invited to facilitate the discussion of the film. Acoma Pueblo members and faculty from ASU's School of Transborder Studies also attended as discussants. I sat toward the back of the room, excited about being able to connect to home and my querencia through this viewing.

I watched the film with a curious familiarity to the debate about Oñate's legacy, coupled with my relationship to New Mexico. My grandmother's first cousin, Pauline Chávez-Bent, has documented our family's history dating to the Oñate expedition. Chávez-Bent was connected to the New Mexico Hispanic Culture Preservation League (HCPL) and invited me to attend a ceremony in 2006 in which she received its Doña Eufemia Award. This organization was founded after a controversy surrounding the statue of Oñate that was placed in Albuquerque as part of the celebration of the four hundredth anniversary of the arrival of his expedition to New Mexico (Horton 2002).

The Chávez family settled in Atarque, New Mexico, located in the north-western part of the state. On the same rock where Oñate's famous line "paso por aquí" is inscribed is an imprint from Juan García, one of the founders of Atarque, that reads: "Juan García pasó por aquí con su familia para poblar el Atarque en el año 1882" (Chávez-Bent 2007, 4). In the mid-1940s, this side of my family migrated to the Gallup and Grants areas in search of employment after my great-grandfather, Juan "Chavitos" Chávez, was no longer able to work as a sheepherder.

I was born in Grants, New Mexico, an economically unstable town follow-ing the uranium boom of the 1950s, where Indigenous and Hispanic com-munities continue to combat the devastating effects of the uranium industry. About twenty miles east of Grants is Acoma Pueblo, the site of the historic 1599 massacre ordered by Oñate. In my early childhood, my family moved to Pojoaque, New Mexico, near present-day Española. I didn't know about Onate's so-called legacy despite being surrounded by it for most of my life.

I heard nothing about this controversy while attending school in Grants, nor was Oñate a topic of conversation when I was growing up in Pojoaque. My siblings and I did, however, take school field trips to places like El Morro National Monument, where Oñate's legacy is carved into Inscription Rock alongside those of more than two thousand others who traveled that historic path and also carved their names in the rock. What I noticed growing up in these spaces was a deep divide between Hispanos, Natives, and Anglo-Amer-icans, which sharply contrasted with any contemporary belief that New Mexico was a tricultural, harmonious state. Those who study New Mexico know the problems with this myth. In Pojoaque, economics divided the rich Hispanics whose families worked in Los Alamos from the poor Hispanos who did not work on "the hill." In Grants, families struggled to survive and fought for jobs in blue-collar industries such as the coal mines, the paper mill, and the prison systems. (With a population of around nine thousand people, Grants is home to two prisons, with another nearby that recently closed.) It was no surprise to me, then, that economics and racial politics drove the nar-rative of Valadez and Ibarra's documentary.

I watched *The Last Conquistador* with this knowledge. At times, I wondered whether people knew I was Nuevomexicana and if they would want me to explain racial politics in New Mexico. As a graduate student, I tended to be an observer rather than a commentator in the classroom, but the film opened me up. I thought about HCPL member Conchita Lucero throughout the film and was angry that she had been chosen to serve as the representative Hispanic. I rejected the privilege that she demonstrated, as well as her lack of interest in healing trauma brought on by colonialism. I questioned whether her querencia, like Oñate's, was also shortsighted. I was familiar with the HCPL through Pauline Chávez-Bent. Though I disagreed with their approach, I attempted to understand how one might feel a deep desire for recognition in the only homeland they have ever known.

As the film concluded, Valadez posed a question for the audience to begin the discussion, "Do you think the filmmaker made this documentary with a colonial mindset?" My hand shot up in the air and I shouted "YES!" The crowd shifted in my direction. I wondered how the audience *saw* me. Did the historical baggage of my querencia make me a target audience for the documentary? Did the filmmakers expect Nuevomexicanos to respond in a particular way? I expressed my disgust at the inclusion of the New Mexico Hispanic Culture Preservation League in the documentary. In an apologetic tone, I said that not all Hispanos think like Lucero and that surely, someone better could have represented the sentiments of Hispanos in this debate, perhaps even those who did not share anti-Indigenous sentiments. Valadez waited for me to finish and retorted, "Well, you have to think about Conchita's position. Her family has been in New Mexico since the 1600s and has a deep investment in the state. She is proud of her background . . ."

I include an ellipsis here because all I heard was justification of Conchita's logic, though now I know Valadez well enough to understand that he likes to provoke reactions to get people to think about all perspectives. His question about a colonial mindset was a loaded one, and likely something he encountered along the documentary tour before arriving at ASU. I remember replying with "Yes, I know . . . My family has the same history," and expressing the feeling that the perceived exclusion of one's own history doesn't give a person the right to deny others of theirs.

The film was the perfect introduction to my doctoral studies because it embodied the complications and questions that now drive my research. The distinct perspectives displayed in the documentary demonstrate where we have come and, more importantly, where we fall short in understanding and appreciating one another's claim to *querencia* and all the complications that arise from it.

The documentary centers on the polemic relationship that was reignited when a series of statues were to be constructed in the center of El Paso, Texas, with the goal of celebrating the history of the Southwest and boosting tourism in the city.[7] The first three statues planned included Friar García, who built the first mission in El Paso; Juan de Oñate, known as the "Last Conquistador"; and Benito Juárez, the only Indigenous president of Mexico. The plan was to place twelve statues to form this memorial.[8] While the Oñate statue itself is not located within the contested landscape of querencia in New Mexico, El Paso is nevertheless significant because it represents another important moment in the history of Indigenous resistance. In 1680, Indigenous communities throughout what is now the state of New Mexico rebelled against Spanish rule and drove the Spanish south. They retreated to El Paso del Norte, or El Paso, before returning to what is now northern New Mexico twelve years later. What ensued in 1692 during the "Reconquista" in Santa Fe and its modern-day celebrations is a conversation for another time.

The fundamental argument in *The Last Conquistador* refers to the statue as a constant reminder of a Spanish colonial past. John J. Valadez and Cristina Ibarra's choosing of polemic sides was strategic and served to demonstrate the viewpoints of different individuals connected to the conflict surrounding the erection of the Oñate statue: Indigenous communities, the self-identified Spanish Americans who formed part of the HCPL, Hispano and Chicano residents of New Mexico and Texas, Anglo-Americans, and John S. Houser— the sculptor—among others.

CELEBRATING OÑATE'S LEGACY

By validating and praising Oñate via a permanent monument, Hispanics and Hispanophiles alike defended his sixteenth-century colonizing project. In the film, Conchita Lucero, a member of the HCPL, says she is thrilled about the edification of the statue. She declares, "It will finally be an unveiling of our history. . . We have a legacy, I think, to be extremely proud of." Lucero's commentary is complicated, as Oñate has occupied similar spaces in the past through pageantry and statues placed prior to 2007. Thus, this was not the first or second "unveiling" of history. A curious viewer of the film may wonder how many unveilings are necessary to render a history visible. Or perhaps one might think about alternative ways to promote history if the number of statues and cultural productions does not yet seem effective.

The film clearly shows Lucero, among others, takes on a colonizing tone and quickly disregards those opinions that do not fall in line with her own. Interestingly, an interplay by the directors portrays the inherent limits of sight/blindness that set up the parameters of the conflict. What one side sees clearly, the other does not. And what becomes apparent, although they use differing strategies, is that neither side can convince the other to see what they refuse to acknowledge. Those who support the Oñate statue use it as a symbol to separate themselves from the Indigenous people and as a tool to refuse their decolonial struggle. By negating one's struggle, there is a discernible atmosphere of racial difference. Viewers are faced with important questions about how they should view historical figures that are marked by their colonial attitudes of racism and indifference. Regarding this, historian John Kessell says in the film: "I think rightly and righteously today we condemn conquest, imperialism, colonialism, and human bondage of any form, but we shouldn't go about damning people four centuries ago who were doing what their societies did, and especially, you know, the idea of the Indians crying victim will bring you immediate attention, and it also leads you to believe that you have attained the moral high ground. And then to use that club to beat up people who are descendants fifteen generations later, seems to me all wrong." According to Kessell, by recognizing themselves as victims, Indigenous people are occupying a position of moral superiority over the previous colonizers, now colonized. This argument, however logical to him, raises important discussions related to the role of historical memory and competing claims to homeland.

Many of those people who celebrate the ideology of the Spanish Empire would say that, instead of focusing on their own oppression, Indigenous people should recognize all the fruits of imperial labor that have been presented to them over time. In a meeting of the HCPL documented in the film, the following arguments are heard in favor of the alleged advantages of Spanish colonization: "Oñate was a hero of the red man, he was not a conqueror. He gathered with all the Pueblo Indians in one spot and created a treaty. Try to find nineteen pueblos anywhere east of the Mississippi; and yet, we are accused of destroying the Indians and they are still here. They are even an ungrateful group. Which one of us hasn't had a benefit of the things that the Spanish brought here? You know what, they [the Spanish] are here, get over it, and deal with it." In this way, the HCPL displays a problematic attitude toward colonized groups, even though its members have fallen from their previous colonizing graces and are working through their own feelings related to cultural erasure. Rather than recognizing the dynamics of colonial relationships, including the element of rebellion as a strategy for anticolonial struggle, the group advocates for an appreciation of Oñate as a heroic man who presented a more favorable fate to the Indigenous people in New Mexico than those who were located farther east. This common defense strategy often sidesteps any progress toward reconciliation.

Romanticizing a Spanish colonial presence in present-day New Mexico is intricately connected to the longevity of the Spanish colonial period in this region. Katherine Verdery (2000) declares that the New Mexican Spanish colonization carries a cultural identity that refuses to surrender: "Identities will be less flexible wherever the process of modern nation-state formation has the greatest longevity and has proceeded the furthest; wherever long-standing nationalist movements have effectively inculcated the sentiment of a single kind of belonging; and wherever colonial states had more extensive and deeper than shallower roots" (37). The cultural and historical politics that arise in the film can be understood as a form of ideological durability. Though these systems are difficult to undo, the decolonial project is necessary to recognize and act in response to historical trauma brought forth by colonialism. In doing so, we create collective spaces of healing that shift the ways we think about colonial legacies.

Thomas H. Guthrie (2013) aptly notes that the politics of recognition in a state that has been doubly colonized have a more nuanced understanding of trauma. He states, "Subaltern groups bear the political and psychological weight of these anxieties, since they must convince others and themselves of their cultural integrity" (12). Now, does this apply equally to Indigenous groups and to Spanish American–identified individuals residing in New Mexico? This is a difficult question in *The Last Conquistador*, as both groups feel their history and culture have been erased. The trauma of colonization is applicable to both, though another's trauma should never be disregarded for the benefit of one's own. However, this is what happens in the film.

INDIGENOUS RESISTANCE

More than recognizing and celebrating a Spanish colonial past as members of the HCPL do and supporting an Anglo-American savior mentality, Native communities of New Mexico look to cure the wounds of the past through recognition of colonial violence. For them, the events of the film are not simply about a statue, but rather a legacy of historical trauma brought upon them during not one, but two colonial periods. The images of Oñate throughout the Southwest are repeated reminders of oppression that, though rooted in the sixteenth century, continue today. Chino comments, "It is not simply a glorification of heritage. We try to celebrate our diversity, but when something demeans another culture, then it crosses a boundary, and that's when people should not be quiet. They should make their voices heard." He counteracts the opinion of the HCPL, saying that the glorification of such colonial history, without recognition of the oppression of the Indigenous, is an open rejection of the history of the dominated and erases important social and cultural communities. "I remember when I first saw the images of that statue down in El Paso," says Chino, "it was such a feeling of anger and disgust. I thought, either a lot of people don't know their own history or, the scary part is, they really do want to honor somebody who was a perpetrator of genocide and violence who slaughtered the people."

David Romo, a writer residing in El Paso, continues by discounting the title given to Oñate, because he believes notions of Spanish conquest still exist: "Some people call him the last conquistador, but he is not the last conquistador. The idea of conquest is one that is very much a part of who we are today. By focusing completely on these notions that make a lot of sense to you, making no attempt to see the other person's point of view, that's how evil comes about." Chino provides additional insight: "Against the wishes of the people, they still continue to put [up] these monuments of racism and shove them into people's faces. That's an example of how the oppression today continues." To combat the imperial ideology associated with the statue, members of Acoma Pueblo, alongside other Indigenous Pueblo communities and all those who stand in solidarity with them, protest its edification and try to convince the city of El Paso not to facilitate this recognition of modern-day colonial violence by allowing it to be placed for the purpose of increasing tourism. The Oñate statue does not serve simply as a reminder of the so-called gains of the Spanish colonizer, but rather represents the glorification of a historical moment in which the community of Acoma was reduced to one-eighth of its population following the 1599 massacre at the hands of the Spanish military forces.

In the film, Romo states, "You're really commemorating that one group of white people took away the homeland of another group of brown people. Is that really the great vision and the great value that America is founded upon?" He makes a valid point in thinking about how notions of querencia function within the Southwest. If statues are an unveiling of Spanish history, as Lucero posits, they also serve as a reminder to the oppressed about not who was here first, but who holds more political and social power in a colonized space, and they continue to promote Oñate's brutal legacy. It is during these moments that contested querencia comes to the forefront and Indigenous groups work to defend a homeland their ancestors inhabited and cared for long before the arrival of colonial empires.

The film is saturated with opposing opinions about the statue and its significance. However, it is easy to distinguish between those who support colonial projects and those who oppose continued celebrations of oppression. Those who support a glorified Spanish past include the self-identified Spanish or Spanish American descendants (Hispanics) and non-Hispanic supporters of the Spanish colonial period whose economic position and cultural neutrality defend a pro-Spanish heritage to promote tourism through a romanticized or glorified view of the past (Guthrie 2013). Contrarily, the Indigenous people of New Mexico show a marked opposition to the celebrations, statues, fiestas, and other events that promote colonial legacies. Throughout the documentary, they repeatedly express their resistance through decolonial struggles.

SHAKY GROUND

Valadez and Ibarra thread the story of John S. Houser throughout the documentary in ways that propose a problematic path to reconciliation. As the film begins, the sculptor comments, "I share the same vision for my work as I would imagine Oñate had for his venture to New Mexico." Viewers who are familiar with the epic poem *Historia de la Nueva México* are aware that Oñate's colonial venture was not without its setbacks; one easily could argue that he was led by a burning ambition to secure a win for the dwindling Spanish Empire. By paralleling Oñate's experience to his own, Houser sets up a relatable narrative that foreshadows continued destruction and a lack of consciousness from a colonizing entity. At the same time, the viewer should be aware of the documentarians' filmic strategy to elicit empathy for Houser's cause. Houser defends his art, declaring that every person can appreciate it for what it is. However, he also recognizes that art is interpreted in distinct manners depending on who views it. This, coupled with the awareness of the historical narrative created in New Mexico since colonial times, motivates the debates about the statue.

The film does not state explicitly the extent to which Houser was educated about Oñate before he began to work on the statue. Nevertheless, he does set himself up as the spokesperson of an ideology embedded in the sculpture as well as any praise or critique from those who support or reject his vision. The ideological implications of the statue as a permanent fixture are well-defined. While people may disagree with the statue at first, Houser is sure that it is something they will grow to appreciate. This has since proven to be false. For those afflicted by the colonial underpinnings of the many Oñate statues that claim space in New Mexico and the Southwest, the film makes it clear that appreciation is not a common sentiment.

As the documentary presents, after years of debate, Houser educates himself about the significance of the conquest and the artistic image of the statue. He recognizes, as the sculptor, that he is participating in colonial oppression. With a supposed newfound consciousness, he asks for forgiveness, saying, "There was a certain blindness in the society of that time and that blindness is still with us today. I had neglected the depth of the injury that had been done to the Native American people and that point now it's too late to rectify. It is a suffering for me, too, to have to carry this, because it is not what I intended for people to get out of this work, but it's something I should have been able to anticipate, and I didn't, and I'm sorry." Although the sculpture cannot be erased or forgiven as easily as his assumed naïveté, the viewers of the documentary can perhaps appreciate Houser's apology at some level.

Some important questions, however, arise in regard to an artist's role in society. If Houser claims not to have known about the sociopolitical and historical conflict rooted in centuries of colonial struggle, can his newfound knowledge and awareness prompt him to make an even bolder move and perhaps advocate on behalf of communities that have been marginalized in this process? If his art communicates conflict between colonizers and colonized, can and would he also then support an anticolonial struggle? How does this reconcile the debate in the film? Houser concedes heroism not to the Spanish colonizers, but to Acoma Pueblo for the struggles they have endured throughout this process. He has recognized a history of oppression. But the statue remains. His project to promote a Spanish imperial legacy and its accompanying ideologies occupies the place designated by its financiers and supporters. As I think about the role of querencia in the documentary, I realize we still have a long way to go. The physical taking of space backed by economic ventures throughout the film mirrors Oñate's original claims to querencia but negates the difficulties in protecting Indigenous spaces subject to colonial violence. Each statue of Oñate placed in New Mexico and the Southwest has been met with protest but, unfortunately, the promise of tourism dollars and the celebration of Spanish glory win out every time.

What does this strategic move by the filmmakers deliver to its audience? Houser, a White man—whose project is supported by a Hispanic and upper-class Anglo society in both New Mexico and Texas—closes the discussion about a historic and heated conflict among Hispanics, Hispanophiles, and Indigenous communities. These moves echo a white savior complex and lends a less-than-palatable sense of closure to the film. Houser learns something through the process, but never resists the placing of the statue because, ultimately, he is self-serving. His legacy, much like Oñate's, is secured.

Under the guise of not offending anyone—and acting as though the artwork itself was the only "offense"—the El Paso City Council, whose city has historical relevance for Oñate's expedition, decided to change the name of the statue. Instead of referring to it as Juan de Oñate, they opted for a more general title. In his book *Pueblos, Spaniards, and the Kingdom of New Mexico* (2008), Kessell explains: "Council members, refusing to withdraw the city's partial funding, nevertheless voted a compromise. They would drop Juan de Oñate's name and call sculptor John Sherrill Houser's gigantic bronze simply *The Equestrian*.[9] Installed in 2006, dedicated on April 21, 2007, and rearing three stories tall above the tarmac at El Paso International Airport, *The Equestrian* surely ranks today as the Southwest's most conspicuous and best-known alias" (184). Another name for a statue associated with a longstanding debate offers no resolution to the conflict that drives the documentary.

The Last Conquistador highlights the tensions of more than four hundred years of New Mexico history with literary origins in the 1610 publication of *Historia de la Nueva México*. The film presents a nonfiltered perspective of a historical debate and radical politics. While this controversy is not new in New Mexico, it adds to national and international conversations about monuments, statues, and the politics of memory. The film demonstrates that longstanding tensions are connected to the ways we claim querencia and how much we are willing to fight in defense of our ideological viewpoints.

The documentary is but another thread in the historical fabric where Oñate takes center stage. I am sure it won't be the last. Although the equestrian statue remains a fixture of the El Paso landscape, the irony lies in the film update provided by Valadez. He notes: "The most remarkable thing that has occurred since *The Last Conquistador* was completed in November 2007 is that nothing has happened. If you go to El Paso you won't miss the Oñate (The Equestrian) statue towering over the U.S. border with Mexico like a Roman god, dominating the sky, singing of the power and glory of empire. All the while, most people who see it have no idea who Oñate is or what he is doing in this 'dusty, isolated border town.'"[10] This cycle is consistent with the lingering debates about Oñate. They surface at different moments in time and expose longstanding tensions between different ethnic groups. John Nieto-Phillips relates this to a sustained emotional and political ideology that is a product of our historical memory. This provides an ideal environment for claiming space and reaffirming identity, however contentious (Nieto-Phillips 2004). The longstanding debate in New Mexico over querencia is rooted in a desire for recognition and a struggle for past and present cultural relevance.

Patricia Marina Trujillo, Corrine Kaa Pedi Povi Sanchez, and Scott Davis (chapter fourteen, this volume) refer to Oñate as a *chispa*, the flyaway piece of hair that keeps resting on your face. You tuck it back, but you know it's bound to get loose again and bothersome. Oñate is a tired, drawn-out character in the story of New Mexico. How do we secure this chispa? And where? Recent national debates surrounding Confederate flags and statues in the South and monuments more generally suggest museums, rather than public spaces, as potential sites of remembrance.[11] And Guthrie (2013) reminds us that these sites serve as an epicenter for the politics of recognition with ties to how we celebrate multiculturalism, specifically in New Mexico. The white supremicist marches and counterprotests in Charlottesville, Virginia prompted social media users and KUNM, a public radio station broadcasting from UNM's Oñate Hall (sigh), to return to the topic of Oñate's legacy in August 2017.

CONCLUSION

As I finished this essay, I could not find a way to break away from the controversy surrounding Oñate that was brought again to the forefront via national conversations on Confederate statues. A recent manifestation of resistance to this narrative was the renaming of the Oñate Monument Resource and

Visitors Center as the Northern Río Grande National Heritage Center, whose vision centers on the economic sustainability of the people of the northern Río Grande.[12] This marks a shift from Oñate's economic claim of landscape and querencia to a shared sense of querencia that celebrates the many cultures that have contributed to the formation of this space. More importantly, it demonstrates an investment in and recognition of the economic structures that were created through centuries of colonial violence in New Mexico and the Southwest. The rededication of this space came to my attention through a Facebook post by Patricia Marina Trujillo on March 2, 2017, where she included a photo showing a new sign posted near the Oñate monument. The sign, a conquistador hat with a line through it, was accompanied by Patricia's hashtag #buenobyeoñate. Though the artist was not known at the time of her posting, it marks a pattern of resistance to the Oñate narrative and a desire to move past exhausted arguments of former Spanish glory that fail to nuance history.

Just as 1998 prompted new conversations about Oñate's legacy in light of the four hundredth anniversary of his arrival, so, too, did more recent events surrounding monuments dedicated to Confederate heroes. In 2017, on the cusp of the Entrada Pageant in Santa Fe for the annual Santa Fe Fiestas held each September,[13] the Oñate statue in Alcalde was vandalized with red paint covering the left foot. On a nearby wall were the graffitied words "Remember 1680" (Bennett 2017). This act demonstrated a continued lack of interest by some in celebrating pageantry and monuments to Spanish colonization and a reminder that this conversation is not a completely silent one and may never be.

In a surprising revelation, the foot that was cut off the Alcalde statue was found by an unnamed man. Simon Romero, writing for the *New York Times*, reported on September 30, 2017 that a mysterious figure met with Cheyenne-Arapaho filmmaker Chris Eyre and himself to unveil the amputated foot. The article notes that Eyre was working on a documentary to tease out the complexities of New Mexico's history via the removal of Oñate's foot and the discussions it had sparked during the previous twenty years. Romero states that in an act of reconciliation, the foot thief "melted down a portion of the foot to make medallions for Pueblo leaders." While the identity of the thief was not known, he made it clear that "he carried out the amputation in 1997 with just one comrade, a Native New Mexican, in solidarity with the Acoma people."

The events surrounding Oñate statues and colonial legacies show that communities, specifically Indigenous peoples and those who labor in decolonial politics, are not easily silenced. Resistance to claiming space via statues, pageantry, or other cultural modes of oppression is an important move in securing querencia for future generations. It is natural for one to want to protect beloved lands and to contest those who threaten it. It also is possible for people today to transcend narratives of conquest rooted in Spanish colonial politics of the sixteenth century. A more nuanced understanding of Oñate's historical narrative and the legacies it celebrates may suggest opportunities for reconciliation and healing rather than glorification. We need to recognize that this is bigger than the removal of statues and monuments. We need to think about how to undo and remove colonial violence and the systemic oppression that plagues our querencia spaces. We need to reaffirm our commitment to querencia while also honoring the querencia that others share in this contested space. A firm commitment to querencia values and protects all those who are committed to caring for it. If we cannot engage in these bold acts and question our own complicity in the colonial narrative, we are doomed to repeat the same weary patterns of our past.

NOTES

1. Manuel M. Martín-Rodríguez, editor of *Historia de la Nueva México, 1610* (2010), affirms, "[A]l cumplirse con el cuarto centenario de la impresión original del poema, y en pleno momento de recuperación histórica de la figura del cantor nuevomexicano, parece más que propicio publicar su obra de nuevo en la misma ciudad que entonces la dio a conocer" (17). [As we complete the four hundredth anniversary of the original printing of the poem and in a moment of historic recuperation of the figure of the New Mexican poet, it seemed more than appropriate to republish this work in the same city that gave it life.] Translation mine.

2. Acoma Pueblo is one of nineteen recognized Indigenous Pueblo communities located in the northwest region of New Mexico, about sixty miles west of Albuquerque. In this essay, I use the terms "Hispanics" and "Hispanophiles" as a way to identify those in the film who align themselves with a celebration of Oñate's legacy. This is in no way a simple task, as these terms do not adequately recognize the complicated nature of identity formation in New Mexico and the Southwest.

3. In "Let's Talk Monuments to Conquistadors" (2017), Maurus Chino (Acoma) notes that he first participated as an activist in a protest of the installation of the Oñate statue near the Albuquerque Museum in 1998. Many Oñate statues that have been placed in New Mexico have been met with protest and many locations have rejected the use of taxpayer dollars to fund such projects.

4. See *Historia de la Nueva México, 1610* (2010).

5. See Michael L. Trujillo (2009) for an insightful discussion of the Oñate statue in Alcalde, New Mexico.

6. The battle at Acoma is described in detail by Pérez de Villagrá in the epic poem *Historia de la Nueva México* (1610). However, many individuals who support Oñate's legacy claim that he did not cut off the left foot of Acoma men aged twenty-five and older following the battle, simply because it did not make sense. Marc Simmons (1991), however, writes a detailed account of the sentencing procedures, which include the punishment of cutting off the left foot; he also notes that this incident should not overshadow Oñate's achievements.

7. Alan Berube and Cecile Murray (2017) report that El Paso, Texas suffers from one of the highest suburban poverty rates in the United States (22.1 percent), based on information from the US Census Bureau. The documentary contrasts the desire for an increase in tourism with shots of the city that represent this statistic. Residents of El Paso who reside in these areas question why the city has not taken steps to improve the living conditions in more poverty-stricken areas of the city (Valadez and Ibarra, 2008).

8. http://xiitravelers.org/.

9. See "Statue to Be Renamed" (2003).

10. http://www.pbs.org/pov/lastconquistador/film-update/.

11. In 2015, protest rallies were held in the South following the killing of nine African Americans at a church in Charleston, South Carolina. These protests advocated for the removal of the Confederate flag as a symbol of a white supremacist ideology. In 2017, controversy about the removal of a Robert E. Lee statue prompted a "Unite the Right" rally. These marchers were met by counterprotestors who represented anti–White supremacist views. These events resulted in larger national conversations about monuments and the ideologies they represent. Oñate monuments in the Southwest were an important part of this conversation.

12. See http://riograndenha.org/index.html.

13. For more on the Santa Fe Fiestas, see Horton (2010).

WORKS CITED

Arellano, Juan Estevan. 2014. *Enduring Acequias: Wisdom of the Land, Knowledge of the Water*. Albuquerque: University of New Mexico Press.
Baumgartel, Elaine. 2017. "Let's Talk Monuments to Conquistadors." KUNM. August 23, 2017. http://kunm.org/post/lets-talk-monuments-conquistadors.
Bennett, Megan. 2017. "Rio Arriba County Statue Vandalized on Day of the Entrada." September 15, 2017. https://www.abqjournal.com/1063880/rio-arriba -county-statue-vandalized-on-day-of-the-entrada-ex-the-left-boot-of-the -statue-of-don-juan-de-ontildeate-was-covered-in-red-paint.html.

Berube, Alan, and Cecile Murray. 2017. "Three Charts Showing You Poverty in U.S. Cities and Metro Areas." September 14, 2017. https://www.brookings.edu/blog /the-avenue/2017/09/14/three-charts-showing-you-poverty-in-u-s-cities-and -metro-areas/.

Chávez-Bent, Pauline. 2007. *Atarque: Now All is Silent*. Albuquerque: Río Grande Books.

"Group: We Have Oñate's Foot." 1998. *Albuquerque Journal*, January 14, 1998. 1.

Guthrie, Thomas H. 2013. *Recognizing Heritage: The Politics of Multiculturalism in New Mexico*. Lincoln: University of Nebraska Press.

Horton, Sarah. 2002. "New Mexico's Cuarto Centenario and Spanish-American Nationalism: Collapsing Past Conquests and Present Dispossession." *Journal of the Southwest* 44, no 1: 49–60.

Horton, Sarah Bronwen. 2010. *The Santa Fe Fiesta, Reinvented: Staking Ethno-Nationalist Claims to a Disappearing Homeland*. Santa Fe: School for Advanced Research Press.

Kessell, John L. 2008. *Pueblos, Spaniards, and the Kingdom of New Mexico*. Norman: University of Oklahoma Press.

Martín-Rodríguez, Manuel M. 2012. "400 Years of Literature and History in the United States: Gaspar de Villagrá's *Historia de la nueva México* (1610)." *Camino Real* 4, no. 6: 13–19.

Nieto-Phillips, John M. 2004. *The Language of Blood: The Making of Spanish-American Identity in New Mexico, 1880s–1930s*. Albuquerque: University of New Mexico Press.

Pérez de Villagrá, Gaspar. 1992. *Historia de la Nueva México, 1610*, edited by Miguel Encinias, Alfred Rodríguez, and Joseph P. Sánchez. Albuquerque: University of New Mexico Press.

———. 2010. *Historia de la Nueva Mexico*, edited by Manuel M. Martín-Rodríguez. Alcalá de Henares, Spain: Biblioteca Benjamin Franklin.

Ramon Resina, Joan. 2005. "Whose Hispanism? Cultural Trauma, Disciplined Memory and Symbolic Resistance." In *Ideologies of Hispanism*, edited by Mabel Moraña, 160–86. Nashville: Vanderbilt University Press.

Romero, Simon. 2017. "Statue's Stolen Foot Reflects Divisions over Symbols of Conquest." *New York Times*, September 30, 2017. https://www.nytimes.com/2017/09/30/us/statue-foot-new-mexico.html.

Simmons, Marc. 1991. *The Last Conquistador: Juan de Oñate and the Settling of the Far Southwest*. Norman: University of Oklahoma Press.

"Statue to Be Renamed: Onate's Controversial Acts Draw Criticism." 2003. Associated Press. *Albuquerque Journal*, November 6, 2003: D3.

Trujillo, Michael L. 2009. *Land of Disenchantment: Latina/o Identities and Transformations in Northern New Mexico*. Albuquerque: University of New Mexico Press.

Valadez, John J. and Cristina Ibarra, dirs. 2008. *The Last Conquistador*. PBS.

Verdery, Katherine. 2000. "Ethnicity, Nationalism, and State Making: *Ethnic Groups and Boundaries*: Past and Future." In *The Anthropology of Ethnicity: Beyond "Ethnic Groups and Boundaries*," edited by Hans Vermeulen and Cora Grover, 33–58. Amsterdam: Spinhuis.

CHAPTER FIVE

Deep Roots in Community
Querencia and *Salt of the Earth*

KAREN R. ROYBAL

In her influential work *Methodology of the Oppressed* (2000), Chela Sandoval asserts, "Differential consciousness . . . emits functioning within yet beyond the demands of dominant ideology" (3). Through this statement, she describes how Third World feminists have created an oppositional ideology that counters the repressive systems of power that have historically attempted to weaken and divide their collective power to make change. This was a particularly salient response to what had occurred during the 1960s and 1970s and extended into the 1980s, decades in which communities of color were fighting for equal social, political, and racial rights and women were confronting fervent gender and racial discrimination within a hegemonic feminist movement. Sandoval's oppositional consciousness and methodology renders visible the hierarchies that firmly established the dominant social order still in effect today.

The rise of police brutality, targeted attacks, blatant gender and racial discrimination, and communities fighting for basic necessities such as clean water and water rights proves that the twenty-first-century US society in which we live is not much different from its jaded past. Though there has been a lack of significant systemic change in response to these issues, communities on both sides of the debate are engaged in increased social activism, and their responses now dominate news accounts, social-media feeds, and discussions across social, political, and geographical borders. These incidents have influenced resistance to hegemonic powers designed to control particular populations and have revealed the various ways in which communities across the nation have banded together to contest multiple forms of subjugation and violence.

These contemporary stories demonstrate a consciousness of opposition reminiscent of the political and social actions of the 1960s, 1970s, and early 1980s; yet if we trace the genealogy of resistance against imperialism and dominant powers, evidence of that consciousness can be found earlier than the Civil Rights era, or what Sandoval labels "The Equal Rights–Reform" era (2000, 56). This chapter employs her notion of oppositional consciousness to map how the 1951 mining strike in Bayard, New Mexico depicted in the film *Salt of the Earth* (1954)[1] exemplifies how, as citizen-subjects, the miners and their wives contested and transformed oppressive powers through their commitment to community, family, and the land—actions that demonstrate how *Nuevomexicanas/os*[2] made their enchanting state of New Mexico *the* center of a significant battle over worker's rights, sanitation, and women's rights. This chapter further suggests that the influence of the Bayard strike does not serve solely as a *recuerdo*, a memory of the past; rather, there remains an enduring battle for social justice in the state influenced by earlier movements significant to Nuevomexicanas/os whose lives are deeply rooted in community and *querencia*—what the late Juan Estevan Arellano called "love of place" (2014, 5).

FIGHTING FOR THE PEOPLE

As members of the "Hollywood Ten," a group blacklisted from the US motion picture industry because of their Communist political beliefs, the filmmakers who wrote, directed, and produced *Salt of the Earth* broke multiple boundaries for the era. The film centers on a group of Nuevomexicano miners and their families who live in a small community in southern New Mexico. Subjected to poor working conditions, unequal pay, and outright discrimination, the miners, with the help of their wives, engage in a strike against their employer, Delaware Zinc, the film's pseudonym for the Empire Zinc Mining Company. The film calls attention to many important issues: the racist treatment of the miners by their employer, the assumed patriarchal control by the miners over their wives, and the importance of querencia and community-based resistance. Director Herbert J. Biberman, producer Paul Jarrico, and writer Michael Wilson made the film amid rampant anticommunist hysteria driven by the early years of the Cold War.[3] James J. Lorence writes: "As Cold War tension mounted between 1945 and 1947, the motion picture industry experienced its own version of combat in the form of a bitter labor struggle that had originated during the war" (1999, 2). The struggle experienced by filmmakers, directors, and other film workers was driven largely by the belief that "Communist influence had tainted Hollywood unionism and threatened to undermine the entire motion picture industry" (Lorence 1999, 2), which was tied largely to big business and capitalism. Built upon a narrative of suspicion, fear, and a significant threat against American essentialism, the ostracism within the industry of the Hollywood Ten began because of their leftist politics, which included working against "fascism, sexism, racism, workplace exploitation, and colonialism" (McDonald 2012, 4). They were later jailed for their actions, which, ironically, were perceived as antigovernment and anti-American, rather than democratic and egalitarian.

In his narrative about the controversy surrounding the Hollywood Ten, Biberman reveals that he was placed by the House Un-American Activities Committee (HUAC) at the center of an anticommunist movement that made him a pariah within not only the Hollywood film industry, but also broader US society. I interpret his opposition to the suppression of the power of the broader public as a similar sentiment to that drawn from Arellano's notion of querencia for place. Just as the Nuevomexicanos Arellano wrote about fought for their land—an extension of themselves and of their community—Biberman was inspired by the profound devotion and commitment in fighting for "the people." As he describes the reasons for standing up to the dominant ideologies that were enforcing what he perceived as fascism, he reveals more intimate details about the eventual dissent among some members of the group. In one section of his narrative, he questions how one of the Ten, who was later revealed to be an informant for the industry and the government, could give up: "Had Eddie [Dmytryk] become tired of fighting for people, of even believing people were worth fighting for?" (2003, 19). The sentiments expressed by Biberman through his self-reflexive analysis depict how, unlike Dmytryk, he remained committed to speaking against the manipulations imposed upon the American people through "Red Scare" rhetoric and continued to contest the constant subjugation of those the dominant capitalist US nation-state did not protect.

The same type of social consciousness demonstrated by the film's creators extended to the lead female actor, Rosaura Revueltas, a rising star in Mexico who held ties to "Mexico's intelligentsia, including Diego Rivera, David Alfaro Siquieros, and her [writer-activist] brother José" (Lorence 1999, 68). Revueltas, another target for the US government based on her political beliefs, confirmed her commitment to ensuring that the film would be completed and disseminated to the broader public despite the government's attempts to deport her to Mexico. She was determined not to back down from intimidation. As noted by Lorence, when "two Immigration Service officers arrested lead actress Rosaura Revueltas on questionable charges of failure to have her passport stamped on entry (a government error) . . . Revueltas concluded that she was seen as 'dangerous' because she had played a role 'that gave stature and dignity to the character of a Mexican-American woman'" (83). Knowing the charges she would face, she demonstrated a differential consciousness in which she addressed not only the political and racial discrimination that challenged the very nature of US democratic ideals, but, through her statement, also emphasized the chauvinistic attitude toward Mexican and Mexican American women at this time, a point to which I will later return.

Perhaps it should come as no surprise that Revueltas would agree to star in a film created by Jarrico, Wilson, and Biberman based upon a Nuevomexicana/o community's tackling the abuse inflicted on them by American capitalist ideologies, influenced by big business that rendered the safety and livelihood of their community invisible. The actress and filmmakers had a history of critiquing racism, capitalism, gender discrimination, and the lack of egalitarianism in their respective societies through their films. Furthermore, they were engaged in their own battle against the labor militancy that dominated the motion picture industry. Hearings by HUAC to identify Communist filmmakers and actors who critiqued the political ideas of the time even subtly meant that they were subject to a form of "thought control" imposed on them by conservative members of the motion picture industry (Lorence 1999, 5).

This form of repression is similar to the actions taken by Empire Zinc over its Nuevomexicano workers. Ultimately, the mining company owners exercised their control and put the lives of the miners working for them at risk in the name of progress, and with no consideration of the impact their actions had on the workers or their families. These actions are in stark contrast to those taken by the filmmakers, who ensured that the miners, their wives, and the labor organizers were an integral part of the making of the film. Kathlene McDonald notes that as writer Michael Wilson crafted the script, he "returned to the mining community to get feedback from the workers; he listened to their suggestions and changed scenes they thought were unrealistic" (2012, 3). By calling attention to the labor issues that affected Nuevomexicano miners, the film provided a realist view of the hazardous work spaces and neglect by Empire Zinc leaders whose focus was on increased production and exploitation of brown bodies and natural resources.

In *The Suppression of "Salt of the Earth": How Hollywood, Big Labor, and Politicians Blacklisted a Movie in the American Cold War* (1999), Lorence argues, "The central theme in *Salt of the Earth* involves the Chicano/Chicana fight for dignity against long odds as workers struggled to improve their lives in a brutal contest between capital and labor" (8). The film indeed directly acknowledges the efforts made by both Nuevomexicanos and Nuevomexicanas in fighting for dignity and respect from the local sheriffs and Empire Zinc representatives and, in the women's case, from their own communities and husbands. Another central theme is the ways in which the Nuevomexicana/o community members demonstrate and defend their querencia, which is attached to their sense of place, their sense of self, and their sense of dignity. In fact, the opening scene firmly establishes the protagonist Esperanza's querencia when she says, "Our roots go deep in this place, deeper than the pines, deeper than the mine shaft. In these *arroyos* my great-grandfather raised cattle before the Anglos ever came. The land where the mine stands—that was owned by my husband's grandfather." Esperanza's articulation of her family's connection to the land exemplifies what Arellano describes when he says that "to understand place, or querencia, one has to know the ground, the rocks, the trees, the flora and fauna"; to know one's roots, he says, means knowing the land "*como mis manos*, 'like my hands,'" and that knowledge is "based on the information stored in my mind and experienced through the senses, that repository of personal and collective memory" (2014, 19).

For Esperanza and the majority of the Nuevomexicana/o community in what she identifies as San Marcos, New Mexico,[4] the land upon which they live is part of their cultural heritage—a *herencia* that drives them to fight for social justice, a point echoed by Lorence when he says the Nuevomexicana/o community in Bayard understood their struggle against Empire Zinc as "an extension of Mexican American culture and community solidarity" (1999, 44). This understanding of place and querencia is in stark contrast to the ties Empire Zinc has to the region and to the people, further reinforced when Esperanza notes: "The Anglos changed the name [from San Marcos] to Zinc Town. Zinc Town, New Mexico, USA." This name denotes that Empire Zinc did not have a deep-seated love for the land, as Esperanza imparts; instead, Zinc Town symbolized the region's wealth of minerals and capital potential, which could be exploited alongside the brown bodies who would perform the labor.

As many scenes throughout the film demonstrate, the Nuevomexicano miners were expendable to the mining company. Early on, for example, a blast and steam whistle are heard. The miners rush to the superintendent's office and are met by Chief Foreman Barton, who attempts to make light of the incident that has just occurred: a defective fuse that caused a blast for a miner who was working alone. Ramón Quintero, the protagonist and spokesman for the group, indicates that miners working alone is a substantial hazard, one that he and his fellow miners refuse to accept. Barton, imprudent and unconcerned with the dangers posed by the working conditions, mocks the miners and indicates that the Super will agree with him, as this is who made the rule for miners to work alone in the first place. Antonio, one of the miners, speaks out against Barton, saying, "Listen, Mr. Barton—there's blood in that mine. The blood of my friends. All because they had to work alone." Another miner, Alfredo, continues: "And nobody to warn the other men to stay clear." Ramón adds, "Foreman wants to get the ore out. Miner wants to get his brothers out. In one piece." This scene reveals the dangers of mining, particularly within the conditions under which the men are forced to work. Perhaps more importantly, however, is that it also reveals the stark contrast in the ideologies of the Anglo mining supervisors and the inferior Nuevomexicano miners. Whereas capitalist and industrialist politics and principles drive the representatives of Empire Zinc, querencia influences the miners, whose lives are on the line each time they enter the mine to defend their "brothers." In much the same way that Arellano describes his querencia as "*la junta*'—the gathering or coming together" of his land, plants, trees, animals, and family (2014, 6), the miners' brotherhood reveals how they come together to defend their community and their lives.

For the miners, collective action and community connection drive them to speak out against the unjust practices that Empire Zinc has imposed upon them. In the scene described above, the viewer is provided with insight into the complex hierarchy of power within which they live. While they maintain control of their homes as the patriarchs of their families, in the contested space of the mine they remain liminal, or in-between. On the other hand, Empire Zinc representatives have no ties to or memories attached to the land; their connection is solely through their investment in exploiting its resources.

Though the miners hold knowledge about the land where the mine is located and the communal way of living upon which their lives were based prior to the arrival of Empire Zinc, in the eyes of the mining representatives, the miners can only remain "in the dark" space of the mine as powerless workers.

The scene depicting the relationship between the miners and the foreman also demonstrates how the foreman's narrative is characteristic of the function of what Louis Althusser labels Ideological State Apparatuses (ISAs) and the roles of subjects within those apparatuses.[5] He defines ISAs as a "reality" of "the (repressive) State apparatus" that "present[s itself] to the immediate observer in the form of distinct and specialized institutions" that are quite simply "*private* institutions" that "*function 'by ideology'*" (1971, 142–45. Emphases original.). Althusser further explains that, within an ISA, "the individual *is interpellated as a (free) subject in order that he shall submit freely to the commandments of the Subject, i.e. in order that he shall (freely) accept his subjection,* i.e. in order that he shall make the gestures and actions of his subjection 'all by himself'" (182. Emphasis original.). At first hearing, the foreman's response in which he indicates that the Super originated the single-worker rule is indicative of the State Apparatus that "functions by violence"; however, the control enforced by Empire Zinc is more closely symbolic of an ISA because the company is a private domain, as is the union of which the miners are a part. Empire Zinc can be considered a subsidiary of the State Apparatus (in this case, the government) that is designed to be governed by laws and regulations that *should* protect its workers. However, the company functions as an ISA in its methods of managing the miners through an ideology based on race and class that dictates labor rights and safety conditions (or lack thereof), which in turn is a system that works to repress the miners.

Closer analysis of the scene between the Empire Zinc employees and the miners (particularly the latter's response) reveals that this situation is much more complex. The representatives of the mining company are continually met with resistance from the miners, making it increasingly difficult for the company to maintain control over them. To put it another way, there is a continual struggle for hegemony. This reading of the scene emphasizes the strength Ramón and his fellow miners exhibit in response to the mining representatives and, more importantly, acknowledges their differential consciousness. In this scene and throughout the film, the miners attempt to ascertain this power through their actions: speaking out on behalf of their rights to company executives, using union meetings to plan their response to unfair working conditions, and, eventually, defending their querencia when they and their wives participate in a strike.

To better understand how the miners resist hegemony, it is important to recognize, as A. Gabriel Meléndez proposes, that we must call "the work [*Salt of the Earth*] a Chicano/a film" (95). This acknowledgment is one way we can continue to understand how the story about the miners, their wives, and the strike against repressive powers reveals Sandoval's notion of differential consciousness at play, for it underscores the tenacity and unity of a Nuevomexicana/o community who banded together to contest their unequal treatment—a *real* community, undergoing *real* oppression. In other words, this story is not just another artificial Hollywood script; it is a narrative about a community in small-town New Mexico whose subjects are "endowed with a 'consciousness'" (Althusser 1971, 167). It is this political consciousness to which Meléndez refers in his reading of the film, and that is indicative of Chicana/o determination. He states that the majority of the nonprofessional cast and extras were local Nuevomexicanos and Local 890 union members (96). Their participation in a film based on their lives is indicative of how the differential consciousness of the Nuevomexicana/o community functioned "within, yet beyond, the demands of a dominant ideology" (Sandoval 2000, 43) that reinforced racial, gender, and class discrimination not only within mining communities across the nation, but also within the "Red Scare" politics and Leftist movement that were simultaneously occurring. Put plainly, their actions reveal that the miners and their wives already were aware of how ideology functioned because of their consciousness, which motivated them to respond differentially.

The struggles of the miners against working conditions based on classism and racism and the filmmakers against censorship in mainstream media emphasize the centrality of both groups in politicizing oppression imposed upon them by dominant powers. For the Nuevomexicana/o community in Bayard, the 1954 film helped bring attention to the fact that in 1951 and 1952 (and most likely before that time) they were being treated as second-class citizens, although they held ties to the land that went back for generations. In this way, the townspeople's actions made visible the new subject position called for by Sandoval, one in which she challenges Althusser's conception of the subject and that serves an "effective and ongoing oppositional struggle" that influences the creation of "coalition politics that are vital" to decolonization (2000, 44). Though she focuses upon the postmodern citizen-subject, I believe her discussion of subject positions is relevant to the transformative actions taken by Nuevomexicanos and Nuevomexicanas in New Mexico. Sandoval further argues, "These subject positions, once self-consciously recognized by their inhabitants, can become transfigured into effective sites of resistance to an oppressive ordering of power relations" (54). Nuevomexicanas'/os' fight for their rights and against racial and gender discrimination, and their strike against Empire Zinc's blatant disregard for their lives and livelihoods is evidence of the ways in which the community developed a consciousness of resistance. In response to their unequal treatment, they claimed their agency and developed an ideological stance that pushed against the social, political, and economic pressures of an American nationalist system that had historically deemed them conquered.[6]

Also at the film's core is the significant issue of gender discrimination, a prevalent issue felt throughout the country in the 1950s. The film brought public attention to the important role women played in their societies and within social movements. Kathlene McDonald notes that the film's writer, Michael Wilson, "challenged the dominant image of women in 1950s mainstream culture: the housewife at the center of the nuclear family" (2012, 3). The ways in which notions of gender are confronted and contested illustrate Sandoval's differential consciousness through the female protagonist, Esperanza Quintero, and the group of miner's wives who enact multiple forms of change.

SELF-CONSCIOUS GENDERED RESISTANCE

Up to this point, this chapter has focused primarily on the ways in which members of the Nuevomexicana/o community in southern New Mexico mobilized themselves as "resistant and oppositional citizen-subjects" (Sandoval 2000, 53). I would like to turn now to the ways in which *Salt of the Earth* renders visible the gender division, mistreatment, and flagrant sexism that remains pervasive in social movements and is evident within patriarchal-based communities, such as those seen in the film. The filmmakers reveal a deep commitment to emphasizing the importance of women to the success of the strike against Empire Zinc, and the film reveals how Nuevomexicanas are forced to navigate literal and metaphorical borders intended to displace them.

Michael Wilson places Esperanza Quintero at center stage. She is the wife of a Nuevomexicano miner, and against her husband's wishes joins the picket line that represents him and other miners who have been treated unjustly by

Empire Zinc. Esperanza, whose name literally translates to "Hope," provides the miners and their families with the hope that conditions will change for them if they fight against what Empire Zinc represents. *Salt of the Earth* provides insight into the racial discrimination prevalent in 1950s New Mexico; more importantly, however, it also reveals how Nuevomexicanas navigated gendered borders. Through their perceived acts of civil disobedience,[7] they revealed that the struggle of the mineworkers had an impact on both men *and* women.

Esperanza's central position in the film challenged the standardized role played by women in 1950s culture, whose lives centered upon domesticity, caring for their children and husbands, and completing household chores such as cooking and cleaning. Instead of further perpetuating this singular role, the film firmly establishes Esperanza's querencia, her relationship to the collective struggles to fight against Empire Zinc, and her connection to place and identity that is not tied to the home. Her connection is to the land, which she confirms in the film's opening scene, noted at the beginning of this chapter: "Our roots go deep in this place, deeper than the pines, deeper than the mine shaft." Esperanza's statement serves as a reminder that "if we lose either memory or landscape, we lose both," because, as Arellano reminds us, "the essence of *Querencia*" is formed when our memory "assume[s] the form of the landscape itself" (1997, 32). The Nuevomexicana/o families who live on the land that Empire Zinc seeks to exploit are tasked with working the land for the company in order to survive in a capitalist-driven economy. They must also preserve their own philosophy and conception of the land, which differs markedly, particularly in how and why they value the land as a community.

Esperanza's position in the film is doubly complex, and reveals the multiple levels of subjugation with which she is faced. While the film's writer underscores how her identity is tied to the land and her Nuevomexicano community, the narrative also reveals how her husband, Ramón, repositions her as tied to the home. Esperanza's work within the collective of women in her community pushes her to fight for equal treatment not only from Empire Zinc, but also from her husband. Throughout the film, she navigates dual borders as a Nuevomexicana in the 1950s: the discrimination from the company that employs her husband and the inequity she faces at home, as her husband's needs and rights take precedence over her needs and those of her family. In a significant scene, as Ramón washes up and prepares to go out for the evening to talk with his fellow miners, Esperanza states that the fire has gone out in the stove. Ramón responds, "Forget it." This prompts his wife to voice her concerns: "Forget it? I chop wood for the stove five times a day. Every time I remember. I remember that across the tracks the Anglo miners have hot water in pipes. And bathrooms. Inside."

Her retort prompts a conversation between husband and wife that demonstrates the stark contrast in their understanding and views of what the goals of the strike should be. Ramón responds bitterly, "Do you think I like living this way? What do you want of me?" Though his question is rhetorical, Esperanza uses the opportunity to further state her case: "But if your union . . . if you're asking for better conditions . . . why can't you ask for decent plumbing, too?" Ramón is clearly aggravated by the conversation and responds tersely, "We did. It got lost in the shuffle." Esperanza cannot believe what she has just heard. Ramón, who continues getting ready to go out, shrugs the conversation off and says, "We can't get everything at once. Right now we've got more important demands." But Esperanza does not let the conversation go that easily. She asks, "What's more important than sanitation?," to which Ramón responds angrily, "The safety of the men—that's more important! Five accidents this week—all because of speedup. You're a woman, you don't know what it's like up there."

While Ramón angrily responds to Esperanza's plea and goes on to list the issues that he and the men have faced that week, Esperanza goes on with her work, lifting a heavy tub of water onto the stove, then lugging it to the dishpan in the sink, all unassisted. Ramón, unyielding in his machismo, ignores the impacts of discrimination on the domestic sphere—a place to which he relegates his wife. Throughout the film, Esperanza is shown chopping wood, caring for the children, and performing other household chores. The issues situated around the impact of sanitation affect not only her, but all of the women and the families in the community. As a group, the women in the film acknowledge what Nuevomexicana character Teresa Vidal asserts when she says, "We got to make them understand—make the men face up to it [the sanitation issues]."

As the film progresses, the women state their case during a union meeting where the men are discussing an upcoming strike. They remind the men that sanitation *is* part of the struggle for equality. The men display mixed reactions, particularly Ramón, who is clearly bothered by the women's actions. The film reveals the resistance the women faced from the men and their inability to see what they perceived as domestic luxuries as part of the struggle for human rights that affected the entire family. The actions taken by the women reflect and are a precursor to "El camino de la mestiza," explained by Gloria Anzaldúa in *Borderlands/La Frontera: The New Mestiza* (1987), because like the *mestizas*, the Nuevomexicanas of the mining community "surrende[r] all notions of safety, of the familiar. Deconstruct, construct . . . She learns to transform the small 'I' into the total Self" (83). Esperanza's development as an autonomous individual is the most significant in the film and is demonstrated most clearly when she asserts, "I want to rise. And push everything up with me as I go." In addition to her own transformation, Esperanza and the group of Nuevomexicanas recognize that the men need them to win the battle against Empire Zinc, as collective action will ensure their victory.

As they launder and hang their families' clothes on *perchas*, or outdoor clotheslines, the women converse about fighting for their rights, demonstrating their process of deconstructing and constructing what would be a more equal representation of the issues at hand in their small town. Teresa Vidal leads the conversation and encourages the women to picket while the men are negotiating in the company office. One of the other women, Consuelo, asserts: "Then both sides will see we mean business." The women's language and actions demonstrate the initial shift in their sense of total Self, most clearly revealed when another woman, Luz, throws the wet clothes she had been hanging to the ground and proclaims, "Listen, we ought to be in the wood choppers' union. Chop wood for breakfast. Chop wood to wash his clothes. Chop wood, heat the iron. Chop wood, scrub the floor. Chop wood, cook his dinner. And you know what he'll [her husband, Antonio] say when he gets home . . . [she mimics him] 'What you been doing all day? Reading the funny papers?'" The women's discussion about their husbands' interpretation of their work and their place within society reveals what Anzaldúa describes as "cultural tyranny," comprising "dominant paradigms, predefined concepts that exist as unquestionable, unchallengeable, . . . transmitted to us through the culture. Culture is made by those in power—men" (1987, 16). However, the Nuevomexicanas in the mining community prove that they are unwilling to accept those conditions, and instead transform them alongside their burgeoning consciousness of resistance.

Although throughout most of the film Esperanza shies away from proclaiming her agency, in a powerful scene toward the end, the greatest indication of her transformation is demonstrated when she stands up to the patriarch of her family and points out how he is discriminating against women just as the Anglo mining representatives are discriminating against him: "'Stay in your place, you dirty Mexican'—that's what they tell you. But why must you say to me, 'Stay in your place'? Do you feel better having someone lower than you?" Ramón tries to quiet her, yet she goes on: "And if you can't understand this you're a fool—because you can't win this strike without me! You can't win anything without me!" The women, especially Esperanza, develop what Sandoval describes as "the ability to self-consciously navigate modes of dominant consciousness . . . not only with the hope of surviving, but with the desire to create a better world" (2000, 104). Their direct action in taking over for the men after an injunction is issued saying that any miner participating in the picket line is subject to termination of employment is evidence of the cultivation of their oppositional consciousness. Their actions are in direct response to the subjugation they faced as marginalized citizen-subjects within and beyond the confines of their domestic spheres. It is *only* because of the women's intervention that the miners successfully win the strike after an arduous struggle with Empire Zinc representatives.

Just like the men in the community, the viewer realizes that the battle could not have been successful without the women's help. At the end of the film, the viewer witnesses what Sandoval labels "the technology of 'democratics'. . . the purposive guiding strategy that is interested in challenging the institutionalization of dominant ideology, and the forms of social and psychological inequity it neutralizes" (2000, 113). This "technology of democratics" is most evident when Ramón tells Esperanza, "You were right. Together we can push everything up with us as we go." This statement signals how Ramón, too, comes to a consciousness in which he understands the "moral and ethical commitment to enact . . . equalizing power between humans" (Sandoval 2000, 113).

As a form of filmic storytelling, *Salt of the Earth* narrates the long history of Chicana/o struggle in the southwest. The film repositions Nuevomexicanas as powerful agents in social activism, invoking a story of hope through Esperanza's narrative and revealing the realities associated with being an ethnic "Other" within the United States' national narrative. Through their work, the makers of *Salt of the Earth* demonstrate the deliberate inequalities in matters of race, space, and discrimination that have persisted over time. The film also invites discussion about the very real issue of gendered borders that continue to impact Chicanas. Just as the filmmakers use alternative sites to produce and situate their narratives, scholars invested in questions of identity, gender, and modes of representation must continue to examine alternative narratives that disrupt stereotypes and myths of women as insignificant to the national narrative. We must (re)position them in a way that acknowledges their value as social and political actors.

Communities throughout New Mexico continue the battle against hegemony imparted through dominant powers designed to dismiss their rights and completely disregard the importance of querencia to the residents whose livelihoods depend on the land, the water, and equality for communities of color. In addition, these communities continue to fight for representation of their stories within dominant narratives. For example, in Albuquerque in 2012, University of New Mexico (UNM) students, staff, and faculty in the Chicana and Chicano Studies Department[8] (where I taught previously), fought to ensure that Ethnic Studies programs, including Chicana and Chicano Studies, Native American Studies, and Africana Studies, were included as part of the university's core general education requirements. At that time, Governor Susanna Martinez began a statewide effort to minimize Chicana/o and Ethnic Studies curricula. Activism enacted by UNM students, staff, and faculty resulted in Ethnic Studies being incorporated into the core general education requirements beginning in 2013–2014.[9] In the north central part of the state, residents of my hometown, Pecos, along with local conservationists, are at the time of this writing engaged in activism against New World Cobalt/Comexico LLC's plans for exploration drilling at the old Tererro Mine site. If approved, this project will not only exploit the mineral wealth of the area, but also have a direct impact on the headwaters of the Pecos River and its tributaries.[10] These struggles, though seemingly divergent, reveal the enduring battle for social justice that remains in New Mexico and the querencia—the deep and abiding love of place—and the "perseverance, resilience, and [sometimes, the] stubbornness" (Arellano 2014, 24) that extends to a deep love for the people of these communities, and that continues to drive the state's communities of color to enact their differential consciousness at a time when their rights are slowly being taken away.

NOTES

1. In this chapter, I refer both to the actual strike in Bayard and the film, sometimes simultaneously. As I read the film, it depicts what originally took place in Bayard when Nuevomexicano miners and their wives participated in the strike against Empire Zinc Mining Company. Typically, in filmic representations of

historical events, the storyline veers from the actual event in substantial ways. I suggest that the *Salt of the Earth* filmmakers made a significant effort (described later in the chapter) to avoid that type of scenario.

2. I use the term "Nuevomexicana/o" in this chapter to describe a regional identity claimed by those who were born and/or raised in New Mexico and who seek/sought to maintain their connection to their New Mexican communities, traditions, and culture. At times, I use the term "Chicana/o" interchangeably to indicate a particular political identity used by those of Mexican descent, which developed as a result of the Chicana/o movement of the 1960s and '70s, in which people of Mexican descent were fighting for their civil rights in the United States. In this essay, I claim that the Nuevomexicana/o miners and their wives demonstrate the same type of political identity shown by those in the 1960s/'70s. Therefore, at times, I identify them as Chicanas/os. I use the term "Mexican American" to identify those who were essentially forced to become US citizens after the signing of the Treaty of Guadalupe Hidalgo if they elected not to relocate south of the newly established US/Mexico border, and those individuals who claim a dual identity as a person of Mexican descent who was born in the United States.

3. In the "Publisher's Preface" to *Salt of the Earth: The Story of a Film* by Herbert Biberman, James Monaco notes that Biberman "was one of nineteen Hollywood filmmakers called to testify before the House Un-American Activities Committee in a show-trial meant to discredit leftist influence in American movies." Further, he states, "In November of 1947 ten filmmakers (eight screenwriters, two directors) were declared in contempt of Congress and sentenced to prison" (7).

4. In the film, San Marcos, New Mexico, represents Bayard, New Mexico, the small town where the strike took place.

5. Althusser (1971) builds his conception of ISAs upon the work of Karl Marx, who defines the role of "the executive of the modern State" in *The Communist Manifesto* (1848/1977) as "*but a committee for managing the affairs of the whole bourgeoisie*" (82). Althusser claims, "What distinguishes the ISAs from what he proposes as the (Repressive) State Apparatus is the following basic difference: The Repressive State Apparatus functions 'by violence,' whereas the Ideological State Apparatuses *function 'by ideology'*" (145).

6. See Lorence 1999 and Sandoval 2000.

7. See Henkel and Fonseca 2016 for an insightful analysis of civility in *Salt of the Earth*.

8. Chicana and Chicano Studies was a program until 2015, when the Faculty Senate Curricula Committee approved departmentalization.

9. See Shah. "Ethnic Studies Hope to Expand Their Curricula," *Daily Lobo.com*, University of New Mexico, April 12, 2018, https://www.dailylobo.com/article /2018/04/ethnic-studies.

10. See "Tererro" 2019 and New Mexico Wilderness Alliance 2019.

Althusser, Louis. 1971. *Lenin and Philosophy and Other Essays*. New York: Monthly Review Press.

Anzaldúa, Gloria. 1987. *Borderlands/La Frontera: The New Mestiza*. San Francisco: Aunt Lute Books.

Arellano, Juan Estevan. 1997. "La Querencia: La Raza Bioregionalism." *New Mexico Historical Review* 71 (January): 31–37.

———. 2014. *Enduring Acequias: Wisdom of the Land, Knowledge of the Water*. Albuquerque: University of New Mexico Press.

Biberman, Herbert. 2003. *Salt of the Earth: The Story of a Film*. New York: Harbor Electronic Publishing.

Henkel, Scott, and Vanessa Fonseca. 2016. "Fearless Speech and the Discourse of Civility in *Salt of the Earth*." *Chiricú Journal: Latina/o Literatures, Arts, and Cultures* 1, no. 1 (Fall): 19–38.

Lorence, James J. 1999. *The Suppression of "Salt of the Earth": How Hollywood, Big Labor and Politicians Blacklisted a Movie in Cold War America*. Albuquerque: University of New Mexico Press.

Marx, Karl, and Friedrich Engels. 1977 [1848]. *The Communist Manifesto*. Mattituck: Amereon House.

McDonald, Kathlene. 2012. *Feminism, the Left, and Postwar Literary Culture*. Jackson: University Press of Mississippi.

Meléndez, A. Gabriel. 2013. *Hidden Chicano Cinema: Film Dramas in the Borderlands*. New Brunswick, NJ: Rutgers University Press.

Monaco, James. 2003. "Publisher's Preface." In Biberman, *"Salt of the Earth,"* 7–12. New York: Harbor Electronic Publishing.

New Mexico Wilderness Alliance. Facebook post, October 16, 2019. https://www.facebook.com/206360852734005/posts/2446837908686277?sfns=mo.

Salt of the Earth. 2004 [1954]. Directed by Herbert J. Biberman. Narberth, PA: Alpha Video Classics.

Sandoval, Chela. 2000. *Methodology of the Oppressed*. Minneapolis: University of Minnesota Press.

Shah, Tasawar. "Ethnic Studies Hope to Expand Their Curricula," *Daily Lobo*, University of New Mexico. April 12, 2018. https://www.dailylobo.com/article/2018/04/ethnic-studies.

"Terrero Drilling Project," Upper Pecos Watershed Association. 2019. https://pecoswatershed.org/tererro-drilling-project.

CHAPTER SIX

New Mexico Triptych
Querencia Etched in Wood, in Media, and in Our Memory

SPENCER R. HERRERA

To provide full disclosure from the start, I confess, I am the only non–New Mexican to contribute to and coedit this anthology on *la querencia nuevomexicana*. It gets worse: *soy Tejano*. For the record, I am proud of being Tejano, which for me is being a *Mexicano* who was born and raised in *Tejas*, a northern frontier of greater México. I did not know, until I moved to New Mexico in 2001, that here Texans are often derided as haughty, uncultured, and even outright aggressive neighbors of New Mexicans. However, this complex relationship started to make sense to me once I began to read and learn about the two states' linked political, cultural, and colonial histories—specifically, how Texas, while a Republic and later as part of the Confederacy, invaded the New Mexico territory in an attempt to seize the land between the Río Grande and Texas's western border.[1] Knowing this, it is understandable why historically many New Mexicans have scoffed at Texans for their arrogant attitudes, misguided by a sense of manifest destiny. After all, the Texans were the ones who tried to steal, by military force, the land from native New Mexicans, to, in essence, rob them of their *querencia* by taking away the land that they loved and that provided their sustenance.

As a native Tejano, generations deep, I can appreciate why New Mexicans have been resistant to trust Texan transplants and look at them with a cautious eye. New Mexicans are keenly aware of the history of encroachment upon their state. Tejanos like myself, who have read and/or listened to passed-down oral histories about our communal loss of language, culture, and land, understand that this was a result of Anglo-American conquest and colonization, eased by the Mexican government's political and military failures. Tejanos have not enjoyed the same fortune as their *Nuevomexicano* neighbors. For, unlike in New Mexico, many Tejano landowners lost much or all of their land holdings as a result of Texan Independence and the subsequent land-grabbing that lasted well into the twentieth century.[2]

Resentment still exists, although it was stronger in previous generations, evidenced by when a Tejano/a elder would see a beautiful piece of land that reminded him or her of México and reminisce nostalgically among like-minded people by saying "That was once ours." Other Tejanos in earshot would understand almost intrinsically what that person meant. It is like the 1935 poem "The Mexico-Texan" by Américo Paredes, which he wrote sarcastically to celebrate Texas's centennial independence from Mexico, with the refrain that repeats this sentiment "The Mexico-Texan he no gotta lan'" (Paredes 1991, 26–27). Paredes, like his Tejano compatriots, knows all too well, as a scholar and a border citizen, how Tejanos lost their land holdings, which were replaced by a sense of second-class citizenry, "A cit'zen of Texas they say that he ees, / But then, why they call him the Mexican Grease?" (26).

Unlike our Nuevomexicano neighbors, Tejanos have a difficult time expressing this same sense of querencia because, although we have a homeland that we love, the vast majority of us have no land. We lost it long ago. This is unfortunate, because land ownership and one's sense of querencia are inextricably linked. For, as the *dicho* goes, "*El que pierde su tierra pierde su memoria*" (He who loses his land loses his memory) (Arellano 1997, 32, translation mine). And without memory of our querencia, it is no wonder why so many Mexican Americans struggle to reconcile with a loss of their cultural identity. For without land, we also lose a sense of who we are and who our ancestors were.

This historical and cultural preface is important to understand, especially for those who are unfamiliar with New Mexico identity politics or know it well enough to compare it as an outside-insider—someone like me, who has lived in this state for more than half of my adult life but cannot and do not claim to be New Mexican.[3] Many Hispanos and American Indians in New Mexico have a strong sense of querencia because their families still own land, even if it is only a small parcel on which they raise a few crops and animals or to which they retain the water rights. Nonetheless, it is theirs and has been so for several generations—in some cases since before recorded ownership.[4] As an envious outsider who continues to feel a strong sense of a *querencia tejana*, it is helpful to develop a clear sense of what *la querencia nuevomexicana* is and why we should protect it. To accomplish this, we must be able to differentiate between a native and nurtured sense of querencia passed on organically through the generations versus a superficial or incomplete identity narrative constructed by outsiders as a justification for political or economic gain.

El Nuevomexicano norteño Juan Estevan Arellano, a renowned advocate for *acequia* communities and respected agronomist and writer, understood this idea of querencia as well as anybody. In his writing, he uses the nurtured sense of querencia to establish a set of values that are indispensable to each other: place, land, character, identity, home. Querencia is the sum of these because, as Arellano shows us, they teach us how to develop "a deeply rooted knowledge" of who we are and where we come from (2012, 158). The simplicity of his message is profound. It describes a cultural and moral stronghold that teaches us how to anchor ourselves within society by drawing strength from our community.

Arellano's sense of querencia expresses a natural and deep love for place and home that represents a symbiotic relationship between a land and the people who inhabit and protect it. This is a healthy practice to create harmony between nature and society. It is a way of life that has been cultivated by generations of Indigenous, Hispano, and Mestizo peoples who came before us and tilled the land. And it was our elders who taught us how to live like this so as to foster a sustainable and healthy way of life that can last for future generations.

In the spirit of respecting *la tierra aquerenciada* that has become my adoptive home, this chapter takes a critical look at the sense of place that has been crafted about New Mexico, mostly by outsiders, and how this relationship and a misguided message can lead to cultural and social dissonance. Specifically, it sets out to paint a New Mexico triptych, a tri-paneled portrait with three different versions of querencia on display. The three panels, a Cold War documentary-style US government film, a state tourism marketing campaign, and a New Mexican Spanish-language poem about an abandoned gristmill, each convey a distinct message and are directed at different audiences. The first panel documents a querencia of the past, the sheepherding tradition of northern New Mexico in the 1950s. The second is a boastful montage of the natural beauty and cultural treasures of present-day New Mexico, albeit an idyllic and incomplete picture of the state's demographically diverse communities. As a metaphor of neglect to which the abandoned mill alludes, the third panel is a painful reminder of how the querencia that we cherish is slowly falling into disrepair. However, the poem's backstory offers a glimmer of hope that it can be partially recovered and preserved for future generations.

Together, these three pieces of a bygone past, an incomplete present, and a recovered memory to help preserve the future teach us that querencia is not what we make it, but what it makes us, a collection of memories of place, people, and traditions.

The first piece in the New Mexico querencia triptych examines the US Information Agency documentary *And Now, Miguel* (1953), directed by Joseph Krumgold.[5] The film was produced by the US State Department during the Cold War. It was designed to show a softer, familial side of the American people. It features a young Hispano sheepherder (*pastor*), Miguel Chávez, and his family in the small northern New Mexico village of Los Cordovas, near Taos, as they prepare for the summer encampment where they graze their sheep in the Sangre de Cristo Mountains. Although the film depicts an idyllic life, it was created as propaganda to defend the "American way of life" and help strengthen diplomatic and cultural ties with our Latin American allies. The film was screened in Latin American countries, particularly in Andean communities where herding traditions were prevalent. Although its cinematography and screenplay give a beautiful depiction of the northern New Mexico querencia, the covert mission of the film was to expand US anticommunism efforts in Latin America.

The second piece critiques the State of New Mexico Tourism Department's 2012 marketing campaign and their construction of cultural pageantry known as "New Mexico True."[6] In the state's attempt to draw out-of-state tourists, the tourism department created billboards, magazine ads, and airport signage, among other forms of media, that point to New Mexico's rugged beauty and cultural treasures as making it a place worthy to visit.[7] However, in highlighting natural wonders and cultural destinations, it creates a superficial façade of a postcard New Mexico that conceals any hint of the social and economic problems that confront the state on a daily basis. The state's objective, to increase tourism, is indeed served by crafting an appealing narrative about New Mexico. However, community issues and governmental responsibilities throughout the state have become neglected and also need to be addressed and remedied.

I argue that, because this messaging paints an incomplete picture, we, the people, our communities, and our government, focus solely on the physical beauty and cultural wealth of New Mexico and ignore the social ills that threaten our well-being. By doing this, we minimize the magnitude of the problems that plague us to the point that we are not addressing them with enough seriousness that would enable us to solve them or at least help alleviate them. For there is a danger that we create when we rely on defining a people and place with a marketing strategy, such as the New Mexico True campaign, or any simplistic, one-sided narrative for that matter. We risk overlooking the marginalized people and impoverished places in our state and ignore the social problems in our community because they do not fit within this true or false dichotomy where everything is "true and good and real."[8]

The third piece, Levi Romero's poem "Molino abandonado" from *A Poetry of Remembrance: New and Rejected Works* (2008), reminds us how to recover an authentic sense of querencia. It is authentic because it is developed from within the community, not crafted by outsiders for political or economic gain. The poem, like much of the poetry in this collection, laments the decline in the sense of community in the small Hispanic villages of northern New Mexico. The cultural traditions, the neighborly love, and the shared sense of community are slowly disappearing. Romero questions what has happened to the people, the villages, and their customs. His description of village life condemns the feeling of emptiness when he states in the poem, "ya no quedan ni migajas / ni tansiquiera una tortilla dura" (Not even crumbs remain / not even a hard tortilla) (144, translation mine). However, we are left with something—our memories of place, people, and community. Fortunately for us, within those memories lies the key to cultural recovery. If we want to rebuild an authentic sense of querencia, which is developed and nurtured from within the family and community, then we need to do the cultural work ourselves. As will be seen, the strongest form of querencia is not etched in wood or in stone, but in our collective memories.

AND NOW, MIGUEL ETCHED IN WOOD

The US State Department documentary-style film *And Now, Miguel* painstakingly details the hard work that goes into sheepherding and wool processing, and the beauty of this family tradition. It shows the Chávez family caring for their newborn lambs, guarding the flock while they graze, the shearing process, and how this occupational knowledge is passed down generationally. But more importantly, it documents the family traditions, *las fiestas de San Isidro*, folkloric dancing that includes la Varsoviana and las Chapanecas, and the deep Catholic beliefs shared by the community. In essence, it records what it meant to live during the 1950s as a *pastor Nuevomexicano* in the Sangre de

Cristo Mountains. It is a beautiful documentation of Nuevomexicanos and their cultural traditions.

But toward the end of the film, this ethnographic storybook narrative changes course. Miguel, the young aspiring *pastor*, finds a letter from the US government addressed to his older brother Gabriel, informing him that he must soon report for military duty. Miguel laments that his brother must leave their home to go off to a faraway and dangerous place. But Gabriel explains to him that sometimes we must make sacrifices and leave the comfort of our family and home to protect a way of life. Miguel narrates the experience of being a *pastor* as a metaphor for his older brother's call to duty:

> He was going because sometimes when there is danger far off, a fox maybe or a wolf, a shepherd must leave his flock to stop the killer before any sheep are lost. Just so, beyond the oceans into which this river flowed, there was now a danger, not only to the sheep, but to our whole family and to all the families like us who live with the freedom to make the wish that was in their hearts like my wish to go to the mountain come true. There are those who would put an end to such a freedom and destroy everyone's wish but their own. Gabriel was going because a shepherd must face them so that one day he and I, we could be pastores together (Krumgold 1953).

The message crafted here is that the American way of life is something to be actively protected. But what about the Chávez's generations-long sense of querencia? Who will stay to ensure that it continues uninterrupted? The narrative hints that one day, Gabriel will return and the family traditions, with everything and everyone intact, will continue. But in reality, this is seldom the case. People, communities, and ways of life evolve. Whether by force due to military conscription or by choice to seek out an education or a job, when people leave their querencias, they also leave behind traditions, some of which cease to be practiced.

And Now, Miguel crafts a narrative with several important messages. It documents a disappearing way of life that might not otherwise have been recorded and made available through the public domain. It also shows how the United States was fighting a subversive cold war against communist influences and was fearful that communism might spread. In this light, we understand that the film was not made to serve as an ethnographic documentation, but rather as propaganda for our Latin American neighbors to create stronger cultural ties between them and the United States while discouraging any anti-American sentiments.

What the film does not address, especially in relation to the preservation of the local querencia, are the challenges that the Hispano pastores have faced over the years. This includes the loss of land, both familial and community land grants, the proliferation of fences that restrict open grazing, and the poverty that has forced many blue-collar *Manitos* (Hispanos from northern New Mexico) to abandon traditional ways of making a living, such as farming and ranching.[9] Many of these workers followed job opportunities in construction, railroad, and general labor in the larger, more prosperous towns of Santa Fe, Los Alamos, and Albuquerque. Others were lured away by contractors who recruited these industrious people to work in the copper mines of Arizona or the beet crop industry in Colorado and Wyoming. Some moved even further, to the fertile pastures of California. This exodus of Hispano natives from their northern New Mexico homeland is what Levi Romero and Vanessa Fonseca describe as the "Manito Trail."[10] It is this historical diaspora of people and culture that made it difficult to sustain the deeply rooted knowledge of place that Arellano describes. But the people persist in their attempt to preserve their culture and way of life.

Despite the economic pressures that threaten the pastoral way of life and the political uncertainties that force young men into the draft to serve in the US Armed Forces, as in the case of Gabriel Chávez, some families manage to maintain their generations-old traditions. Because his father needs help on the ranch to fill the void left by his older son's departure, young Miguel earns the right to work alongside the men in his family. Together, they lead their flock to the Sangre de Cristo Mountains, where they will camp for the summer and the sheep will graze in green pastures. Like the other Chávez sheepherders before him, Miguel gets to carve his name on the aspen tree, as a form of pastoral *con safos*, a signature *Miguel pasó por aquí* (Miguel was here). Hence, the film's title *And Now, Miguel*. Unfortunately, with the economic climate quickly changing after WWII due to modernization and interstate migration, the agricultural and ranching traditions began to dissipate as a viable way of life for New Mexican families.

Considering these cultural and economic changes, was Miguel the last *pastor* in his family to carve his name into the aspen tree? Did these New Mexican families, as the film's narrative suggest, get to "live with the freedom to make the wish that was in their hearts," or were they forced to make tough decisions

FIGURE 6.1 *And Now, Miguel* US Information documentary film still, 1953.

and eventually sell their land and abandon this way of life? What happened to the Chávez family querencia? To avoid detracting from its intended message, the film does not address these types of questions that certainly must have arisen at some point.

Through mass media, whether it be Cold War–period black-and-white film or modern digital advertising, those in power can manipulate a message to advocate for their way of life. The crafted message often obscures any truth that may weaken their position. The target audience is not primed to examine the complexities surrounding the various issues or be open to different viewpoints, but rather is groomed to buy into a specific narrative. So although the message points to a shared value (e.g., the freedom to make the wish that is in your heart come true), it is really about achieving a political agenda.

This is what the US Information Service (USIS), later the US Information Agency (USIA), accomplished with the production of this film and others like it.[11] According to A. Gabriel Meléndez in *Hidden Chicano Cinema* (2013), "the motives of the USIA during the Cold War were straightforward, as can be seen in the ideas that the agency wished to convey to the world about the United States" (107). I argue that the motives may have appeared straightforward, but the US government was also striving to receive a political return on their investment for making these films. The main points that the USIA wanted to convey about life in the US included:

Americans are nice people.
America is generous and altruistic.
America is democratic.

In America all races and creeds live happily together.

Americans don't consider it beneath a man to work with his hands.

Americans believe in equality for other people.

American life has a spiritual quality.

Americans are a cultured people.

The U.S. economy is successful.

America is a peaceable country. (Meléndez 2013, 108)

It is noteworthy that strength of economy is toward the end of the list. Most of the ideas conveyed here deal with notions of community and culture. This was deliberate to avoid projecting a high standard of living and material wealth, because the USIA did not want to portray a sense of boastfulness (Meléndez 2013, 108). To this end, it was important to foster a message of family unity, hard work, and selflessness, all themes highlighted in the film. And equally important as molding this message was disseminating it to their targeted audiences.

Outside of the film's narrative, Gabriel Chávez, the older brother, did actually report for military duty. However, he received a ROTC student deferment. Upon the advice of Ernesto Gutiérrez, a New Mexico State University (NMSU) county extension agent in northern New Mexico, Gabriel enrolled at NMSU in 1953. He graduated with a BA in Agricultural Science in 1956. It was while he was a student that Gabriel began to participate in the distribution and screening of *And Now, Miguel* by becoming a goodwill ambassador for the US State Department, visiting every country in Central and South America. In a serious commitment to convey the US message of altruistic democracy, Ernesto Gutiérrez accompanied Gabriel for about eighteen months and together they traversed Latin America, screening the movie and presenting the book. They visited particular groups with whom sheepherding, familial cohesion, and rural experiences would resonate, such as the Altiplano and other Indigenous communities of Bolivia and Peru (Meléndez 2013, 110–11). They screened a Spanish-language version of the movie, hoping to make some diplomatic inroads with the people of these regions. The showing of the film was a way for the US government to influence neighboring Latin American countries through the peaceful process of what in diplomacy is referred to as soft power.

Joseph F. Nye, Jr. (2006) coined the term "soft power" in 1990, decades after the US government was already implementing this practice as part of its foreign policy. As he explains, "Power is the ability to alter the behavior of others to get what you want." According to Nye—and many politicians and philosophers would agree—"There are basically three ways to do that: coercion (sticks), payments (carrots), and attraction (soft power)." To put it simply, soft power is cultural power. Nye explains that a country develops its soft power through three distinct resources: "its culture (in places where it is attractive to others), its political values (when it lives up to them at home and abroad), and its foreign policies (when they are seen as legitimate and having moral authority)." Seen in this light, the US government sought to protect its interests and expand its hemispheric influence through sticks and carrots, which also allowed them to avoid major armed conflict with other world powers during a contentious cold-war period.

However, it was the soft power of cultural attraction that the government hoped to portray in the film *And Now, Miguel*, which developed into a key strategy of US foreign policy. The American way of life (i.e., the American Dream) was transformed into the narrative that defined who we are as a people and a culture, as documented through government-sponsored films and Hollywood productions. *And Now, Miguel* is a clear example of how the US government attempted to craft an image that it wanted to convey to the world, particularly in Latin America during the Cold War era.

Joseph Krumgold, *And Now, Miguel*'s director and author of a children's book with the same title based on the film, stated that one of the purposes of the US government-sponsored film was to show that "the family unit still constituted as an economic and a social unit that was highly important . . . that it was a unit of cohesion in this country." According to Krumgold, his "assignment was to find a farming family that did this and [he] started the search in Oklahoma and went west looking for them" (Meléndez 2013, 108–9). However, it was not the Protestant, Anglo-American, Midwestern family that came to present the ideals of Americanism in Krumgold's work or for the US State Department, but rather a Catholic, Spanish-speaking family from a rugged and isolated area in northern New Mexico. It is ironic that a Hispanic family from this region became the symbol of the American family unit, considering that New Mexico had only been granted statehood in 1912, forty-one years prior to the film's release.

Even though the Chávez family experience is an authentic one, it was not representative of most US families of that time. Most Americans were not Spanish-speaking sheepherders living in the Sangre de Cristo Mountains. To find the ideal "unit of cohesion" was clearly a laborious, interstate effort. Thus, although the Chávez family way of life was real, it was not a truthful representation of the "American way of life" for most Americans. Nonetheless, the US government was able to paint a picture of American life that most likely resonated with many Latin American communities. Unfortunately, that way of life, just a generation later, had disappeared for most New Mexicans.

"NEW MEXICO TRUE" ETCHED IN MEDIA

I first encountered the marketing campaign "New Mexico True" on a billboard as I was walking through an airport terminal in Texas a few years back. The campaign has become much more robust in its scope, with short documentary videos, certifiable New Mexico True merchandise, New Mexico True Trails (e.g., Burrito Byway and Green Chile Cheeseburger Trail), tourism toolkits to promote scenic and cultural "assets," and even contests such as the New Mexico True Hero. The campaign, especially in the Southwest and neighboring states, remains prevalent in airport terminals on digital billboards and in retail shops, where travelers can buy jewelry, textiles, arts and crafts, food, alcoholic beverages, and other products with the New Mexico True certified mark, declaring it a product made in the state. Every time I see a billboard advertising the brand, whether along the highway or in an airport terminal or in an airline magazine, it manages to catch my attention and make me wonder who and what exactly defines this notion of New Mexico True.

On the surface, the campaign is founded on sound economic policy, which is to help create jobs and generate tax revenue. It is important that the state have a successful marketing campaign, because New Mexico relies heavily on tourism income. In fact, Governor Susana Martinez announced in October 2018 that "the state's tourism industry had a $6.6 billion impact on the New Mexico economy in 2017," which her office described as the largest in state history. The governor called tourism "a key economic driver" and said the "$6.6 billion number represents a 3.2 percent increase from the year prior. Tourism's economic impact has grown for the past seven years consecutively." The New Mexico tourism industry also generates nearly $660 million in state and local tax revenue per year (Randall 2019). Much of this growth was attributed to the New Mexico True marketing campaign. Martinez went on to share how "This means more jobs and better opportunities for New Mexican families." These "better opportunities" now equal more than one hundred thousand jobs in the leisure and hospitality sector ("Governor" 2018). These jobs filter into industries across the state, including lodging, recreation, entertainment, food and beverage, hospitality, and retail, and represent one in twelve jobs in New Mexico (Peerman 2016).

To be clear, all of these economic indicators that lead to job growth and a larger tax base are good for the state of New Mexico. Nevertheless, Jim Peach, an economist at New Mexico State University, cautions that despite the overall positive data, the "wages in leisure and hospitality are low. You've got hotel clerks, maids, casino workers being paid $396 a week. Whereas manufacturing jobs are twice that and engineering nearly five times that number" (Peerman 2016). Peach commends the success of the tourism industry in New Mexico with some reservation, but his point is well taken. Yes, there has been job growth in this sector, but it is not leading to a more prosperous middle class that earns a living wage. Despite the increase in hospitality jobs, New Mexico's economy has still not recovered from the great recession. In fact, "The state's jobless rate was 6 percent in December 2017, according to preliminary estimates. Alaska is the only state doing worse. The nation's rate was 4.1 percent, a 17-year low" (Cole 2018). The state's unemployment rate did improve to 5.1 percent as of February 2018, but so did the national rate, to 3.8 percent (Hedden 2019).

To compound the effects of the high unemployment rate, wages have not kept pace with inflation. There are now more people living in poverty in New Mexico than in late 2007 and more children in families who receive public assistance. Due to the lack of higher-paying jobs, "Some of New Mexico's youngest and best-educated workers are moving to states with better prospects—not just Colorado, but Texas, Utah, Washington and more" (Cole 2018). Bill McCamley, Cabinet Secretary of the New Mexico Department of Workforce Solutions in Governor Michele Luján Grisham's administration, has duly noted this, stating "We're behind our neighbors. We consistently have lower wages and higher unemployment" (Hedden 2019). Without better-paying jobs, New Mexico's economy will remain stagnant, the tax base will not grow to meet its needs, and the citizens of the state will continue to suffer the consequences.

I want to reiterate that the economic impact of tourism on the state of New Mexico is a positive contribution. The New Mexico True marketing campaign is, in part, responsible for some of the gains. And, to the credit of the state tourism office, it is a clever campaign. However, when we get past the attention-diverting billboards and glossy magazine articles with beautiful images of natural landscapes and spontaneous moments of joy and wonder coupled with witty language about soulful moments, we have to start asking ourselves what it means. Who and what is New Mexico True and where do you find it?

Even though this marketing campaign only began in 2012, I find an interesting correlation with the US government-sponsored film *And Now, Miguel* from nearly sixty years earlier.

Just as in modern political times, it is not how things truly are that is important, but how they can be made to seem and to what end. More than half a century after the release of *And Now, Miguel*, the government's propaganda efforts have transitioned from a political agenda to an economic one. It is now New Mexico's state office of tourism that produces videos, billboards, and print media to promote their "New Mexico True" brand that is geared toward consumers, not political alliances or cultural connections. As the state tourism website for the brand asserts, and this is at the core of their message, the purpose of "New Mexico True" is to "seek what is true" and "push past what we know to be false." The brand narrative, as defined by the "New Mexico True Manifesto," continues by asking some poignant follow-up questions:

> We are all travelers. We seek what is true and we push past what we know
>   to be false.
> The question is: where to go? What place is true and good and real?
> Where is the place that will speak to us, crystal clear, in a voice that is
>   familiar and kind?
> Where is true found . . . and false forgotten? Where? New Mexico, True.

These deep, soulful questions are set in white lettering on a turquoise background. This lies underneath a large photo of what looks to be an American Indian woman wrapped in a traditional Navajo-style blanket, wearing white moccasins, standing on top of a rock formation facing the sun with her back toward the camera.

My questions in response to these rhetorical questions are: "How do we go about seeking what is true? How do we differentiate what is true from what is false? Are there places that incorporate all of the elements of what is true and good and real? Even if we could find this geographic nirvana, why would we ever return? Why remain a tourist and not become a local?" The marketing campaign does not provide any substantive answers to their questions or

FIGURE 6.2 New Mexico True tourism Guideline Agreement advertisement. Image courtesy of New Mexico Tourism Department.

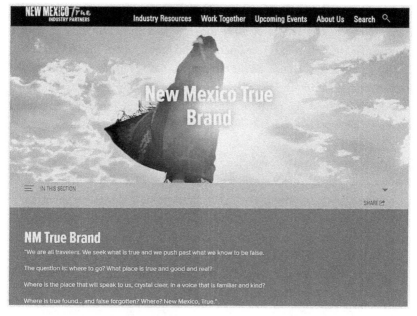

FIGURE 6.3 New Mexico True tourism website main page advertisement. Image courtesy of New Mexico Tourism Department.

mine. As travelers, it is up to us to figure this out. But one thing is for sure, according to the marketing narrative: we know that the answers can be found in New Mexico.

Fortunately, the state tourism office, along with the original marketing company from Austin responsible for much of the early marketing campaign material, assists local communities by offering them a detailed formula that can help their visitors discover these truths for themselves. For a community

FIGURE 6.4 New Mexico True tourism Guideline Agreement advertisement. Image courtesy of New Mexico Tourism Department.

to participate in this branding promotion, it must employ the logo template (XYZ is New Mexico True) created by the state, as outlined in the New Mexico Tourism Brand Guideline Agreement, found online under the section "How to Use New Mexico True." The next key step is to create a message tied to the local campaign effort. The visual effect is made even more powerful when tied to a question about the purpose behind a visit. As the guideline agreement explains, this must be a part of the combined message. The instructions read:

> There is always a true-false question. The questions are rhetorical. True is always the answer. There is no answer of False in New Mexico True. The tone of the campaign is aspirational. We are talking about something that is ultimately personal. The answer should be obvious. So the first thing the campaign does is allow the consumer a chance to think about something. "Can a state be a soul mate?" Can you think about this place like an old friend, a place where you find out who you are? Here is another example: the visual is a tribe performing a traditional dance. The headline reflects the higher values of the show "Your spirit will also dance." For a simple but powerful alternative, you may choose to customize this sentence to your destination: Gallup is New Mexico True. Ruidoso is New Mexico True. This one works every single time.

The campaign asks a question that has either a true or a false answer. Generally, the question is lofty, like "Can a place in New Mexico be a soul mate?" The answer is "true." "Can a sunrise change the way you look at everything else?" "True." "Can a place you visit once haunt you or perhaps inspire you for the rest of your life?" "True." The questions are rhetorical and, in many cases, illogical because there is only one answer. Per the guideline agreement, the answers are always "True."

So how do we push past what is false, as the marketing campaign suggests? What I have learned by working with different cultural practitioners over the years is that we accomplish this by being there, among *la plebe*, as Levi Romero calls them, and in the community. We simply cannot accept at face value what we are being told and sold. We must crave more and seek it out for ourselves. This does not mean to search for what we are told is true, but rather to seek opportunities to learn, take in, ask questions about, and respect the shared knowledge by listening to the people tell their stories. We must learn to do this if we want to live in a healthier society. For there is a critical dilemma that we create when we rely on defining a people and place with a marketing strategy (or any simplistic, one-sided narrative, for that matter). This is that we ignore the problems in our community because they do not fit within this true-or-false dichotomy of adventure feeding the soul.

The textual narrative embedded within the New Mexico True campaign cannot, however, successfully craft this message by itself. It is just one key element in a combined effort to forge this propagandistic message. As Gregory Ulmer explains in his book *Electronic Monuments* (2005): "The basic unit of signification in [Jacques] Lacan's theory is not the sign, but the emblem, given that his counterexample has the tripartite structure of this genre (slogan + picture + commentary)" (21). Lacan's theory explains how people connect a word, a sound, or an image to a concept. Ulmer argues that out of these three, it is the emblem (image) that is the driving force behind this theory and how we form meaning:

> The success of the emblem or ad depends on the use of codes shared by
> the audience. E.D. Hirsch called these shared codes "cultural literacy"—a
> superficial knowledge of an encyclopedia of information that, he said, it was
> the job of the public schools to teach. Emblems assumed a knowledge of the
> classical tradition, for example, including an awareness of stock images selected
> from the tradition and fixed into iconic poses and gestures. The historical
> literacy stories are miniaturized in the emblem into one pose that expresses
> the fundamental significance, and atmosphere, of the narrative (122).

In accordance with the tripartite formula of slogan + picture + commentary, we can see below in this simple New Mexico True advertisement of how the three parts come together to craft and deliver a message.

FIGURE 6.5 New Mexico True tourism guideline advertisement slogan. Image courtesy of New Mexico Tourism Department.

Slogan = New Mexico True
+ picture = Zia with photo image
+ commentary = Adventure that feeds the soul
───────────────────────────────────
= New Mexico is a true or false (black or white) place

The signification or meaning behind this message is that New Mexico always represents what is true and good and real. There is no false in New Mexico True. Yes, it is true that New Mexico is known for its stunning high desert sunsets, a world-renowned hot-air balloon fiesta, and the beautiful architecture of its plazas and Indian Pueblos. But it is also true that New Mexico ranks poorly in many social well-being categories dealing with poverty, education, and child welfare. Herein lies the danger of such a one-sided constructed message: we fail to see the complete picture of who we are and thus ignore our social ills.

What happens when we question this narrative formula and begin to look beyond this true/false dichotomy? This is what Catholic Health Initiatives–St. Joseph's Children, a faith-based nonprofit organization, has begun to do with their own campaign called "New Mexico Truth." As they state on their website: "As New Mexicans we love the natural wonders of our state, but we can't take credit for how deep the Carlsbad Caverns are, how white the White Sands are or how high Wheeler Peak is, but we can take responsibility for the wellbeing of our children. New Mexico is ranked 49th in children's wellbeing, we can't stand for this! We need to take responsibility for this and understand that this is a part of our New Mexico Truth." Some of the basic facts to which they draw attention include: "New Mexico ranks 49th in children's wellbeing; New Mexico has the highest rate of children living in poverty in the nation; 58% of our 3 and 4 year olds are not enrolled in preschool; 77% of our children

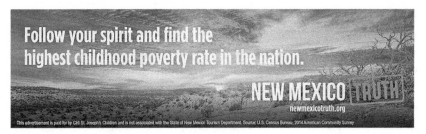

Follow your spirit and find the
highest childhood poverty rate in the nation.

NEW MEXICO TRUTH
newmexicotruth.org

This advertisement is paid for by CHI St. Joseph's Children and is not associated with the State of New Mexico Tourism Department. Source: U.S. Census Bureau, 2014 American Community Survey

FIGURE 6.6 New Mexico Truth website advertisement. Image courtesy of New Mexico Truth Educational Campaign, CHI–St. Joseph's Children.

are not proficient in reading by the 4th grade; 41% of our children are raised in single-parent families." Clearly, these truths affect our state's well-being, especially in the long-term socioeconomic outlook.

In their New Mexico Truth campaign, CHI–St. Joseph's takes this same signification formula and turns it on its head to exploit the shallow messaging, such as in the following satire of the New Mexico True campaign. The New Mexico Truth campaign makes valid points: The state's natural wonders, although beautiful, cannot address our social ills. It is up to us to fix them. How we go about this is open to debate, although the approach should be multipronged. We should identify good practices and propose effective policies to improve the well-being of our communities, especially our children, as it relates to education, health, and poverty. Only then, after we make serious inroads into improving our social well-being, especially for our most vulnerable populations, can we begin to point to our New Mexico truths with a sense of pride.

"MOLINO ABANDONADO" ETCHED IN OUR MEMORY

As a literary and cultural studies scholar who focuses on Chicanx themes, I believe in the power of cultural knowledge and the value in the expression "la cultura cura" (culture cures). I have seen firsthand how cultural traditions passed on through generational knowledge can and do make significant, positive changes for individuals and their families. However, this type of cultural work must be done together, as a community, to achieve maximum potential for change. The end goal should be to (re)build the community as a unit of cohesiveness, not a collection of individuals living in proximity.

To achieve the re-creation of a cohesive community unit, we must learn how to recover the livable public space. Paul Virilio states that the key to accomplishing this "lies in reorganizing the place of communal life." The first step in this process, he claims, "is to counter the image by recreating speech, recovering language, and writing" (Qtd. in Ulmer 2005, xix). In other words, we must not just create a rhetorical space of New Mexico True, but build a sense of community where people are nurtured through the messages that we send, in a language that is native to us, and through re-creating these images and narratives ourselves by writing about them and preserving them.

When we learn to see and think more deeply, we can begin to untangle the messages embedded in the codes of cultural literacy, such as those used in the New Mexico True campaign. We can thus decipher a tourist photograph of people consuming culture and nature as an incomplete representation and false staging of a place and its people. Instead, to better appreciate the spirit of New Mexico's people and cultures, we must learn about the region's deep historical memory and respect the value of place that defines the sacred space of where two or more people gather in the name of community. Levi Romero, the New Mexico Centennial Poet Laureate, examines this idea of *lo sagrado* (the sacred) in his poetry. His poem "Molino abandonado" (2008) demonstrates how the recollection of a communal memory can help recover the place of communal life.

It was during an excursion to the small northern New Mexico town of Apodaca as part of a poetry workshop that Romero was inspired to write a poem about this idea of place and memory, themes present in much of his poetry. He asked the students to pick an object full of character from a bygone era to write about. It was there that he saw an old abandoned gristmill and wondered what it must have been like when people once used it.[12] Aaron Griego, a village elder, told Romero that when he was a child the locals would use the mill to process their crops. Griego recalled the sense of joy they experienced while they worked and sang together. Singing enabled them to pass the time and created a sense of community.

Unfortunately, during that visit, Griego could not recall any of the song lyrics they used to sing. However, he told Romero that he would tell him what he could remember upon his next visit. Romero did return, and the village elder, true to his word, shared with him a key stanza from the song's refrain: "sopla viento, sopla más / y la paja volará / ahí preparado el banquete / pa' todo el que vaya entrando" (blow wind, blow more / and the chaff will fly away / there's the prepared banquet / for everyone who enters) (Romero 2008, 144).[13]

There is much cultural knowledge passed on through this four-line stanza. It teaches the listener about the afternoon breeze and its role in helping to clean the chaff from the grain. It also reminds us about the sense of community and how it was paramount to the village's identity during that period. They worked together, sang together, and broke bread together. This is evident in its description of the harvest banquet in which they celebrated their bounty. The invitees were not limited to a special few honored guests; the community gathering was open to anybody who wanted to partake in the festivities. This is querencia in its purest form. In the spirit of Arellano's description of querencia, this memory of a people and culture describes a deeply rooted knowledge of place where one feels safe and at home. It is a sacred place, where two or more are gathered in the name of community. The problem is, as the poem's title conveys, although the mill once functioned as *el molino comunitario*, it is now *el molino abandonado*.

The abandoned mill, at one time "con su rueda en el agua / ahora, se usa de dispensa" (with its wheel in the water / now, is used as storage) (145). This acts as a metaphor for the lost sense of community. How do we recover "la historia / de un pueblo / hecha polvo" (history / of a town / made into dust) and set the stone wheel back into motion? We can do so by singing the lyrics that we know, even if we only recall one stanza. If the key to reorganizing the place of communal life lies in re-creating speech, recovering language, and writing about it, then we must do as Romero and other *poetas del pueblo* have modeled for us. We must read poetry and sing songs and create dialogue aloud because it will serve as the seed of love in times of darkness. Romero closes the poem before one last refrain by stating that "el pueblo [queda] sin molino" (The town [remains] without a mill) (146). However, it is easy to envision the situation the other way around, that *el molino queda sin pueblo* (the mill remains without a town). The molino has remained; it is la plebe who have abandoned it. But through remembering, as alluded to by Romero's book title, we can recover a fragment of our communal identity, and with it, regain a piece of our beloved querencia.

CONCLUSION: ON RESTORING QUERENCIA

As we can now see, the marketing formula of slogan + picture + commentary does not produce cultural truths, but rather convenient, albeit incomplete portraits of who we are. And however earnest their attempt to reflect a positive image of New Mexico and its people, in the end, cultural truths cannot be fully revealed through propaganda like the film *And Now, Miguel* or crafty marketing campaigns such as New Mexico True. Instead, traditional ways of knowing are developed through the sharing of knowledge and preserved through generational continuity.

Like the people who once gathered around the village molino with a sense of community and the pastores who carefully tended to their flock in *And Now, Miguel*, today's New Mexicans must learn to protect their culture on their terms if it is to endure for future generations despite the rapid changes due to growth and technology that threaten cultural traditions. For the people to reestablish a healthy sense of querencia, they must embrace the totality of their homeland and not just the visitor's guide points of interest, engage in cultural and language maintenance, and tell their stories in their own words. This is how the molino becomes relevant again as a metaphorical symbol of where two or more gather in the name of community.

Our ancestors provided us with the blueprint for how to accomplish this. For this way of life, or any life worth living, is etched in our memories, not in wood or stone. It takes hard work and consistent effort to maintain what is dear to us and pass it on for future generations. We must keep moving forward, *adelante*, toward an imperfect place that makes us question the rhetoricity of simple and incomplete thoughts. In this spirit, we must search for truth in people, not propaganda. That's the beauty of our querencia for *Nuevo México* or wherever you may call home, not just because of its natural wonders, but because it's the place we love, and because of the community of people with whom we share it.

NOTES

1. In 1841, the Republic of Texas, under orders from President Mirabeau B. Lamar, launched the ill-fated Texas–Santa Fe Expedition led by General Hugh McLeod to gain control of Mexico's northern province of Nuevo México, particularly the Santa Fe Trail. It failed miserably: the men were captured and marched to Mexico City, where they were imprisoned, most of them eventually being released. Texas attempted other unsuccessful invasions of Mexico's northern territory. In 1842, the Mier Expedition of 261 men was defeated by the Mexican Army. In 1843, the Warfield and Snively expeditions attempted similar Santa Fe campaigns, both unsuccessful. The US Army disarmed Snively's men because they were interfering with

the Santa Fe trade route and had murdered a Mexican trader, Antonio Chávez. This ended the Republic of Texas's military forays into New Mexico (Wroth). In 1861, during the Civil War, Jefferson Davis commissioned General Henry Hopkins Sibley to lead a brigade through New Mexico to capture Colorado and California for the Confederacy. Sibley's Brigade defeated the Union soldiers near Fort Craig in the Battle of Valverde in 1862 and later seized Albuquerque and Santa Fe. At Glorieta Pass, Sibley's Texans beat a federal force of Colorado "Pike's Peakers" on March 28, 1862, but lost their entire supply train to a raiding party of Union troops. Forced to evacuate the territory, Sibley began a disastrous retreat through the San Mateo Mountains, losing a third of his men in New Mexico. It was the largest Civil War battle to take place in the Rocky Mountains region, which became known as the "Gettysburg of the West" (National Park Service).

2. See Armando Alonzo (1998) for more information on the history of Tejano land ownership and loss.

3. With many New Mexicans being generations-deep citizens of the state, the question arises as to when one is allowed to call oneself native to the region. Levi Romero argues that you become part of a place when you can point to the graves of relatives buried in the local cemetery. This being the case, I hope that I never become a Nuevomexicano, but remain a transplant. One day, my children can then visit my gravesite and feel an attachment to the place where I am buried.

4. Acoma Pueblo is the oldest continuously inhabited community in North America, established in 1150 AD (Sky City).

5. The film was so well received that the Thomas Y. Crowell publishing company asked the director, Joseph Krumgold, to write a children's book based on the film. The book was published in 1953 and won the Newbery Medal for excellence in American children's literature in 1954. A mainstream Hollywood movie released in 1966 with the same title and also based on the book was directed by James B. Clark.

6. The New Mexico True marketing campaign was developed by the Austin-based company Vendor, Inc. in 2012. Since then, other companies, including the Santa Fe firm Talweg Creative, have been involved in refining this message (Brodsky, 2012). Talweg has been more cautious in their approach on how they market New Mexico. To their credit, they have toned down the rhetoric of true versus false. Instead, their focus tends toward creating one's own story worthy of sharing with others. As such, the critique in this chapter lies mostly with the earlier campaign strategy and narrative and not Talweg Creative.

7. Although the marketing campaign attempts to attract out-of-state tourists with its airport terminal signage and airline magazine ads, it was travel around New Mexico by New Mexicans that represented one-third of all visits in 2014 when the state reported record-high visitation levels (Dyer, 2015).

8. The "true and good and real" phrase is part of the New Mexico True manifesto.

9. For a general overview of the issue of grazing and land rights, see Donald Dale Jackson's "Around Los Ojos, Sheep and Land are Fighting Words" (1991).

10. For more information, see www.followmanitotrail.com.

11. See Dizard (2003) for more information on the propaganda efforts of the USIA.

12. According to Levi Romero, the *molino* was known as "El molino de los parciantes." Although it was managed by one individual, it belonged to all the members of the local community ditch system. Romero's *tío*, Silviano Griego, operated the molino when it was in working order.

13. All translations from "Molino abandonado" are mine.

WORKS CITED

Alonzo, Armando. 1998. *Tejano Legacy: Rancheros and Settlers in South Texas, 1734–1900*. Albuquerque: University of New Mexico Press.

Arellano, Juan Estevan. 1997. "La Querencia: La Raza Bioregionalism." *New Mexico Historical Review* 7, no. 1: 31–37.

———. 2012. "*La Cuenca y La Querencia*: The Watershed and the Sense of Place in the *Merced* and Acequia Landscape." In *Thinking Like a Watershed: Voices from the West*, edited by Jack Loeffler and Celestia Loeffler, 151–91. Albuquerque: University of New Mexico Press.

Baca, Marie C. 2018. "Tourism Impact on NM Continues to Grow." *Albuquerque Journal*, October 10, 2018.

Brodsky, Rivkela. 2012. "Texas Firm Keen on Tourism Campaign." *Albuquerque Journal*, January 30, 2012. https://www.abqjournal.com/84227/texas-firm-keen-on-tourism-campaign.html.

Catholic Health Initiatives–St. Joseph's Children. "New Mexico Truth" Educational Campaign. http://newmexicotruth.org/.

Cole, Thom. 2018. "New Mexico's Lost Decade: State Mired in Economic Problems since Great Recession." *The New Mexican*, February 3, 2018.

Dizard, Jr., Wilson. 2003. "Telling America's Story." *American Heritage* 54, no. 4 (August/September): 41–48. http://www.americanheritage.com/content/telling-america%E2%80%99s-story.

Dyer, Jessica. 2015. "Instate Tourism Accounted for 30% of 2014 Visits." *Albuquerque Journal*, July 2, 2015.

"Governor Susana Martinez Identifies Tourism for Increased Investment." 2018. *Las Cruces Sun News*, January 10, 2018.

Hedden, Adrian C. 2019. "New Mexico's Unemployment Rate Higher than National Average, Lower in Oil and Gas Counties." *Carlsbad Current Argus*, April 2, 2019.

Jackson, Donald Dale. 1991. "Around Los Ojos, Sheep and Land Are Fighting Words." *Smithsonian* 22, no. 1 (April): 37–47.

Krumgold, Joseph, dir. 1953. *And Now, Miguel*. Motion picture. Washington, DC: United States Information Service.

Meléndez, A. Gabriel. 2013. *Hidden Chicano Cinema: Film Dramas in the Borderlands*. New Brunswick, NJ: Rutgers University Press.

National Park Service. "Battle of Glorieta Pass." https://www.nps.gov/peco/learn /historyculture/copy-of-battleofglorietta.htm.

New Mexico Tourism Department. 2012a. "New Mexico Tourism Brand Guideline Agreement." http://media.nmtourism.org/sites/default/files/New-Mexico -Tourism-Brand-Guideline-Agreement.pdf.

————. 2012b. "New Mexico True Brand." https://www.newmexico.org/industry /resources/nm-true-brand/.

Nye, Jr., Joseph F. 2006. "Think Again: Soft Power." *Foreign Policy*, February 23, 2006. http://foreignpolicy.com/2006/02/23/think-again-soft-power/.

Paredes, Américo. 1991. *Between Two Worlds*. Houston: Arte Público Press.

Peerman, Lucas. 2016. "New Mexico, Las Cruces See Record Tourism Numbers." *Las Cruces Sun News*, October 23, 2016.

Randall, Randy. 2019. "It's NM True: Tourism Benefits All New Mexicans." *Albuquerque Journal*, April 1, 2019.

Romero, Levi. 2008. *A Poetry of Remembrance: New and Rejected Works*. Albuquerque: University of New Mexico Press.

Sky City Cultural Center. "History of Acoma Pueblo." http://www.acomaskycity .org/main.html?pgid=11.

Ulmer, Gregory L. 2005. *Electronic Monuments*. Minneapolis: University of Minnesota Press.

Wroth, William. H. 2014. "1841 Texan–Santa Fe Expedition." http://http://new mexicohistory.org/2014/01/22/texan-santa-fe-expedition-1841/.

This section focuses on the efforts of Nuevomexicanas and Indigenous women who define and defend querencia through the politics of memory. The authors illuminate the need to tell stories and to enact memory as a way to combat erasure. In doing so, they show that the female body, cultural practices, and claiming space are integral components in the protection of querencia. In chapter seven, "(Re)Signifying Gender and Sexuality for the Nuevomexicana Historical Body: The Politics of Reading Place in *Women's Tales from the New Mexico WPA: La Diabla a Pie*," Bernadine Hernández centers on the narratives of women whose bodies were used for debt peonage in nineteenth-century New Mexico. She cites several important historical documents to support her argument, including an 1857 Territorial Supreme Court ruling defining the ambiguous labor system of debt peonage for Juana Analla, an indebted servant, who was allowed to take back her daughter, Catalina Bustamento, who was being held in bondage. Hernández also uses contrasting literary narratives from *Women's Tales from the New Mexico WPA* to understand the relationship between the symbolism, metaphor, and allusion specific to New Mexico writing in relation to how gender and sexuality are constructed through place.

By examining historical cases and literary stories collected by the Work Projects Administration (WPA) that outlined the boundaries of debt peonage, Hernández prompts us to think about how the material economic relations of the state of New Mexico were linked to the construction of gender, land, place, and labor. She argues that poor Nuevomexicanas occupied a complex site of contestation in that their bodies served a dual function within the debt peonage system: first, they produced work and resources for the *patrones* (owners), and second, they reproduced the worker through childbirth. Hernández asserts that, in contrast to elite landholding Nuevomexicanas, poor Nuevomexicanas negotiated and contested the typical boundaries of gender and sexuality while also challenging conventional feminist theories. She argues that debt peonage was a sexual economy that built racialized civility and capital, where idealized femininity and the fraught social figure and sexual utility of the Nuevomexicana were in contention. In this chapter, she demonstrates through legal cases and WPA stories specifically how the body serves as a site of memory and querencia, while also helping the reader to understand the complexities of gender and sexuality in New Mexico from the late 1800s through the mid-1900s.

In chapter eight, "Erasing Querencia from Los Alamos: Racist and Sexualized Portrayals of New Mexican Women and Place in the Television Series *Manhattan*," Myrriah Gómez considers another element of labor for native New Mexican women who worked in Los Alamos, New Mexico, during the development of the atom bomb. Her analysis looks at the difference between the location and space of Los Alamos as a way to understand and preserve notions of querencia under erasure in the television show *Manhattan*. Gómez argues that the series threatens querencia by erasing the complex relationship between local people and Los Alamos and by rendering the voices and experiences of New Mexican women as invalid. Her chapter effectively reinserts New Mexican voices into the history of Los Alamos and opens conversations about local women laborers who were connected to the Manhattan Project. She argues that, as a fictional television show, *Manhattan* creates yet another pop-cultural representation that works toward undoing Nuevomexicana/o and Native querencias in and around Los Alamos through its portrayal of the town as undesirable, godforsaken, and ambiguous in its cultural identity. Throughout this chapter, Gómez juxtaposes the fictional representation of the female characters in *Manhattan* with interviews with Nuevomexicanas and Indigenous women who worked at Site Y during the 1940s. She does this with a firm recognition of the complexities of querencia and bioregionalism, noting that the memory associated with Los Alamos by way of its inhabitants and/or neighbors is under threat of erasure by television shows such as *Manhattan*, which create a false narrative of what it was like to live and survive in this space. Ultimately, she shows that that fictional representation of space confuses the relationship that native New Mexicans maintained with the lands that they called home. These women are disconnected from their physical homeland and sense of querencia. Therefore, they rely mainly on their memories as a way to connect to a space they once considered their home.

In "Mestiza Consciousness a la MeXicana in Ultima and Agueda Martínez: Bridging and Legitimizing Querencia in the Borderlands," Norma A. Valenzuela furthers conversations on displacement and belonging. As a central thread in her chapter, she explores the connection between two homelands: Torreón, Mexico and Alburquerquito, a word her father uses to refer to Albuquerque. As a transnational MeXicana, Valenzuela offers her *testimonio* as a way to bridge a history of living in distinct spaces that are anchored in common cultural practices. Her lived experiences serve as a testament to generational bonds formed with her grandmother, a querencia space she remembers fondly by way of *dichos* (proverbs), storytelling, and *curanderismo* (folk medicine).

Using Gloria Anzaldúa's concept of *Nepantla* (in-between spaces), Valenzuela explores how her transnational identity allowed her to appreciate querencia in the borderlands. For her, querencia is a journey of discovery that is informed by memory in multiple spaces and shaped by academic and personal experiences that allowed her to be more aware of the complexities of home and belonging. Valenzuela validates her querencia through a reflection on Chicana/o literature and culture, utilizing figures such as Rudolfo Anaya's fictional character Ultima and Agueda Martínez, a weaver from northern New Mexico, to understand shared cultural experiences between her home community of Torreón and her family's later home in Albuquerque. She reflects on the cultural practices of language, food, burying umbilical cords, and agricultural work to better understand the vast similarities between two distinct geographical spaces, both of which she claims as her querencia. She is reminded of the reasons why her family chose to call Albuquerque their home in the 1970s. Memory thus becomes an important aspect of Valenzuela's personal journey as she uses a variety of narrative forms to frame her lived experiences. Even more present in her analysis and testimonio is the enduring strength of her maternal ancestors and those cultural and literary *mujeres* (women) from Nuevo México who worked so diligently to pass on knowledge and cultural understanding so that the family did not forget its querencia—and so that they might guard it fiercely and call it their own.

The chapters included in this section call to our attention the paths that Nuevomexicanas have paved for future generations of cultural warriors and scholars who look to them for inspiration and guidance. Nuevomexicana women have embodied querencia in the ways they challenged the use of their bodies through debt peonage, by holding on to querencia when homelands were co-opted by external interests, and by creating legacies that help us to understand our own borderlands identities in nepantla spaces. Through a careful analysis of memory as querencia, Hernández, Gómez, and Valenzuela are also creating new pathways as Nuevomexicanas.

CHAPTER SEVEN

(Re)Signifying Gender and Sexuality for the Nuevomexicana Historical Body

The Politics of Reading Place in *Women's Tales from the New Mexico* WPA: *La Diabla a Pie*

BERNADINE HERNÁNDEZ

In 1867, the US Federal Government prohibited debt peonage in the Union. This decision came after two essential rulings by the New Mexico Territorial Supreme Court that set the foundation and the boundaries of debt peonage in the United States. Debt peonage was an important social and economic system in the contemporary Southwest that was invested in labor control and the evolution of the Americas through racial capitalism. New Mexico was a focal point of the debt peonage debate because the system did not have a clear definition. It was not slavery and it was not free labor, but lay at the interstices of these two economic and labor systems. While it favored the cis heterosexual male, there was a feminine and sexual component of debt peonage that has yet to be uncovered. Poor Nuevomexicana women were at the center of it.[1] In framing two foundational court cases heard by the New Mexico Territorial Supreme Court, *Jaremillo v. Romero* and *Bustamento v. Analla,* and two short stories from the Works Progress Administration, this chapter contends that debt peonage was a sexual economy that built racialized civility and capital, where idealized femininity and the fraught social figure and sexual utility of the Nuevomexicana woman were in contention. Straddling the line between black feminists' theory of sexual economies and Marxist feminists' notions of productive and reproductive labor, it looks at the way poor and racialized Nuevomexicanas occupied a dual capacity, not only in the production for their families, but also for reproducing children for the economic system of debt peonage that ushered in our global capital moment and provides an alternative history of the borderlands. These women became a site of the resignification of gender and sexuality in that they upheld the domestic sphere and the workforce, all while producing for their families; their gender and

sexuality were sites through which empire and the nation-state were reproduced and both exemplify the turmoil of pleasure and power. Their body politic contested the threatening of *querencia* and their sense of place anchoring
them to New Mexico, setting the foundation for the judicial ruling of debt
peonage in the Union. While there are no fictional stories to my knowledge
that center the female within the economic system of debt peonage, the 1930s
WPA short stories allow one to read the archives metonymically in relation to
the utility of the Nuevomexicana body and her connection to place.

Women's Tales from the New Mexico WPA: La Diabla a Pie is a book of stories
collected from the community of New Mexico through a program designed
to help destitute writers during the Depression. An oral history program in
the late 1930s and early 1940s that was attempting to recover New Mexico's
Spanish-Mexican past for the modern US state, this New Deal project was
a federal initiative that employed eligible writers to collect, transcribe, and
submit stories about New Mexico's folktales. The Works Projects Administration, formerly the Works Progress Administration, was known locally as *la
diabla a pie* (the devil on foot). Similar projects took place in rural states across
the US, particularly in the Deep South, where the tradition of collecting slave
folk narratives—living traditions—goes back to the time of Reconstruction.
The New Mexico WPA stories are just as complex. Tey Diana Rebolledo and
María Teresa Márquez published their volume of New Mexico WPA stories in
2000 via the Recovering the US Hispanic Literary Heritage Project, through
which more than sixty story collections compiled by Annette Hesch Thorp
and Lou Sage Batchen are accessible. The WPA narratives and the complicated position of Thorp and Batchen in collecting the stories relay how race,
gender, class, and sexuality shaped New Mexico, the US empire, and the most
intimate spaces that uncover the political positionality of the Nuevomexicana
woman.[2]

As previously stated, not many stories center on the economic system of
debt peonage. "The Panic of 1862" and "Mateo y Raquel" frame the racialized and sexualized female body on the borderlands and in New Mexico. In
stark contrast to the utility of the elite landholding Hispana who consolidated white femininity and was consecrated as both the symbolic center and
boundary marker of the nation as "home" and "family," the WPA stories bring
to the forefront the sexual utility of the poor Nuevomexicana body of that
time. For poor, racialized Nuevomexicana women, their bodies signified an
expansive charge that exemplified the theoretical and practical discomforts

of pleasure and power. The Nuevomexicana body was a deceptively complex site, because it unveiled how their biological capacities were linked to their status and place in New Mexico. As race emerged as a heritable category that defined social reality, their reproductive lives were signified by their public location in the space of capital accumulation in New Mexico, rather than in the private space of the domestic.

The Federal Writers' Project was a "back-to-work" project where writers collected materials for a series of State Guides. The main component of the project was to interview older residents, those who gave information to "document the culture and history as a 'human interest' section of the guides" (*Women's*, 2000, xix). The first collection and writing of data began in 1933 under the Civil Works of Art Project. While the interviewers and writers tapped the vein of folklore and culture, many of them didn't speak the language of the people of New Mexico, which was Spanish, and even with the little Spanish they did know, could not recognize, as Rebolledo states, the "jocularity and linguistic playfulness of the phonetic and mimetic representation" (xxii). Along with this misinterpretation of the information, the interviews tended to romanticize New Mexican culture and the land. However, even with these problems, the representation of periphery populations within New Mexico weaves a rich narrative of the negotiation of memory and querencia.

Memory and querencia are intricately tied to how these economic systems resignify the Nuevomexicana body and delineate a hierarchy of social relations. The WPA stories allow us to think about place, history, and memory together because they (re)remember the past of nineteenth-century New Mexico through the dispossessions and inequalities of the twentieth century. Thus, the Nuevomexicana body is a site of resistance where her dual capacity as a gendered and sexualized woman upholds and maintains the domestic space, the borderlands, and the US empire. Her memory produces querencia in that she creates a new gendered and political identity up and against "proper" femininity. The Nuevomexicana female body becomes a site of contestation and power through her subjugation. The New Mexican home is equally contradictory, because the social realities of the Nuevomexicana household take on multiple meanings in the past through her dual capacity and, in the present, as her racialized sexuality signifies the remaking of her "femaleness."

On memory, Kerwin Lee Klein states, "Where we once spoke of folk history or popular history or oral history or public history or even myth we now employ memory as a meta historical category that subsumes all these various terms" (2000, 128). Memory went from an archaic mode of being to a remaking of historical imagination. Memory—and, more specifically, a critical memory that intervenes within a conventional historical narrative—maintains close ties with other forms of folk, mythological, oral, and popular histories and establishes an inextricable link among a past, present, and future while (re)mapping history. Because American history is fraught with one-sided and limited viewpoints, a critical memory that establishes links to the past is crucial. Geographically speaking, New Mexico is a location where multiple histories collide as a result of colonization and settlement. Memory is oftentimes paired as an antithesis or antonym of history. This erroneous pitting of the terms suggests that memory is positioned counter to history at any moment. On the opposite end of the spectrum, memory can serve as a synonym for history, often "softening" the latter term while giving it a relatable connotation. While memory can certainly add depth and context to traditional historical accounts, Klein suggests, "We need to reconsider the relationship between historical imagination and the new memorial consciousness, and we may begin by mapping the contours of the new structures of memory. Memories appeal to us partly because they project an immediacy we feel has been lost from history" (2000, 129). From a Chicana feminist perspective, the uncovering of the gender and sexual condition of the Nuevomexicana within debt peonage is a retrofitted memory.[3] This is a new gendered political identity produced through history that creates contestatory identities and political practices, a type of querencia. Thus, memory complicates structural systems of oppression but does not necessarily function completely outside of these ideological systems. History is not a linear model of isolated events that collapses into the present. With New Mexico occupying such a conflicted historical space in the Southwest, it seems necessary to turn toward a politics of critical memory to interrogate the (mis)constructed histories of violent colonization, racial, gender, and class conflict, and dispossession. (Re) remembering the residual economic system of debt peonage in New Mexico unveils the distinct social relations and gendered and sexual condition of racialized sexuality through the dual capacity of the Nuevomexicana body and uncovers her political position through geography, place, and personhood. The following discussion exemplifies how gender, sex, and the geography of New Mexico uphold a specific way of life while fighting for autonomy in the poor Nuevomexicana's homeland.

The notion of productive and reproductive labor aids us in thinking about how the poor, racialized Nuevomexicana body had a dual capacity that Karl Marx and even Marxist feminists have failed to see. Marx notes that productive labor is any form of labor that produces surplus value, which can constitute a tangible commodity or merely a service.[4] For him, only labor power has value and is a commodity. Reproductive labor has use value but no exchange value; therefore value comes only when labor power produces. Thus, reproducing labor power falls outside of the category of value and it becomes naturalized as social labor and not as a productive process of capital. Reproduction (labor that mysteriously happens and is "natural") is nonvalue and production is value. However, the poor, racialized Nuevomexicana resignifies the limits of nonvalue reproductive labor, an indirect way of approaching the history of the borderlands. The dual character of reproductive labor has a formal appearance, which is attached to a racialized ideology of colonialism and its hidden real function that centers racialized gender reproduction and production. To think of the economic system of debt peonage as a sexual economy is to unveil the nuanced ways gender and sexuality are utilized in relation to the poor, racialized Nuevomexicana and to rethink how she reproduces the worker (through her indebted children) and produces for the worker (through her reproductive labor in survival).

I am deploying the term "sexual economies" in this chapter, as it is tied to the debt peonage labor system for the Nuevomexicana body. Adrienne Davis (2002) first coined the term and delineated that, under slavery, reproduction was integral to the plantation economy. Black reproduction yielded economic profits, creating value for the slaveholding class. Enslaved black women gave birth to white wealth.[5] Masters established enslaved women as sexual outlets to perform sexual labor. Davis states, "Black women's sexuality and reproductive capacity [was] for white pleasure and profit" (2002, 104). Black women could be sexually terrorized in order to coerce economic work or discipline enslaved men. The legal "unrapeability" of black women within the institution of slavery and their differently gendered process through the middle passage were all part of the sexual economy of chattel slavery.[6] Davis defines sexual economies as "reproducing the slave workforce through giving birth and serving as forced sexual labor to countless men of all races" (105). The sexual and reproductive exploitation of the institution of slavery helps us understand that it was a violent economic structure that was gendered and sexualized as well as a racial institution for economic and market relations. Within the institution of slavery, Davis states, "crossing gender boundaries" through physical labor marked a differentiation of "feminine" and "masculine" as ungendering.[7] This violent mode of production still foregrounded the slave woman's gender and demonstrated how embedded their sexuality was in slavery's economic market. The children of slaves followed the mother and were foundational for the economy to reproduce itself. This converted enslaved women's reproductive capacity into work serving economic interests and produced much of the rural workforce in parts of the United States. The slaves in the South served as the labor supply and also as capital assets, where the law and market converted reproductive capacity into capital creation. I define sexual economies as modern/colonial structures, enacted through sexual and economic systems (in certain historical moments overdetermined by racial miscegenation and violence) that build racialized civility and racialized capital.[8] I link sexual violence, colonial/expansionist conquest, and economy to the production of settler subjectivity in New Mexico, where idealized femininity and the fraught social figure of the elite landholding "Mexican American" woman are sites through which empire and nation-state were reproduced in contention with subjugated bodies.

Expanding upon Davis' definition of the sexual economy of slavery, I deploy the term to think about the economic system of debt peonage and the lasting effects it had on racialized gender and sexuality in the Southwest. The tasks that peons performed under bondage depended on their gender, age, and strength. It was not always the case that women and children performed the menial tasks and domestic work while the men did the hard labor outside, as herdsmen and field hands. Males made up most of the peons in the Southwest. A peon's family was indebted indefinitely because of his peon status. When the male could no longer work or needed more hours than he could provide individually, the *patrones* (bosses) used his family, mostly sons, to continue payment to his account, which could never be rectified. While the majority of the stories regarding debt peonage in the Southwest center on the male peon, using a reading strategy that interrogates the gaps and silences, it becomes clear that debt peonage also affected the peon's wife and shaped her gender and sexuality.

While conversations surrounding westward expansion were happening in relation to the place of slavery in the newly annexed territories of northern Mexico after 1848, many lawmakers did not know how to categorize or think about debt peonage, or involuntary labor, in the Southwest. Debt peonage became a mainstay in this region by the 1800s. Scholars maintain that it was a regionally specific system in Mexico and Latin America that was not limited to race. Historians have questioned the institution of debt peonage in the Southwest and some say it was not fully established under Spanish and Mexican governance. However, it is recalled in oral testimonies.[9]

What the region did have was something different than debt peonage: the *encomienda* (labor system of the Spanish colony) and *repartimiento* (a noun form stemming from "an American Indian hired to work"). These systems under Spanish colonialism spanned from British Carolina to French Louisiana, Spanish New Mexico, and Alta California.[10] The Spanish crown targeted Indigenous populations for cheap labor. The Native or Indigenous slavery particular to the Southwest resulted in the *genízaro* population who settled mostly in northern New Mexico in places such as Abiquiu and Taos. Elite landholding families kept these Native or Indigenous slaves, who were different than peons, well into the 1880s as the *encomienda* and *repartimiento* systems became extinct because of disease and the transfer of private enclosures, haciendas, and ranchos. Rebolledo (2002) notes that from the sixteenth to the late nineteenth century, "The use of these Indian servants was rationalized, unlike the African slave experience, by the fact that they were 'adopted into the family' and their souls saved by Christianizing. These 'slaves' were kept within the family, were not sold from person to person, and were sometimes able to barter for their freedom. Many of those released became detribalized Indians, called *genízaros*, who later formed townships" (132). The Spanish crown renounced the encomienda and repartimento system in the 1600s (though not Native or Indigenous slavery particularly), but patrones on haciendas, ranchos, and communal land property needed human labor at cheap prices. Debt peonage was one of the fastest-growing labor sources. In the Southwest, this was characterized by work in agrarian and pastoral areas and in its earliest Latin American manifestations targeted lower-class, racialized citizens.

The racist undertones of letting this minority-majority territory in as a state was at the forefront of political conversations before and after the Civil War. Some scholars have asserted that debt peonage was one reason why New Mexico was not granted statehood earlier. However, government's so-called repulsion at the "savage" coercive labor practices of New Mexicans was a racist attempt to wrest control of equal social and political rights from the "mongrel" Mexicans. Although Congress was split on the slavery debate in New Mexico, many members saw it as a potential source of revenue. "New

Mexico's representatives to Congress were issued a warning—unless New Mexico supported slavery, proslavery legislators would vote against New Mexico becoming a state" (Menchaca 2010, 226). New Mexico would not become a slave state, though they did not abolish Native slavery or debt peonage at this time.[11] The practice was prohibited by the US government in 1867 rather than with the signing of the Thirteenth Amendment in 1865, which supposedly liberated all persons subjected to slavery and involuntary servitude. However, convict leasing and debt peonage remained in practice well into the twentieth century in the South.

Shelley Streeby (2002) traces the history of debt peonage as appearing linguistically in "English in the mid-nineteenth century as a way of describing an array of labor arrangements" (192). Alan Knight (1986) states that from the late colonial period to the early nineteenth century there were two forms of peonage: coercive and noncoercive, or traditional (45–46). However, William Kiser (2014) notes that peons performed tasks and the patrones "paid all their laborers' tributes, advanced them money, clothed them, gave them medical attention . . . and thus kept permanent debt accumulating" (171). These scholars state that debt peonage in the Southwest was coercive and functioned as a form of bondage: family members, particularly sons, were indebted once a father or mother died with a debt. By contrast, David Weber (1982) maintains that a peon could "end his obligation by paying off his debt and his condition was not hereditary" and thus not a voluntary servitude (212).

Many elite families in the Southwest attempted to mask peonage as a "system of apprenticeship or voluntary servitude," as territorial representative of New Mexico Miguel A. Otero wrote in his letters.[12] Congress and other elected officials of the US did not have any intention of banning peonage because it was completely misunderstood in the discourse of slavery and free labor. They justified keeping New Mexico, which was mostly Hispano, at bay for statehood given the "mongrel" actions of bondage or peonage. This was obviously a ruse that had racist underpinnings, as the US settler nation-state was not looking for equality for black or Native people. Lieutenant Philip St. George Cooke, accompanying General Stephen W. Kearny's expedition of conquest in August 1846, noted that "the great boon of American citizenship [is] thus thrust . . . upon eighty thousand mongrels who cannot read—who are almost heathens,—the great mass reared in real slavery, called peonism" (qtd. in Kiser 2014, 173).

This feudal system set the foundation for other modes of production to come. The capital invested in peons was minimal, and thus provided more leverage for the debt system based on the masters' provision of health care and clothing; the landowner also gave them small advances, which the peons could never pay off and were added to the debt incurred throughout their lives. Patrones did not own the peon's physical body as in slavery, only their labor; thus peons were valuable for their productive work and were not a commodity themselves. Kiser (2014) states, "Unlike most Southern slaves, peons did sometimes receive monetary compensation for their work, but their meager earning went toward satisfying the debt owed, and compounding interest ensured permanent bondage. Average adult male peons earned between $2 and $5 per month . . . Such stipends never came in the form of hard currency, but were instead applied directly toward the cost of food and clothing at the master's store" (175). The patrones inflated the prices of goods and, in this way, increased a peon's debt, holding them in bondage for a longer period. Peons in the Southwest could also be transferred, but usually in an open forum, as was the case with slavery.

In 1857, the New Mexico Territorial Supreme Court defined the ambiguous labor system of debt peonage as a class of "servants, menials, or domestics, 'bound' to some kind of 'service' for the payment of their debts due to their masters" (*Jaremillo*, 194). This ruling came after Mariana Jaremillo left her service to José de la Cruz Romero, a resident of the County of Bernalillo in New Mexico. Romero filed suit against Jaremillo because she owed him $51.75 at the time she left. At the time, The New Mexico Territorial Supreme Court was attempting to outline peonage in stricter terms. Even so, it remained a labor system trapped at the interstices of slavery and free labor. Slavery established a system of economic growth in North America, but debt peonage was not so clear in its form and function.

As stated earlier, debt peonage came out of vassalage from Spanish rule. The conditions of the peon in Mexico originated in the workings of the repartimentos. However, when José de la Cruz Romero sued Mariana Jaremillo for abandoning her work and service to him, owing the sum of $51.75 advanced to her, the court was unable to find any law creating and defining duties and rights or civil and domestic relations under the specific domination of "peon." The invariable rule was that the peon could discharge himself from service by the payment of his indebtedness to his master, and the master never supposed he had any right to refuse to receive his pay from his peon and still hold him in service. Interestingly, the language in this court case states that peons were "not any particular color, race, or caste of inhabitants," although the ruling reveals that they "generally had none or small amounts of property" (*Jaremillo* 1857, 194). The lower class of individuals the court case classified as peons were linked to a racialized population in the Southwest who were made up mostly of American Indians, mulattos, and mestizos.[13]

While New Mexico did not stand in for the entire Southwest, it became the focal point that set the foundational boundaries, definition, and legislation of debt peonage in the region. This 1857 case distinctly maps out the terms of debt peonage in the United States, and states that all free men and women, when no legal impediment existed, could enter into this type of contract. The only way a peon could leave his or her master during the time of service was mutual consent, injury or a similar reason, or if the master kept the peon's account in an ambiguous manner so that he or she could not understand him. As a side note, the court ruling stated that parents could not contract away the services of their children, except if this was agreed upon beforehand. This is the vaguest part of the ruling and, it seems, for good reason. If a peon died, usually from excessive punishment or malnutrition, his oldest son would usually be contracted to take the position of the deceased parent. This was not "legal" and was reserved for special contracts and circumstances, but it was a norm for many peon families.

After the 1857 court case outlining debt peonage for the US Federal Government, the arrangement became a mainstay in the United States until it was abolished in 1867, two years after the signing of the Thirteenth Amendment. However, many wealthy landowners in New Mexico did not follow the law that required them to emancipate their peons. And while this economic system was about labor control, there remained a gendered and sexualized component that has yet to be uncovered. The peripheral sexual and gendered condition of debt peonage consolidated labor control and race in nineteenth-century New Mexico.

While *Mariana Jaremillo v. Jose de la Cruz Romero* outlined the conditions of debt peonage, it was *Marcellina Bustamento v. Juana Analla* in the same year that mapped out the way sex and gender were central to its economic system. This case paved the way to interrogating the sexual economy of debt peonage, kinship ties within the institution, and the legality of bondage of a minor. Catalina Bustamento was a child born out of wedlock between a *patrón*, Carpio Bustamento, and his peon, Juana Analla. In the case, the judge stressed that Catalina was the illegitimate child of Carpio, but the power dynamics within the case that reveal the discomfort of pleasure and power were never questioned or examined. Bustamento's wife, Marcellina, took Analla to court because she claimed the child belonged to her and that she wanted to keep her in her care, in all probability to utilize her labor. When the judge asked Marcellina Bustamento if she planned to use the child as an indebted servant, she refused to respond, though she did state that Catalina had not been detained illegally and was there of her own free will, as a child. Bustamento stated repeatedly that Analla was a woman of "immoral habits and conduct, and unfit to have the care and custody of the said Catalina" (256). The judge, James J. Davenport, ruled that Catalina Bustamento had been illegally detained as a peon and told the court "that the biological mother, despite her marginalized social status as a peon, retained legal guardianship over her child and that neither the father nor the surrogate mother could claim the girl as a servant . . . Thus, Davenport granted protection to the bond between mother and child and in so doing rendered a stunning legal blow to a tradition of servitude and fictive kinship that had proliferated in the Southwest for over two centuries" (Kiser 2014, 182). Interestingly, the judge likely ruled for the girl to be returned to Analla not because of kinship and blood ties, but because Marcellina Bustemento did not respond to the allegations that she was holding the child in peonage and servitude.

While this decision in 1857 began to shed light on the sexual and gendered condition of debt peonage in the Southwest, the implementation of laws was slow-moving. These foundational cases for the present-day US Southwest were legitimized through New Mexico and exemplify how the meditating forces of economies, social formations, and cultural practices shape the Nuevomexicana body. How can we think about the cultural practices and production in New Mexico as seen through these historical cases? The resignification of the Nuevomexicana body and the issue of kinship in relation to sex, sexuality, and querencia is exemplified in the WPA stories from *Women's Tales from the New Mexico WPA: La Diabla a Pie.*

Two WPA stories filed in 1949 recall the nineteenth-century debt peonage system and are significant for this chapter. The first, "The Panic of 1862," is about the Perea family of Las Placitas, New Mexico. The constant threat of Texans raiding New Mexican *ranchos* due to the unresolvable border conflict between the two territories is at the forefront of this story. What is most interesting about it is the narrative about the peons who worked on the Perea rancho. It informs the reader, "A small army of natives at and around the town of Bernalillo were practically in bondage to Don José Leander Perea, head of the family" (1). The household had Native slaves and also peon workers in bondage. The narrative goes on, "In fact the room was a store, which supplied the needs of the Perea household, and at which every peon round about had a charge account. The peons lived in little adobe houses of their own, on land outside the Perea estates or in the native villages in the vicinity. What they earned was applied on their accounts at the Perea store. Eight dollars a month was standard wage for the men" (1). As the story lays out the conditions of the peons, we get a glimpse into how the family of a male peon is utilized. After the small town hears of the Texans raiding New Mexico, the Pereas all flee to Colorado and leave the peons to protect their ranchos. The peons help them with the packing of bags and the carriages. They also help barricade the house and are given orders as what to do when the Texans arrive: "The youths of the peons were left to guard the house and the adjoining property. They were to stick to their duties, no matter what" (3). Although it was illegal to use an indebted person in this way, this did not stop most New Mexicans who held peons.

As stated, if a debtor were to die without satisfying his debt, his wife and children were required to assume it. While the condition of debt peonage was not supposed to carry a hereditary element, it did nonetheless. The children in "Panic" guard the house as ordered. While the mother is not present in the story, it is her reproductive capacity that provides the labor force of those in bondage; her sexuality finances an economy from which she is removed. When the Perea family returns to New Mexico, the Don finds out that someone has stolen a fortune that he and his son buried in the middle of the rancho. They automatically blame the children for taking the treasure. "Without warning the youths left to guard the house were dragged into the fearsome presence of the Don José and his son Pedro. They were scared half to death" (4). While no one is ever found to be guilty, the children are still punished, and are forced to incriminate peons who were not even at the rancho, who are subsequently flogged.

The 1857 *Bustamento v. Analla* case underscores the economic relations of the territory that were tied to place and labor. It resignified the Nuevomexicana body politic by shifting how people understand the materiality and management of gender and sexuality in relation to sexual violence, production/reproduction, and proper femininity. The other WPA story, "Mateo y Raquel," tells about a man named José María who was also held in bondage by

Don José Leander Perea. His debt was left to José María by his father and would be carried on by his son, Mateo. Here again, we see the reproductive capacity of the peon's wife, even if she is not in bondage with her husband. The story states that José María received five dollars a month, an average of about sixteen and two-thirds cents a day, with no days off because he was a sheepherder. (The other ranch hand had Sundays off if there was no urgent work.) Food was provided to the family but was minimal and just enough to keep them going. The "debt" to the store of the patrón was what kept the institution of debt peonage going, because it was the law that the peons purchase whatever they needed from the patrón. The story reads, "It was the privalege [sic] and the custom of the rich dons to see to it that such [debt] grew rather than diminished. The law was on the side of the rich dons, in fact, they were the law unto themselves. They must have the labor of the poorer class (los peones) and they laid down all the rules of the game" (1).

As the story progresses, José María goes in late to work and is flogged and beaten by the patrón. He cannot take the conditions of his bondage any longer and escapes. He "knew all about his debt to his patron and how his patron held money far above the life of any peon" (3). When he is captured and sentenced to hang, his son, seventeen-year-old Mateo, takes his place in the fields. It is 1836. By the time of the American invasion in 1848, the institution of debt peonage was so embedded in the Southwest it would take another twenty-one years for the peons to see their freedom.

While Mateo is at work acquiring more debt, it is his wife, Raquel, who becomes the center of the story, as she raises their family, clothes them, teaches them, and raises goats for their sustenance. Mateo cannot do anything but work for the patrón and use his labor to build the landowners' rancho and provide the animals he trades and sells. Raquel is the one producing and reproducing for not only her own family, but the family of Mateo's patrón, even though she is not an indebted peon. Interestingly enough, the metonymic meaning of the archive rests in the symbolic meaning of the goats that Raquel maintains to keep the family alive: in addition to production and survival, with their fertility, vitality, and ceaseless energy, they represent Raquel's dual capacity and reproductive labor. The generative power of the representation and symbol of the goat speaks to the abundance and duality of Raquel's positionality within New Mexico and the utilization of her racialized gender and sexuality. While Mateo's five dollars a month is applied to his store credit, Raquel keeps her family alive with goatskin clothing and bedding and goat's milk and meat. Her productive labor produces a livable situation for her family. She makes use of her labor to sustain her children and husband and her reproductive capacity to reproduce the free labor force of peons.

The productive capacity of racialized sexuality is utilized as an exploitative tool. Marxist feminist Leopoldina Fortunati attempts to unpack reproductive labor as she examines the transition from precapitalism to capitalism. Like Fortunati, I am thinking about an older economic form, debt peonage, and the reproductive labor capacity inherent to it that constructs the sexual economy constitutive of the emergence of capitalism, while acknowledging that it is a precapitalist condition. However, the institution of debt peonage and the rancho and hacienda system of land grants were involved in capitalist accumulation as well. How, then, do we think about the condition of racialized lower-class women like Raquel within the institution of debt peonage?

Fortunati (1995) argues that the aim within specific communities through the previous modes of production was the reproduction of individuals and the production of use-value (2). The aim was the production of exchange value, that is, the creation of value for value. Fortunati takes a close look at where production appears "as the creation of value [while] reproduction appears as the creation of nonvalue . . . posited as natural production" (2). In an attempt to expand upon Marx and rethink female reproduction, she thinks through how the reproduction of individuals implies the reproduction of labor power because bodies have exchange values only and cannot create value for themselves. Thus, bodies can only "present themselves in relation to their capacity to produce" and are offered as a "commodity by [the person in] exchange for [the body's] exchange-value" (5). Debt peonage, while a residual mode of the economy, reproduces the conditions for capitalism and exists within it simultaneously. This allows us to rethink Fortunati's critique of Marx's production by remapping how a mestiza within debt peonage (whether a peon or a wife to a peon) had a dual characteristic through not only her gendered, racialized labor, but her racialized sexuality and reproductive function.

The peon was not a commodity, but occupied a unique position where he earned a low wage but never saw it, as it went directly toward his bill at the store of the patrón, who moderately clothes and feeds him. Raquel's reproductive capacity, as the wife of a peon, yields economic profit for the patrón by producing children who will become peons. Even though it is illegal to force the children into bondage after their parents are dead or cannot work, reality tells a different story. As the story comes to a close, "Mateo became very ill.

He could not work. His pay was cut off and he was told to get out. And as all the curandera's yerbas failed to cure him he was ordered to send his son Juan to take his place and assume the just debt to the patrón, and likewise add to the account at the store" (8). As Mateo's body becomes literally useless while his livelihood depends on it, Raquel maintains the familial structure by having more children to take her husband's place. The sexualized and gendered economic status of mestiza women within a system of debt peonage before and after 1848 produced much of the workforce in the Southwest.

The tension in these two narratives reveals and then attempts to hide the inherent contradictions in Nuevomexicana female subjectivity and the economic systems that revolve around the historical conditions of racialized gender and sexuality. The juxtaposition of the elite landholding Hispanas with the mestiza peons exemplifies a rich history of social, economic, and political entanglements that were constructed by Spanish colonialism and sustained by US imperialism. The dual function of racialized gender and sexuality informed by the sexual economy of the contemporary Southwest is always in contention and relation to the elite landholding Mexican American women who later become dispossessed by the US empire. The collision of the romanticized and factual past of New Mexico comments not only on the changing place, dispossession, and displacement of Nuevomexicanas, but also on gender and sexual norms in the racialized labor systems of the past. To be a poor, racialized woman in the territory of New Mexico signified "womanhood" differently because of her position within power, the domestic space, and economies of the Southwest. However, she was and still remains the pillar of her family.

NOTES

1. "Hispanas," "New Mexicans," "Nuevomexicanas," and, later, "Mexican Americans" are all terms used to describe the people of New Mexico who occupied (genealogical) spaces during Spanish colonialism, Mexican rule, and finally US Empire. For the purposes of this chapter, I will be utilizing "Nuevomexicana" because in the nineteenth century "Hispana" was a term reserved for elite landholding New Mexican women and New Mexico was still a territory, so "Mexican American" does not apply.

2. Annette Hesch Thorp and Lou Sage Batchen were both long-term residents of New Mexico when they started collecting stories for the WPA. Neither woman was fluent in Spanish and both used translators; however, as Tey Diana Rebolledo (2000) points out, neither collector nor translator shaped the final version of the narratives.

3. Maylei Blackwell coins the term "retrofitted memory" in *Chicana Power: Contested Histories of Feminism in the Chicano Movement*.

4. Marx, *Capital* (1867).

5. Davis 2002.

6. The militaristic codes of law during slavery made the black female an "owned" body incapable of claiming rape by a master.

7. See Spillers 2002, where she discusses the structures of colonial violence such as slavery that was perpetuated on Black females whose gender was not considered, only the quantity and the reproductive value of her body.

8. I am utilizing Jennifer Morgan and Kristen Fischer's definition of sex in the colonies in "Sex, Race, and the Colonial Project."

9. I am speaking of colonial rule under Spain and Northern Mexican governance in what is now the US Southwest. Shelley Streeby (2002) states, "Although "Southern [Mexican] plantations" were the "great bastions" of classic, coercive debt peonage, "traditional peonage, in which the worker was not necessarily tied to the hacienda by extra economic coercion and in which debt did not always function as a bond, was more common, especially in Northern Mexico" (193).

10. *Repartimientos* involved the Spanish crown distributing Native labor so they could regulate labor relations more specifically. *Encomiendas* were the granting of land and the use of the people on it by the Spanish crown; this was formally abolished in 1730 but was ineffective much earlier.

11. The old order under Mexican governance abolished Black slavery in 1834, but not Native slavery.

12. See Miguel A. Otero's letter to the editor printed on January 12, 1861 in the *Santa Fe Weekly Gazette*.

13. Martha Menchaca states in her book *Recovering History, Constructing Race: The Indian, Black, and White Roots of Mexican Americans* (2010), "Though by law the *criollo* racial category was reserved for whites, it was common for parish priests to register *mestizo* children of means as *criollo* by including in the baptismal registry only the race of the father" (65).

WORKS CITED

Blackwell, Maylei. 2011. *Chicana Power!: Contested Histories of Feminism in the Chicano Movement*. Austin: University of Texas Press.

Davis, Adrienne. 2002. "'Don't Let Nobody Bother Yo' Principle': The Sexual Economy of American Slavery." In *Sister Circle: Black Women and Work*, edited by Sharon Harley, 103–27. New Brunswick, NJ: Rutgers University Press.

Fortunati, Leopoldina, and Jim Fleming. 1995. *The Arcane of Reproduction: Housework, Prostitution, Labor and Capital.* Brooklyn, NY: Autonomedia.

Kiser, William S. 2014. "A 'charming name for a species of slavery': Political Debate on Debt Peonage in the Southwest, 1840s–1860s." *Western Historical Quarterly* 45, no. 2: 169–89.

Klein, Kerwin Lee. 2000. "On the Emergence of Memory in Historical Discourse." *Representations* 69 (Winter): 127–50.

Knight, Alan. 1986. "Mexican Peonage: What Was It and Why Was It?" *Journal of Latin American Studies* 18, no. 1: 41–74.

Marcellina Bustamento v. Juana Analla. 1857 [1911]. In *Reports of Cases Argued and Determined in the Supreme Court of the Territory of New Mexico, January Term 1852 to January Term, 1879.* Vol. 1, edited by Charles Gildersleeve, 255–62. Chicago: Callaghan & Co.

Mariana Jaremillo v. José de la Cruz Romero. 1857 [1911]. In *Reports of Cases Argued and Determined in the Supreme Court of the Territory of New Mexico, January Term 1852 to January Term, 1879.* Vol 1, edited by Charles Gildersleeve, 190–208. Chicago: Callaghan & Co.

Marx, Karl. 1992 [1867]. *Capital: Critique of Political Economy,* Vol. 1. London: Penguin.

"Mateo y Raquel." 2000 [1949]. In *Women's Tales from the New Mexico WPA: La Diabla a Pie,* edited by Tey Diana Rebolledo and María Teresa Márquez, 358–64. Houston: Arte Público Press.

Menchaca, Martha. 2010. *Recovering History, Constructing Race: The Indian, Black, and White Roots of Mexican Americans.* Austin: University of Texas Press.

Morgan, Jennifer, and Kirsten Fischer. 2003. "Sex, Race, and the Colonial Project." *Sexuality in Early America. The William and Mary Quarterly* 60, no. 1, third series: 197–98.

Otero, Miguel. 1861. "Letter to the Editor." *Santa Fe Weekly Gazette.* January 12, 1861.

"The Panic of 1862." 2000 [1949]. In *Women's Tales from the New Mexico WPA: La Diabla a Pie,* edited by Tey Diana Rebolledo and María Teresa Márquez, 396–491. Houston: Arte Público Press.

Rebolledo, Tey Diana. . 2000. "Introduction: The Federal Writers Project." In *Women's Tales from the New Mexico WPA: La Diabla a Pie,* edited by Tey Diana Rebolledo and María Teresa Márquez, xix–liv. Houston: Arte Público Press.

———. 2002. "Las Hijas de la Malinche: Mexicana/India Captivity Narratives in the Southwest, Subverting Voices." In *Nuevomexicano Cultural Legacy: Forms, Agencies & Discourse,* edited by Francisco A. Lomelí, Víctor A. Sorell, and Genaro M. Padilla, 129–50. Albuquerque: University of New Mexico Press.

Scott, Joan. 1991. "The Evidence of Experience." *Questions of Evidence: Proof, Practice, and Persuasion across the Disciplines,* edited by James K. Chandler,

Arnold I. Davidson, and Harry D. Harootunian, 363–87. Chicago: University of Chicago Press.

Spillers, Hortense J. 2002. "Mama's Baby, Papa's Maybe: An American Grammar Book." In *Black, White, and in Color: Essays on American Literature and Culture*, 203–29. Chicago: University of Chicago Press.

Streeby, Shelley. 2002. *American Sensations: Class, Empire, and the Production of Popular Culture*. Berkeley: University of California Press.

Weber, David J. 1982. *The Mexican Frontier, 1821–1846: The American Southwest under Mexico*. Albuquerque: University of New Mexico Press.

CHAPTER EIGHT

Erasing Querencia from Los Alamos

Racist and Sexualized Portrayals of New Mexican
Women and Place in the Television Series *Manhattan*

MYRRIAH GÓMEZ

In the series premiere of the WGN America television series *Manhattan*, Liza
Winter, botanist and wife of physicist Frank Winter, attempts to decorate her
yard for a party. Trying to hide her frustration with the wind, she sarcastically
tells her Tewa maid, "There's no place like home."[1] The maid shakes her head
and responds in Spanish: "*Lo siento*" (I'm sorry). In this scene, Liza mocks
Los Alamos, New Mexico, as a suitable place for Manhattan Project newcomers, the people who lived atop the Pajarito Plateau during the early 1940s
after local residents were displaced from their farms and had their access to
ceremonial sites revoked. Despite the description of the show by *Manhattan*'s
writers as a "true-life science fiction story" (VanDerWerff 2015), viewers get
two seasons of White outsiders complaining about the desolate landscape
as Los Alamos transforms into a militarized scientific space. This chapter
interrogates the roles of fictional Native American female characters in *Manhattan* and compares them to real New Mexican women who worked on the
Manhattan Project. Using New Mexico scholar Juan Estevan Arellano's definition of *querencia*, I contend that the television series threatens querencia by
portraying native New Mexican women in racist, sexualized ways and erasing
their voices and histories from the telling of the Manhattan Project story.

Arellano (1997) discusses bioregionalism, or our basic understanding of
place, "the immediate specific place where we live"[2] in the context of how the
Los Alamos National Laboratory has transformed the way New Mexicans
view place. Since its inception in 1942, when Los Alamos was condemned
to become Site Y of the Manhattan Project, the laboratory has represented
an ominous place in northern New Mexico spatial poetics. Arellano writes:
"What is happening in Los Alamos today began with memory, but we are on
the verge of losing our memory. If we lose our language, we will lose most of

our environmental history. Never! Our memory has now assumed the form of the landscape itself. This is the essence of Querencia, if we lose either memory or landscape, we lose both" (32). He places bioregionalism, the understanding of the place we live, in direct conversation with another term: querencia, which he describes as "that which gives us a sense of place, anchors us to the land, and makes us a unique people" (35). He tells us that the intimate understanding of environmental history that New Mexicans have of Los Alamos is associated almost entirely with memory. *Manhattan* threatens that memory by offering a fictional and inaccurate representation of the roles of local laborers in Los Alamos during the Manhattan Project and places under erasure Nuevomexicanas/os'[3] and Native Americans' relationship to the space and landscape of Los Alamos.

The erasure of querencia is prominent in *Manhattan*. The series begins in 1943, with military and civilian employees (mostly scientists) and their families arriving at the gates of Los Alamos to start a secret project. It ends in 1945 at the Trinity Test, when Manhattan Project scientists exploded the nuclear device, nicknamed "Gadget," between Alamogordo and Socorro, New Mexico. Everything that occurs in the show between arrival and detonation is based loosely on what actually happened on the Hill.

In an article published in *Popular Mechanics* magazine, "What *Manhattan* Gets Right, and Wrong, about Los Alamos," Andrew Han writes, "In real life, Los Alamos was kind of a dumpy camp and the government really didn't want people to know it was there. The town, partially selected for its remoteness, was built on the site of a boys' ranch school 40 miles from Santa Fe. Secrecy was paramount and the project went to great lengths to prevent the release of information." It frustrates me to admit that Han is right about the perception of Los Alamos, but his statement is incorrect in the sense that it is evasive. It is true that the federal government created a makeshift city that many transplants viewed as a "dumpy camp." The pipes froze during the winter, and the roads were so muddy that, at times, cars were stuck for days. The town was selected partially for its remoteness, but it met no other stipulations to be the ideal location for Site Y other than having access to a reasonable labor force. The original buildings were remnants of the Los Alamos Ranch School (LARS), an elite school for boys, but LARS was not the only entity that occupied space on the Hill at the time of condemnation. In fact, more than thirty Nuevomexicano farming families were displaced from their properties there when the US Army removed them; some removals were conducted violently.

Additionally, much of the land condemned by the Manhattan Engineering District for the Manhattan Project was sacred to local tribes, including the Pueblos of San Ildefonso and Santa Clara. Historiographies of the Manhattan Project and Site Y, in particular, fail to acknowledge Nuevomexicana/o and Pueblo presence in Los Alamos or the people's relationship to the land. Both historiographies of Los Alamos and pop cultural representations, including *Manhattan*, place querencia under erasure.

MANH(A)TTAN: THE FICTIONAL PORTRAYAL OF SITE Y OF THE MANHATTAN PROJECT

The central theme in this television series is not the making of the atomic bomb, although that is an important storyline. The premise is a fictional depiction of daily life in Los Alamos between 1943 and 1945 of the Manhattan Project, complete with nuclear secrets, extramarital affairs, and murder. The central message of the show is that military personnel and scientists and their families, many of whom became civilian workers, were cloistered on the Hill for two years while scientists built the bomb(s). They could leave the Hill with a day pass only to Santa Fe, but even that was difficult to obtain. The only people allowed to come and go from the Hill, in real life and in the series, were the local day laborers, who were primarily Nuevomexicana/o and Indigenous; however, male laborers are completely erased from the historical narrative in the series, and female laborers are depicted as unintelligent (and sometimes unintelligible) "Indian maids." In other words, *Manhattan* presents Los Alamos as a secret city surrounded by an Indian reservation, which fails to address the complicated land tenure of various neighboring Pueblos and Nuevomexicano communities. The show does not acknowledge the presence of the Spanish-speaking Nuevomexicanas/os who lived in nearby villages. Interestingly, most of the Pueblo women in the show speak Spanish, not Tewa, but the reason for that is unclear to viewers.[4] Thus, the show creates a fictional storyline about scientist and civilian life in Los Alamos behind the fence—people who despised their surroundings and complained about the "godforsaken" place where they had been coerced to live to serve their country and bring an end to the war.

Straying from traditional historiographies, biographies, and memoirs of Los Alamos that attempt to portray events there exactly as they occurred, *Manhattan* deviates from historical accuracy. The ever-growing body of work on Los Alamos[5] often focuses on the scientific aspect of the project and fails to acknowledge civilian personnel other than the scientists who also worked there at this time. Creator and executive producer Sam Shaw attempts to address the lacuna with this show. He states:

> But what really interested me as I got to get more and more immersed in the
> subject matter was the experience of all of these other thousands of people in
> this secret town whose stories I hadn't really seen before. And a lot of them,
> for me, were people who were marginalized in the official histories. I was really
> interested by the question of what it was to be a spouse in this town. What
> it was to be uprooted from your life and dragged to this mysterious, secret
> city on top of a dead volcano, surrounded by barbed wire fences, and not have
> your partner be able to tell you what it is he's working on at the end of the
> day when he comes home. The kind of story that we wanted to tell certainly
> involves the history and involves the science, but ultimately isn't a docudrama
> and certainly not a technical history of the development of the bomb, fasci-
> nating as that is. It attempts to be a character story about the inner lives of
> this ensemble cast. From the very beginning, the approach was to populate
> this carefully researched, historically accurate world with fictional characters.
> (VanDerWerff 2015)

In doing so, Shaw creates a storyline that attempts to portray a fascinating life inside the fences of Los Alamos. It certainly involves the development of the bomb but focuses on the "inner lives" of the characters. One problem remains: the civilian characters continue to be scientists and their wives and children, the people who were "dragged to" Los Alamos. Spanish-speaking Nuevomex-icanas/os are erased entirely from Los Alamos in this show, with the excep-tion of one Nuevomexicano who tries to rape the wife of a lead scientist at a party. While "Indian maids" do appear in *Manhattan*, they are sexualized as deviant or stereotyped as dumb. Native American men also make appearances as middlemen between one maid, Paloma, and her employer, Frank. In this way, they are depicted as savages who connive a head scientist into trading a car to keep his extramarital affair a secret. Put plainly, the depiction of local Nuevomexicanos and Native Americans in the show is racist.

Manhattan begins with the main characters arriving in Los Alamos for a secret government project. Two teams have been created on "the Hill": the implosion team and the gun-model team. The implosion team includes Dr. Frank Winter, the leader; Dr. Sidney "Sid" Liao, who is killed after being set up by Frank; Dr. Helen Prins, the only woman scientist on the Hill; Paul Crosley, an aspiring British scientist; Jim Meeks, who is involved with Soviet spies; and Louis "Fritz" Fedowitz, a goofy scientist who accidently ingests plutonium. Frank Winter moves to Los Alamos with his wife, botanist Dr. Liza Winter, and their daughter, Callie, who detests the place more than any other character in the show. Liza is unable to conduct her research in Los Alamos but ultimately finds a role in the Project when she begins to research the effects of radiation on humans and plants. The second team—the designers of Thin Man, a plutonium gun-type nuclear bomb—is led by Dr. Reed Akley until he commits suicide. One member of his team, Dr. Charlie Isaacs, comes to the Hill with his wife Abby, arguably the show's most complex character, and their toddler son. Other characters emerge around the major players, including Robert Oppenheimer, depicted as a cheating husband and a brooding scientist. Finally, there are the "Indian maids," including Paloma, the Tewa maid who works for the Winters. Only one other Tewa maid, Mrs. Ortiz, is called by her name.

PALOMA: THE "INDIAN MAID" AND FRANK WINTER'S MISTRESS

Paloma, played by Tailinh Agoyo, whose roots are Blackfeet and Narragansett (Klein 2015), appears sparingly throughout the first eight episodes of Season 1. We first see her in Episode 1 helping Liza Winter hang sheets. Liza tells Paloma (whose name we do not learn until Episode 6), "There's no place like home. How many drunken physicists do you think we can cram into that shack?" Paloma responds to her: "Lo siento."[6] At this point in the show, and really until Episode 6, it is not clear whether Paloma is Tewa or Nuevomexicana.[7] She speaks Spanish, and she is dressed in a cotton dress with a floral pattern. Her dark hair is pulled back into a low bun, and she wears coral-and-turquoise earrings that are beaded into teardrops.

Dwanna L. Robertson (2015) writes, "Oppressors must transform into victims whose actions are portrayed as brave and necessary. Racial discourse accomplishes both of these goals. Indigenous Peoples become othered as heathens, savages, or beastlike beings that are incapable and inferior and, therefore, easily forgotten." (124). Just as the Native American men in this show are depicted as savages, Paloma is depicted as a beastlike being, both incapable and inferior, whereas Frank Winter is portrayed as a victim whose actions are brave and necessary. At the end of Episode 1, Paloma sits next to him in his car. Frank starts his final monologue by saying, "There's something I need to tell you." He goes on to describe the atomic bomb project in which he is engaged. He describes the bomb as "the endgame," suggesting that the US must build the weapon before any other country. After his very long description of both the project and the bomb, he ends by saying that the work must be completed at "whatever cost." When he says this, he looks over at Paloma in the passenger seat. She shakes her head and struggles to find a response. Finally, she says, "No inglés." She caresses Frank's shoulder and strokes his face. She turns to open the car door and glances back at him once before stepping out. She walks to the door of her adobe house; which viewers can see illuminated by the car's headlights through the windshield. Again, she glances back at Frank, who is smoking a cigarette, before she opens the door, enters the small home, and shuts the door behind her. Frank takes another drag of his cigarette before extinguishing it. He turns off the headlights and gets out of the car. The episode ends as Frank shuts the door and walks toward Paloma's house.

Despite the language barrier and their inability to effectively communicate verbally, Frank is having an affair with Paloma, and the audience learns this quickly. Frank's monologue at the end of Episode 1 in which he states his task to build the bomb at "whatever cost" includes the opportunity to cheat on his wife. The audience learns throughout the show that it is common for other scientists and their spouses to cheat on each other. Charlie and Helen have an affair, Abby and Elodie[8] have an affair, and Oppenheimer has an affair, not to mention the other unscrupulous amounts of sex on the Hill, including by members of the Women's Army Corps (WACS) who prostitute themselves out to scientists and male soldiers. Several things make Frank and Paloma's affair different than the others, primarily that Paloma becomes the foreshadowing tool for the show's writers and director to convey information about the bomb project without involving other characters. She is Frank's sounding board. She is inconsequential, or at least there are no immediate consequences for Frank telling Paloma secrets that he cannot tell Liza. In fact, Paloma, the Spanish-speaking Indian maid who lives in a one-room mud house, is a perfect foil for Liza, the PhD who is hospitalized after her mental-health breakdown in Los Alamos after trying to busy herself with meaningful work. Frank is safe with Paloma, but Paloma is not safe with Frank. As viewers learn in Episode 5, a G2 military intelligence agent is spying on the affair.

He returns in Episode 8 to threaten Paloma and her family. Because of this threat, she is forced to stop working for the Winters and leave her job as a day laborer in Los Alamos. She is easily forgotten. Her disappearance is initiated in Episode 5.

Episode 5 foreshadows the final episode of the series, in which Frank uses his radio skills to break into the tower at the Trinity site in an attempt to stop Meeks, who is working with the Soviet spies, from destroying the test. Toward the end of Episode 5, Frank arrives at Paloma's house with a radio wrapped nicely in brown paper—a present. He tells her, though she never indicates that she understands, that he used to work at a repair shop where he worked on radios. This information foreshadows the final episode of the series; it is how viewers know that Frank has infiltrated the Trinity communication system. After plugging the radio into the wall at Paloma's house—because apparently her old, one-room adobe home has electricity[9]—Frank switches the radio on and walks over to Paloma, who is sitting on the bed. She reaches up and strokes his chest. He takes her hand and embraces it between his own hands. The scene shifts to the spy sitting in a car outside the house. When the scene flips back inside, a fire burns in the fireplace and candles flicker atop the bedside sconce. Frank is sitting upright on the side of the bed wearing an undershirt and boxer shorts. Paloma sits up, entirely naked, and places her arms around Frank's neck. The glow of the fire and the shadows blocks everything but the outline of Paloma's dark, naked skin. Here Paloma is sexualized, but she also becomes the enemy. Viewers are expected to hate her for seducing Frank Winter away from Liza, the only wife of any of the scientists who treats the local women somewhat decently as well as being an intelligent woman herself.

The other scientists' wives in Los Alamos are condescending, cruel, and racist to the maids, all of whom are depicted as Native American. In Episode 4, four wives sit in a living room while their maids give them manicures and pedicures. One Native American maid sits on the floor and another sits on an ottoman giving two of the wives pedicures; both wives have drinks in their hands. The first wife says, "No, no, no. First you shape the nails, then you soak, or they'll get too soft. Shape. Then soak. Understand?" She looks beyond the maid at her friend sitting next to her, who says, "Gosh, ten thousand years in this country and they still don't speak the language."[10] But the maids do speak English in the series, as they did in real life. During season two, one of the maids, whose first name we do not know but whose last name is Ortiz, is working at one of the scientists' houses. While she vacuums, two women sit at the kitchen table talking about spies on the Hill. One wife says, "Speaking of Indians, what's your girl doing to the Hoover?" to which the other responds, "I dunno. Praying to it? She probably thinks it's a god."[11] The racism is not meant to be indicative of the real racism that women experienced on the Hill. Rather, it is intended to be ironic and funny, especially in this scene. As Robertson says, Indigenous people "become heathens," and that is how the Native American women are portrayed in this show.

Manhattan's characters, especially the racist wives, are unaware of the relationship that the locals had with Los Alamos before they intruded. The maid referenced above, Mrs. Ortiz, did not think the vacuum was a god. Instead, her people had found Los Alamos to be an important spiritual site for them. Arellano (2007) would define their feelings for the space as querencia: "A place where one feels safe, a place from which one's strength of character is drawn, where one feels at home. Even the bull in the bullring prefers a certain place within the plaza where he fixates his gaze and to which he will retreat once he is wounded to rest and feel safe" (50). But in *Manhattan*, with the racist wives and predatory men like Frank Winter, Los Alamos is no longer sacred and no longer safe.

The manner in which the wives disrespect their maids throughout *Manhattan* is consistent with representations made by other outsiders during that time. Bernice Brode was the wife of Robert Brode, a physicist at Site Y of the Manhattan Project. Her recollection of the maids in her memoir, *Tales of Los Alamos: Life on the Mesa 1943–1945* (2007) might have served as a reference for *Manhattan*. She writes, "Things like vacuum cleaners defeated [the maids], but they understood linoleum floors and our Black Beauty stoves and made them shine. They talked little, although most of the Indians knew three languages—English, Spanish, and their native Tewa. What they thought of our strange town, or our houses—many of them with Indian rugs, pottery and paintings—we shall never know" (52–53). Brode and others downplay the work of the Native American women who worked in Los Alamos. They did not understand Native American culture, and many of her comments about the local Indigenous population suggest that their Native neighbors performed for the Anglos' entertainment. She was disconnected from the relationship that Indigenous people historically had with Los Alamos. She writes, "I think the Indians, especially, loved their daily trips to this other world" (54). But it was the Anglo newcomers who did not understand the world of the native New Mexicans. For this reason, they inaccurately recorded history without using the opinions or feelings of local people.

REAL WOMEN LABORERS IN LOS ALAMOS

Beginning in 1942, local women were incorporated as part of the labor force at Site Y. They were recruited as housekeepers and caregivers for the scientists and their families. It became difficult to negotiate the pride they took in their jobs and the realization that they were doing menial labor. Because they were satisfied with having employment in Los Alamos, they did not attempt to challenge existing power structures. Some scholars have recognized the contributions of women to the Manhattan Project, but most of these studies[12] recognize women who migrated to Los Alamos for this purpose, neglecting the local women who worked at Site Y. In real life, both Native American and Nuevomexicana women worked on the Hill. Some were day laborers while others lived on the Hill, sometimes with scientists' families.[13] In her 2015 interview with nuclear historian Alex Wellerstein and physicist David Saltzberg on "Getting History and Science Right on 'Manhattan,'" Robin Burks states, "A common misconception about the Manhattan Project is the idea that it was solely helmed by men. Other fictional depictions of Los Alamos have either shown only men working, or women just as secretaries and the like." In the same article, Wellerstein acknowledges that women filled "very important roles" but admits that not many people today are aware of how many women worked on the project. He says, "Women played very, very key roles and, unfortunately, because of the way people like to tell these stories about science in the 1940s, they get written out of the story" (Burks 2015). But even the studies that recognize women in the Manhattan Project and Site Y blatantly dismiss the local women who worked on the Hill.

Local women worked as maids in two different capacities: Indigenous women often worked as day laborers and Nuevomexicanas as live-in maids. I offer the statements from one Santa Clara woman and two Nuevomexicanas to illuminate the discussion of how local women actually performed work in Los Alamos, which proves contrary to the racist and sexualized depiction of maids in *Manhattan*.

Florence Singer was approximately thirty-three years old when she began working in Los Alamos as a maid around 1945. The idea to work there was recommended to her by another Santa Clara woman, Cristina Naranjo, who worked with Singer's mother making pottery. Singer recalls Naranjo telling her to go work in "Alamo," because "that's how they used to just say Alamo" for Los Alamos. Pueblo women stood on the side of the road and waited for someone to pick them up. Naranjo had told Singer to tell the person at the gate that she was "going to where the ladies work" (Singer 1992b). Singer remembers that once there, she was assigned to different houses. The women worked a half-day in one house and a half-day at another; that was how it worked every day, and every day they worked in different homes. During her time as a maid, she worked for the Bradburys, the Oppenheimers, and the Tellers, among others. In her interview with Theresa Strottman, Singer mentions repeatedly that she and other Native American women were assigned to different homes every day, and that they did not "go to these houses every day or stay steady with them," which contradicts the nature of Paloma's relationship with the Winter family in *Manhattan*.

Recalling her treatment by the Los Alamos wives, Singer clearly remembered being paid a dollar and a half for each half-day's work, which, she says, was enough to buy groceries. The day would start with coffee at the kitchen table with the woman of the house. Then Singer would ask the woman, "Where do you want me to start?" (1992b). She recounts an interaction with the Divens family, whose son David once asked his mother if she "was sure Florence was an Indian." When his mother assured him that she was, he asked: "Well, where are her feathers? Where are her feathers, then? She don't have feathers" (1992b). That is how she recalls becoming a regular employee for the Divens family.

Racism was strewn into the daily interactions between Pueblo women and Manhattan Project families in ways that might be considered microaggressions today; however, contrary to the mistreatment that Paloma and others experience in *Manhattan*, Singer remembers being treated kindly by most of the people on the Hill. She says, "Some, you could just go right to their door. You'd just know what kind of people they are. They greet you. They tell you, 'Come on in.' Just real nice. Others you can tell as soon as you get to the door that maybe you wouldn't like them. I'm sorry to say that, but there's, there were not too many like that. But people, you find, you know, different kind of people. But anyhow, I enjoyed working up here" (1992b). In this interview, Singer does note one family with whom she had problems, but she never returned to work for them after they treated her badly.

She does recall, however, other racist experiences on the Hill. Once, two children were following an Ohkay Owingeh woman who was walking down the street. They "kept saying everything to her" including, "Oh, you dirty Indian." Singer turns the remark around by telling her interviewer with a laugh, "Sure we know we are Indians, but I don't know which way we're dirty or what" (Singer 1992a). She counters that racist remark by explaining how some of the families on the Hill were dirty—including the family with whom she had problems—and relied on her and the other maids to clean their homes for them.

Another significant point regarding Florence Singer is that she was a fluent English speaker and went on to become a bilingual teacher. In an interview with Dohn Chapman,[14] Singer explains where she learned English. She says:

> I went to school to learn English. I didn't know a word of English and where I went to school at the Indian School in Santa Fe, they were strict. They were strict with us. They would get after us, they would punish us if we were talking Indian. We had to learn to Speak English. We'd be punished for every little thing if we spoke Indian. No way but what we had to learn English. After I finished Santa Fe, I went to Albuquerque to school and that was another place, too, that was strict. Of course, we already knew then how to speak English a little (Singer 1992a).

Nevertheless, she endured "punishment" for "talking in Indian" throughout her process of learning English. After boarding school, she spent time working in Ignacio, Colorado, where she improved her English because no one else there spoke Tewa. Singer's experience of what was probably corporal punishment for speaking her native Tewa at the boarding schools might have made her life in Los Alamos easier, but the point that she was mistreated for speaking her Native language is a reality. Not speaking English is mocked in *Manhattan*.

Native American women hitched rides to Los Alamos every day until the later years, when a bus was contracted. Nuevomexicanas' service functioned somewhat differently. Many of them worked as live-in maids. This experience is completely erased from *Manhattan* in favor of an exotic Native American maid. During an interview with Theresa Strottman, Nuevomexicana Frances Gómez Quintana says, "I was born and raised in El Rancho, but my education was very limited. If education were only based on books, mine was limited due to an ill mother and being left with the responsibility to raise and educate my brothers and sisters. My education did not end but began with extensive regard in childcare experience . . . [This] has been my wealth of education" (Quintana 1992). Education for Nuevomexicanas at that historical moment in El Rancho depended largely on the family and the collective community. Family life was the only way of life. Whether it was caring for younger siblings or helping in the fields, knowledge was embodied by the familial duties that a woman performed.

Ironically, when Quintana went to work on the Hill, her entire ontology shifted. When asked if she united with her sisters, who also worked on the Hill, she responded: "No, most of the time we were all working. Even though both sisters lived up here, like Lydia lived with the Gordons and Viola lived with J. A. D. Muncy who was a business manager for the Lab. She took care of children there in the evenings, too, so we didn't have very much free time. When I had free time, I'd go and clean house for Mrs. Wilson who was a schoolteacher. And Peggy Felt was a schoolteacher. I'd help them in the evenings wash dishes or clean house or that's what I used to do." Quintana emphasizes that two of the women whose houses she cleaned were schoolteachers. And whereas she answers the earlier question about her education being restricted to childcare experience, she views education differently than she had before, as now schoolteachers symbolize education, but her relationship to them was as their housekeeper. When asked if Los Alamos altered her life in any way, she responded: "Yes it did. It was very educational. I learned a lot from people, I met a lot of good friends and I've had them for many years now." Quintana's definition of education changed again once she was employed in the mailroom at the Laboratory. For Nuevomexicanas, educational opportunities such as these allowed them upward mobility, even if they remained at the bottom of the hierarchy in the Los Alamos social structure.

Quintana's sister, Lydia Gómez-Martínez, began working in Los Alamos as a babysitter, but by the time she was in high school she was doing technical work. She tells an interviewer (1991) that during Christmas vacation and in the summer, she worked for the X division, which was and still is the weapons division. In fact, she worked on making weapons and worked with weapons parts in 1943. She says, "When I worked at x7, we knew we were working with detonators, so we knew it was a weapon. We just never spoke to anyone about what we were doing 'cause it was highly classified."

Gómez-Martínez's parents would not allow her to stay in the dormitories available for Site Y employees, so she lived with a Carl Gordon and his family. After high school, she left her home community of El Rancho to attend

York College in Nebraska, but she eventually returned and continued to work for x7. She explains, "Well, we worked with detonators and I did a lot of inspecting. I worked at a microscope all day where I inspected those parts to make sure the diameter was the right diameter." However, in this interview, conducted by Theresa Strottman in 1991, Strottman was not concerned with the type of technical work accomplished by Gómez-Martínez; rather, she was curious about her interaction with people in Los Alamos. Whereas we could have learned a significant amount of information from Gómez-Martínez about the type of technical work accomplished by Nuevomexicanas, we learn, instead, about the Fermi family. Gómez-Martínez says, "Mrs. Fermi, I think her name was Laura, was a wonderful, very, very sweet person. She would always have a box of candy for me there to eat while I was working. I have very good memories of the family. He was a short, very pleasant man and I just really enjoyed working for him" (Gómez-Martínez 1991). Much of the information garnered from Valley Nuevomexicanas in Strottman's series of interviews from the 1990s focuses on men like Enrico Fermi, regarded as the father of the hydrogen bomb.

Any of these three women, or others like them, could have served as examples for how to include local women in the reimaging of Los Alamos. Instead *Manhattan* portrays local women in racist, sexualized ways.

QUERENCIA: A UNIQUE PEOPLE AND THEIR DEEPLY ROOTED KNOWLEDGE

The creators of *Manhattan* had plans from the beginning to use the landscape as an integral part of the story.[15] The show's writers could have easily done this by telling the backstory of Los Alamos. They could have examined the history of Nuevomexicanos on the Pajarito Plateau, dating back to the 1742 Pedro Sánchez Land Grant (Ebright 1993). They could have acknowledged the Pueblo presence on the plateau, which dates back to the 1150s CE (Hoard 2009). Instead, they called the people of Site Y the "homesteaders on the Atomic Frontier" (St. John 2015), ignoring the historical significance of homesteading on the plateau. The 1862 US Homestead Act allowed Nuevomexicanos to regain land in Los Alamos after losing much of it to Texas cattle farmers. The local people had an intimate relationship with the land that they held sacred. That relationship is not examined in *Manhattan*. Although Shaw says its creators had the "brilliant insight to make the landscape of New

Mexico a part of the story," the landscape is not part of the story except when the characters describe how much they hate Los Alamos. At one point, Frank Winter tells his daughter, "This isn't our home, Callie. This whole neighborhood is just cheap plaster and wood. In a couple of years, we will be back in Princeton. And this? This will all be Indian land. Like it never happened."[16] Nuevomexicana/o tenure in Los Alamos is erased, as well as the fact that the land has never been returned to its original occupants in its entirety.

In Episode 6, after Paloma fails to show up to work at the Winters' home, Frank and Liza leave the Hill to find her. They learn that Paloma's brother has died in the war. She asks Liza if Frank can take her family to the Hill, behind the fence, to do a ceremony for her brother on their ancestral lands. Frank and Liza take Paloma and her family behind the fences of Site Y. Frank is in one vehicle with some of Paloma's family, and the remaining family members follow him in a truck. The trucks stop in a remote location, where a Tewa man tells Frank and Liza that they must wait while the family performs the ceremony. He tells them, "You don't have the authority to witness the releasing rite."[17] When they return, the Tewa man thanks Frank and asks him, "Do you know Robert Frost, professor?" Frank tells him that Liza "reads him," at which point the Tewa man recites part of a Frost poem entitled "Mending Wall." In it, two neighbors argue over the construction of a wall that divides their property. One neighbor keeps saying, "Good fences make good neighbors." The Tewa man, who remains nameless, recites this part of "Mending Wall" to challenge the US government's decision to separate Los Alamos from its Indigenous neighbors, to separate Native Americans and Nuevomexicanas/ os from their lands. After reciting the second half of the poem, he ends with his own comment, "Maybe I just never met the right fence." He says this to highlight his discontent with the fences that surround Los Alamos, which prevent the rightful residents from accessing holy sites and kill their memory of the place and the ceremonies associated with it.

Historically, fences have created the relationships between the *location* of Los Alamos and the *space* of Los Alamos. Like the speaker in "Mending Wall," the Tewa man, a relative of Paloma, does not see the need for the fence because the fence separates his people from the *space* that Los Alamos represents. The building of the fence has created a new *space* in the location of Los Alamos, one that alienates Indigenous people. The wall is a built thing; it is also a boundary. Martin Heidegger (1954) notes, "A boundary is not that at which something stops but, as the Greeks recognized, the boundary is that from which something *begins its presencing.* . . . Space is in essence that for which room has been made, that which is let into its bounds. . . . Accordingly spaces receive their being from locations and not from 'space'" (italics original). Thus, Los Alamos received its being, the essence we now associate with it, from the location of Site Y, not from the space itself, just as native New Mexicans developed their querencia based on cultivating and worshipping the land. As Arellano (2007) says, "It is that which gives us a sense of place, that which anchors us to the land, that which makes us a unique people, for it implies a deeply rooted knowledge of place, and for that reason we respect our place, for it is our home and we don't want to violate our home in any way" (50). No longer is Los Alamos a space where local people feel safe—not in the show and, for many native New Mexicans, not in real life, either.

One of the many problems with *Manhattan* is that it erases querencia. It does this in a number of ways. It disassociates the local people from the land; however, it does show a brief relationship when Paloma's family asks to return to the land to perform the ceremony for her brother. It erases Nuevomexicanas/os from Los Alamos entirely. It sexualizes Native American women in a space that was once familiar to them. Arellano (1997) contends that Los Alamos destroyed the rural economy and replaced it with an "economy based on fantasy" (36). It created a consumer society that has replaced local people's intimacy with the land.

The danger of *Manhattan* is that, by giving a fictional representation of Site Y of the Manhattan Project, it further confuses the relationship that native New Mexicans had with the space of Los Alamos. As it transformed into a location for science, it was built using fences to separate Indigenous people from their ancestral homeland. Our querencia that was once rooted in Los Alamos will continue to fade as we lose either memory or landscape or both. Today, Los Alamos National Laboratory is still surrounded by fences, and Nuevomexicanas/os and Native Americans from nearby villages and pueblos continue to be alienated from their ancestral homelands.

NOTES

1. Episode 1: "You Always Hurt the One You Love."

2. Kirkpatrick Sale, *Dwellers in the Land: The Bioregional Vision* (San Francisco, California: Sierra Club Books, 1985, 42), quoted in Arellano 1997, 32.

3. I use the term *Nuevomexicana/o* throughout this chapter to refer to a population of Spanish-speaking New Mexicans and their descendants who trace their Spanish

lineage and who rejected the term Mexican American after the signing of the Treaty of Guadalupe Hidalgo in 1848. This nomenclature is especially used in northern and central New Mexico, although it is also found in the southern part of the state among Hispanic, Hispana/o, and Mexican American populations. The term refers to an identity more than an ethnicity, what Erlinda Gonzales-Berry and David R. Maciel (2000) call "a people who for centuries have occupied a particular region which they have come to see as their homeland, albeit a contested one" (5). Like Gonzales-Berry and Maciel, I also find this term to "best identif[y] a culture and a people whose roots reach deep into the brown earth of their homeland and across its cultural borderlands" (7).

4. In a full-length manuscript currently underway, I explain how nuclear colonization is the third major period of colonization in New Mexico. Spanish (1598) and American colonization (1848) are generally accepted as its first two major periods of violent takeover. *Manhattan* neither traces nor explains how the violent period of Spanish colonization resulted in Spanish becoming a common language spoken in Pueblos along the Río Grande, particularly in northern New Mexico.

5. See, for example, *109 East Palace: Robert Oppenheimer and the Secret City of Los Alamos* by Jennet Conant, *The Making of the Atomic Bomb* by Richard Rhodes, *Manhattan Project: The Birth of the Atomic Bomb in the Words of Its Creators, Eyewitnesses, and Historians* by Cynthia C. Kelly, *In the Shadow of the Bomb: Oppenheimer, Bethe, and the Moral Responsibility of the Scientist* by Silvan S. Schwer, and *Critical Assembly: A Technical History of Los Alamos during the Oppenheimer Years, 1943–1945* by Lillian Hoddeson et al.

6. Episode 1: "You Always Hurt the Ones You Love."

7. Despite this description of a potential *mestiza* or even *genízara* character, Paloma is neither. She is created deliberately as a Native American woman, but her rendering as such is ambiguous.

8. Elodie Lancefield is the wife of a scientist but also, and more importantly, Abby's female lover.

9. It is documented in several places that Los Alamos scientists installed electricity in some Pueblo homes. The number of homes and the names of families are not documented. Of course, this information is not explained in the series, and viewers are left to question how or why Paloma has electricity in her one-room adobe.

10. Episode 4: "Last Reasoning of Kings."

11. Episode 20: "Behold the Lord High Executioner."

12. See *Inside Box 1663*, Eleanor Jette; *Their Day in the Sun: Women of the Manhattan Project*, Ruth H. Howes and Caroline L. Herzenberg; Brode 2007; and *Standing By and Making Do: Women of Wartime Los Alamos*, Jane S. Wilson and Charlotte Serber.

13. The differences between the positions of the Native American women who worked as day laborers and the Nuevomexicana women who worked as live-in

housekeepers and childcare workers create another hierarchy that remains to be examined.

14. Both the Strottman and Chapman interviews with Florence Singer were recorded as part of the *Remembering Los Alamos: World War II* series. Chapman's interview was recorded several days after Strottman's, but the exact date is unclear based on the holdings I received from the Los Alamos Historical Society archives. I would like to credit the Los Alamos Historical Society for providing me with these transcripts.

15. "From the beginning it was Tommy Schlamme's brilliant insight to make the landscape of New Mexico a part of the story" (Sam Shaw in St. John 2015).

16. Episode 8: "The Second Coming."

17. Episode 8: "The Second Coming."

WORKS CITED

Arellano, Juan Estevan. 1997. "La Querencia: La Raza Bioregionalism." *New Mexico Historical Review* 72, no. 1: 31–37.

———. 2007. "Taos: Where Cultures Met 400 Years Ago." *Grantmakers in the Arts Reader: Ideas and Information on Arts and Culture* 18, no 1 (Spring): 49–56.

Brode, Bernice. 1997. *Tales of Los Alamos: Life on the Mesa, 1943–1945.* Los Alamos, NM: Los Alamos Historical Society.

Burks, Robin. 2015. "Interview: Alex Wellerstein and David Saltzberg Discuss Getting History and Science Right on 'Manhattan.'" *Tech Times*, August 6, 2015. www.techtimes.com/articles/74658/20150806/interview-with-alex-wellerstein-and -david-saltzberg-discuss-getting-history-and-science-right-on-manhattan.htm.

Ebright, Malcolm. 1993. *Land Grants and Lawsuits in Northern New Mexico.* Albuquerque: University of New Mexico Press.

Gómez-Martínez, Lydia. 1993. Interview by Theresa Strottman, November 9, 1991. "Remembering Los Alamos" archival collection, Los Alamos Historical Society.

Gonzalez-Berry, Erlinda, and David R. Maciel. 2000. Introduction to *The Contested Homeland: A Chicano History of New Mexico*, edited by Erlinda Gonzales-Berry and David Maciel, 1–9. Albuquerque: University of New Mexico Press.

Han, Andrew. 2014. "What *Manhattan* Gets Right, and Wrong, about Los Alamos." *Popular Mechanics*, July 28, 2014. www.popularmechanics.com/culture/tv/a3109 /what-manhattan-gets-right-and-wrong-about-los-alamos-17033716.

Heidegger, Martin. 1954 [1997]. "Building, Dwelling, Thinking." In *Rethinking Architecture: A Reader in Cultural Theory*, edited by Neil Leach, 100–9. New York: Routledge.

Hoard, Dorothy. 2009. *Historic Roads of Los Alamos.* Los Alamos, NM: Los Alamos Historical Society.

Klein, Rebecca. 2015. "Moving Photos Show Native American Children Defending the Earth." *Huffington Post*, April 21, 2015. http://www.huffingtonpost.com /2015/04/15/tailinh-agoyo-warrior-project_n_7066438.html.

Quintana, Frances Gómez. 1993. Interview by Theresa Strottman, January 4, 1992. "Remembering Los Alamos" archival collection, Los Alamos Historical Society.

Remembering Los Alamos: World War II. 1993. Los Alamos, NM: Los Alamos Historical Society.

Robertson, Dwanna L. 2015. "Invisibility in the Color-Blind Era: Examining Legitimized Racism against Indigenous Peoples." *The American Indian Quarterly* 39, no. 2 (Spring): 113–53.

Shaw, Sam, creator. 2014. *Manhattan*. Lionsgate Television, Skydance Television, and Tribute Studios.

Singer, Florence. 1992a. Interview by Dohn Chapman, 1992. "Remembering Los Alamos" archival collection, Los Alamos Historical Society.

Singer, Florence. 1992b. Interview by Theresa Strottman. April 11, 1992. "Remembering Los Alamos" archival collection, Los Alamos Historical Society.

St. John, Allen. 2015. "This Incredible Act of Violence: Showrunner Sam Shaw Discusses Season 2 of wgn America's 'Manhattan.'" *Forbes*, October 20, 2015. https://www.forbes.com/sites/allenstjohn/2015/10/20/this-incredible-act-of -violence-showrunner-sam-shaw-discusses-season-2-of-wgn-americas-man hattan/#6bbafc64371e.

VanDerWerff, Todd. 2015. "Radioactive Coyotes and Poisoned Apples: The Strange History of the Manhattan Project." *Vox*, August 7, 2015. www.vox.com /2014/10/17/6993305/manhattan-project-facts-wgn-manhattan-interview-sam -shaw-season-finale.

CHAPTER NINE

Mestiza Consciousness a la MeXicana
in Ultima and Agueda Martínez
Bridging and Legitimizing Querencia
in the Borderlands

NORMA A. VALENZUELA

> Because I, a *mestiza,*
> continually walk out of one culture
> and into another,
> because I am in all cultures at the same time,
> *alma entre dos mundos, tres, cuatro,*
> *me zumba la cabeza con lo contradictorio.*
> *Estoy norteada por todas las voces que me hablan*
> simultáneamente.
>
> GLORIA ANZALDÚA | "Una lucha de fronteras"

I am a walking contradiction.
JUAN ESTEVAN ARELLANO

HOW I, A TRANSNATIONAL MEXICANA, BRIDGED CULTURAL
PRACTICES AND ANCHORED *QUERENCIA* IN TWO PLACES—
TORREÓN AND *MI ALBURQUERQUITO*

I still remember the day, as a graduate student, when one of my professors told me that I should contact the newly hired Chicana faculty member who wanted to meet with all the Chicano students. This was the first time any- one had verbally labeled me as a Chicana. This marking pushed me to re- think my conception of identity and its ties to the place that saw me grow up: Albuquerque, Nuevo México, a place that also helped me understand the importance of *querencia.* In Juan Estevan Arellano's (2014) words, querencia is the "understanding of place . . . the love of place" (5). My querencia for Albuquerque began as a way to feel connected to a place after the trauma of being torn from my maternal family in México and traveling thousands of miles *pa'l norte* (to the North). Similar to the sentiment expressed by Arellano and Gloria Anzaldúa in the quotes with which I began this chapter, my head buzzed with contradictions. According to Anzaldúa, we are "[i]n a constant state of mental nepantilism, an Aztec word meaning torn between ways, la *mestiza* [being] a product of the transfer of the cultural and spiritual values of one group to another" (1987, 100) which we use as a survival practice in the Borderlands. As I considered her concept of nepantilism, I questioned: So, was I a Chicana or a Mexicana? When and how had the two mixed? When did my *mestiza* (mixed-heritage) consciousness develop, which then allowed me to ground my querencia? How do I make sense of all those voices that speak to me simultaneously? And how does one learn to utilize querencia as a resistance strategy to reconfigure a survival space?

To answer such contradictions, I examine in this chapter the intersectionality of race, gender, class, and nation as sites of contestation, and discuss how my lived experiences have enabled me to understand how I became a transnational MeXicana by bridging cultural practices that allowed me to anchor querencia in two nations. To demonstrate querencia in practice, I turn to Rudolfo Anaya's novel *Bless Me, Ultima* (1972) and the documentary *Agueda Martínez: Our People, Our Country* (1977). The narratives guiding this novel and film document the lived experiences of two powerful Nuevomexicanas, Ultima and Agueda, by centering their relationship to the earth, their family, and community. Querencia allows the women to survive in rural New Mexico. I compare my own history as an (im)migrant with their experiences as a central way to reveal how querencia is grounded in the mestiza consciousness I use to understand and make sense of remapping my memories in Albuquerque.

Thus, I explore specific cultural practices, such as language, spirituality, religious, and food customs performed in the quotidian life of the Borderlands to anchor my own querencia in two geographical spaces: Albuquerque, New Mexico and Torreón, Coahuila, México. In this in-between space, I learned to maneuver between clashing cultures by learning the dominant language, values, beliefs, and way of life, yet simultaneously resisting total assimilation by maintaining my heritage culture and language and grounding my sense of place—my querencia—in 'Burque.

In much the same way that Ultima and Agueda demonstrate querencia by embracing their culture, language, and love of place, my querencia begins in northern México, where my unschooled grandparents educated me through *dichos* (proverbs), storytelling, spirituality, and *curanderismo* (healing). Equally important in my understanding of querencia is my experience growing up in *Alburquerquito* (as my *bracero* father so lovingly calls it), where I was surrounded by strong, sexually liberated Chicanas who spoke Spanish a little differently. I grew up living and breathing northern Mexican Spanish from my working-class family. Discovering Anzaldúa's essay "How to Tame a Wild Tongue" (1987) freed me because it taught me to value my linguistic hybridity.

In Albuquerque schools, my peers were Diné, Apache, or Pueblo Indians, as well as African Americans. I appreciated, valued, and lived within this *mestizaje* of languages and cultures. In recognizing this valuable diversity, Anzaldúa articulated *la facultad* as "the capacity to see in surface phenomenon the meaning of deeper realities, to see the deep structure below the surface." I consider her observation that "Those who are pounced on the most have it the hardest—the females, the homosexuals of all races, the dark skinned, the outcast, the persecuted, the marginalized, the foreign" (60) in order to map the disciplinary exploration of my experiences in colonized spaces that enabled me to understand and recognize my own social positioning within Albuquerque society, and to think further about the ways that Nuevomexicanas such as Ultima and Agueda provide evidence of nepantilism, la facultad, and querencia in practice. Northern New Mexico and northern Mexico thus become a bridge to my lived experiences and connect my querencia in negotiated spaces within the Borderlands. As Anzaldúa aptly notes of mestiza consciousness: "From this racial, ideological, cultural and biological cross-pollinization, an 'alien' consciousness is presently in the making—a new mestiza consciousness, *una conciencia de mujer*. It is a consciousness of the Borderlands" (99). This critical consciousness informs my positionality within two geographical spaces connected by hundreds of years of history, both worlds converging in the Albuquerque of the late 1970s and 1980s.

In telling my story, I look to Arellano (2014), who reminds us that querencia is his family's "odyssey, but more than that it's a person's journey in search of querencia, of breathing and living querencia, of defining querencia, both with words and with pick and shovel, with poetry and by planting trees" (6).

Mapping the journey of myself and my family allowed me to anchor my querencia and embrace both my Mexicanidad and Chicanidad. In reflecting on my journey, I have learned that I cannot separate who I've become from what I consider my querencia to be—my love and respect for and ties to Albuquerque. My memory of the city that saw me grow up and that shaped me into the MeXicana I am today was formed by the natural landscapes of the Sandías (the supposedly dormant volcanoes), the Río Grande, the *acequia* (irrigation ditch) near Nana's house, the educational institutions that I attended (Taft Middle School, Valley High School, and the University of New Mexico), and such social phenomenon as the lowriders driving by slowly on 4th Street and cruising down Central, mass on Sundays at Guadalupe, and the *cholos* and *cholas* (gangsters) from Juaritos, Duranes, or Martínez Town. I am very cognizant of Arellano's underscoring of querencia as being "aware of the landscape which carries the memory of those who came before me" (2014, 6). In my case, it was my father, José Tobías Valenzuela López, and several of his brothers who fell in love with Albuquerque during the 1960s.

BLESS ME, ULTIMA: QUERENCIA THROUGH ULTIMA'S TEACHINGS

The first time I saw my heritage culture validated and at center stage was in my high-school Honors English class, when we read Rudolfo Anaya's *Bless Me, Ultima*. I was engrossed with the novel and its themes because Ultima and her cultural practices reminded me of my life in northern México. Ultima was the grandmother, the healer of the community, the respected elder. The love that she had for her family, her community, and specifically for Antonio was palpable. Antonio's love for Ultima was like the love I had for my maternal grandmother and the family I had not seen in eight years. Ultima's teachings through dichos, spirituality, respect, values, and love for the earth was like the querencia my grandmother Fidencia had instilled in me and my sisters.

I grew up within two geographical spaces connected by El Camino Real, which traveled from Mexico City all the way to Santa Fe. During the Spanish colonial period, New Mexico was part of the farthest northern frontier, relegated to isolation. Similarly, Coahuila and Durango were key states during the Mexican Revolution and were also on the periphery, seen as untamable. The Valenzuelas (my father's side) lived in Yermo, Durango, a small desert town right on the Camino Real. The Pulidos (my mother's side) settled in the city of Torreón, Coahuila, during the late 1960s after traveling in boxcars, to build and maintain the railroad. My father loved his forsaken Yermito, but the only thing that grew there was cactus, and during the second phase of the *Bracero* Program, he enlisted. That's how he made his way to Albuquerque.

Being raised on the US side of the border anchored me in these two geographical spaces, where my maternal grandmother's teachings of spirituality, curanderismo, and other cultural practices developed my sense and love of place. Cordelia Candelaria (2004) describes culture as "such learned and socially constructed systems as language, religion, food and cooking, clothing, arts and crafts, sports, and myriad other shared characteristics that unite people into recognizable categories of social identity" (659). It was the intersectionality of these social identities that allowed me to survive within the Borderlands. In Anzaldúa's words (1987), "[t]he new *mestiza* copes by developing a tolerance for contradictions, a tolerance for ambiguity. She learns to be an Indian in Mexican culture, to be a Mexican from an Anglo point of view. She learns to juggle cultures" (101). I learned to juggle cultures because I come from the Sonoran Desert, where *los bárbaros del norte* (the barbarians from the North) thrived and where people live on the periphery in the land of barbarians, a term used by Mexican elites. The Mexican *norteños* (Northerners) had to learn to survive in a hostile environment far away from Mexico City, and where food and water were as precious as gold. Like the Nuevomexicanos from up north, all we had was the land, our family, community, and traditions.

Set shortly after his older brothers returned from World War II, *Bless Me, Ultima* is the coming-of-age story of Antonio, taking place in rural northern New Mexico. The novel describes the ties to the land—querencia—from different perspectives between the Luna and the Márez families, who are at odds when it comes to identity. Those of us who have grown up in the countryside are keenly aware that a person's family name ties them to a specific geographical location, and how esteemed that lineage will be seen. Similar to the family conflict between Antonio's parents, my family was also in constant conflict. My mother's family was in the city, but my father's was in the countryside, *en el rancho*. Whenever my father was home from Albuquerque, we would travel to his hometown, Yermo, Durango, located on the old main road that connected Mexico City to Santa Fe, the Camino Real. This lasted until he and my mother agreed that the family should be together, and made the difficult decision to travel *pa'l norte*. My maternal family was never happy with that decision, but they respected it. It was not until almost a decade later that we saw them again.

Education for their daughters was what pushed my parents to journey north. I still remember that warm summer evening the day before we left Yermo, and my Tía Mayela—my dad's youngest sister—telling me that we were really going to like school in Albuquerque because they provided free breakfast and lunch. I have always loved school, and my mother tells me that my first steps were toward the schoolhouse in Yermo. I began school in Torreón, Coahuila, but all I remember is white-and-blue uniforms and saluting the flag every Monday.

My schooling experience in Albuquerque began at Larrazolo Elementary School—named after New Mexico's fourth governor, Octaviano Larrazolo—in the South Valley. Like Antonio on his first day of school, I was frightened, nervous, and shy. It was a traumatic experience because the language was unfamiliar, and no one in my family could help me with homework because they did not speak English and had only a first-grade education. I eventually became a proficient English-language learner because of the strong foundation I had in my first language. Yet I am still haunted by what Anzaldúa (1987) affirms: "Until I can take pride in my language, I cannot take pride in myself . . . Until I am free to write bilingually and to switch codes without having always to translate, while I still must speak English or Spanish when I would rather speak Spanglish, and as long as I have to accommodate the English speakers rather than having them accommodate me, my tongue will be illegitimate" (81). Only in that middle space—in Nepantla—do I feel like I can switch between codes and not be judged as deficient in either. My working-class Mexican Spanish is akin to the way Nuevomexicanos speak, incorporating sixteenth-century Spanish, and therefore it is directly tied to my identity and sense of place. Neither of the varieties is incorrect or deficient. It is a living language that has sustained us through centuries of turmoil, and our "secret language," as Anzaldúa terms it, has been used as a tool to resist the hegemonic language, whether it be standard Spanish or English.

The importance of language in maintaining ties to my linguistic and cultural identity is also evident in the mestizaje of Indigenous practices, such as the curanderismo and Catholicism that are central to my family's beliefs and querencia for both Albuquerque and Torreón. In México, my family did not attend church, but in Albuquerque we went to Sunday Mass because it was a place that felt comfortable. Mass was given in Spanish and so our spirituality was validated, as was our heritage language. This language validation was important because, as Anzaldúa states, "ethnic identity is twin skin to linguistic identity—I am my language" (1987, 81).

In the same way that Antonio pays homage to *"La Virgen de Guadalupe* [who] was the patron saint of [his] town" (Anaya 1972, 13), a symbol of his spirituality, my maternal family was devoted to *la Virgen de Guadalupe*, whose symbolism in the Americas is very important. La Virgen represents the mestizaje of the Indigenous and Spanish; her apparitions to an Indigenous man enabled the indoctrination of millions of Indians. Lupita, the endearing name that many Indigenous, Mestizo, marginalized, working-class Mexicans call her, is the patron saint who gives them hope. The love, strength, and mestizaje of la Virgen is another aspect that linked my lived experiences and cultural ties to the characters in *Bless Me, Ultima*, particularly the relationship between Ultima and Antonio.

Reminiscent of my maternal grandmother's relationship to the earth, Ultima's spiritual connection to the land anchors her sense of place, which can be seen in her cultural practice of curanderismo and its importance of utilizing the land's gifts for healing. In one teaching, Ultima "spoke to [Antonio] of the common herbs and medicines . . . shared with the Indians of the Rio del Norte. She spoke of the ancient medicines of our tribes, the Aztecs, Mayas, and even of those in the old, old country, the Moors" (42). Likewise, my *abuelita* (grandmother) Fidencia respected plants and herbs just as Ultima taught Antonio: "[E]ven the plants had a spirit, and before I dug she made me speak to the plant and tell it why we pulled it from its home in the earth. 'You that grow well here in the arroyo by the dampness of the river, we lift you to make good medicine'" (39). My grandmother taught me the importance of nature's healing powers. I still drink *hierbabuena* (spearmint) for an upset stomach or *manzanilla* (chamomile) for cramps. If I feel the onset of a cold, I make some *hierba del marrano* (oshá) to cure me. Ultima's teachings tie Antonio to the land, the *llano* (plains) and *el pueblo* (hometown) and she educates him so that he will love and respect the land and recognize it as provider and life-sustainer.

In another instance, Ultima's ritual of burying an infant's umbilical cord is a manifestation of tying the child to the land and his destiny. During Antonio's birth, Ultima tells his mother, "I will bury the afterbirth and the cord that once linked him to eternity. Only I will know his destiny" (6). I am also tied to the land because my *ombligo* (umbilical cord) is buried in the soft brown earth of my maternal grandmother's backyard, right underneath the waterspout. It is an Indigenous tradition that links us back to Mother Earth, where we will return. Ultima embodies querencia via ancestral rituals and cultural practices and through their mestizaje; she anchors her querencia in rural northern New Mexico. It was these same shared cultural practices and elements of resistance that I used to make sense of place within New Mexican society.

AGUEDA MARTÍNEZ: QUERENCIA AND THE IMAGERY
OF FOOD AS IDENTITY MARKERS

While the narrative guiding *Bless Me, Ultima* parallels my early life in many interesting ways, it was not until a visit to the Indian Pueblo Cultural Center in Albuquerque in the mid-1990s that I encountered another narrative that so closely resembled the querencia and connection I felt with New Mexico's countryside . . . *desde* (from) Albuquerque. The National Hispanic Cultural Center was screening *Agueda Martínez: Our People Our Country*, a short 1977 documentary about the life of seventy-seven-year-old Agueda Martínez, who worked on her ancestral lands in Medanales, Nuevo México, during the late 1970s. I immediately recognized the arduous work that Agueda did daily to maintain her ties to the land, her Spanish-language preference, and the love for her family. The content and images of the film reminded me of my own family, similarly invested in the importance of harvesting the land that sustains us physically, spiritually, and emotionally.

My ancestors also lived off the land. My abuelita Fidencia herded goats, walked the llano to pick wild cactus and hierbas, and cut mesquite wood to light the makeshift stove she used to cook. Growing up in the Sonoran Desert, water was precious and treasured. In Yermo, I accompanied my mother to the cistern to collect our weekly ration of water. Agueda, too, points out the reasons for which she would rather have her water source, firewood, and restroom outside: "I still don't want anything inside the house because that would hurt my natural habits and the system of my body." It's clear that Agueda understands the healthy benefits of her way of life, especially the importance of water and the river that provides it. In developing my own sense of place, the presence of the river was symbolic because I knew it could swallow and take lives. I learned early in life to be careful, because the spirit *La Llorona* is ever-present near bodies of water. Yet the river also gives life. Water is powerful: it cleanses and purifies. It also connects and divides my

two querencias. For me, crossing the Río Bravo to get to the US was important because, in my young child's mind, I felt the river had followed me to
Albuquerque and become the Río Grande.

Nuevomexicano film scholar A. Gabriel Meléndez describes *Agueda*
Martínez as an "eloquent *testimonio* of a life of fortitude and self-sufficiency,
one of humble but noble purpose," stating that it is one of the "first films to
align the landscape and humanscape of northern New Mexico's rural Indo-
Hispano communities" (2013, 166). My reading of the film is that it is the
second Chicana/o film other than *Salt of the Earth* (1954) that centers on a
Chicana, Nuevomexicana, and mestiza voice, because it is directed by Chicana film director Esperanza Vásquez and narrated in English by Chicana
actor Carmen Zapata.

Agueda Martínez anchors her ancestry to the land that she cultivates. Her
querencia for the land and the traditional ways, and how she seeks to maintain them, demonstrates how she survives in Nepantla, that middle land between the nation-state and her quotidian reality. She embodies the "Mexican
American women from the Southwest" Pat Mora (1993) describes as "desert
women. We 'know about survival . . . / Like cactus / we've learned to hoard.'
We hoard what our mothers, our *tías*, our *abuelitas* hoarded: our values, our
culture" (53). Agueda's way of surviving in the rapidly changing New Mexican
society of the 1970s was to care for her ancestral land, which would then be
passed on to future generations of Martínezes. That is the reason she taught
her daughters and grandchildren how to cultivate their *herencia* (heritage)
and the best practices to care for the ranch. She teaches her grandchildren
when chiles and vegetables are ready to be picked, and which hierbas were
used for their medicinal properties, telling the audience, "You have to know
herbs well." Agueda underscores that "Indians were better experts with herbs
than we are [today]," and claims lovingly that "Grandparents are the ones
that teach you": they are patient and loving, unlike parents, who spank their
children to discipline them.

Self-sustaining Agueda begins her narrative by situating her ancestry, stating that "*Era buena vida*" (It was a good life) back in the old days. All of her
knowledge comes from her Navajo ancestors, whom she proudly claims were
weavers and ranchers. She continues the tradition of working the land that
sustains and nourishes her, because, as Mora explains, "By incorporating the
strength and stubbornness of *nuestras antepasadas*, 'our foremothers,' we create
and claim our space" (1993, 71). Querencia for her ancestral land allows for

survival in the Borderlands. It emphasizes that work does not tire her because she has made her life through her work.

Another example of Agueda's querencia is that she prefers a wood stove to a gas stove. As she tells the viewer, they're less expensive, provide warmth, and cook better-tasting food. She cooks traditional meals such as tortillas, beans, chile, potatoes, and *atole* (corn gruel), for "[f]ood is more than a basic source of nutrients, it is also a key component of our culture, central to our sense of identity" (Koc and Welsh 2002, 46). Like Agueda, for me food is central to my understanding of who I am. Corn, chile, potatoes, and beans nourish my soul, but also remind me of my ancestral past. Corn is one of the most sacred foods in Mesoamerica because it nourished Indigenous tribes both physically and spiritually, through ritual practices. In the kitchen scenes, we see that Agueda uses her hands to mash the chile and put it and the corn into the *molino* (grinder). She even provides the viewer with a couple of recipes. I still remember the old hand-operated molino my grandmother used to grind corn and chile. She didn't like to use a blender because the food "didn't taste the same."

Agueda's tortilla preparation and cooking resembled my grandmother's, even though we only ate flour tortillas on Sundays, when my mom's oldest brother would come into town from working on the railroad. During this special time, everyone would gather in the kitchen to joke, gossip, and cook. The sense of place that these gatherings offered was crucial in anchoring my *querencia* through specific cultural practices that bridged my "two worlds." From my childhood perspective, I was fascinated at how large my grandma could roll out and stretch the tortillas with her hands, quickly throw them on the *comal* (griddle), press them, and then toss them onto her beautifully decorated handmade *servilleta* (napkin). The images I have of my grandmother are those of a busy woman who was always working and rarely sat down to watch television, yet loved to *platicar* (chat) and tell stories. My abuelita's stories always taught us about our elders. She would tell us about our great-great-grandma Petra Cano, who cooked for the *Villista*s (those that fought for Pancho Villa) and wove and sold palm baskets during *La Revolución* (Mexican Revolution).

One of my favorite stories was about great-grandma Goyita, who gave birth on the side of the dirt road that led to great-grandpa's work. She was a *partera* (midwife) and disliked doctors because, as she would say, "uno nomás va por un dolor de muela, y luego, luego, le dicen que se encuere. Pa' que quieren que se encuere uno si va por un dolor de muela?" (one goes for a toothache, and immediately they [the doctor], ask you to remove your clothes.

Why do they want us to get naked if we are just going in for a toothache?). Through my abuelita's storytelling, I learned about the strength and persever-ance of the *mujeres* (women) in my family. Her storytelling was better than any television show. Similarly, Agueda does not really care much for watching television. She would rather sit and talk with her grandchildren and other family, or whoever is visiting, and this is how she gets her news.

During the long winter months, Agueda weaves serapes and rugs, a skill and way of life that was passed down from her Navajo ancestors. She points out that her daughters are also weavers, and that they sell these artistic creations to make a living. Agueda proudly states that her designs are unique because she visualizes them in her head and never copies from any other design. I, too, remember my grandmother crocheting and making table covers and tortilla warmers to finance my youngest aunt and uncle's schooling. My grandma did not know how to read or write, but all she had to do was look at a pattern to memorize it, and would then make it her own by adding her unique stitch. Seeing the images presented in *Agueda Martínez* further bridged my querencia and validated my existence and sense of place in Albuquerque.

In another scene, Agueda discusses the difference between atole and ch-aquegue, notes that chaquegue is an Indian recipe, and emphasizes her Indig-enous roots: "We may consider ourselves Mexican, or Hispanics or whatever we want but we are more Indian." To me, Agueda's claims made perfect sense because my maternal side of the family was Indigenous—they used a *metate* (grinding stone) to grind chile and corn and a *molcajete* (mortar) to grind spices and make green chile sauce. They could cook over a wood stove, clean and eat *nopales* (cactus), and find the best hierba to cure any ailment. Here I recall Glenabah Martínez's (2010) findings to underscore the importance of cultural representation and Indigenous knowledge for members of marginal-ized Native societies.

Agueda's cultural practices are legitimate and reference my MeXicana po-sitionality. They do count as knowledge because they are part of my being, and part of the way I make sense of who I am within contemporary New Mexi-can society. Thus, for me, the scenes in the kitchen remind me of my grand-mother's *cocina* (kitchen)—the smells, tastes, warmth, love, and intrigue—all emotions I felt in that private space. Here, I recall Anzaldúa (1987), who re-minds us that "[t]here are more subtle ways that we internalize identification, especially in the forms of images and emotions. For [Anzaldúa] food and certain smells are tied to [her] identity, to [her] homeland" (83). My hunger to find images, stories, or artifacts that bridge and connect my life in Albuquerque was particularly important to my sense of identity and my ability to preserve my heritage culture, language, and other cultural practices. In the words of Arellano, querencia, then, is that "love of place, that sense of place defined by the texture of biting into a recently plucked green chile, the smell of tortillas cooking over a piñón fire on my grandmother's old wooden stove, the color of a ripe tomato waiting to be sliced" (2014, 6). The combination of using all my senses allowed me to remap memories and anchor my querencia *aquí y allá* (here and there). Agueda's querencia for her ancestral land is clear when she states that "land is a blessed thing because it produces the food that I have, the clothes I wear, 'cause it produces the cotton, it maintains the sheep that produce the wool, the cow that's the meat and the milk."

MI ALBURQUERQUITO

My journey of discovery of querencia for Albuquerque is defined by shared cultural practices such as language choice, spirituality, the religious and food customs that I experienced while growing up in the North Valley, and my mother's constant reminder "así lo hacía/decía tu abuelita" (that is how your grandmother did it/said it). My language use and my bilingualism are fundamental to my concept of querencia. In Albuquerque, I learned to codeswitch when gossiping with my sisters because everything just made more sense. I learned that it was not disrespectful to use the Spanish pronoun "la" in front of a woman's name because that's how la Nana, la Libby and other Chicanas used it.

At Nana's house, I learned that Uncle Ofo "*se fue al servicio y duró 5 años*" did not mean "he was in the bathroom for 5 years." I learned that the Treaty of Guadalupe Hidalgo of 1848 guaranteed Nuevomexicanos the legal right to speak Spanish, but due to the push for Americanization, speaking Spanish was perceived as a deficit and the language was figuratively ripped from our communities' tongues. Just because some Nuevomexicanos looked "more Mexican," it did not mean they spoke Mexican Spanish. Growing up in Albuquerque, I learned to call all soft drinks "cokes" and to sprinkle *caló* (Chicano Spanish) into my sentences because I heard it from the cholos in school, which brought memories of my family in Torreón.

Life in Albuquerque was learning the rituals of our family, including that we used layaway at Kmart and shopped for groceries at Bag-n-Save. It was buying Mexican products at the flea market on Old Coors before the *carnic-erías* (meat markets) opened throughout the city. Surviving in Albuquerque was looking out for *la migra* (border patrol) while walking to school because we did not have *papeles* (papers). It was meeting the nicest Chicana employees at Blake's Lota Burger, who always gave my sisters and me free meals.

In Albuquerque, I recognized that my Indigenous roots were reflected in the Navajo, Apache, and Pueblo people I met at HiLo Supermarket—the women with long, wide skirts that were similar to my great-grandma Goyita's *naguas*. In Albuquerque, I felt safe making a cross on a baby's forehead so I would not *"hacerle ojo"* (give it the evil eye), just like my abuelita Fidencia taught me. In 'Burque I realized that my dad's nickname of *"el negrito"* from the Mexican game *La Lotería* (Mexican Bingo) fit him perfectly because he indeed looked like the Black people we encountered. But most of all, it was realizing that our stay in Albuquerque was not going to be temporary. I understood that we were not going back to Torreón after several Christmases came and went. Instead, we would load up my Uncle Ramón's truck with presents for our family. He was the first Valenzuela to get his "papers" so that he could cross the border legally.

Accepting that realization allowed me to remap my memories and create my own story. This anchored my querencia in and for Albuquerque. Here, the words of Arellano resonate: "For my history is not from east to west but rather from south (Zacatecas and Aguas Calientes) to north or vice versa. Today La Villa de Albuquerque is the heart of that cross, the Big I is that which connects us in all directions. In a way the Camino Real, or Royal Road, and the Santa Fe Trail intersect here" (2014, 23). In my case, it was my father, José Tobías Valenzuela López, and his brothers, Ramón, Gerardo, and Beto. They all fell in love with Albuquerque during the 1960s and decided to make New Mexico their home. They all worked as silversmiths for "el Joe" and learned to make Indian jewelry using silver, gold, and precious stones like turquoise. In the early '80s, they began to work for Kabana Inc. in sweatshop conditions with little pay.

ROUTES/ROOTS: ON BECOMING A TRANSNATIONAL
MEXICANA IN THE BORDERLANDS

To begin building upon my lived experiences and my anchoring in querencia, I situate myself in relation to this work by considering Anzaldúa's articulation of la facultad, which is what has sustained me as a first-generation immigrant to the US, one who serves as translator and cultural broker between the dominant culture and my ethnic community. Therefore, in my articulation of querencia, I remapped my memories of Torreón and replicated them in Albuquerque. Like the countless number of immigrants to New Mexico who, as Arellano (2014) describes, were "[n]ostalgic for their homeland" and "wanted to replicate their 'habits,'" (193) I also wanted to re-create my cultural practices in my adopted place in order to anchor my sense of space.

My name is Norma Angélica Valenzuela Pulido. I am the first member of the Valenzuela family to earn a college degree, yet the most important education I received was from my elders. They were all educated outside the traditional classroom. Similar to my concept of education in the "nontraditional classroom," New Mexican Indigenous educator Glenabah Martínez discovered four powerful discourses in the construction of an educated Native person during her interviews with Indigenous youth and teachers: the "two worlds metaphor, cultural representation and mainstream signifying practices, Indigenous knowledge, and youth recognition of the politics of what counts as knowledge" (2010, 26). I utilize her two worlds metaphor to describe how I, too, inhabit two worlds, two cultures, and two languages in which I have learned to navigate and coexist in Mexican and US societies.

My Indigenous maternal grandmother, Doña Fidencia Hernández de Pulido, did not know how to read or write. She signed with a cross the way the Spanish colonizers taught the Indigenous converts. My abuelita Fidencia's wisdom, intelligence, and storytelling were fundamental during my formative childhood. Through her storytelling, and specifically her dichos, my sisters and I learned about respect toward others, values, and morals. Some of the dichos that my abuelita taught us and role-modeled for us as children that I completely understand at this stage in my life are: "*cuando tú vas, yo ya vine*" ("when you go, I already went") and "*como te ves, me vi, y como me ves, te verás*" ("as you see yourself, I saw myself, and as you see me, you will see yourself"). As a child, I remember my abuelita telling my aunts and uncles these dichos so that they could understand that with age comes wisdom and knowledge, as well as respect from younger people. Another dicho that she used taught us not to judge people and that we should never "*escupir al cielo porque te cae en la cara*" (spit up at the sky because it will fall on your face). We learned to value the land we lived on and the animals that resided on it. We learned about discipline, hard work, spirituality, and healing. Our abuelita taught us to help others. *"Hacer el bien sin mirar a quien"* (do good no matter who is watching): through this saying, grandma taught us to share our food and not be stingy with each other and with people in need. She instilled in us pride in being women and working-class Mexicanas. This is the cultural capital I brought with me to Albuquerque on September 16, 1979. Tara Yosso (2005) calls this "community cultural wealth" and describes it as "an array of knowledge, skills, abilities and contacts possessed and utilized by Communities of Color to survive and resist macro and micro forms of oppression" (69).

In Albuquerque, the linguistic registers of the *Chicanas chingonas* (fierce Chicanas) I encountered were dissimilar to my own family's. Here, I want to emphasize that there is linguistic resistance to colonial purity in Chicano communities. For me, it's crucial to value the varieties of spoken language in Chicano/Mexicano communities, such as mixing Spanish and English or using caló to communicate. I myself grew up in a working-class Mexican norteña family and speak "different" than the Mexicans from the middle of the country. I live and breathe Spanglish or Chicano Spanish because we speak a "language which [Chicanos] can connect their identity to, one capable of communicating the realities and values true to themselves—a language with terms that are neither español ni ingles, but both. We speak a patois, a forked tongue, a variation of two languages" (Anzaldúa 1987, 77). These varieties of spoken Spanish value and corroborate my language experience and that of many of my peers and their ancestors.

Resembling Arellano's goal in his "attempt . . . to create a collage with words . . . based on [his] memory of the land that has molded [him], showing what it is to live in a rural space in northern New Mexico inhabited by ghosts and memories of [his] ancestors for centuries" (2014, 6), as I grow older, the more entrenched Nuevo Mexico has become in my blood. It's been over thirty years since I arrived in Alburquerquito and discovered my querencia for the Land of Enchantment that molded me into what I am today: a bilingual, bicultural, transnational MeXicana activist scholar.

CONCLUSION: QUERENCIA A LA MEXICANA

In this chapter, I have remapped my personal journey to create a collage of words and images based on my memories. I have examined how Ultima, Agueda, and I, a contemporary MeXicana, negotiate querencia in the Borderlands, and more specifically in northern New Mexico and Albuquerque.

Historically, Chicanas have looked south to make sense of who they are as subjects existing in this region. I, on the other hand, look to northern Nuevo México to provide me with ways to legitimize my positionality within contemporary Albuquerque society. At a very early age, I utilized la facultad to see beyond surface meaning, which then allowed me to develop querencia and build bridges in order to make sense of being part of two cities within two nations via a mestiza consciousness. I had to learn to live in "two worlds" because I knew my stay in Albuquerque and, by extension, the United States, was not going to be temporary.

Writing this essay from Manhattan, Kansas, has been a very emotional and heartfelt process. Describing my journey has allowed me to embrace who I have become—a MeXicana—and like Juan Estevan Arellano I want this writing to be about "knowledge and wisdom . . . of perseverance, resilience, and stubbornness . . . of traditional knowledge being the main thread" (2014, 24). As a first-generation US resident and with the rise of hate and overt acts of racism, xenophobia, homophobia, and violence of all sorts due to the 2016 presidential election, it is even more imperative that I share my story. The space and place I currently inhabit is the ancestral land of the Arapaho, Comanche, Kansa, Kiowa, Missouri, Osage, Otoe, Pawnee, and the many other tribes who were relocated here by the US government. I stand in solidarity with all groups who have made US cities, towns, and urban and rural spaces their own querencia.

WORKS CITED

Agueda Martínez: Our People Our Country. 1977. Motion picture. Directed by Esperanza Vásquez. Los Angeles: Educational Media Corp.

Anaya, Rudolfo. 1972. *Bless Me, Ultima.* New York: Grand Central Publishing.

Anzaldúa, Gloria. 1987 [2012]. *Borderlands/La Frontera: The New Mestiza.* 4th Edition. San Francisco: Aunt Lute Books.

Arellano, Juan Estevan. 2014. *Enduring Acequias: Wisdom of the Land, Knowledge of the Water.* Albuquerque: University of New Mexico Press.

Candelaria, Cordelia. 2004. "Race and Ethnicity." In *The Encyclopedia of Latino Popular Culture,* edited by Cordelia Candelaria, Arturo Aldama, and Peter J. García, 653–59. Westport, CT: Greenwood Press.

Koc, Mustafa, and Jennifer Welsh. 2002. "Food, Identity, and the Immigrant Experience." *Canadian Diversity* 1, no. 1: 46–48.

Martínez, Glenabah. 2010. *Native Pride: The Politics of Curriculum and Instruction in an Urban Public School.* New York: Hampton Press.

Meléndez, A. Gabriel. 2013. *Hidden Chicano Cinema: Film Dramas in the Borderlands.* New Brunswick, NJ: Rutgers University Press.

Mora, Pat. 1993. *Nepantla: Essays from the Land in the Middle.* Albuquerque: University of New Mexico Press.

Salt of the Earth. 1954. Motion picture. Directed by Herbert J. Biberman. Independent Productions.

Yosso, Tara J. 2005. "Whose Culture Has Capital? A Critical Race Theory Discussion of Community Cultural Wealth." In *Race Ethnicity and Education* 8, no. 1: 69–91.

This section emphasizes literature and cultural production as a mode of resiliency for tribalized and *genízaro* Indigenous communities in New Mexico. While focusing on questions of Native and Indohispano cultural homeland from distinct perspectives, C. Maurus Chino, Jonathan Wilson, and Moises Gonzales advocate for a careful consideration of our connection and obligation to homeland as a mechanism to sustain cultural practices and traditions. For these authors, cultural performance, via the sustained practices of Indigenous communities over time, the production of poetry, and the organization of societies is integral to our understanding of cultural resilience and sustainability within the spirit of *querencia*. However, as the authors demonstrate in their work, this is not an individual endeavor.

Part IV begins with C. Maurus Chino's conceptualization of Acoma Pueblo as a beloved space. His chapter, "Ak'u, Beloved," leads the reader into a journey through Acoma by describing the landscape and creating connections between it and other Indigenous communities throughout North, Central, and South America. In sharing his childhood memories, he informs the reader that an appreciation and reverence for the land and for Acoma as Mother is integral to his sense of place.

Chino's chapter also serves as a testament to the continuity of Acoma, a community that has survived colonial undertakings and remains committed to the prayers, songs, and ceremonies that have endured in this space. The cultural capital of Acoma Pueblo is shared with Indigenous communities through Chino's own participation in activist struggles with his Indigenous brothers and sisters in the Americas. As an artist and an activist, he regularly calls out systems that seek to erase the querencia of his beloved land. He reminds the reader that Acoma was never conquered by the Spanish; rather, the people have survived in spite of it.

Acoma is one of the longest continually inhabited Indigenous communities in the United States, and this factors greatly into how Chino envisions his querencia. In the early part of his chapter, readers get a sense of what it is like to experience Acoma and to grow up there. Later, he expands on homeland by including the shared cultural practices of Acoma with other Indigenous communities who resided and continue to reside in places like Chaco Canyon,

Paquimé, and Chiapas, among others. Chino relates his travels to these places, reminded continually of the powerful connection these spaces share with his own homeland. The chapter ends with a critique of Spanish colonialism both globally and within New Mexico, and the ways in which Indigenous identity is framed more recently, in Chino's view, as a co-opting strategy within the state. This can be read as a new challenge for Acoma and for all tribal communities in New Mexico to reassert their presence and resilience, as well as a larger call to those invested in the state to focus on its current social ills rather than expend energy on glorifying Spanish colonialism.

In his chapter "Homeland Security: Sustaining Indigenous Culture and People through Narrative (Re)Remembering and Future (Re)Imagining in Simon Ortiz's *Men on the Moon* and *Woven Stone*," Jonathan Wilson argues that Simon Ortiz's (Acoma) narratives are not only a coping mechanism for watching the land of his people disintegrate from its traditional glory without any recourse, but a way of reminding Natives that the Western concepts of ownership and control are temporary. Wilson establishes a trajectory of Native American writing that investigates the causes and outcomes, both present and future, of occupied homelands, and analyzes storytelling as a way to (re) remember and (re)imagine connections to place. The question of representation and cultural, historical, and spiritual erasure, among other forms of invisibility through the imposition of another culture's dominating presence, is at the center of Wilson's work.

Wilson focuses on strategies of cathartic writing and analyzes how Native Americans process larger national and global issues and concerns of colonialism through storytelling. He looks at the rhetorical strategies of Simon Ortiz's writing and contends that Ortiz's cathartic method moves readers to process historical trauma and to remain hopeful about the spirit of Native resilience in a geopolitical space where colonization has significantly shifted the cultural landscape of Indigenous communities in New Mexico. For Wilson, Ortiz's writing does not convey a predominantly negative outlook on life; rather, his narratives build a dream of what the future can hold for the land and its inhabitants, while still acknowledging the atrocities that already have occurred under the pseudo-legitimacy of Western ideology and power. The cathartic process in which Ortiz engages allows him to acknowledge, heal, and react to US policies that have resulted in the contamination of the land and attempts to disconnect Native Americans from traditional values. Though Ortiz writes from a personal and communal perspective, he also invites readers to engage in storytelling as an important mode of resilience and, as Wilson states, as a way to connect past, present, and future through narrative.

In "La Querencia: The Genízaro Cultural Landscape Model of Community Land Grants in Northern New Mexico," Moises Gonzales utilizes querencia as a concept to deploy a historical organizing framework for traditional Indohispano, or *genízaro*, land-based communities. As he argues, the Nuevomexicano cultural landscape is composed of three primary components: the natural system, the physical system, and the cultural social system. These systems work in balance to maintain traditional forms of knowledge, cultural production, and traditional government in genízaro communities throughout northern New Mexico. For Gonzales, the concept of querencia is a reciprocal complex of interconnected relationships between these three systems that helps to maintain the cultural homeland of Nuevomexicanos.

Gonzales first relates his own experience working in Abiquiu, New Mexico on a mapping system that would better explain how querencia functioned in this community as a system of cultural resilience. He then extends the querencia landscape model to his own genízaro community, the Cañón de Carnué Land Grant, located in the Sandía Mountains. Gonzales traces the historical trajectory of this land grant to Spanish colonial times and relates to the reader the importance of community involvement in maintaining querencia at all levels of the cultural landscape framework. He argues that the success of a framework like this depends on the ways that all systems work in harmony to promote cultural resilience.

The case study of the Cañón de Carnué Land Grant community demonstrates the interconnectedness of natural systems (mountain ranges, arroyos, streams), physical systems (land grants, grazing areas, community land grants), and sociocultural systems (Carmelites, ceremonial dancers, artisans) in maintaining querencia in genízaro communities. The concept of querencia is often mistaken as a simple term connected to place. Through these systems, Gonzales presents a more complex and historical approach to querencia that considers the importance of community work based in collective action. These systems converge and rely on one another to successfully transmit notions of querencia. They also serve as a teaching model for younger generations who may have become disconnected from more traditional forms of community organization and unity.

Gonzales' work with the querencia cultural landscape model is rooted in his own process of learning from those who shared knowledge of these systems and who have influenced his own work. As he notes, the goal of the research produced in his chapter is twofold: to develop new ways of understanding the value of the landscape from a land-based perspective and to use traditional localized knowledge forms to legitimize and sustain Indohispano/genízaro land-based practices. The framework Gonzales provides here can serve as a valuable resource for readers who are interested in interdisciplinary approaches to community networks and sustainability.

The chapters in this section demonstrate the importance of cultural landscapes rooted in connections to land and land-based practices. Through the analysis of storytelling, activism, and global Indigenous connections and the visual framework of querencia, Chino, Wilson, and Gonzales demonstrate the varied ways that Indigenous and Indohispano communities in New Mexico enact a politics of resilience rooted in communal and historical knowledge and continuity—particularly when these practices are threatened by outside forces. In doing so, they also produce knowledge and awareness that can be passed on to future generations.

CHAPTER TEN

Ak'u, Beloved

C. MAURUS CHINO

"*Amuu Hanu, eh Amuu, Haatsi.*" Beloved People, and Beloved Land. We hear this at Acoma often. It may come up in private conversation when we speak about preparations for the prayers or in everyday terms when the people talk about the planting of the fields or the hope for rain. When the land is in deep drought, people may simply say, "*amuu haatsi*," beloved land. And always we hear it during times of ceremony when the prayers and songs, without exception, mention the Land and the welfare of the People. These values have guided the People from the beginning. The deepest belief of the People revolves around the Land and our harmony with the universe and our creator. The Land and the People are inseparable, one and the same. This is the meaning of *Amuu Hanu, Amuu Haatsi*.

Acoma, the "Sky City" in northwest New Mexico, sits atop a 350-foot sandstone mesa with sheer sides. It is one of the oldest continuously inhabited communities in North America. (The Hopi village of Old Oraibi, at least as old, is the other.) *Ak'u* (Acoma) and Zuni are the two most western and isolated Indigenous city-states in New Mexico, with Hopi the farthest west in Arizona. Ak'u, Zuni, and Hopi are also the most independent-minded city-states because of their physical isolation. Despite speaking three totally different languages, all three have always kept in close contact, sharing culture and religion. Acoma has survived raids by the nomadic tribes. It has survived forced conversion to Christianity and attempts by the conquistadors to destroy it. It has persevered through the Spaniards' attempts to turn the Acoma People into mirror images of themselves. To this day, Ak'u has remained relatively unchanged despite constant external threats.

The Acoma People are a matrilineal society. Women take a central role in the welfare of the family. All land and property belong to the females and ownership is passed down traditionally to the youngest daughter in the family. We belong to the clans of our mothers and we say we are children of the clans of our fathers. Acoma People did not use surnames before European contact. We identified ourselves by telling our Indian names, which clan we belonged to, and the clan of our father. Today, even with surnames, we inquire about clan if we do not know the other person.

Acoma is part of the Keres-speaking People. Keres is an isolate language, meaning there are no known connections to any other language. The Keresan People include the present-day tribes of *T'amaya* (Santa Ana), *T'siya* (Zia), *Ko'tyit* (Cochiti), *Kewa* (Santo Domingo), *Kawaika* (Laguna), and *Kat'ishtya* (San Felipe). Sharing this land with the Keres are the Towa, Tewa, Tiwa, Zuni, Hopi, Apache, and Diné. Toward the east, past the natural boundaries of the Sandia and Manzano Mountains, are the Kiowa and Comanche. To the north, at the southern tip of the Rocky Mountains, are the Ute People.

Ak'u sits fixed in a beautiful valley with verdant corn fields watered by rain runoff from the surrounding hills, providing a rich contrast to the dark green of the cedar trees. The land is high semiarid desert and mountain country with average rainfall of about twelve and a half inches per year. Ak'u is surrounded on all sides by sandstone cliffs that radiate crimson, red browns, burnt orange, and yellow ochres. In the high desert air, these colors turn deep cobalt blue and violet in the distance. At over six thousand feet above sea level, the trees include cedar and pinion in the lower elevations. As one travels higher, a transition in vegetation is easily noticeable as it changes to juniper, oak, ponderosa pine, spruce, and, at more than nine thousand feet in elevation, aspen.

The air is crystalline, with objects sharply in focus. If you allow yourself, it is possible to feel the infinity of your existence. The land, at first, may appear empty and barren until the movement of crows flapping between pinion trees and sandstone cliffs breaks the still frame and, suddenly, you realize the Land lives and breathes. The sharp trill of rock wrens echoes off the steep canyon walls. Hawks and buzzards use the warm updrafts as they circle higher and higher in search of food. A tarantula moves across an animal path in beautiful, slow, and jerky smoothness.

Power resides here. All of it is Holy. We were led from our previous existence in the North to our place, the sandstone monolith we refer to as *Haak'u*, or "prepared." We say it was here waiting—prepared for us. Ak'u comes from the word haak'u. *Ak'ume* means People of Ak'u. The word Acoma comes from Ak'ume. At Acoma, we say, Ak'u is and always was.

Communication radiated in all four directions; ideas were exchanged. While survival before Spanish invasion was never easy, an intimate knowledge of the Land provided the People with the means for survival. It was possible to not only survive, but to thrive through shared ideas of architecture, agriculture, and astronomy. Celestial knowledge was useful for the guidance in timing the changing seasons and engaging in ceremony. Some evidence of this sharing can be seen in the architecture of Chaco Canyon, *Washbushuka*. The exquisite stone masonry displays a unique architectural detail—the use of a T-shaped doorway. A T-shaped doorway is not stronger structurally in any architectural sense. There had to be another reason for its use. I have heard from others that it was a doorway of power, which I took to mean spiritual power. Like Chaco, Acoma used the T-shaped doorway and, today, they can still be found in some of the older homes.

Many years ago, on a group field trip, I went to visit the ruins of Paquimé in the northern state of Chihuahua, Mexico. Paquimé was part of the same Mogollon culture, linked to other Mogollon sites in Arizona and New Mexico. In many ways, it looked much the same as many so-called Pueblo ruins in New Mexico. However, there were some major differences. Mayan influence could be seen in the ball court, a feature prominent in the many Mayan ruins. Paquimé was a trading center. They raised parrots in stone cages for trading in the North. They also manufactured corn-grinding stones, *metates*, from a very fine-grained volcanic basalt. I saw one such stone that seemed ready to trade. It was about one foot high by two feet long. There was a one-inch groove cut where the *mano*, or grinding stone, could fit. It seemed brand-new. I imagined a stone like that would last for centuries, a family heirloom to be passed down the generations—a precious and useful tool to be shared with stories of its origin and our connection with our relatives to the South. The similarities of culture and stonemasonry between Paquimé, Ak'u, and Chaco were very strong, but the one similarity that stood out the most for me was the use of the T-shaped doorway.

During a trip to Mexico in 2004, of which I will speak later, I was part of a group of activists who drove down to Chiapas. We went as representatives of First Nations North and South, an organization that promoted unity between the Indigenous Peoples of the Americas. We were there to help the Zapatistas celebrate the ten-year anniversary of the 1994 uprising in San Cristóbal de las Casas, Chiapas. We took one day off after we reached the highlands in Chiapas. In a day-trip, we drove down to the jungle to see the Mayan ruins of Palenque. The mountain air from Chiapas was cool enough that we drove without air conditioning and the windows rolled down. The drive was easy. There wasn't much traffic, though often we would see the ubiquitous Toyota trucks (we never saw any other make of vehicle) with Mayan passengers sitting in the back. We reached the jungle and the ruins of Palenque in the early afternoon. When I got out of the vehicle, I became acutely aware of the incredible, almost suffocating humidity and the roar of the howler monkeys in the treetops. The heat, the lush vegetation, and the sounds of the jungle made me intensely aware, in that moment, how far away my world of Ak'u was. I made my way up the steep steps of the largest temple and, breathing heavily, sat looking out over the other temples. The tourists, antlike specks far below me, wandered between the temples. It was easy to imagine what Palenque may have looked like in the zenith of its existence, as ceremonies were being conducted, visitors arriving and leaving, and markets abuzz with activity.

Rested, I walked quietly into the dark, damp, musty-cool interior. In one room, murals, barely visible, crumbling with age from the thousands of years past, covered the heavy stone walls. These paintings in oxides of reds, yellows, and blacks were human figures and stylized symbols, depicting what seemed to me a religious ceremony. I wondered if I should even be there, and respectfully, I left the room. I continued farther into the temple, and there it was again . . . the T-shaped doorway. I was affected greatly by this. I could see clearly the architectural link among Chaco, Acoma, Paquimé and, there in southern Mexico, Palenque, all geographically and culturally connected.

The T-shaped doorway is but one of the many links between the Indigenous Americas. In New Mexico, the Indigenous city-states, though physically isolated, were part of a social network that radiated to the four directions. Communication with other tribes was widespread. We traded with the Maya People to the South and acquired precious stones, seashells, and sacred parrots for ceremonial use and personal adornment. Abalone shell was obtained from the tribes on the West Coast. Contrary to the belief of Spanish colonizers, our existence was not soulless nor half-empty. We were not waiting to be discovered by Columbus or any so-called Spanish conqueror. We were not, as Pope Benedict so ignorantly stated during a trip to South America in 2007, "silently longing" for Christianity (Colitt 2007). Rather, ancient cultures in the Southwest were vibrant. The incredible diversity of Indigenous languages and cultures was possible because the People, even in the struggle for survival and conflict, allowed for differences in beliefs. Ceremonies were respected, and, in many instances, ceremonialism was shared and borrowed.

All of the land was spoken for. All Indigenous People had their tribal boundaries in the form of natural landmarks—usually mountains or rivers. Even now, one may walk in any direction away from our present cities and find evidence of Indigenous People. Sooner or later, one will find pottery shards, worked flint stones, or—if one is lucky—an arrowhead. There was no one place where the People were not. By one conservative estimate, there were eighteen million Indigenous People on the North American continent and millions more in Central and South America and the Caribbean Islands.

INVASIONS

When Columbus blundered into the New World with Spanish soldiers, all Indigenous People soon experienced a violent cultural shift. Our world was changed forever. Beginning with the Caribbean Islands, the indiscriminate slaughter of the People began. Before each battle, the Spanish soldiers read *El Requerimiento* (The Requirement)—an absurd act considering that no Indigenous Tribe or Nation understood it. Nevertheless, as an act of authorization for the Spanish invasion, this statement of Christianity and allegiance to the Spanish Crown was read. It states, in part, "I certify to you that, with the help of God we shall powerfully enter into your country and shall make war against you in all ways and manners that we can, and shall subject you to the yoke and obedience of the Church and of their Highness. We shall take you and your wives and your children, and shall make slaves of them . . . And we shall do all the mischief and damage that we can, as vassals who do not obey and refuse to receive their lord and resist and contradict him" (Hanke 1949, 33). This was the bent of the Spanish psyche from the beginning.

From 1496 to 1518, the Indigenous population of the Caribbean Islands fell from eight million to twenty thousand as a result of genocide and disease brought by the Spaniards. By 1535, the Native population in the Caribbean was considered extinct, (Cook and Borah 1971), though the People there still exist. The Caribbean Islands were only the beginning. Millions more Indigenous People in Central and South America were set to perish through genocide and pestilence brought by the Spanish. They were on a collision course with untold suffering as the bloodbath of Spanish discovery spread southward.

The butchery at the hands of the Spanish conquistador Juan de Oñate in the North American Southwest had not even begun. Oñate, so revered here in the Southwest, had yet to cause human suffering.

DEFENDING HOME

Rumors of great wealth in land, gold, and human souls brought Oñate north to present-day New Mexico along an ancient Holy Road the Spanish named *El Camino Real.* In April 1598, he and his soldiers arrived at present-day El Paso, Texas from Zacatecas, México. Oñate, accompanied by Franciscan friars, stopped just short of the Río Grande and held a formal ceremony and Catholic Mass (Weber 1994). In accordance with the Spanish laws of discovery, he formally claimed ownership of all lands and natural resources north of the Río Grande and held all Indigenous People in subjugation to the Spanish Crown. It was not love of land. It was not any profound sense of *querencia* that brought Oñate north to present-day New Mexico. It was Spanish lust for land, weath, and human souls that brought him there, nothing more. For the Acoma People, this defines a fundamental existential difference in how we perceive our worlds. The Land does not belong to us; we belong to the Land.

In October of 1598, only six months after the arrival of Oñate, the first major confrontation with the Spanish occurred. In that battle, thirteen Spanish soldiers were killed, one of them a nephew of Oñate. The humiliating defeat quickly brought a larger retaliatory force bent on punishing and destroying Acoma. In the bitter cold of January 1599, an epic battle ensued, lasting three days. From Spanish historical accounts, the massacre at the hands of professional armored soldiers using horses, cannons, muskets, and war dogs (150-pound *presa canarios* trained to eat human flesh) resulted in the butchery of more than eight hundred men, women, and children (Hammond and Rey 1953). When the Acoma People determined the battle to be lost, so great was the despair of their Beloved Ak'u being destroyed that many killed themselves rather than submit. Most people simply cannot comprehend the sorrow and despair that can turn a people to suicide rather than submission. I say that only people who have a deep and intense connection to the land can know this love to and of place. Ak'u is our mother.

How can this be possible—this inhumanity? Acoma was a microcosm of the inhumanity that took place in the Americas. Yet the trauma we experienced is no less than what our Brothers and Sisters endured to the South. To

FIGURE 10.1 C. Maurus Chino, *Ak'u, Beloved Ak'u, Ancient of Days*. Oil on canvas, 40"× 40". Artwork courtesy of C. Maurus Chino, Acoma Pueblo.

use the word "butchery" in reference to Oñate and the conquistador invaders is to use the word in a literal sense. When Acoma warriors had their right feet chopped off in punishment for resisting Spanish violence, this act was butchery. Many of the horrific and unspeakable details of the savagery my Acoma People endured in 1599 I have left unsaid. What good would it do? What must be remembered and acknowledged is that the horrors perpetrated on my People were committed by Spanish soldiers in the name of God. The Catholic Church who deemed war at Acoma as just is no less culpable. Who has the right to commit murder in the name of God?

Guwaatsi Hauba! Du shinume K'a aimais'iwa dagaashi. Dyaami Hanu s'uda. Usraatra waashdi s'uda etyu. Maurus Chino es'e, Merikana shiya. Greetings Everyone! My name is K'a aimais'iwa. I belong to the Eagle Clan. I am a child of the Sun Clan. Maurus Chino is my American name.

AT THE NORTH DOOR

I grew up in McCarty Village, *Diitsiama* (North Door) in our language. It is one of three farming villages about fourteen miles north of Old Acoma.

Diitsiama and Acomita, *Diichuna* (North Stream), about seven miles to the east of Diitsiama, are the oldest villages still in use. The newest village, Anzac, *Diyabuni Shuku*, identified simply as "the place at the Northwest End," is approximately five miles west of Diitsiama. These farming villages relied on the permanent water source of the *Chuna*, the Río San José. The sources of this once-beautiful stream are springs to the north of Diitsiama. The Chuna is not a big stream, only several feet deep in places, but it was cold enough and deep enough to support trout. I fished in that stream with my uncles, brothers, and cousins. Our beloved Chuna was clear and cold, and when we swam or waded in the water, we could feel fish brushing against our legs. I have many beloved memories of that precious stream, now ruined by the pollution of the City of Grants, when during the Uranium Boom of the 1960s the city grew too fast and was not able to keep its sewage treatment in check and untreated wastewater was dumped into the waterway. The Chuna cannot support fish any longer. There are no more frogs or dragonflies. The memories of that precious stream are now too painful to tell.

In many ways, in my youth, growing up in Diitsiama was idyllic. My generation and the generations before knew an unspoiled and quiet land. Neighbors were not so close, but close enough that you could hear the far-off sound of wood being chopped on a cool, still autumn evening. The ax–wood *thunk* out of sync with the woodchopper's swing is now only a memory of a more simple time.

I lived with my extended family a few miles apart from the main village. We were all Eagle Clan in our original cluster of three homes, held tightly together by our family matriarch, my grandma Mamie. We were a close family and I grew up playing various children's games with siblings and cousins. Although we lived separated from the main village, we were not isolated. Relatives frequently stopped by, and evening meals would sometimes turn into social events. And, often, my mother would send me, a young boy of maybe six or seven, to an aunt's house several miles away. I would run with a note in my pocket—an invitation to dinner!

About a mile west of where we live, the land makes an abrupt shift. Mesas at this point start to change in elevation from the foothills of the sacred North Mountain *Kaweshdima*, Mount Taylor on today's maps. At over eleven thousand feet, Kaweshdima, an extinct volcano, is the highest point in the Cibola National Forest. At a certain point directly west of McCarty Village is a narrow opening between the lava flow of Kaweshdima, impassable to anything but slow and careful foot traffic and the mesas that start the climb toward Ak'u to the south. This narrow opening is the "doorway." It is where McCarty Village gets its Acoma name, Diitsiama, the North Door. Life movement—human, water, and animal—was all directed through this doorway. Today, Interstate 40, the BNSF Railroad, and the El Paso Natural Gas Company all follow this same path. Only now, explosives used in the construction of the interstate have blasted open wide the ancient doorway.

It was on these mesas that my uncle and I would spend many hours hunting or just walking. I was very young then. I remember holding on to my uncle's back pocket so I could keep up with his fast pace. His left back pocket always frayed in that year or two when I needed the help. Later on, as I grew older, I walked those same hills with my brothers and sisters and cousins. And much later, when I became a father, I took my daughter on those walks.

One summer midmorning, my daughter and I started on a long hike, our lunch and water slung in a pack over my shoulder. We set out walking the same trail I had walked countless times. Memories of my youth appeared in my mind. Like old-time sepia photographs, mental images appeared blurred, then were instantly replaced by another, as I recognized a familiar turn or dip in the trail. I set a slow pace so she wouldn't tire, and we made our way up to the west mesa. It took real effort for us to climb to the mesa top. Once there, we sat on the edge, rested, and looked down at the valley. Kaweshdima, Snow Mountain, loomed benevolently to the north of us. I held her hand and I cautioned her to be careful as we tossed small stones over the edge.

We continued walking. I carried her on my shoulders when she tired. We stopped when we reached the edge of a small box canyon and sat on warm, bare rock. The natural rock basins at the cliff edge were mostly dry, but the deeper ones still held some water from a rain several days earlier. The bits of twigs, dark sand, and dried cedar berries rolled around the bottom of the basins when we touched the cool water. It smelled like rain. The very essence of the previous rainstorm and the Land were contained in those small pools. I remember clearing the sticks and rocks away from under a pinion tree and patted together soft mounds of pine needles so we could sit and rest in the cool shade. We ate our lunch and, when we were done, I showed my daughter how to chew the small, round, hardened bits of pinion pitch we found under our tree. I remember saying to her, "Keep chewing until it becomes soft." After crumbling, it would take on a soft, chewy consistency. I told her how we chewed this as children when we wished for and did not have store-bought gum. We lay back and picked out animal shapes in the enormous monsoon cumulus clouds building over the mountains to the west and went to sleep with the scent of the pinion and cedar trees and the earth carried by a soft summer breeze.

As a child, I attended McCarty Day School. It was a US government–funded school. I was a good student, and in the five years I spent there, I excelled in my work, though I can say now as I look back that I was not happy. I saw no use for school. I was happier and more interested in my surroundings outside the classroom. I learned, from watching other kids, that the schoolyard was strewn with soft stones containing iron oxides. The colors were mostly various shades of reds, browns, and yellows. When you were lucky, you might find a special one—a deep, rich purple. I drew pictures on the sidewalk with my classmates during lunchtime or recess. I knew then that I would be an artist. I played the rough-and-tumble games of our schoolyard but, many times, I wanted only to draw on the sidewalk. I saved those rocks in my pocket, always on the lookout for a good color. Sometimes I would walk alone up to those beloved hills, with my colored rocks in my pocket, and draw on the smooth sandstone.

AN UNEXPECTED TURN

I became an activist in 1992. I was reading the *Albuquerque Journal* one morning and came across a story about the creation of a monument to Juan de Oñate, the Spanish invader who made war and massacred my Acoma People in 1599. The proposed monument was to be erected in Alcalde, New Mexico, where Oñate had a home. I can remember that morning very clearly—the visceral reaction I felt to learn about Oñate's monument. I didn't know what to do. I wondered if anyone was going to do anything about it. I made calls and soon found out that all the people I spoke to felt the same way I did, but no one was taking action. I decided in that moment that if anything was to be done, I should not look to anyone to do it. It was up to me to do something.

That moment was life changing. As a painter, I did much of my work in solitude. Most people know me in that way. Taking action for political or social reasons was not in my character. But over the next few days, I realized that I could not ignore the situation. I wrote a letter to then Secretary of the Interior Manuel Luján. In my naïveté, I thought I might make a difference.

After all, the story in the paper had called the monument "proposed." I soon found out, when I received a certified form letter from the office of Manuel Luján, that the funds had been appropriated and the project was a done deal. My letter had not made a difference at all. My first action and failure might have ended my activism right then and there. But something inside me had changed, and I started to address the issues of racism and revisionist history here in New Mexico.

I founded an organization—the Southwest Indigenous Alliance (SWIA). Our early membership was mostly friends and family. We began to protest in the streets. We protested the conquistador monuments and celebrations in Santa Fe, Albuquerque, and El Paso, Texas, where we were sometimes outnumbered by the police. We organized conferences and symposiums. We allied ourselves with other organizations such as Vecinos United, Stop the War Machine, First Nations North and South, Veterans for Peace, the Tricentennial Truth Alliance, and Voices against the Wall (activists from the Tohono O'Odham Nation in southern Arizona). In addition to these issues directly related to Indigenous Peoples, SWIA tackled issues of police brutality, the antiwar movement, and US/Mexico border violence.

THE ROAD SOUTH

In late December 2004, I joined other activists from New Mexico and Pine Ridge, South Dakota. Our trip was organized by First Nations North and South, an organization to promote alliances between Indigenous People of the Americas. There were five of us, two young Lakotas (male and female), a Diné woman, and a young woman from Peru who went with us as an interpreter. We later added three more to the group when we reached southern Mexico. We drove to Chiapas, Mexico, to help the Zapatistas celebrate the ten-year anniversary of the 1994 Zapatista Uprising in San Cristóbal de las Casas when, on New Year's Eve, Indigenous tribes from surrounding areas rose in armed conflict to fight for equal rights and against the subjugation endured since Spanish invasion. The Zapatista Movement takes its name from the Indian Mexican Revolutionary leader Emiliano Zapata.

We drove from Albuquerque, New Mexico through Ciudad Juárez, Chihuahua, Saltillo, Tampico, and Veracruz, and then inland into the southern mountains of México. We passed numerous Mexican Army checkpoints, many with teenage soldiers who uneasily and nervously handled automatic weapons. The whole country was on alert, suspicious, it seemed, of activists driving to Chiapas.

From Tuxla Gutiérrez, our road rose sharply. It seemed we were driving into the clouds as the two-lane highway zig-zagged up the mountain. We passed Mayan villages, some with big hand-painted signs at the entrance, proudly proclaiming their Zapatista identity. At one such village, we stopped to rest. We walked around the small plaza, the *zócalo*, and communicated through our interpreter. We may have been seen as foreigners—who knows?—but we felt accepted. We were all Indians, after all. On impulse, we decided to ask to see the village leadership or elders. We were treated kindly and were asked to wait. Soon, we were introduced to one of the community leaders. We formally introduced ourselves, showing the proper respect when younger individuals address elders. We told him where we were from and why we were there. He listened politely and welcomed us. I remember telling him as we were getting ready to leave that, as I walked around his village, I saw many of my nieces and nephews running around. He laughed, and we agreed with him when he said, "We are all related."

We drove on and reached San Cristóbal de las Casas, a beautiful old highland Spanish colonial town. There, we rested and spent a few nights in relative comfort in a hotel that had a large banner on the lobby wall, "Basta! y Basta!" (Enough! is Enough!), referring to the Zapatista demands of Indigenous equal rights. We went sightseeing, visited the common marketplace for provisions to contribute when we reached the Zapatista camp, and took one day off to drive down to the jungles of Palenque in southern Chiapas. At the Mayan ruins, I saw the same T-shaped doorways I have seen in Chaco, Acoma, and Paquimé.

OVENTIC, ZAPATISTA STRONGHOLD

We left San Cristóbal in the early morning and finally reached our destination in the afternoon. Oventic, one of several Zapatista camps in the mountains, is the largest and de facto capital of the Movement. We surrendered our passports at the gate. To our surprise, they were simply and without fanfare thrown into a cardboard box along with all the other passports. We were then allowed to enter. People from all over the world and of all races were arriving. Most impressively, the Zapatistas were coming. They all wore their signature black bandanas, which covered their lower faces, revealing only their eyes.

Wearing the bandanas was not an act of concealing their identity: it was a way of showing their commitment to the Zapatista Movement. There were young people and old people, people from the mountains and from the Lacandón jungle. Many arrived riding in the back of Toyota pickup trucks, which local entrepreneurs used as self-appointed public transportation on those isolated mountain roads; their trucks were fitted with a framework on the back, over which a canvas or plastic tarp could be stretched to protect the riders from the sun and rain. One *peso* per person!

We requested and were granted a meeting with the leadership, who met with us in the main building. Two men and one woman were seated at a homemade table. They wore their black bandanas like badges of honor. After formal introductions, we told them why we were there. We spoke of our gratitude to their People in welcoming us and reaffirmed the belief that all Indians are related. We offered the gifts we had brought, sacks of beans and rice. We shook hands.

ACOMA AND MAYA

The nights in Oventic were cold and damp and the afternoons warm. The mornings were clear and cool. Then, like clockwork, midmorning brought in a dense, heavy fog. It was so thick that it was difficult to see more than ten or fifteen feet away. The fog muffled noise and made it seem as if people were speaking in hushed tones. Ghostly figures shuffled through it slowly and carefully. Movement was kept at a minimum. It just wasn't safe. The ground was often wet, and the mountains were incredibly steep. There were no level areas. Even the corn fields we passed as we drove through the mountains were planted on hills as steep as a forty-five-degree angle. On the journey to Oventic, I stopped our van near one of these. A woman was sitting outside her home. She sat husking corn, the pile beside her a mound several feet high. I walked up to her and nodded hello. She smiled in return. I motioned to her that I wanted an ear of corn. I tried to give her a couple of pesos, but she refused and smiled as she gave the corn to me. I carefully wrapped and stashed it away in my pack like a treasure. I gave the corn to my brother when I got home and told him the story. He was farming back then. When I saw him again, he told me he had planted that corn mixed with his Acoma corn seeds. It felt good to hear that Acoma and Maya were intertwined by the very earth.

We spent several days in Oventic. The camp was abuzz with excitement for the New Year's Eve celebrations. All of us hoped that our camp would be the place Subcomandante Marcos would come and speak. Though he did not speak in our camp, we celebrated nonetheless. It was a proud moment for me when I was one of the people who stood on the stage and addressed (through an interpreter) the crowd of revolutionaries, activists, human-rights observers, citizens, and, I'm sure, undercover police.

A SACRED CONNECTION

One foggy midmorning, quite unexpectedly, we were blessed to see a dance by Mayans from the Lacandón jungle. They walked single-file into one of the buildings and lined up in front of an altar that had been set up against the length of one wall, where flowers and objects I could not see clearly were set up. Each dancer had a gourd rattle in one hand and a tie of flowers in the other. Their clothing was white, with woven belts tied around their waists and handwoven straw hats from which parrot feathers hung down the brim, concealing their faces. Wooden rifles carved in the shape of AK-47s, painted black, were slung across their backs. They danced in unison in front of the altar, a medium-paced cadence, one foot lightly touching the earthen floor as the other lifted slightly. They kept time with their Maya song and danced in perfect rhythm, their feet pounding the earthen floor as they made a quarter turn to their right, then, facing the altar, a quarter turn to the left. They repeated this until the song ended. With hand motions, they blessed the people.

I stood there, stunned, and wept. I thought of Beloved Ak'u and how it is always present with me in spirit, no matter where I am. That Maya dance reaffirmed in me, in the deepest way, my belief in Indigenous spiritual connections among all Indians. I felt a profound sense of love and commitment that I have known only in the shared sacred ceremonies of my Acoma People. I was proud to be with my Mayan brothers and sisters. I looked about and saw pride in People maintaining cultural identity. Though the Maya People may have, like us, endured forced subjugation and forced Christianity, that day I saw a People who were not conquered at all. I heard many Maya dialects spoken in that camp. The ceremony many of us had witnessed had nothing to do with Christianity and everything to do with the Maya People. Those Indians rose in armed conflict, those brave women, men, and children who, like us, took matters into their own hands to say, "We are not conquered at all."

"Conquest" is not a word I prefer to use when describing shared histories in the Southwest. It glorifies a violent and brutal past. It implies, of course, that Indigenous People were conquered, which is not true at all. If we had been, we would be a Spanish-speaking people; we would have forgotten our original language. We would have pushed aside the religion and beliefs that have sustained us for thousands of years. We would simply be dark-skinned mirror images of the Spanish. Christianity was forced on the People. It must be remembered that adopting it was a way of survival at a time when practicing our own religion meant punishment by death.

People ask me now and then why it is that I have a Spanish surname, and whether that is proof that I am somehow related to the Spanish. I think they mean to ask if I am related through blood, or if I was given the "Chino" surname as a connection to my slave masters. The suggestion makes my blood boil. No, I say, I am not connected to the "Chino" family. Whoever they are or wherever they come from is no concern of mine. Generations ago, we picked surnames in order to get on the US census rolls. Acoma names were too difficult for outsiders to pronounce. Acomas were given a list of names, and it just so happened that the name "Chino" sounded good enough or was maybe just convenient enough for my father's family. We still have our traditional names, and every newborn is given an Acoma name. However, many people, including myself, continue to use our *merikana* (Acomanized American) name out of convenience and survival outside of Acoma.

REMEMBER THIS!

Our original beliefs were never forgotten. The Prayers and Songs that have sustained the People continue today. Indigenous cultures here in the Southwest remain intact, not because we were granted our rights, lands, and freedoms by the Spanish as I hear and read so often, but because Indigenous People forcibly took back our cultural and religious independence and kept it. The Revolution of 1680 came about violently for these very reasons. The use of forceful actions to maintain our cultural freedom is hardly ever mentioned in scholarly works and never by the so-called New Mexico Hispano elite who hold themselves to self-perceived and imagined heights of conquistador glory.[1] There is, of course, a good reason why the People's resistance is hardly ever mentioned: to acknowledge Indigenous cultural sovereignty minimizes and threatens to deconstruct the careful historical revisionism that recounts the glory and benefits of Spanish colonization. I say there were none at all. To mention our resistance contradicts the overall public perception of the People as meek and subservient. "Conquistador"—I abhor the very word!

ON INDIGENOUS IDENTITY

There is a new appropriative social movement among Hispanos in New Mexico in which many self-identify as "Indigenous." Recently, I attended a lecture at the Indian Pueblo Cultural Center in Albuquerque. It was part of a series called "The Counter Narrative." The lecture, titled "Genes R' Us: DNA, Identity, and Genealogy in the Southwest," implied, considering the venue, Indigenous DNA ancestry. All other Indian People I spoke to felt the same way. The title did not mention "Genízaro" ancestry.

The room was packed and, from where I sat, there seemed to be an equal number of Indigenous and non-Indigenous people. Neither of the two panelists, Moises Gonzales, associate professor of architecture at the University of New Mexico, and Gregorio Gonzales, PhD, or the organizer of the event, Miguel Torrez, was qualified to speak specifically on Indigenous ancestry. I never heard any mention of Indian DNA ancestry. They directed the lecture exclusively to a discussion of their Genízaro identity. They spoke forcefully of their "Indigenous" identity and their pride in inheriting Spanish land grants. They were oblivious to the fact that these lands are, in fact, Indian lands stolen from the People. They continued to speak of their Indigeneity until I spoke up and reminded them what it means to be Indigenous. There are four requirements: a traditional or original land base, an Indigenous language, a tribal self-government, and an official tribal recognition from other Indigenous People as Indigenous.

There is a time and place for Genízaros to speak and be proud of their identity. If I saw a notice of a lecture on Genízaro identity and were interested, I might attend. I might support them if the venue were right, though I will never support their bid for Indigeneity, for it is a false claim. As it was, the Genízaro panelists very rudely and disrespectfully sabotaged an event for their own agenda.

Often, the efforts of those individuals who want to recognize themselves as Indigenous is an insidious attempt to claim Indigenous lands and natural resources. As an activist, I organized many actions protesting conquistador celebrations in New Mexico and West Texas. Many of our actions happened in the mean streets and in front of hostile crowds. Many brave Chicanas and Chicanos stood with us. We never saw any proud Genízaro-identified groups, nor did any Hispano person or organization help in our complete denial of conquistador glory. Hispanos have always refused to join the Indigenous Struggle of Resistance, yet the movement of many of these same people proudly claiming to be Indigenous gathers strength.

A claim to American Indian ancestry is one thing; almost anyone can do it. A claim to Indigenousness is quite another. In North, Central, and South America, only Indian People (here I use the term "Indian" to refer to the Indigenous People of the Americas) can refer to themselves as Indigenous. It is a misnomer, of course, but as "Indians" we can say we now own the term. Anyone born in the United States can claim to be native. However, to be very clear, in the Americas, only Indian People are Indigenous.

CONCLUSION

Southwest history obsesses over the so-called Spaniards here in New Mexico. We all know they came from Mexico, not Spain, and that many were probably part Indian even then. Historians obsess over events long past, in search of imagined glory that was never theirs in the first place. They desperately want vindication for a violent past, saying times were different then. They cling to any connection to Spain—our state flag waves proudly in its colors of gold and scarlet. In Santa Fe, even dark-skinned Hispanos are Caucasian. They clench desperately the idea of Spain and, when convenient, profess their love of "sense of place" over this holy Land when, instead, it is the love of possession of history and possession of place, concepts not akin to Indigenous worldviews.

It is so easy for many in New Mexico to condemn the Jewish Holocaust and to shake their heads in self-righteous disbelief that we, as a country, have taken this long to condemn Confederate monuments. And yet, rarely is anything said about the obscene Spanish monuments that are shoved in the faces of all, except by Indians who "can't let the past go."

Many Hispanos, when speaking about Indian protest, say that we "need to move on." All the while, they continue to pay homage to the unspeakable horrors of a savage time. Many people refuse to see that New Mexico obsesses over a violent and brutal past, pouring millions of tax dollars into celebrating a butcher, Juan de Oñate, and ignoring our social ills.[2] The very society and the communities we live in are mired in perpetual violence. I read somewhere that the sickness of violent cultures is that they celebrate violence. This sick obsession has produced a disturbing reality. Read the newspapers any day of the week. We cannot blame our sick society on today's Mexican immigration. New Mexico has been sick and corrupt since the very moment Oñate crossed the Río Grande. For too long, a twisted and false view of our shared history has been shoved in the faces of us all. We have to change the story. We are not a defeated people and we were never conquered. The so-called Spanish are not victors.

For me, and I believe for all Indian People in New Mexico, the here and now is the most important thing. The actual doing and carrying on of our beliefs in the present time is of utmost importance. The obsession to remember and to commemorate the past as specific events is not as important as our continuance as a cohesive People. And what of those brave Acoma men and women who defended and carried us through the darkest of times? Who they were individually is not as important as what they preserved—our very continuance. We continue to believe in the Land and to believe the Beloved Land is our Mother, both metaphorically and literally. The People were nearly destroyed in 1599, but the Prayers and Songs were not forgotten. We had the absolute courage and belief to not forget who we were. We are firmly rooted to this Land.

We were born to this Land. We belong to it.

NOTES

1. In this chapter, I use "Hispano" to refer to New Mexicans of Spanish/Hispanic heritage who support colonial projects and who have worked against Indigenous People.

2. In May 2018, Española mayor Javier Sánchez and eight Española city council members voted to repeal city government authority to organize the Española Fiestas. See Bennett 2018.

Bennett, Megan. 2018. "Española Bows out of Fiesta, Oñate Commemoration." *Albuquerque Journal*. May 31, 2018. https://www.abqjournal.com/1178932/espanola -council-cuts-commemoration-of-conquistador-onate.html.

Colitt, Raymond. 2007. "Brazil Indians Offended by Pope Comments." *Reuters World News*. May 14, 2017. https://www.reuters.com/article/us-pope-brazil-indians /brazils-indians-offended-by-pope-comments-idUSN1428799220070514.

Cook, Sherburne F., and Woodrow Borah. 1971. *Essays in Population History: Mexico and the Caribbean*, Volume 1. Berkeley: University of California Press.

Hammond, George, and Agapito Rey. 1953. *Don Juan de Oñate, Colonizer of New Mexico, 1595–1628*. Albuquerque: University of New Mexico Press.

"History of the Archdiocese of Santa Fe." Archdiocese of Santa Fe. http://archdiosf .org/asf-history.

López de Palacios Rubios, Juan. 1513 [1949]. *El Requerimiento*. In *The Spanish Struggle for Justice in the Conquest of America* by Lewis Hanke, 33. Philadelphia: University of Pennsylvania Press, 1949.

Weber, David J. 1994. *The Spanish Frontier in North America*. New Haven, CT: Yale University Press.

CHAPTER ELEVEN

Homeland Security

Sustaining Indigenous Culture and People through
Narrative (Re)Remembering and Future (Re)Imagining
in Simon Ortiz's *Men on the Moon* and *Woven Stone*

JONATHAN WILSON

The cathartic quality of writing is well-established.[1] Numerous studies document how the creation, evolution, and reading or viewing of narratives works to bring peace and hope to individuals.[2] However, unlike personal stories of trauma, most Native accounts are derived from a communal space or place. Such a fact complicates how writing translates or transforms into more than traditional definitions of catharses. For Native writers, they are not simply putting pen to paper to work through their own psychological, physical, and emotional triggers or disturbances: they are writing to address and process these ailments within the scope of a specific people who have been oppressed, abused, and marginalized by colonization and, as a corollary, subjected to institutionalized discrimination. As Gloria Bird (Spokane) describes it, "writing remains more than a catharsis; at its liberating best, it is a political act. Through writing we can undo the damaging stereotypes that are continually perpetuated about Native peoples. We can rewrite our history, and we can mobilize our future" (1998, 30).[3] Catharsis, in this case, is then just an initial step to defining or (re)imagining Native peoples in the future by (re)remembering their past through narratives, or as Jean-Michel Vives (2011) puts it, should "be understood not so much as a mechanism of discharge linked to abreaction, but rather as the actual analytical process itself during which the Subject is 'unveiled' and thus faced with the enigma of his own desire" (91). Within the scope of a community/people as Subject, "desire" is identity and place. However, accomplishing such a task is not without its complications and negotiations.

The modern world does not offer Natives in the United States a geographical or psychological position in which to reconfigure their identities.

It thrusts them headlong into a foreign power and ideology. Their lands are in "trust" of the US government, and to exist in the contemporary world, they must function in a society and economic system that suppresses them. Thus, the reality of staying in the same place and viewing the destruction of or, at least, the marked change in the structure of their land and people adds to the complexity of addressing the constraints of a dominant belief system that values Native homelands from a monetary/conqueror's perspective.[4] Simon Ortiz's work challenges this viewpoint through the careful examination of land and the people who are connected to it. At the same time, his narratives also give them hope—hope for a future that wisely notes the encroachment of the past on the present in order to envision a future for Native peoples and their homelands. In fact, from one "trained in literary studies," Arnold Krupat (1995) contends that "some of the most important experiments in ethnocritical historical writing today . . . are coming from the poets," such as Simon Ortiz (169).[5]

My argument is that Ortiz's narratives are more than a coping mechanism for watching the land of his people disintegrate from its traditional quality and value: his stories obligate the audience to reidentify with the land and each other via his careful depictions of both Native tragedy and hope in order to (re)remember the past and (re)imagine the future.[6] His narratives are more than self-reflections or creative writing; they are both "the resolution of a certain, merely personal conflict, [and] the revelation of a higher, more general, human truth in the phenomena of life," and it is the "arousal of tragic emotions . . . [that] raises self-reported tension and anxiety" and necessity for action (Vygotsky 1971, ix; Khoo and Oliver 2013, 267). In Khoo and Oliver's terms, catharsis fosters "a richer self-understanding in the context of lived experience," but it is also "understood as *emotional* clarification . . . [that] promotes insights into common humanity, especially through recognition of the pain and suffering of others" (268, author's emphasis). They write that clarification is "an insight-gaining psychological phenomenon, and it involves three components: (i) emotional engagement, (ii) self-reflection, and (iii) an awareness of human suffering for understanding what is good not only for oneself but also for others" (268). Narratives, then, are not simply words without merit. They are connected to the human condition and the forthcoming conditions of humanity. For Ortiz, the "good not only for oneself but also for others" is coupled directly with securing and identifying with homeland.

In twenty-first-century New Mexico, the sovereignty of the land and people are relegated to words, but, as Leslie Marmon Silko reminds readers at the end of *Ceremony* and Khoo and Oliver argue in their work above, words have power. It is in this power, within the narratives, that Natives can create and re-create themselves into future images by negotiating the realities of the past and present. N. Scott Momaday's *Way to Rainy Mountain* (1969), Silko's *Almanac of the Dead* (1991) and *Ceremony* (1977), and Louise Erdrich's novels known as the North Dakota Saga are a few of the most famous works in a longer thematic timeline that address the actualities of (re)defining identity and place in light of colonization. In reaction to such works, criticism on the subject has been extensive; various scholars have dedicated their labors to both historical and theoretical research on space and individuality and how they intersect for Natives who exist in a variety of new or developing circumstances.[7]

Anastacia Schulhoff's article "More than Native American Narratives: Temporal Shifting and Authentic Identities" (2015) catalogues how Native "storytellers construct subversive narratives that challenge the Native American stereotypes, mythologies, and formula stories that circulate through the dominant culture" (166). Her study examines 103 stories "told by Native American elders, historians, storytellers, and song carriers" and, more interestingly, tackles the overriding stereotypes that pervade "American consciousness about Native Americans . . . The Indian princess, the Native warrior, the noble savage, the failed environmentalist, . . . the aggressive yet defeated drunk" and "the wealthy and greedy Indian Casino owner" (168). Such a study in social sciences is complemented by Reginald Dyck and Cheli Reutter's contentions in *Crisscrossing Borders in Literature of the American West* (2010). Dyck and Reutter offer a "compact argument for the adoption of new paradigms and new models for the study of the West. These promise to maintain the commitment of the New Western history to recovering the stories of repressed groups while also assuming the responsibility to reveal the hidden political and economic struggles that motivate discourses of various kinds" (qtd. in Petzak 396).

With this notion in mind, Nicholas Petzak applauds Dyck and Reutter's attention to Simon Ortiz's work, specifically how the anthology "valorizes Ortiz's allegiance to oral traditions, literary inventiveness, [and] celebration of Acoma identity" (396). However, the most promising implications of Dyck's, Reutter's, Petzak's, and Schulhoff's works is the idea that Western theory

(Aristotle's catharsis, in the case of my argument) and Native stories and criticism should not remain independent of each other in both range and application. In fact, such a suggestion was made by Arnold Krupat in 1995, when he noted that "efforts [in ethnocritical history] should assure that American histories and Native American narratives need no longer engage each other at cross-purposes" (170). More succinctly, Andrew Wiget (1991) states that "the study of Native American literatures—both the oral and written traditions—has resisted theory." However, "following [James] Clifford and [George E.] Marcus, to view the ethnographic project more suspiciously—this trust in social science is being reevaluated in a way that creates a climate more hospitable to theory" (476). For my intentions, I do not discount criticism by or on Natives or devalue ethnocriticism or theory. Instead, my claims hinge on the fact that all viewpoints are necessary to understand the "perspectives of the actors involved" in (re)remembering Native pasts and (re)imagining Native futures (Raymond DeMallie, 1995, qtd. in Krupat 169).

Ortiz's work enters the above conversation by concisely and precisely tackling the issue of converging cultures and peoples in the context of the modern world by writing from the perspective of an American (from the American continent) rather than branding himself as a Native or activist writer. He is all and neither: He is a Native writer who was born into a colonized world, and he is a marginalized voice, but as Ortiz confirms, he "wanted to have a universal appeal, i.e., not limited to Native American boundaries simply because I was a Native American writer writing about the life I knew" (1984, 65). It would then be irresponsible of me to shun any interpretation of his work—critical, theoretical, or historical—because the cathartic nature of his writing serves the greater population of the defined region, rather than any subset or group defined as either dominant or subjected. As Marjane Ambler puts it: "Like good writers anywhere, they [Native writers] touch universal themes. Turning their experiences into poetry and short stories, they use the creative medium as their catharsis, purging their lives of pain to enable them to focus upon the future" (1999, 1). While Ortiz's work is definitely a form of Native activism, his rhetorical mode of delivery is significant to note because it accounts for the actuality of Native/"Native"[8] lives and how they influence or are influenced by competing cultural values on a daily and social basis. As Maria Turri argues in "Transference and Katharsis, Freud to Aristotle" (2015), "Transference allows for the representation and expression of repressed emotions through the reenactment of past relational dynamics" (368).

Ortiz is, then, not a proponent of reverting to "the blanket Indians," to use Samson Occom's term, nor does he promote the notion that assimilation is key to continued Native existence or relation to homeland(s); he uses the historical backdrop (past relational dynamics) of Natives and Westerners to critique and express his hope for the present and future. His work is constructed in a schema of the truth at present: the narrative of a people, the land, and how and what they mean to each other within the larger scope of a communal voice that is in search of identity, affirmation, and place. However, to achieve such an objective, his stories require readers to revisit sites of historical communal trauma—colonization's negative alteration of the land and people—in order to "'work through' . . . repressed emotions, bringing into effect the transference cure" (Turri 2015, 369). However, "cure" is a strong word to use within this context. In Ortiz's work (and that of other Native writers previously mentioned), catharsis does not necessarily denote a perfect outcome. In fact, in David Purnell and Jim Bowman's view, "Narrative conclusions can be optimistic and have catharsis, but not end with a 'happily ever after'" (2014, 175). Focusing on individual and communal growth rather than the fantasy of the unattainable, Ortiz's stories give his readers a glimpse into a world community that appreciates and complements the land, yet his underlying sentiments continually focus on challenging an ideology that has physically or spiritually separated him and his people from their homelands.

The Native tribes of the southwestern United States remain in the land of their ancestors, but they no longer have legal or social rights to such places and spaces.[9] They were not relocated via a Trail of Tears, nor were they eradicated from the eastern seaboard like so many Natives during the British colonization of the Americas. Instead Ortiz and other Native peoples of the Southwest are relegated to a state of perpetual liminality within the scope of their lives. They can see, feel, and breathe in the land of the old and new, the past, present, and future, but they do so with the knowledge that their homeland is forever changed by colonization and its ideological, economic, and cultural attributes. It is here, in this in-between space, that Simon Ortiz works to reestablish connection to his past, culture, and homeland by writing the story of his people and himself. As Jerome Rothenberg (2015) notes, Ortiz "has continued over the years as a major figure in the still active American Indian literary renaissance and in the 'new American poetry' over all. [In fact,] it is hard for [Rothenberg] to imagine a genuine ethnopoetics without his [Ortiz's] authoritative voice [and] presence" (1).[10]

Using his literary background and private experience in the workforce as a muse, Ortiz's short stories emphasize the importance of an intimate relationship with the land and its Indigenous/non-Indigenous peoples. As he states, "I do know the fact of my present *reality* as a person with an Acoma heritage, and I know the circumstances, experiences, events that I as a personal and social entity have gone through, including many changes" (1999, ix, emphasis mine). This "reality" is the environmental and psychological place Ortiz and people like him occupy. This space is one of marginalization, minimization, oppression, and silence within the Western context. However, Ortiz does not convey a predominantly negative outlook on life; rather, his narratives build a dream of what the future can hold for the land and its inhabitants, while still acknowledging the atrocities that have already occurred under the pseudo-legitimacy of Western ideology and power.

In a bit of layered performance, Ortiz cleverly employs voyeurism in the plot of "Hiding, West of Here" to transfer emotions to the page and back to the reader/viewer. Since the audience is privy to the protagonist's secret view of a Native American ritual, the main character and the reader are both "hiding" and equally privileged to experience catharsis by "watching" the act. The protagonist states, "[U]sually I come up that road from Grants into Lobo Canyon, following the little creek running by the road, then up this way. And I drive off the road a ways on a little dirt road that nobody ever uses much and I sort of hide" (Ortiz 1999, 191). It is in this place (hiding) that he sees an act he believes to be sacred: "They'd gone over by a rock that was split in half. A huge rock, even the halves were big . . . They stood by that huge split rock for a long, long time . . . I could hear something. It was a kind of sing-song . . . Praying, that's what I figured" (195). The narrator states, "It seemed like I was part of what the Indians were doing. Like they wanted me to be even though they didn't know I was there" (195). This relationship—although seemingly unknown to the Natives in the scene—makes the protagonist an active participant in the action of the story, and we (the readers) become just as important to creating meaning as the viewer and the chanting Natives.

As Purnell and Bowman argue, "resolutions come as the pages are un-folded, but the narrative is not a finished manuscript; it represents a *moment in time*" (Ortiz 1999, 176, emphasis mine). It is in this moment that the land, the people, and their connection become equally significant characters in the story. The audience sees all elements function in relation to each other with-out a chasm: they are one with each other because their view of the world is interdependent. In other words, they sustain each other in this "moment in time," but the instance does not exist without Ortiz's "telling," which is necessary for cathartic clarification, in Khoo's and Oliver's sense of the term. For "the shapes of time are determined by our ongoing experiences and actions in which we project or portend the future and retain the past" (David Carr, qtd. in Purnell and Bowman 2014, 176). Ortiz's emphasis on the connection between land and people manifests in varied ways, but his reliance on the narrative to underscore the significance of his message to the reader is never abandoned.

In "The Way You See Horses," a father and son become emotionally closer through the shared assembly and flight of a kite. While the father and son create what is traditionally considered an inanimate object, the elements of the environment cause the kite to become almost creaturelike: "The boy held it in his hands and looked it over. The kite flapped some in a gust of wind. It felt alive, almost like a live animal or bird" (Ortiz 1999, 40). The teaching and learning of how to create or how to build a relationship is not relegated to the characters. The land is more than scenery; it is an associate in creating a specific lens of interpretation. The boy observes, "It's the same way the clouds seem to be real close, like my kite is touching them. It's the way you see them." His father replies, "Yeah . . . It's the way you see them" (43). Perspective and performance take on dual significance in this interaction: the father and son view the clouds and kite in relation to the land, and the audience sees all events of the story as a way to redefine themselves within the context of the narrative. The mimetic function of the tale makes it "real," in the sense that it replicates humanity. The "written word" (the reader's view) is then interchangeable with the characters' interpretation because both derive meaning from their relation to and interaction with the land, people, and telling of the story.

Moving in a different contextual direction, "Crossing" depicts the United States' wrongful appropriation and contamination of sacred Native lands that existed virtually unharmed before colonization. As Americans moved west, Native territories were forcibly taken away and their concepts of "homeland" were replaced with Western notions of ownership and socioeconomic prowess. Native American author Samson Occom (1723–1792) notes this significant difference in value during early English colonization: "I am afraid the poor Indians will never stand a good chance with the English in their land controversies, because they are very poor, they have no money. Money is almighty now-a-days, and the Indians have no learning, no wit, no cunning; the English have all" (qtd. in Weaver 1997, 51). Ortiz reiterates this sentiment centuries later when he states, "It was after the railroad came, I think. Things were so poor. The people were sick. There wasn't much to eat. There was little useful farming land left. The men decided to leave the Pueblo to find work" (1999, 184–85). Yet Ortiz's tone differs from Occom's: Ortiz seems to point out a fact, while Occom's statement only laments reality.

In "Happily Ever After," Purnell and Bowman state, "endings" definitely "point to potential futures," but "not everything ends well . . . Sometimes, things just end" (2014, 175). This concept is key to understanding Ortiz and other Native writers' work because a "happy ending" has not been afforded to them. In fact, within the large schema of treaties and even "civil rights,"[11] Natives have not received any redress or satisfaction from the foreign government that oppresses them.[12] In *Treaties Made, Treaties Broken*, Helen Oliff cites that over five hundred treaties were signed with Indigenous peoples in the United States from 1778 to 1871, and all were "changed, broken, or nullified when it served the government's interest" (qtd. in Toensing 2013).[13] Adding insult to injury, the United States boldly voted against the UN Declaration on the Rights of the Indigenous People, which the rest of the General Assembly adopted on September 13, 2007 (Toensing 2013). It later endorsed the statement, but failed to address the context and content of the declaration in any fashion: No treaties were revisited, and no treaties were upheld. Ortiz's work seems to consider such modern realities, because his pieces do not deal in the fantastical, in the sense of conveying sentiments toward a "happy ending," or even suspended belief in the actualities of the current state of Native affairs. Instead, "the story . . . is ongoing and becomes a way for readers to make sense not only of themselves but of others as well" (Purnell and Bowman 2014, 177). And, as Purnell and Bowman assert, "narrative accounts of unresolved life events are important, and narratives that do not follow traditional scripts can be as healing as narratives of reconciliation" (178).

In "Men on the Moon," which gives its title to his short-story collection, Ortiz uses the interaction of a modern convenience and an aging Native man to emphasize such an idea. While technology changes the literal context of his home, the protagonist's perspective on life still adheres to Native values and beliefs because, as L. S. Vygotsky (1971) puts it, "the resolution of a certain, merely personal conflict, the revelation of a higher, more general, human truth in the phenomena of life" is revealed (ix). On Father's Day, Faustin receives a television set. The picture that appears before him is the second Apollo moon landing. This leads to a question-and-answer session between Faustin and his grandson Amarosho, who has recently been "educated" at an American school:

> Are those men looking for something on the moon, Nana? he [Faustin] asked his grandson.
>
> They're trying to find out what's on the moon, Nana. What kind of dirt and rocks there are and to see if there's any water. Scientist men don't believe there is any life on the moon. The men are looking for knowledge, Amarosho said to Faustin.
>
> Faustin wondered if the men had run out of places to look for knowledge on the earth. Do they know if they'll find knowledge? he asked.
>
> They have some already. They've gone before and come back. They're going again.
>
> Did they bring any back?
>
> They brought back rocks, Amarosho said. Rocks. Faustin laughed quietly. The American scientist men went to search for knowledge on the moon and they brought back rocks. (Ortiz 1999, 5)

The mere idea that men had to travel to the moon to discover knowledge is absurd to Faustin's Native viewpoint. Why would man have to escape the earth to locate "knowledge," when questions that have plagued society and the earth have gone unanswered for centuries? The fact that the scientists bring back rocks, of all things, exemplifies the irony, because rocks are building blocks of the earth (Faustin's homeland) and, as such, already sacred to Native Americans. The narrative can then be read as type of tragic humor. Khoo and Oliver state that "emotional clarification consists of two components operating in tandem: emotional engagement with a tragic narrative and related (concurrent and retrospective) self-reflection" (2013, 269). "Men on the Moon" encompasses both qualities, while drawing attention to how the narrative addresses the relationship of the land to Natives and (re)imagining how oneself engages with the world around them.

Ortiz's aptly named "Home Country" works in the same vein: the narrative emphasizes how "meaningful affect in response to a protagonist's distress may bring about a decrease in self-critical judgments." According to Khoo and Oliver, "the evocation of meaningful affective states, in response to others' distress, may facilitate self-compassion . . . a form of reflection that, in contrast to self-blaming, involves the following interrelated components: feelings of connectedness with other human beings, self-kindness, and mindfulness" (2013, 271). While "Home Country" works to express how Natives have become dislocated from their own people and, as a corollary, their homelands, the narrative simultaneously reinforces the idea that Natives can reconnect to culture and the land through (re)remembering the past.

This idea is set in motion by the death of a young Indian girl's mother. During her mother's illness, the girl recalls the state of affairs on the reservation: "Well, there was that feeling that things were changing, not only the men, the boys, but other things were changing" (Ortiz 1999, 15). These cultural and physical alterations placed restrictions on Native Americans' movements and/or reassigned them to locations that were, at times, wholly outside of their traditional comprehension of home: Upon her mother's demise, the young girl is quickly persuaded by an Anglo home-health-care nurse to leave the only place she has ever known to seek employment at a distant Indian School. She thinks, "Hardly anybody at home was working at something like that—no women anyway. And I would have to move away" (16). It is at this juncture that Ortiz, again, shifts the narrative's focus on (re)remembering the past to create a viable future by illuminating the girl's need to revert to her childhood, a point in time where she was embraced by the world and family around her: "I wanted to be a little girl again, running after the old man [her grandfather] when he hurried with his long legs to the cornfields or went for water down to the river" (18). In Native novels, William Bevis (1987) argues, "coming home, staying put, contracting, even what we call 'regressing' to a place, a past where one has been before, is not only the primary story, it is a primary mode of knowledge and a primary good" (582). Thus, for the sake of her spiritual, emotional, and mental health, her family, and the land, the girl needs to remain in at least psychological proximity to the people and place she has always known.

In "Something's Going On," the Native characters of the story initially attempt to assimilate into Western culture, but their plans are dramatically derailed when the patriarch of the family murders his Anglo employer. While such a deed is atrocious, Ortiz carefully draws attention to the underlying causes of the man's actions: The protagonist returns from an "American" war to find his wife and children destitute and living on a government reservation. Furthermore, he has been maimed in the fighting, and the repercussions are seemingly debilitating: "With crutches, his walk was jerky and awkward and he would often come to a halting stop" (Ortiz 1999, 60). Such an outcome is both physically and psychologically appropriate to the character's circumstances: "According to Freud, the merit of . . . transference is to allow the representation of an emotion which would otherwise remain repressed . . . [and] manifest itself as a symptom impinging on the patient's health" (Turri 2015, 374). However, when reading the story from the perspective of a communal narrator, the "symptoms" of such trauma are more than the aftermath of serving in the war, the individual's corporeal and mental wounds and resulting impairments: they represent the poverty of the people and their dislocation from the land caused by the man's removal from his family and home. Simultaneously addressing both of these issues, Ortiz's protagonist is unencumbered by his injuries in "the fields and pastures and mesa meadows, [where] his movements were smooth and fluid" (60–61). This drastic change in physical ability and, as a result, psychological easement relates how cohesion with homeland facilitates rather than hinders the Native man. In "Catharsis and Other Heresies," Thomas Scheff states that "the effectiveness of a cathartic technique for pathological bereavement (unresolved grief), called 're-grief therapy,' also supports the validity of catharsis" (2007, 100). For Natives, the loss of identity, place, and homeland are central to this "unresolved grief." To reconcile the Native psyche to its plight and condition, they must rely on the influence of and connection to the land, even if such an endeavor, in this case, depends upon the depictions and plot of a narrative.

Still, ever the realist, Ortiz is careful to remind his readers of the past and present and how internal as well as external forces have worked against their retention of the land and psychological connection to it: "As if disease and musket—both imported by whites—could not mow down the Indian fast enough, the fire water crept in and began to gnaw their vitals, debasing their morals, lowering their dignity, spreading contentions, confusions and death" (Weaver 1997, 63). When Harry J. Brown, the protagonist of "The Panther Waits," drunkenly determines to say something "important," the effects of alcohol lull him from his thoughts. He knows that something must be done, something must be said in regard to the land and people, but he is unable to find the words: "Sit down, I want to show you something," he tells narrator Jay. "And he pulled out this piece of paper. It was just an old piece of paper, sort of browned and folded, soft looking like he's carried it a long time. Listen, he said, and then he didn't say anything" (Ortiz 1999, 99). Brown seems to have no connection to his homeland because he is not able to conceptualize or (re)imagine himself within the scope of his environment. He is lost in his own home, a fact that Natives struggle with daily.

This character's case is crucial to understanding how and why catharsis is important, or even necessary, to Natives and their homelands in the contemporary world. In the Dewey-Mead model of communication, the authors propose that "[c]ollective repression of emotions may be one of the main causes of largescale violence" (Scheff 2007, 98). If Brown is, indeed, a paradigm of current Native existence, he is endowed with only two modes of recourse for his predicament outside the realm of violent retaliation: forgetting his people, the past, and the sacredness of the land, or reconnecting to those elements via (re)remembering and (re)imagining himself and them within the modern context. In "Discarding Sympathy, Disrupting Catharsis: The Mortification of Indigenous Flesh as Survivance-Intervention," Jill Carter (Anishinaabe) states, "The act of story-and-relationship-making among ourselves and with others is . . . an act of love; it is what maintains us, (re) creates us, and ultimately what defines us" (2015, 413).

Fittingly, in "The Panther Waits," the overarching theme of storytelling or story (re)telling emphasizes the importance of both Native unity and (re) creation in relation to homeland. Brown states, "You Indians must be together and be one people. You are all together on this land. This land is your home and you must see yourself as all together. You people, you gotta understand this. There is no other way we're gonna be able to save our land and our people unless we decide to be all together" (Ortiz 1999, 100). In the complete collection *Men on the Moon*, only three stories begin with quotes, and only "The Panther Waits" uses the serious and poignant words of Tecumseh to reiterate the significance of Native solidarity to sustain themselves: "That people will continue longest in the enjoyment of peace who timely prepare to vindicate themselves and manifest a determination to protect themselves whenever they are wronged" (97). The fact that such a message prefaces the drunken meanderings and "recollections" of the characters is beside the point. If anything, the importance of the content that is conveyed is even more significant because even the dullness of alcohol cannot dissuade the teller, Harry J. Brown, from delivering the message he knows to be true. He states, "They keep coming, and they want to take our land and our people. We have told them we cannot sell our mother earth, we cannot sell the ocean, we cannot sell the air, we cannot give our lives away" (100). In the same vein as Tecumseh's words, Brown advocates for active resistance against the oppressor: "We will have to defend these things, and we must do it all together. We must do it. . . . Listen" (100).

While Brown is in the middle of what one can only classify as an alcohol-induced diatribe, his meaning is not lost on his audience. They are not only engrossed, but they comprehend him. They become part of the story: "But what Harry was saying with his serious story voice put something there, I think. When I looked over at Taft again, he was nodding his head again like he understood perfectly what Harry J. Brown was saying" (101). It is this entrenched message that remains with Jay through Brown's telling and Jay's retelling (reimagining) to his friends, Billy and Sam. In turn, the reader becomes a new participant in the narrative. The piece, then, implies a type of challenge: Retell the story another time and/or never (dis)remember the story. As Jay remembers at the conclusion, "The two brothers were talking about the Americans coming, and they wanted the Indians to be all together so they could help each other fight them off. So they could save their land and their families and their ways. That's what I remembered a while ago. I thought I'd forgotten, but I don't think I'll ever forget" (101). By the simple act of retelling (reimaging) the story of the inebriated Harry J. Brown, Jay ensures that he and other Natives never discount the message, regardless of the origin of its repetition.[14]

"LOVE, ANGER, AND SIMON ORTIZ'S POETRY"

Standing before the children, I realized that what I do as a writer, teacher, and storyteller is to demystify language, and I smiled (Ortiz 1992, 3)

What I want is a full life
for my son,
for myself,
for my Mother,
the earth (Ortiz 1992, 56)

In the same manner as his short stories, Ortiz's poetry emphasizes the significance of the connection between people and homeland. However, his poetry—in both form and message—is a verbal explosion that attacks and disassembles the notion that the land and its inhabitants are psychologically separate. This type of linguistic analysis was used by early Russian Formalist critics (Viktor Shklovsky, Roman Jakobson, Boris Tomashevsky, Boris

Eikhenbaum) who believed that where "practical speech facilitates access to information by making language as transparent as possible, poetic speech contorts and roughens up ordinary language and submits it to what Roman Jakobson called 'organized violence,' and it is this roughening up of ordinary language into tortuous 'formed speech' that makes poetry poetry rather than a weather report" (Rivkin and Ryan 1998, 4). Ortiz uses this type of "organized violence" to appeal to his readers in short bursts of anger, art, compassion, and clarity that are tailored to express his belief that homeland is a living organism that must be carefully used and always respected.

In "My Father's Song," the land is an important part of a family unit rather than a resource to be depleted. While Ortiz writes this poem from his personal experience, the emphasis on the links among people, the land, the narrator, and language is clear: "I remember the very softness / of cool and warm sand and tiny alive / mice and my father saying things" (Ortiz 1992, 58). The description of the sand and the "tiny alive mice" illustrates the significance of the land's power to affect all creatures—both human and animal. The relation of this interaction is important because, as Ngugi wa Thiong'o states, "language is . . . inseparable from ourselves as a community of human beings with specific form and character, a specific history, a specific relationship to the world" (qtd. in Weaver 1997, 13). Ortiz later comments on this same idea: he "had been born into a people who knew and lived this way of life, who had accepted us as children of the human family, who were now entering a stage of life that required appropriate responsibilities and maturity" (Ortiz 1984, 59). He speaks of "responsibility" and "maturity" as indispensable and interrelated concepts that must be understood and addressed for his people to (re)remember and (re) imagine themselves and their connection to the land via the narrative medium. It is in this "opportunity to articulate such acts of resistance and to remember and articulate these moments of meaning in the midst of colonization's disordered assault" that one discovers "a vital, life-affirming act that connects the fallen ancestor, the current survivor, and the future descendant in a ceremony of mourning and a celebration of Indigenous endurance" (Carter 2015, 419).

In the poem "Buck Nez," Ortiz presents all life as equally meaningful and dependent on the land and each other. To illustrate, he recounts his journey home with a small puppy for his son:

You slept against my neck,
curled by my soul. Once,

I awoke to a tiny whimper,
and I worried
that I should feed you
when I had nothing to eat
myself. (Ortiz 1992, 55)

Ortiz's narrative creates an interaction where the puppy is not a mere animal, but an entity close to his "soul." It is something that has touched him in some fashion. Ortiz needs the puppy's proximity to bring about levity and cohesiveness with the world around him. Even though he is poverty-stricken, he is more concerned with satisfying the puppy's hunger than his own—the animal is a codependent, rather than a liability. The language of the poem is also a powerful step toward illuminating Ortiz's thematic commentary on land, people, and the power of the narrative. At its most fundamental and significant points, Ortiz's work conforms to Gerald Vizenor's term *survivance*: "an active sense of presence [in the world], the continuance of native stories, not a mere reaction, or a survivable name" in resistance to the "dominant mythos that continues to craft, support, and disseminate tragic fictions about a vanished/ing, 'primitive' People" (qtd. in Carter 2015, 419). It is then fitting that Ortiz pens a poem that literally and literarily creates an entity out of the land to stand as both a "presence" and a reminder of Native communalism.

In "A Story of How a Wall Stands," Ortiz details his experience of working with his father to create a stone wall by utilizing the gifts of the land that surround them.

He [Ortiz's father] tells me those things,
the story of them worked
with his fingers, in the palm
of his hands, working the stone
and the mud until they become
the wall that stands a long, long time. (1992, 145)

These lines not only give the reader insight into a precious father/son relationship, but also show the possibility of man and nature to form a bond that will last for "a long, long time." Furthermore, the fact that Ortiz and his father use their hands instead of tools to work the mud and stone depicts an elevated level of closeness that one can achieve with the land. While such poems obviously promote harmony between land and people, Ortiz's works in *Woven*

Stone also respond, much like his short stories, to the travesties that have and are plaguing the environment today.

Within this dialogue, Carter claims that Native "vigils, memorials, survivance-interventions, and performative mounds are in alignment and in conversation with each other" (2015, 432). Ortiz's "wall" acts in this performative manner: it is a solid structure (memorial) that represents Natives and the land. As Carter contends, "through the survivance-intervention, then, Indigenous people can fully realize and declare our existence in the present moment and so imagine ourselves and our nations in the future" (419). However, in order to accomplish this feat, it is necessary to return to the site of trauma. As Turri argues, applying Freud's theory of transference to Aristotle's tragic catharsis "allows for the representation and expression of repressed emotions through the reenactment of past relational dynamics" (2015, 95). In this case, Native oppression and subjugation are transferred to Ortiz's poems to reenact the tragic national dynamics of US and Native American interaction.

In the poem "It Was That Indian," Ortiz clearly demonstrates how the United States government refuses to take responsibility for destroying the Earth's natural beauty and resources and humankind through pollution. The town administration of Grants, New Mexico, at first honors Martinez (Navajo) for his early detection of uranium on the outskirts of Grants:

> Tourist magazines did a couple spreads
> on him, photographed him in Kodak color,
> and the Chamber of Commerce celebrated
> that Navajo man. (Ortiz 1992, 295)

But reverence for Martinez's discovery is short-lived after the multiple and compounded negative side effects of uranium mining become well-known:

> Well, later on,
> when some folks began to complain . . .
> lack of housing in Grants,
> cave-ins at Section 33,
> nonunion support
> high cost of living
> and uranium radiation causing cancer, they—the Chamber of Commerce—
> pointed out
> that it was Martinez

that Navajo Indian from over by Bluewater
who discovered uranium. (296)

The Grants Chamber of Commerce, which had previously recognized Martinez's find as an achievement worthy of magazine articles and photo spreads, retracts its initial enthusiasm and transfers the horrors of uranium mining back onto Martinez. In Martinez's time (the 1950s), the toxic effects of uranium exposure were not wholly known, and while the effects of contact with the substance are still somewhat inconclusive, repeated and high-dose exposure is lethal to all forms of life. Sadly, an investigation into the effects of uranium exposure on Native workers, awarding of reparations, and a study of how the process of mining drastically transformed the land were not initiated until 2012.[15]

In reaction to such historical injustice, Ortiz states that "it is not only a matter of preserving and protecting Indian lands as some kind of natural wilderness or cultural parks; rather, it is a matter of how those lands can be productive in terms which are Indian peoples to make, instead of Indian people being forced to serve a U.S. national interest which has never adequately served them. Those lands can be productive to serve humanity" (1992, 360). For many Natives, only through his narrative can they—the readers and their communities—learn of such atrocities, address them, and, most importantly, process them through catharsis in order to obtain both insight and wisdom in the matter. Stories are much more than information: they are a way to acknowledge, heal from, and react to US policies that have contaminated the land or made it inaccessible to Native Americans.

Drawing attention to a specific locale in "That's the Place Indians Talk About," Ortiz recounts how Coso Hot Springs was previously "a sacred and healing place for the Shoshonean peoples" (1992, 321). This blessed place is, for many tribes, the site of miraculous medicine that promotes good health. In fact, it is widely believed that the mysterious waters can cure the Shoshonean people of any ailments that might afflict them:

Children, women, men,
we would all go up there.
You drink that water, it makes you well.
You put it on your hands, face, all over,
and you get well, all well. (321)

Unfortunately for Natives, the United States did not merely enclose the sacred springs, but used the land for testing that could potentially do irreversible harm to their delicate ecosystem. While this "fountain of youth" may seem farfetched by conventional Western thinking, the fact remains that the United States had no right to deny access to the springs to Natives, who formerly possessed the territory until the US Cavalry built a fort at Coso "to stop Indians from attacking the Coso miners during the 1860's" ("Historic" 2002, 1). These miners were gold hunters who pleaded for and received US Army protection while drastically transforming both the consistency and composition of the land.

In the end, Natives of Coso Springs submitted to American expansionism. The conflict was settled when miners at Darwin agreed to provide jobs to Native Americans at the local smelter in return for the use of the spring ("Historic" 2002, 1). The Shoshonean people's land, culture, and labor was bought for a wage, which ultimately allowed them to survive, but never live. Furthermore, the ecological consequences of acquiescing to Western demands for use of the springs were either ignored or unrealized. The springs themselves are located "within the China Lake Naval Station. Like Los Alamos Scientific Laboratories in New Mexico, the naval station is a center for the development, experimentation, and testing of U.S. military weapons" (Ortiz 1992, 321).

However, Ortiz is careful to remind his readers that reconception, and therefore (re)imagining, is key to creating a positive future out of past oppression and subjugation:

Hearing,
that's the way you listen.
The People talking,
telling the power to come to them
and pretty soon it will come.
It will come,
the moving power of the voice,
the moving power of the earth
the moving power of the people.
That's the place Indian People Talk About. (1992, 324)

The "voice" here is undeniably linked to the land, and it is through that relationship that both can once again obtain power in this world. The narrative (the telling and reading) creates a space of catharsis, but it also advocates a new world order in which the storyteller is indebted to the land for the story. The emotional range and limits of the catharsis are defined by its ability to purge emotions connected to oppression and marginalization, and the aftermath creates an opportunity for growth: reconnection to the land and people through (re)imagining who they are within that context.

Simon Ortiz is, for the sake of the planet and its people, intelligently and productively creating new[16] routes of criticism that combine literature and psychology in a fashion that questions the direction of the world in its present state and addresses how the racial and ecological injustices that have happened can be corrected or abated. He speaks with the heart of an educator, philosopher, student, and citizen of the world when he states that corn "is a food, gift, seed, symbol, and it is the very essence of humankind's tending and nurturing of life, land, and product of physical, mental, and emotional work. Corn cannot be regarded as anything less than a sacred and holy and respected product of the creative forces of life, land, and the people's responsibilities and the relationships. And when loss and waste are spoken of, it is in the same mythic proportion because it is totally serious business that life should not be destroyed" (Ortiz 1992, 346). Therefore, all things living and nonliving, human and nonhuman, share equal "responsibility" and depend upon each other for livelihood and productivity. Their relationship cannot be swung out of balance without causing catastrophe—losing one's home, space, place, and identity. Ortiz's writing, although steeped in the reality of contemporary Native American life, works to reeducate his readers on the importance of acknowledging both the past and present circumstances for Indigenous peoples. It also creates a theater in which they can process such actualities to (re)remember how their Native ancestors interacted in and with the land and (re)imagine how contemporary Natives might positively redefine home within the aftermath of colonization.

In "Transference and Katharsis, Freud to Aristotle," Turri (2015) elaborates on this idea: "In the transference it is the reattribution of the aroused affects to a past relationship which cures through an elaboration of meaning which allows the patient to take a view on this emotion from a distance wherein he can reflect on them as signifying a part of his history and reevaluate their validity for the here and now" (376). Within the Native American context, Ortiz is not simply the architect or the patient: the Native community as a whole learns through such (re)remembering to (re)imagine a new future through catharsis. Such an objective is not an easy task to accomplish, but it is necessary to secure a psychological and literal home in the modern world, and therefore "a necessity for the survival of a society in the long run" (Scheff 2007, 100). For Natives, then, the process of catharsis is not a solution: it is the initial step toward (re)creating and actualizing themselves within the scope and notion of their homelands.

NOTES

1. "Aristotle's theory of tragic *katharsis* is the most ancient theory describing the effect of the theatrical experience on the audience. It is set forth in the Poetics (1449b24–28) and it states that tragedy is 'a representation [*mimesis*] of an action which is serious, complete . . . and through the arousal of pity and dear effecting the *kartharsis* of such emotions'" (qtd. in Turri 370, author's emphasis). Arnold Krupat (1995) elaborates on this concept in his article "American Histories, Native American Narratives" when he quotes Raymond DeMallie, former president of the American Society for Ethnohistory. In his address, DeMallie claims that "if we are to understand history as lived reality, it is essential to understand the perspectives of the actors involved" (169).

2. The term "catharsis" originated with Aristotle and evolved with Freud, but for the sake of my contentions, Guan Soon Khoo and Mary Beth Oliver's studies and M. G. Turri's contentions are paramount. While the former tackle the subject matter from the "*Scientific Study of Literature*" and the latter from a traditional psychological perspective, both parties' definitions of catharsis complement the notion that it is more than a simple "purging" of emotions through mimesis. (Note: Quotations are intentionally used around the journal title because such a feat as it describes seems theoretical, at best).

3. Anastacia Schulhoff reiterates this sentiment when she states, "Attempting to create an 'authentic' and less marginalized identity for these storytellers is a political, social, and cultural act that has very real everyday consequences" (169). Schulhoff is referenced at length in the body of this essay, but her contentions are important to insert here because they so closely support Gloria Bird's view from a social sciences perspective. In fact, she notes that "narrative research has become popular in the social sciences because people make sense of others, their selves, and their social worlds through stories" (167).

4. The Acoma Pueblo page of the Sky Center Cultural Museum & Haak'u Museum website claims that "since 1150, Acoma Pueblo has earned the reputation as the oldest continuously inhabited community in North America." This time is debated by fifty years on both ends of the spectrum, but the pueblo's name means "a place always prepared."

5. Krupat specifically mentions Ortiz's *From Sand Creek* (1981).

6. The terms (re)remembering and (re)imagining are used because a substantial percentage of Native Americans do not have a historical or even literary context for their own past because of external powers, such as boarding schools, or internal influences, such as the need for social acceptance via assimilation. Each contention and its categorization is debatable, but those are arguments for another time. I am simply explaining that in order to (re)imagine themselves outside of the oppression of colonization, they must have a historical (or literary, in this case) basis for reconceptualizing themselves and their homeland in a positive, communal manner.

7. Lee Cuba and David Hummon's "Constructing a Sense of Home: Place Affiliation and Migration across the Life Cycle," John Gamber's "'Outcasts and Dreamers in the Cities': Urbanity and Pollution in *Dead Voices*," and, most notably, William Bevis's "Native American Novels: Homing In" investigate the causes and outcomes (and future outcomes) of how Natives living in these occupied homelands must (re)remember and (re)imagine themselves and the world through the lens of storytelling.

8. In this article, the term Native without quotation marks describes Native Americans. "Native" is a label for non–Native Americans who live and work within the same geographical confines.

9. In a bit of irony, the United States Supreme Court, during the *Carpenter v. Shaw* (1930) case, declared that Natives were "weak and defenseless people who are wards of the nation, dependent upon its protection and good faith" (qtd. in Johansen and Lewis 2015, 4). Unfortunately, such "protection" and "good faith" seem to be both arbitrary and mostly in favor of Western idealism.

10. Jerome Rothenberg's 2015 comments in "Poems and Poetics" elaborate on his careful work with fellow editor Diane Rothenberg on "Song/Poetry and Language—Expression and Perception" in *Symposium of the Whole: A Range of Discourse toward an Ethnopoetics* from 1983.

11. See the General Allotment Act of 1887, the failed American Indian Movement's "Trail of Broken Treaties" from 1972, and, most recently, Gale Toensing's 2013 article "Honor the Treaties" in the newspaper *Indian Country Today*.

12. See also Bruce Johansen and Thomas Lewis' "Native American Treaties and the Supreme Court." They trace the application of Article III of the United States Constitution to Native treaties, and how the Supreme Court has insisted that "treaties were not necessarily meant to endure in perpetuity."

13. Ari Kelman takes this fact a bit further in her article "'We Are All Americans': Native Peoples in the National Narrative." She quotes post–Civil War reformer Ely Parker, who suggests "in his report on frontier violence, the federal government's lack of commitment to its treaty obligations, the presence of traders with unfettered access to Native peoples, and incompetent local officials created a great deal of bureaucratic bungling and unnecessary blood shed" (668).

14. "Origin of its repetition" is used here to clarify that the story is continuous.

Harry J. Brown does not define the story or the telling of it. In fact, the text makes clear that he is reading it from a folded old piece of paper.

15. "The Radiation Exposure Compensation Act ("the Act" or "RECA"), 42 U.S.C. § 2210 note (2012) established an administrative program for claims relating to atmospheric nuclear testing, and claims relating to uranium industry employment. The Act delegated authority to the Attorney General to establish procedures and make determinations regarding whether claims satisfy statutory eligibility criteria." However, it should be noted, according to the same publication, that this act was only established "as an expeditious, low-cost alternative to litigation."

16. Notions of catharsis have recently reemerged in the field of psychology that complement Aristotle's original version of the term. While Freud's interpretations of both "catharsis" and "transference"' are equally important to this argument, the convergence of the above ideas is deemed "new."

WORKS CITED

Adams, T. E. 2008. "A Review of Narrative Ethics." *Qualitative Inquiry* 14, no. 2: 175–94.

Ambler, Marjane. 1999. "Of Innocence and Catharsis." *Tribal College Student Art, Writing, and Expression*. August 15, 1999. http://tcjstudent.org/introduction-1999.

Bevis, William. 1987. "Native American Novels: Homing In." In *Recovering the Word: Essays on Native American Literatures*, edited by Brian Swann and Arnold Krupat, 580–620. Berkeley: University of California Press.

Bird, Gloria. 1998. "Breaking the Silence." In *Speaking for the Generations: Native Writers on Writing*, edited by Simon Ortiz, 25–45. Tucson: University of Arizona Press.

Carter, Jill. 2015. "Discarding Sympathy, Disrupting Catharsis: The Mortification of Indigenous Flesh as Survivance-Intervention." *Theatre Journal* 67: 413–32.

Cuba, Lee, and David Hummon. 1993. "Constructing a Sense of Home: Place Affiliation and Migration across the Life Cycle." *Sociology Forum* 8, no. 4: 547–72.

Gamber, John. 2007. "'Outcasts and Dreamers in the Cities': Urbanity and Pollution in *Dead Voices*." *PMLA* 122, no. 1: 179–93.

"Historic Military Sites." 2002. Historic Military Sites Information, 5 April 2002. http://www.nawcwpns.navy.mil/~epo/hms.html.

Johansen, Bruce, ed. 2015. *American Indian Culture: From Counting Coup to Wampum*. 2 vols. Santa Barbara, CA: Greenwood.

Johansen, Bruce, and Thomas Lewis. 2015. "Native American Treaties and the Supreme Court." *Encyclopedia of the American Indian Movement*. Pasadena, CA: Salem Press, 3.

Kelman, Ari. 2014. "'We Are All Americans': Native Peoples in the National Narrative." *Reviews in American History* 42, no. 4: 661–69.

Khoo, Guan, and Mary Beth Oliver. 2013. "The Therapeutic Effects of Narrative Cinema through Clarification: Reexamining Catharsis." *Scientific Study of Literature* 3, no. 2: 266–93.

Krupat, Arnold. 1995. "American Histories, Native American Narratives." *Early American Literature* 30: 165–74.

Ortiz, Simon. 1983. "Song/Poetry and Language—Expression and Perception." *Symposium of the Whole: A Range of Discourse toward an Ethnopoetics*, edited by Jerome Rothenberg and Diane Rothenberg, 399–407. Berkeley: University of California Press.

———. 1984. "Always the Stories: A Brief History and Thoughts on My Writing." In *Coyote Was Here: Essays on Contemporary Native American Literary and Political Mobilization*, edited by Bo Schöler, 57–69. Aarhus, Denmark: Seklos.

———. 1992. *Woven Stone.* Tucson: University of Arizona Press.

———. 1999. *Men on the Moon.* Tucson: University of Arizona Press.

Petzak, Nicholas. 2010. Review of *Crisscrossing Borders in Literature of the American West*, edited by Reginald Dyck and Cheli Reutter (New York: Palgrave Macmillan, 2009). *Western American Literature* 44, no. 4: 396–97.

Purnell, David, and Jim Bowman. 2014. "'Happily Ever After': Are Traditional Scripts Just for Fairy Tales?" *Narrative Inquiry* 24, no. 1: 175–80.

Radiation Exposure Compensation Act. 2012. 42 U.S.C. § 2210 note.

Rivkin, Julie, and Michael Ryan. 1998. "Introduction: 'Formalists.'" *Literary Theory: An Anthology.* Chichester, UK: Blackwell.

Rothenberg, Jerome. 2015. "Jerome Rothenberg: Poems and Poetics." Jacket 2. https://jacket2.org/commentary/jerome-rothenberg.

Scheff, Thomas. 2007. "Catharsis and Other Heresies: A Theory of Emotion." *Journal of Social, Evolutionary, and Cultural Psychology* 1, no. 3: 98–113.

Schulhoff, Anastacia. 2015. "More than Native American Narratives: Temporal Shifting and Authentic Identities." *Narrative Inquiry* 25, no. 1: 166–83.

Toensing, Gale. 2013. "'Honor the Treaties': UN Human Rights Chief's Message." *Indian Country Today*, August 24, 2013.

Turri, Maria. 2015. "Transference and Katharsis, Freud to Aristotle." *International Journal of Psychoanalysis* 96: 369–87.

Vives, Jean-Michel. 2011. "Catharsis: Psychoanalysis and the Theatre." *International Journal of Psychoanalysis* 92: 1009–27.

Vygotsky, L. S. 1971. *The Psychology of Art.* Cambridge, MA: M.I.T. Press.

Weaver, Jace. 1997. *That the People Might Live.* New York: Oxford University Press.

Wiget, Andrew. 1991. Review of *Narrative Chance: Postmodern Discourse on Native American Indian Literatures* by Gerald Vizenor (Norman: University of Oklahoma Press, 1993). *Modern Philology* 88, no. 4: 476–79.

CHAPTER TWELVE

La Querencia
The Genízaro Cultural Landscape Model
of Community Land Grants in Northern New Mexico

MOISES GONZALES

INTRODUCTION

Querencia is a common vernacular concept used by Indo-Hispano people of the Northern Río Grande Bioregion to describe their connection to a homeland. In the late 1990s, the term began to make a more formal academic presence to describe an Indigenous Chicano land ethic connected to cultural landscape. In 1997, an article entitled "La Querencia: La Raza" was published by Juan Estevan Arellano, who was one of the principal members of *La Academia de La Nueva Raza*. Arellano pushed the scholarly evolution of the concept from a common vernacular meaning into a scholarly theoretical framework used to describe a complex cultural landscape. This reframing of querencia inspired many young New Mexican land and water activists such as Paula García of the New Mexico Acequia Association, Miguel Santistevan, and myself in my own work on the land-grant movement to adopt the concept as a movement framework. Today, the next generations of scholars from the Upper Río Grande region continue to build on the cultural landscape framework of querencia in order to construct strategies for the protection and resiliency of land grant and *acequia* (ditch or irrigation canal) based communities.

The purpose of this chapter is to describe the concept of querencia as a cultural landscape framework of resiliency embedded in land-grant communities throughout New Mexico and to explain how this model can be used a tool of analysis to help Indo-Hispano communities develop intergenerational capacity for the perseverance of cultural production in northern New Mexico. In 2014, a group of land-grant and acequia scholars met to develop a methodology for creating a description of elements that identified the natural and cultural attributes found in communal land grants and acequia landscapes. To

my knowledge, this was the first time New Mexico cultural landscape scholars such as Devon Peña, José Rivera, Juan Estevan Arellano, Sylvia Rodríguez,
Enrique Lamadrid, Nejem Raheem, Arnold Valdez, and I, along with other
interdisciplinary scholars, set out to map the attributes that define the land-
grant and acequia cultural landscape (Raheem 2015, 559).

The goal of this research was to develop new ways of understanding the
value of the landscape from a land-based perspective and extract traditional
local knowledge to legitimize the land-use practices of Indo-Hispanos
as sustainable. Moving forward from this experience, I have worked on
plaza restoration and community development projects in various *genízaro*
(pan-Indigenous groups of the Southwest) communities throughout New
Mexico, such as Abiquiu, Pueblo Quemado (present-day Córdova), Embudo, and San Antonio de Las Huertas, as well as my own community in
the Cañón de Carnué Land Grant east of Albuquerque. Graduate students
from Chicana and Chicano Studies, scholars at the Southwest Hispanic Research Institute (SHRI), and physical planning students from the Resource
Center for Raza Planning in the School of Architecture and Planning at
the University of New Mexico (UNM) and I have built on the community
mapping methodologies developed in Embudo to expand and understand
the relationships between natural, social-cultural, and built environments.
This chapter demonstrates how querencia is a system of cultural landscape
resiliency in New Mexico. The model is explicated and demonstrated at and
examines how this research methodology can be applied at the community
scale, such as in the genízaro settlement of the Cañón de Carnué Land Grant.

LA QUERENCIA LANDSCAPE MODEL

The process of transforming the localized term of querencia from the meaning of "love of place" into a cultural landscape model has been in evolution
by regional scholars since the 1990s. The post-1960s evolution began in the
late 1960s with *la academia*, but was analyzed deeply by Arellano (1997), Peña
(1999), Lamadrid (2003), Rivera (2005), and Rodríguez (2006). Each of these
scholars examined and described the cultural landscape as a process of cultural production and performance, bioregionalism, environmental resiliency,
and community governance, as well as reciprocity through community mutual societies. Although they do not cite querencia explicitly in their work,
these scholars use concepts and systems from the *merced* (land grant) and

MAP 12.1 Bernardo de
Miera y Pacheco, Alcaldía
de Alburquerque (Carnué
context map), 1779.

acequia social institutions and community rituals to describe the historical
connection of communities to a regional landscape. More recently, scholars
such as Nejem Raheem have been unpacking the landscape framework of
querencia and developing ecosystems services model for the protection of
upland cultural resources in the Upper Gallina Watershed and the upper Río
Grande watershed. In the last few years in my work as an urban designer,
I have started to deconstruct the highly complex systems embedded in the
cultural landscape of northern New Mexico in developing historic restoration
plans for the Plaza de Cerro in Chimayó (Gonzales 2017, 68–88), as well as
ongoing work in the Pueblo de Abiquiu.

While working with some students in the SHRI summer community learning and engagement field school at UNM to restore the plaza in Abiquiu, I
I realized the project would need to involve a variety of community stake-
holders. Abiquiu is a high-mountain genízaro community that still owns approximately sixteen thousand acres as a communal land grant. In order for

the community to implement a historic restoration plan for the plaza, the project would need to engage with the entire Abiquiu community to fully understand local knowledge. I told my students that we would understand the historic morphology of the plaza better through understanding the querencia of Abiquiu. During a class session, I recognized that we needed to deeply deconstruct the elements that informed querencia through the natural systems, the physical elements of the community, and the social-cultural systems that collectively inform a cultural landscape. For the next month, we developed a cultural mapping assessment to map the querencia of Abiquiu from its plazas (town squares), *moradas* (prayer chapels), acequias, confraternities, and Indigenous cultural societies. This process allowed us to develop an understanding of the community's capacity to maintain the cultural landscape and build system resiliency. From this experience, I have refined the querencia landscape model as a tool to understand cultural resiliency in other genízaro communities, such as my own in the Cañón de Carnué Land Grant, located in the Sandía Mountains.

The querencia model is a synthesis of cultural landscape elements that New Mexican scholars have identified and I have adapted into an analytical mode for understanding community resiliency. The three major systems that make up the querencia landscape model are the Natural System, the Physical System, and the Social-Cultural System. The Natural System is a community's natural landscape, which consists of the following elements: *sierras* (mountain ranges), *montes* (mountains), *cerros* (foothills), *lomas* (hills), *arroyos* (ephemeral washes), *llanos* (plains), *altitos* (uplands), *bosques* (riparian zones), *ciénegas* (wetlands), *ríos* (rivers), *riítos* (streams), and *ojitos* (springs).This Natural System was organized in the seventeenth century into a land management and a built environment system, which I label as its Physical Systems. The 1680 *Recopilación de las leyes de los reinos de las Indias*, otherwise known as the Laws of the Indies, prescribed the foundation for the spatial organization of the physical built environment, as well as land management principles.

The Physical System of querencia includes mercedes, *solares* (house lots), *suertes* (farm plots), *baldidos* (commons shared among various settlements), *ejidos* (common lands), *propios* (town reserve lands), *dehesas* (common grazing areas); acequias and their components: *la presa* (the main head gate), the *acequia madre* (mother ditch), *sangrías* (lateral ditches), *compuertas* (head gates for the diversion of water), and *desagues* (channels or outlets at locations along the acequia madre to divert water back into the river or another acequia);

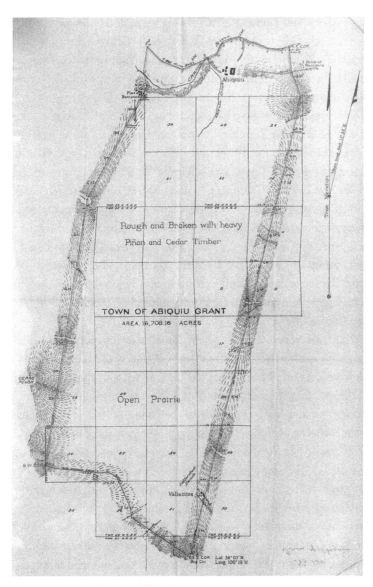

Abiquiu

Rough and Broken with heavy
Piñon and Cedar Timber

TOWN OF ABIQUIU GRANT

AREA 16,708.16 ACRES

Open Prairie

CERRO
PELON

Vallecitos

Lat. 36° 07' N.
Long 106° 19' W.

MAP 12.2 Historic Pueblo of Abiquiu land grant boundary patent.
Map courtesy of the US Survey General.

and building systems and landmarks such as plazas, *salas* (community halls), moradas, *capillas* (chapels), *camposantos* (cemeteries), *calvarios* (processional prayer routes, such as stations of the cross), and *rutas de ceremonía* (ceremonial routes). Finally, the highly complex Social-Cultural System works to maintain and sustain both the Natural System and the Physical System in communities. This is organized by governance, confraternities, ritual societies, and artisans. It is by no means hierarchical, but is a collaborative for the maintenance of community structure. The Social-Cultural System is organized by the following typologies: *El Concilio de la Merced* (Land Grant Council), *La Comisión de la Acequia Madre* (Acequia Commission), *mayordomo* (ditch boss), *parciantes* (irrigators on an acequia system), *ganadores* (grazers), *cofradías* (confraternities, or ritual dance societies), *Carmelitas* (Carmelites), *Los Hermanos de La Fraternidad Piadosa de Nuestro Padre Jesús Nazareno* (The Brothers of the Pious Fraternity of Our Father Jesus the Nazarene, also known as *Los Penitentes* and *Los Hermanos*), *danzantes* (ceremonial dancers), *mayordomos de las fiestas* (caretakers of community feast days), *curanderas* (healers), *artesanos* (artisans), and *músicos* (musicians).

The concept of querencia is a reciprocal complex of interconnected relationships among these three systems that helps maintain the cultural homeland of Nuevomexicanos. The resiliency and maintenance of the community is based on maintaining the cultural landscape, such as irrigable crops in the suertes and hunting and wood-gathering in the ejidos, as well as the collaboration of the social institutions. Community moradas and capillas would not be maintained if not for the work of la Hermandad and las Carmelitas through mutual aid. The complex social organization in the community has *tareas de obligación* (obligatory community work contribution), which translates to individual contribution to the entire community. For this reason, the contemporary use of the word querencia as a term referring to the identity of New Mexican people is problematic because it overromanticizes the concept without placing the true meaning in collective action of maintaining the landscape and the individual's role to the entire community. The use of querencia as a concept associated with the connection to place is misunderstood because, in a cultural landscape, the concept is more related to the fulfillment of one's tarea, and therefore is more a process than a state of being. The state of being is expressed as a result of the process of collective community action. The cultural landscape model of querencia requires a highly sophisticated relationship between governance and social organization.

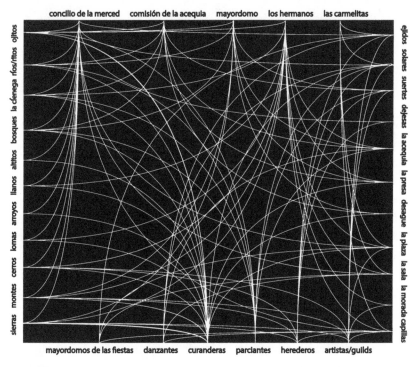

concilio de la merced · comisión de la acequia · mayordomo · los hermanos · las carmelitas

ejidos solares suertes dejesas la acequia la presa desague la plaza la sala la morada capillas

sierras montes cerros lomas arroyos llanos altitos bosques la cienega ríos/ritos ojitos

mayordomos de las fiestas · danzantes · curanderas · parciantes · herederos · artistas/guilds

FIGURE 12.1 Moises Gonzales, Data visualization mapping system of complexity in the Querencia Cultural Landscape Model, 2017. Courtesy of Moises Gonzales.

QUERENCIA MAINTENANCE THROUGH *TAREA*
AND *DELIGENCIA* (WORK EFFORT)

In the high-mountain genízaro communities of northern New Mexico—Abiquiu, Cañón de Carnué, Pueblo Quemado (Córdova), and Placitas (San Antonio de Las Huertas)—have relied on the social organization of obligación since at least the eighteenth century, when high-mountain community land grants were established to serve as buffer settlements against nomadic Indian raids for the larger settlements of Santa Fe, Santa Cruz, and Albuquerque and organized in town governmental units. The Leyes de las Indias that established land-grant settlement in New Mexico required each merced to be run by a *Concilio de Merced* (Land Grant Council) elected by the community members to manage the natural system of the ejidos and baldidos and assign solares, as well as maintain the physical systems of the central plaza. Additionally, the concilio maintains the community salas and manages the grazing of stock and hunting and gathering of resources on the common lands. The acequia governance system, also a governmental entity of the community, manages the irrigation infrastructure and the land related to the acequia network—ríos, riítos, and ojitos—and maintains the physical systems related to them—acequia madre, presas, desagues, and *tanques* (water reservoirs). The acequia commission leaders are elected by the parciantes and a mayordomo, who "manages" the water distribution of an acequia system in the community.

Religious and ritual societies form the next segment of social organization and are responsible for maintaining elements of the natural and physical world of local communities. These groups are made up of cofradías and leaders chosen to maintain social structure. The former are organized along gender lines, such as the *Cofradía de Nuestra Señora del Carmel* (or simply *Las Carmelitas*) for the women, and *los hermanos penitentes* for men. Beyond their duties in private ceremonial rituals and serving as spiritual guides to the entire community, the hermanos are tasked with maintaining the social order and community consensus. In addition, they maintain the physical elements of the moradas, ceremonial ritual routes, as well as important physical landmarks. Las Carmelitas are organized as a religious devotional society; however, their historical role has been to leverage community economic assets to care for less-fortunate families and community members in need of assistance. They served as the community social safety net long before public governmental assistance ever existed: they helped place orphans into permanent families, provided financial security to widowed community members, and ensured that the elderly were cared for in the community.

The mayordomos of community fiestas also help uphold social order in the community because they are obligated to maintain the parish church and community capillas and organize annual Catholic feast days, which involve the collaboration of community social structures. They are also tasked with raising funds from the community to maintain these churches and chapels. Ritual dance societies associated with many Genízaro communities in the upper Río Grande Bioregion also play an important role in the social order of community. Groups such as the *Matachines* (Matachín Dancers) and *Los Comanches* (Comanche Dancers) are vital beyond production and maintenance of cultural memory and performance during saints' days: they also teach and reinforce the oral traditions, social norms, and community structures to younger members. The *curandera/os* (traditional healers) are also a segment of querencia social society because they have learned the relationships among the natural, physical, and spiritual worlds. The obligation of the curanderos is to serve as spiritual guides and healers to all community members. Historically, curandera/os have been the most knowledgeable about the entire natural system of the cultural landscape because the wild and domestic plants used for traditional healing are harvested across all the natural typologies from the bosques, suertes, and sierras. Loss of knowledge in this organization can have lasting negative impacts on how the Concilio de la Merced makes decisions on land management. For example, if the knowledge about the use of medicinal plants is lost, so is the knowledge of how the plant is managed in the communal landscape.

Artisans and craft guilds once existed in every community in the Río Grande Bioregion. According to the 1790 census of New Mexico, weavers and carders were common occupations among Nuevomexicanos at a period of time when weaving production had probably reached its peak (Olmstead 1975). In the eighteenth and early nineteenth centuries, trade into central Mexico was limited, while trade on the plains with the Comanche, Utes, and Kiowa was more common. Therefore, the lack of regional trade required that communities be self-reliant. Localized pottery such as *tinaja* (large storage jars), Carnué gray utilityware, embroidery, weaving, woodcarving, and tanned buffalo skins for clothing and moccasins were commonly produced by individual artists and guilds in genízaro frontier settlements. According to Adeliada Chávez, describing community production in the Sandía Mountains in the nineteenth century, "Aside from all these labors there was weaving of wool into cloth, and the making of it into garments for the women and children and into shirts for the men. Many skins of animals tanned to perfection by a member of the great household were made into breeches for the men and boys and leggings and *tewas* (moccasins) for the whole clan. The work of the skins was a fulltime employment for one member of the household" (qtd. in Rebolledo and Márquez 2000, 167). The work of artisans historically and today best represents the material culture of querencia through the metal arts, woodworking, pottery, and weaving throughout the Indo-Hispano homeland.

The purpose of deconstructing querencia as a cultural landscape model is to explicate the natural, social, and cultural order of communities in northern New Mexico and demonstrate how this order maintains cultural resiliency. Conversely, the deconstruction and understanding of the cultural landscape as a typological network of relationships and collaboration between a complex social and natural world helps us understand querencia. The model is not only a framework for understanding querencia, but also an analytical tool to help inform how high-mountain villages maintain culture and identity. Therefore, querencia is deeper than a connection to place and homeland, but is a highly collective process working to sustain a *nacimiento*, a place one is born into with an obligation to participate in its maintenance.

THE CARNUÉ LAND GRANT: A BRIEF HISTORY

The Cañón de Carnué Land Grant east of the Villa de Alburquerque, in the Sandía Mountains, is one of several genízaro settlements that exist today. It was initially established as a buffer settlement in 1763. Its purpose was to protect the entrada from attacks by the Utes, Comanche, and Apache. The land grant was envisioned by Governor Tomás Vélez Cachupín as providing opportunity for Genízaros to acquire land, but also serving a purpose to the colony (Gonzales 2014, 583–602). Governor Cachupín believed that establishing community land grants for Genízaros was a way to move this landless Indigenous population living in servitude into land ownership. "During those years, *Genízaros* were living, not only in Abiquiu but also neighboring Ojo Caliente, in Santa Fe, Trampas, Ranchos de Taos, [and] Carnue(l), in a number of Río Grande Indian Pueblos and in various plazas of the Belén and Tomé Area" (Swadesh 1974, 31). Genízaro communities became important vehicles for the assimilation of captive Native Americans into Spanish colonial life and their indoctrination into Catholicism (Córdova 1976).

In much of New Mexico's literary history, scholars have seldom recognized or appreciated the role of genízaro land-grant communities in the defense and buffer protection of both Pueblo Indian and Hispano settlements along the upper and middle Río Grande valleys. Ned Blackhawk, a Western Shoshone scholar, in his book *Violence over the Land: Indians and Empires in the Early American West* (2006), affirms the importance of genízaros in sustaining settlements in New Mexico. According to Blackhawk, "Over time, genízaros constituted upward of a third of many northern towns and played central roles in the fortification and defense of the colony. Indeed, the sustained incorporation of Indian captives into colonial society led to the eventual creation of northern villages capable of buffering New Mexico from nomadic attack.

Originally born into or descended from northern Indian societies, genízaros helped defend colonial society from raids from northern communities" (57).

The importance of Genízaro epistemology in the conceptualization and theorization of querencia is that it occupies another space outside of the Pueblo Indian and Hispano imaginary and places it directly in relation with equestrian and plains nations such as the Ute, Diné, Apache, Comanche, and Kiowa. As Blackhawk reflects, "genízaros continued to maintain social relations with northern Indian communities, and when Indian rancherías visited, former and now Hispanicized captives and their children reconnected with family and friends, sharing their respective languages and customs, as well as new stories and older memories" (113).

Like many frontier settlements of the eighteenth and early nineteenth centuries, these communities were often abandoned temporarily and resettled due to constant attack by nomadic raiding bands of Utes, Navajos, and Apaches (Archibauld 1976, 313). By the late 1700s, Carnué had suffered many attacks and been abandoned and resettled by additional landless mixed-class Genízaros, as well as the children of the original settlement (Gonzales 2014, 583–602). In 1819, under pressure from prominent local families of the Río Abajo to protect grazing land, along with the desire for landless Genízaro, Coyote, and Genízaro/Mestizo population to acquire lands, the Spanish officials once again opened the Carnué Land Grant for settlement as a new land grant. The people who responded were landless mixed Indigenous populations from Los Padillas, Valencia, Belén, Atrisco, Los Ranchos de Albuquerque, and Alameda (Rodríguez 1997, 125). In many cases, the petitioners were seeking opportunity and escape from servitude and peonage. Two settlements were established, one in Carnuel at the mouth of the Tijeras Canyon and the other, San Antonio de Padua, on the east slope of the Sandía Mountains. The boundaries of the grant were described by Josef Mariano de la Peña, secretary for Governor Facundo Melgares, as "the entrance of the Cañón de San Miguel de Carnué to the Tijera, the width of the canyon west to east and here South to North as far as the cross set up to the North of San Antonio" (SANM I, Reel 27, Frame 864–68). At San Antonio and Carnué, two defensible compact plazas were established measuring fifty *varas* (yards) square, and solares were assigned there. On February 5, 1819, suertes were assigned in Carnué along the Rito de Carnue (Carnue Creek), and on February 26 of that same year, suertes were assigned at San Antonio de Padua.

The two fortified plazas were constructed as a community project, as was the organization of churches within the walls of the plaza. It is apparent that the construction of an acequia system was a collective project by community members of the entire land grant. Also, both acequia systems were hydrologically connected with two independent acequias, which explains the collective water management across all community members. According to the Spanish Archives of New Mexico, evidence supports strong local collaboration in managing community systems in terms of governance and collective action. On April 21, 1819, an ordinance was issued for San Miguel de Carnué and San Antonio that stated:

> 1st Point. All the waters shall be worked in common letting them run as far as the last settlement.

> 2nd No one shall make dams to stop the water to the damage of another, but shall irrigate in his turn day or night in order that all may irrigate equally, without preference.

> 3rd All surplus waters should be discharged into the common ditch and arroyo running from above downward without anyone raising dispute or questions since all are equal and enjoy the same privileges.

> He who shall violate any of the three said points and shall not observe them, will at once be exiled from the settlement, as in like manner will be he who brings in another who is not of those set down in the list and possession . . .

> Notice: I again repeat that the work of the public square is also common among all, in proportion to the measurements made and all general works. Complied with and obeyed . . .

> Juan Bautista Duran

The order is understood as a recommendation to Lieutenant Alcalde of Albuquerque by Juan Bautista Durán, head of the Concilio de Merced of the land grant, and written by an official government scribe, the aforementioned Josef Mariano de la Peña (SANM 1 Reel 27, Frame 903). The purpose was to enforce the obligation of water sharing, as well as the construction of the walled plaza. The document represents the role of local governance by the land grant and acequia, as well as the expected contribution of reciprocity by community members to support the settlement.

During the 1820s and into the 1830s, farming was difficult because of the short growing season, limited water supply, and constant attacks by the Apaches, Navajo, and Utes. According to an agricultural report conducted by the Alcalde of Albuquerque in 1819, the entire community produced 183 sacks of dry corn, 122 *almudes* (bushels) of wheat, 8.5 almudes of corn, 4 strings of chile, 33 hands of tobacco, 336 onions, and 205 pumpkins (Melgares 1819; SANM I Reel 27, Frame 912). The community had more success in maintaining livestock, such as sheep and goats, for the production of dairy and protein, utilizing the ejidos and dehesas as common grazing areas. However, due to the intense nomadic raids of the early nineteenth century, a limited number of animals could be grazed. This number was usually figured on how many head could be moved inside the walls of the fortified plaza at San Miguel de Carnué and San Antonio.

By the late 1820s, due to constant raids on San Miguel de Carnué, the settlers of Carnué were assigned solares and suertes and resided permanently in San Antonio. This resulted in a better-fortified settlement. Father Francisco Leiva issued a permit to construct the capilla de San Antonio in 1823, which was completed some time in the 1830s (Dart 1980, 42–45). It is believed that the morada was built north of the plaza on a *solar* of the Gutiérrez family (50). Sustaining the land grant was difficult during this period. Francisco Ignacio de Madariaga, assessor of New Mexico, urged the departmental assembly on July 20, 1837 to cancel the rights of settlers in San Antonio de Carnué, San Antonio de Las Huertas, and Manzano because of continued abandonment (SANM I, doc 1148). Wealthy ranchers of the east Albuquerque mesa, as well as Isleta and Sandia Pueblos, depended on these communities to protect their large cattle herds. At this time, the settlers constructed improved fortifications, but the constant raids continued to occur.

The economic stability of the Carnué Land Grant in this period was not from the ranching and farming that occurred on the grant, but the economic value that came from the buffalo hunts on the *llano estacado* (staked plains). Al Dart points out that the "growth of San Antonio was linked with the industries that brought in residents, and also caused San Antonio residents to be absent for the greater or lesser stretches of time. From the beginning, men customarily were absent from the settlement for months at a time, hunting buffalo and trading on the plains" (1980, 54). Men would typically leave to the plains after the feast of San Miguel, observed on September 29, and would not return until Christmastime. They would skin the dead buffalo and dry the meat for the haul back to San Antonio. They also brought products such as bread, corn meal, and metal to the plains to trade with the Comanches for captives, usually children and women of Ute, Kiowa, and Apache background. The buffalo hides supplied much of the clothing used in the community, such as moccasins, breechcloths, and leggings; they were also used to make a type of warrior shield known as a *chimal*. A complex network of artisans in the village tanned the hides and made clothing.

These times were dangerous for women and children in San Antonio, which was under constant attack by the Apaches. Many children who were taken in these raids were adopted into the tribal community. Other captive women and children were sold to families in the Albuquerque area for servants, and many were adopted into families in the community. This economic system existed until the decimation of the buffalo by the US Army, in conjunction with the forced settlement of Plains Native Americans onto reservations. The last buffalo hunt and raid by the Apaches into San Antonio was most likely during the 1860s.

The end of the Mexican War in 1848 and the end of the buffalo hunts shifted the land use and economic system of the Carnué Land Grant. By the 1860s, the population began moving out of the fortified walls of San Antonio back to San Miguel de Carnué, and to newly formed settlements such as Tijeras and Cañoncito. During this time, the economy shifted back to agriculture, in the form of grazing and small-scale farming. The grazing of sheep, cattle, horses, and goats became the economic base of the community. San Miguel de Carnué, now known as Carnuel, became well-known for the production of goat cheese called *quesón*, which was sold throughout the middle Río Grande Valley. All through the 1880s and 1890s, the Carnué Land Grant was pushing its case to have the US government recognize the ninety thousand acres held by the community. However, following a US Supreme Court decision, the land grant was reduced to a mere two thousand acres. The land-grant council was forced to accept a patent incorporating only the suertes and solares.

In 1894, Carnué, along with six other community land grants, was affected by the US Supreme Court ruling known as US vs Sandoval. This reduced the total claims of the six land grants (San Miguel del Vado, Cañón de Chama, Galisteo, Petaca, Santa Cruz, and Don Fernando de Taos) from a combined area of 1.1 million acres collectively to about 16,000 acres (GAO, 113). The Supreme Court ruled that the common lands were really owned by the sovereign

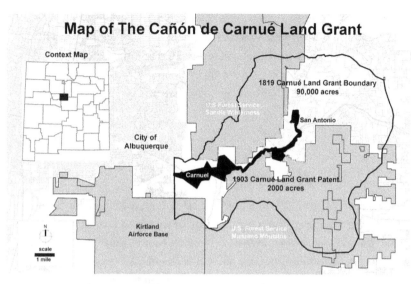

Map of The Cañón de Carnué Land Grant

Context Map

1819 Carnué Land Grant Boundary
90,000 acres

U.S Forest Service
Sandia Wilderness

San Antonio

City of
Albuquerque

Carnuel

1903 Carnué Land Grant Patent
2000 acres

N

scale
1 mile

Kirtland
Airforce Base

U.S. Forest Service
Manzano Mountains

MAP 12.3 Moises Gonzales, Land loss of the Carnué Land Grant, 2017.
Map courtesy of Moises Gonzales.

government of Spain and that therefore, as the people resided in the sovereign nation of the United States, the titles to the common lands now belonged to the US government. However, this decision acknowledged that justice should be sought to find an equitable solution to the 1,120,417.76 acres left out of communal ownership for the six land grants. Congress has yet to consider the recommendation of the Supreme Court. However, a study by the General Accounting Office in 2004 recommended that Congress consider providing a remedy to this longstanding issue.

Through the early 1900s, ranching and small-scale farming continued to be the basis of the local economy. The lost common lands north of Carnué and east of San Antonio became part of the Cibola National Forest, which in 1964 was given a wilderness designation. Those to the South are also now controlled by the Forest Service. In the early 1900s, the land-grant heirs formed a grazing cooperative and were given a community grazing allotment in former common land controlled by the USFS. In 1941, "there was a total of 130 head of cattle, 113 head of horses and 747 goats. Of this, 517 head of goats [were] authorized to graze on the National Forest." In 1949, the Forest Service eliminated the communal grazing allotment, arguing, "They being so close the unlimited labor market in Albuquerque can better do without this grazing livestock" (USFS 2015, 1–2). Since World War II, San Antonio had been losing population to Carnuel, which today has a population of approximately 1,200 residents, the majority land-grant members. Despite the attack on common land-grant ownership for over 160 years by the US government, this community tucked into the Sandía Mountains still maintains querencia and serves as an example of resiliency.

QUERENCIA CULTURAL LANDSCAPE:
INVENTORY AND ANALYSIS

The Querencia Cultural Landscape Model is both a framework for understanding the complex cultural organization of land-based communities of the Upper Río Grande and an inventory research tool to measure the resiliency and capacity of communities. So far in this chapter, I have described the typology of land and water systems in the cultural landscape and the social networks that maintain them. In my work as a community land-grant member in the Carnué Land Grant, a genízaro scholar, and an urban design professional working throughout the region, I have found it useful to understand the relationship of resiliency to the level of community participation in maintaining the cultural landscape.

In the past few years, while working in summer field research schools through SHRI's Building Community Capacity through Community Based Learning Initiative, I have mentored students on how to utilize this model as a tool to measure community capacity in community projects in Córdova, Chimayó, and El Pueblo de Abiquiu. Community capacity is the human capital in a local community needed to sustain and maintain community systems. In 2017, the SHRI Summer Field Research School class entitled "Querencia" conducted an in-depth inventory of the historic Embudo Land Grant building from the earlier work of Nejem, et.al. (2014).

For the purpose of this chapter, this is a brief analysis of findings I conducted in my own community querencia inventory of the Carnué Land Grant using the framework model. I accomplished this by developing a cultural calendar associated with the social organization of the community. I developed this concept from Alfonso Ortiz (1998), a pueblo scholar who used this framework to describe the annual cultural cycle related to the Tewa pueblo cultural organization.

The cultural annual cycle, an analytical tool to understand the querencia

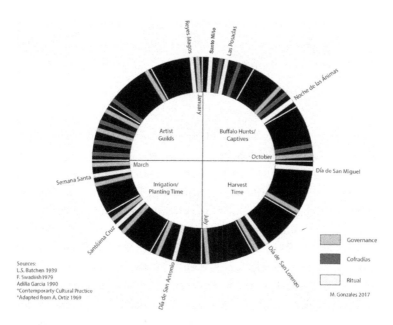

Sources:
L.S. Batchen 1939
F. Swadiish 1979
Adlila Garcia 1990
*Contemporarty Cultural Practice
*Adapted from A. Ortiz 1969

(Labels around calendar, clockwise from top:)
Reyes Magos
Santo Niño
Las Posadas
Noche de las Ánimas
Día de San Miguel
Día de San Lorenzo
Día de San Antonio
Santísima Cruz
Semana Santa

(Month labels:)
January
March
July
October

(Inner segment labels:)
Artist Guilds
Buffalo Hunts/ Captives
Irrigation/ Planting Time
Harvest Time

(Legend:)
Governance
Cofradías
Ritual

M. Gonzales 2017

FIGURE 12.2 Moises Gonzales, Cultural calendar of the Cañón de Carnué Land Grant, 2017. Courtesy of Moises Gonzales.

framework through historical and contemporary practice, was created as a way of understanding the various social organizational structures in the Carnué community. It provides an understanding of the cultural events held throughout the year and the community structures associated with them. The model reflects on cultural practices of the eighteenth and nineteenth centuries and how they are practiced today, as well as the adaptations in cultural practice that have occurred. In developing the annual cycle based on the inventory of social organization, natural and physical systems, and how these systems interact during the act of cultural practice, analysis can be made as to what elements of the querencia model are resilient and what elements are in distress. For example, if a cofradía struggles to maintain members such as la Hermandad, then the structure can become distressed and affect participation in maintaining querencia, which would be reflected in diminished cultural practice in the annual cycle. My study broke out the annual cycle of the Carnué Land Grant along a calendar year and analyzed the function and role of the governing bodies, cofradías, and days of community cultural ritual connected to the cycle of seasons. The findings revealed that overall, the querencia system is resilient in Carnué; however, the community will need to build capacity among some social organizations, as some have become distressed.

GOVERNANCE AND THE ANNUAL CYCLE

The governing systems of Carnué Land Grant consist of the Board of Trustees, the *Acequia Madre de Carnuel* for the town site of Carnue(l), and the *Acequia Madre de San Antonio de Padua*. Each acequia commission appoints a mayordomo who regulates the water distribution of the acequia during the irrigation season. The governance of the Carnué Land Grant is operational year-round, with a monthly membership meeting of the heirs held the first Sunday of every month. The board consists of five elected trustees who serve terms of four years and are elected in even-numbered years in April. The board of trustees is responsible for the management of all communal property in the land grant, which includes all the land elements in the merced except for the solares and the suertes. The board of trustees of Carnué follows the New Mexico State Statutes governing land grants as a political subdivision of the state (New Mexico Compilation Commission 2017). The role of the acequia commissions is to ensure an adequate irrigation water supply as well as maintain the acequia infrastructure.

The acequia commission consists of three members and is elected at an annual meeting of parciantes in March. They then appoint a mayordomo. The governance role of the acequia is usually from March through August, during the growing season. Before New Mexico became a state in 1912, the Carnué community had a constable, who served as the land-grant law enforcement officer and was appointed by the board of trustees.

All governing institutions are still functional and have community participation. However, relating to the acequias, in the last twenty years there has been a decline in the interest in farming, recruitment, and capacity-building by members of the land grant. Also, prolonged drought in the Sandia watershed has greatly impaired the water flow in the San Antonio acequia system. Capacity-building among youth, as well as supported improvements, will need to be addressed to deal with the some of the distress in analyzing the acequia systems. Currently, the governing systems are represented in the annual calendar and functioning according to their obligation of governance and managing the land and water resources.

The cofradías and ritual societies that exist today are the Women's Guild ("the Guild," historically called las Carmelitas), los Hermanos (also called la Hermandad), los Mayordomos de Capillas/Fiestas, los Matachines, and the recently revived Comanchitos. The largest society in Carnué is the Women's Guild, made up of the adult female members of the community, whose role is primarily mutual aid. The Guild is highly active in all aspects in the community and is active in raising money to maintain the camposantos, supporting families in need, developing women's leadership roles in the community, and organizing the winter bazaar held annually for all the children of the land-grant community. Since wwii, this has been the strongest and most influential organization in the community. The rise in power and influence of the Guild resulted from the decline of the organization of los Hermanos. In my own experience, a person is only elected to the board of trustees because of the political power held by the women in the community.

La Hermandad, or the brotherhood, is one of the most important institutions in the Carnué Land Grant. It began with the establishment of the morada in San Antonio de Carnué in the early 1800s. Because the church in San Antonio was far from the parish church in San Felipe de Neri de Alburquerque, los Hermanos administered much of the function of the church in the nineteenth century. They also maintained the social order of the community, since law enforcement was nonexistent except for the land-grant constable. In addition, they conducted training and leadership development for those who would go on to serve in other leadership positions in the community. Dart (1980) describes la Hermandad in San Antonio as "the lay brotherhood popularly called the *penitentes* [who] carried on Socio-religious activities to supplement the functions of the church. Comforting the sick and holding prayer vigils for them, conducting wakes for the dead and burying them, and organizing work crews to help those in need were the year-round charitable-religious functions of the brotherhood, in addition to their Lenten–holy week observances" (62).

During wwii, the rate of men serving in the military affected the number of members in the morada. When men returned from military service, they didn't always join cofradías or other ritual societies. This reduced the participation, although the decline may have started a decade earlier, when film-maker Carl Taylor secretly filmed a movie entitled *The Lash of the Penitentes* in San Antonio in 1936. This act angered a young man from San Antonio by the name of Modesto Trujillo, so much so that it led him to murder Mr. Taylor. In retaliation for the murder, Hollywood released the film in June of 1937, exposing the rituals of los Hermanos. It is believed the organization of la Hermandad condemned the action by the brotherhood of San Antonio de Carnué (Meléndez 2013, 75). Factionalism among los Hermanos is believed to have led to the decline of the morada, and it was demolished in the late 1950s, the saints and ritual items moved to a capilla in the small community of Bartolo Baca. In 2008, members of La Morada de San Jose de Los Ranchos de Atrisco de Alburquerque, with the initial help of Fr. Thomas Steele, petitioned the Carnué Land Grant for a site on which to establish a new morada. Since then, los Hermanos have been serving the community in the manner that los Hermanos of Carnuel once did, including the reestablishment of religious rituals and processional routes.

The cofradías of the Women's Guild and la Hermandad play an important role of social organization and regulating socially accepted behavior in the community. Today, many young families are not as formally active in the Catholic Church and rely on la Hermandad to assist in family rosaries and wake services, as well as provide financial help in time of need. The group's presence in Lenten rituals is recognized and Hermanos are asked to lead ritual processions for feast days. The Women's Guild is still active in the mutual aid of families in need and actively fundraises in the land-grant community. Because of its members' leadership roles, women have recently held leadership positions in other community organizations, including the board of trustees. These cofradías have maintained very important roles historically and currently within the cultural annual calendar of the merced.

RITUAL SOCIETIES

The ritual societies of the Carnué Land Grant—the mayordomos de las capillas, Los Matachines, and the recently revived Comanche Dance—are the entities tasked with maintaining the historic capillas and performing the cultural ritual dances during the feast day rituals. They work collectively to maintain significant cultural and spiritual sites, and are a key component of the cultural calendar.

The mayordomos de las capillas are the caretakers of each of the historic chapels located within the Cañón de Carnué Land Grant and organize annual fiestas. They are a married couple in good standing with the Catholic Church and are recognized leaders in the community. They serve in the role for one year. At the end of each community's feast day, a ceremony takes place that passes the responsibility to the new mayordomos. The incoming mayordomos immediately begin fundraising for the maintenance and repairs of the chapels. They are also responsible for organizing the feast day Mass, the procession to sacred sites, and the Matachín dances, and providing the food for the feast day celebrations. The ritual annual calendar includes the feasts of El Día de La Santísima Cruz on May 3rd at the Santo Niño Church in Carnuel, El Día de San Antonio de Padua on June 13th in San Antonio de Carnué, El Día de San Lorenzo in Cañóncito on August 10th, and El Día de San Miguel on September 29th in Carnuel. It ends at Christmas time with las posadas and the Christmas feast of Santo Niño, which historically coincided with the Comanche dances, Comanchitos, in remembrance of Genízaro captives initiated into the community.

Los Matachines is a ritual dance society that performs a public dance during the saints' days for all the east Sandia Mountain communities, but has its origin in San Antonio de Carnué. The Matachines likely arrived in the Carnué Land Grant by way of Isleta Pueblo and Sandia Pueblo, where many early San Antonio families have matriarchal lines through intermarriage. The dance is practiced primarily in Pueblo native communities in New Mexico, but also in communities such as Alcalde, Bernalillo, El Rancho, and Tortugas (Rodríguez 2009). The leaders of the Matachines are known as the *monarchas* (monarchs), representing the Aztec king Montezuma. They are responsible for organizing practices, selecting *danzantes* (dancers), and mentoring and training youth from the community to join the matachín society. Historically, there was one monarcha from San Antonio de Carnué, but later there were two, with a leader in Carnuel. Before the Second World War, only men were allowed to be danzantes; however, during the war women ensured that the ritual performances continued despite a lack of male dancers in the community. Los Matachines serves as an initial training ground for the youth of the community to develop the querencia of Carnué.

Los Comanchitos was historically another dance society that existed in the region but declined during WWII. At that time, it is believed, a segment of the group's dance was added into that of Los Matachines (Lamadrid 2003, 256). The Comanchitos performs a ritual Comanche dance during the Christmastime posadas and on Christmas Eve for the Santo Niño. Although until

FIGURE 12.3 Carmen Chávez Gonzales, Matachines dance,
San Antonio de Padua, 1935. Photo courtesy of Moises Gonzales.

FIGURE 12.4 Alicia Lueras Maldonado, Comanchitos de la Sierra, 2016.
Photo courtesy of Alicia Lueras Maldonado.

recently the dance had not been performed in decades, the Comanche songs had been preserved and sung as lullabies to children, and portions had been recorded in 1950 and were maintained in the Robb Music Archive at the University of New Mexico. In December of 2016, the Comanchitos were revived and performed in the town site of La Madera in the Sandía Mountains, with a procession led by Hermanos from La Morada de San Miguel de Carnuel. The dance is significant to the remembrance of captive Kiowa, Apaches, and Utes who were adopted into land-grant families as Genízaros of the Sandía Mountain region.

The ritual societies are important to maintaining querencia in the Carnué Land Grant. Overall, the mayordomos and Los Matachines have maintained their cultural roles. The Matachines adapted after WWII to be gender-inclusive and continue to be the primary mode of initiation of youth into the cultural organizational structure of the Carnué community. The recent revival of Los Comanchitos demonstrates the area's deep connection to cultural memory and resilience and brings back the understanding of the group in the cultural calendar. However, an observation made while the capacity of the mayordomos was being examined suggests they may be in early stages of distress because younger land-grant families are less involved in the formal aspects of the Catholic Church. This trend will also place more focus on la Hermandad to conduct ritual events.

GENÍZARO LAND GRANTS: QUERENCIA, RESILIENCY, AND IMPLICATIONS

Querencia is a powerful community concept of the Indo-Hispano homeland of northern New Mexico and Southern Colorado that has engendered the preservation of land-grant and acequia communities. As discussed in this chapter, many New Mexicans relate to this concept in the vernacular as a deep connection to place. La Academia de la Nueva Raza was founded in 1969 in Embudo, New Mexico by Dr. Tomás Atencio and sociologist Facundo B. Valdez, two of the first scholars to develop a theoretical scholarly framework for concepts such as la querencia, according to Patricio García of Río Chama (Interview 2017). Juan Estevan Arellano emerged from a group of young scholars who were beginning to further develop a land and water framework to better understand the concept. In the late 1990s, Arellano published groundbreaking scholarship on querencia as a land ethic framework.

Throughout the next decade, scholars further developed the concept from a range of academic disciplines. During this time, Dr. José Rivera and I set out to work with Arellano to develop a comprehensive mapping of querencia in the Embudo Land Grant that explicated the cultural landscape. Unfortunately, Estevan died on October 29, 2014.

Since Arellano's passing, I have continued constructing the Querencia Cultural Landscape Model, building on the concepts of creating a typology of a Natural, Physical, and Social-Cultural System that defines the cultural landscape of New Mexico. Over the years, the SHRI at the University of New Mexico has funded summer field research schools in Plaza del Cerro at Chimayó, Pueblo Quemado in Córdova, and the Pueblo de Abiquiu. My students and I have begun to further develop the Querencia Cultural Landscape Model as an analytical model to understand community resiliency and community capacity.

In this chapter, I demonstrated how this model can be applied to the Genízaro land-grant community of Cañón de Carnué to understand community complexity, relationships, and distress in community systems. The landscape model is now being used as a legitimate research methodology that crosses the many disciplines of social sciences, design and planning, anthropology, and the humanities. More importantly, I believe this model can be a reflective community participatory research tool that engages with land-based communities in evaluating their natural and cultural systems and developing strategies to strengthen resiliency.

While engaging in this research, I realized how resiliency extends across communities through the network of land-based Chicana/o communities throughout New Mexico as a free flow of traditional knowledge and cultural memory. For example, the Las Huertas Land Grant in Placitas has assisted families of the Carnué grant in reviving the Comanchitos. In turn, the Comanchitos de la Sierra from Carnué are assisting in the revival of Comanchito dances in Atrisco. Matachines in Carnué have danced in fiestas in Atrisco, Chimayó, and Córdova. Hermanos from Embudo and Atrisco have helped to revive La Hermandad and reestablish a morada in Carnuel. Since the early years of establishing querencia as an academic framework by La Academia de la Nueva Raza, my hope has been that our scholarly knowledge continues to expand. In the summer of 2017, Nejem Raheem, Levi Romero, and a group of Chicana/o students revisited the work begun by Arellano to complete the Querencia Cultural Landscape Model inventory in the form of a querencia community mapping of Embudo. The work we continue to do honors the memory of Juan Estevan Arellano and Academia founders Tomás Atencio and Facundo Valdez.

WORKS CITED

"La Academia de la Nueva Raza." 2017. Social Networks and Archival Context (SNAC), University of Virginia. https://snaccooperative.org/ark:/99166/w6tj5bot.

Archibald, Robert. 1976. "Cañón de Carnue: Settlement of a Grant." *New Mexico Historical Review* 10, no. 4: 313–28.

Arellano, Juan Estevan. 1997. "La Querencia: La Raza Bioregionalism." *New Mexico Historical Review* 72, no. 1: 31–37.

Blackhawk, Ned. 2009. *Violence over the Land: Indians and Empires in the Early American West.* Cambridge, MA: Harvard University Press.

Cordova, Gilberto Benito. 1979. "Missionization and Hispanicization of Santo Tomas Apostol de Abiquiu, 1750–1770." Doctoral Dissertation, University of New Mexico.

Dart, Al, ed. 1980. *Archeological Investigations at San Antonio de Padua, LA 24, Bernalillo County, New Mexico.* Santa Fe: Museum of New Mexico Contract Archeology Section.

García, Patricio, Río Chama Acequia Association. 2017. Personal interview on the early years of La Academia de la Nueva Raza. May 22, 2017.

Gonzales, Moises. 2014. "The *Genízaro* Land Grant Settlements of New Mexico." *Journal of the Southwest* 56, no. 4: 583–602.

Gonzales, Moises, et al. 2016. "Cultural Landscape Strategies for Restoration of the Plaza Del Cerro, Chimayó, New Mexico." *International Journal of Heritage Architecture* 1, no. 1: 68–77.

Lamadrid, Enrique R. 2003. *Hermanitos Comanchitos.* Albuquerque: University of New Mexico Press.

———. 2015. "Cautivos y criados: Cultural Memories of Slavery in New Mexico." In *Linking the Histories of Slavery: North America and Its Borderlands*, edited by Bonnie Martin and James F. Brooks, 229–56. Albuquerque: School for Advanced Research Press.

Little, Helen, Elfego Sánchez, and M. García. 1950. *San Luis de Gonzaga Indita, Tijeras, New Mexico.* John Donald Robb Field Recordings. Center for Southwest Research, University of New Mexico. http://econtent.unm.edu/cdm/compoundobject/collection/RobbFieldRe/id/5976/rec/68.

Meléndez, A. Gabriel. 2013. *Hidden Chicano Cinema: Film Dramas in the Borderlands.* New Brunswick, NJ: Rutgers University Press.

New Mexico Compilation Commission. 2004. "Management of Spanish and Mexican Grants," from NM Stat § 49-1-1 (2013). https://law.justia.com/codes/new-mexico/2013/chapter-49/article-1/.

Olmsted, Virginia. 1975. *New Mexico Spanish and Mexican Colonial Censuses, 1790, 1823, 1845.* Albuquerque: New Mexico Genealogical Society.

Ortiz, Alfonso. 2012. *The Tewa World: Space, Time, Being, and Becoming in a Pueblo Society.* Chicago: University of Chicago Press.

Peña, Devon G. 1999. "Cultural Landscapes and Biodiversity: The Ethnoecology of an Upper Río Grande Watershed Commons." In *Ethnoecology: Situated Knowledge/Located Lives,* edited by Virginia D. Nazarea, 107–32. Tucson: University of Arizona Press.

Raheem, N., et al. 2015. "A Framework for Assessing Ecosystem Services in Acequia Irrigation Communities of the Upper Río Grande Watershed." *Wiley Interdisciplinary Reviews: Water* 2, no. 5: 559–75.

Rebolledo, Tey Diana, and María Teresa Márquez, eds. 2000. *Women's Tales from the New Mexico WPA: La Diabla a Pie.* Houston: Arte Público Press.

Resource Center for Raza Planning, University of New Mexico. 2015. "Mutualismo: A Community Based Approach Preservation of the Pueblo de Abiquiu." Summer Urban Design Studio, School of Architecture and Planning. https://digitalrepository.unm.edu/crs_rio_chama/6.

Rivera, José A. 1998. *Acequia Culture.* Albuquerque: University of New Mexico Press.

———. 2010. *La Sociedad: Guardians of Hispanic Culture along the Rio Grande.* Albuquerque: University of New Mexico Press.

Rivera, José A., et al. 2015. "Irrigation and Society in the Upper Río Grande Basin, USA: A Heritage of Mutualism." In *Irrigation, Society and Landscape: Tribute to Tom F. Glick,* 443–57. Valencia, Spain: Editorial Universitat Politècnica de València.

Rodríguez, Sylvia. 2009. *The Matachines Dance: A Ritual Dance of the Indian Pueblos and Mexicano/Hispano Communities.* Santa Fe: Sunstone Press.

Spanish Archives of New Mexico and Mexican Archives of New Mexico (SANM). Surveyor General Report Collection. Microfilm, Reel 7. n.d. New Mexico State Records Center and Archives, Santa Fe.

Swadesh, Frances Leon. 1974. *Los Primeros Pobladores: Hispanic Americans of the Ute Frontier.* Notre Dame, IN: University of Notre Dame Press.

Treaty of Guadalupe Hidalgo: Findings and Possible Options Regarding Longstanding Community Land Grants and Claims in New Mexico. 2004. Report, GAO-04-59. Washington, DC: General Accounting Office of the United States.

US Forest Service, Cibola National Forest and Grasslands. 2015. "Gross-Kelly Grazing Allotment." Briefing Paper, June 16, 2015. 2 pp.

Air, water, food, fire, and shelter. These are the five basic elements that people need to survive. But to do more than just survive, to live and prosper as part of a community, we need one more thing: stories. The first five essential elements protect and nourish the body. Stories nourish the soul. Without stories, we would not know when it is time to plant or harvest, how to bring life into this world, or even how to fall in love, fall out of love, and then forgive and make up. Stories provide us a means for how to relate our experiences and share our memories. In this section, with Kelly Medina-López's discovery of her own authentic querencia, Patricia Marina Trujillo, Corrine Kaa Pedi Povi Sanchez, and Scott Davis's kitchen table revolution, and Levi Romero's *manito* trail odyssey, the authors' words convene at the confluence to form one inalienable truth: stories matter. And we know that they really matter when they're still being told even after we're gone.

Kelly Medina-López's chapter "La Llorona as Querencia: Shared Stories and Sense of Place" reminds us about something that many writers face: questions of authenticity and the dreaded imposter syndrome. After several drafts of writing her essay about querencia, Medina-López realized that her querencia is not the same as expressed by many of her manito counterparts (northern New Mexicans). She then began to question whether her essay had a place in this anthology about New Mexican querencia, but soon realized that her story and sense of identity is just as valid and valuable as anyone else's. If anything, her experience exemplifies why the editors chose a newer generation of burgeoning scholars to participate in this project. The veteran voices are well respected, and their ideas have been widely disseminated. However, a new generation of scholars have proven their ability to reinvigorate scholarship on querencia.

What Medina-López learned through this process is that, out of the many shared identity markers of New Mexicans, it is perhaps the value of stories and storytelling that unite them the most, whether someone is from the north or south. One story in particular that she mentions as a binding cultural icon is that of La Llorona. As she notes in her essay, even the damming of the Río Grande at Elephant Butte could not stop the flow of stories. Although colonial histories, manmade barriers, and playful stereotypes may separate southern New Mexicans from their northern compatriots, stories connect us. After her long search, it's as if La Llorona has finally found her lost children who have been dispersed all throughout the state.

Corrine Kaa Pedi Povi Sanchez, Patricia Marina Trujillo, and Scott Davis's chapter "The Revolution Begins at La Cocina!" builds on Medina-López's idea of questioning the what and where of querencia through storytelling. This chapter uses a unique methodology to disseminate the authors' message. They chose to forgo the standard academic format to which most readers of such anthologies are accustomed. Instead they "utilize 'kitchen table organizing' as a praxis-oriented theory introduced by Joy Harjo and Gloria Bird in their groundbreaking collection *Reinventing the Enemy's Language* (1998)." Although every chapter in this book has something to offer our readers, this one provides a breath of fresh air for those who want to feel as though they're at the kitchen table listening to these stories firsthand. Through this inclusive method, everybody gets to share in the storytelling, even Jeanie the carhop, whose voice adds to the conversation as she takes the group's order through the intercom at the Sonic in Española.

The dialogue, although full of laughter and good spirit, also grapples with some serious issues. In discussion about Juan Estevan Arellano's concept of querencia, Sanchez agrees that she feels deeply at home within her Tewa homelands, but questions the idea about feeling safe, especially as a Native woman. She is right to express such sentiment. Why have we not, as nations, communities, and even families, protected our women from harm? How can we expect anyone to love a place when it does not always or consistently love them back? Through this lively discussion, Sanchez and Trujillo invite us to see their worlds and begin to understand their daily struggles. Scott Davis, the white male discussant in the conversation, is not without a voice among these two strong women. You can feel him listening intently and ruminating on this idea of querencia. His response is sincere and refreshing. For him, the idea is new, and because of that he does not share, at least to their degree, the deep sense of place for where they live. But you can feel that he wants to. He is hopeful that maybe his grandkids or their children will know and understand querencia.

After several "kitchen table style" meetings at various locations in Española, the trio of friends accomplished something more valuable than what the editors requested of them. Through honest and open conversation while they broke bread, they also became more human. Their words remind us that sometimes we don't need a revolution of ideas, just a drink refill, a bowl of chips and salsa, and some friends with whom to share it. And lots of stories.

Levi Romero's chapter "Following the Manito Trail: A Tale of Two Querencias" documents the manito diaspora from northern New Mexico to Wyoming and other parts of the southwest. *Following the Manito Trail* is an oral history documentation project Romero conceived after meeting his wife's relatives in Riverton, Wyoming for the first time and that was inspired by his meetings in the following years with other manitos from Wyoming whose families and sense of querencia originate from New Mexico. What he found most astounding when he met his wife's family and other manitos in Wyoming was how pronounced New Mexican culture was in their homes and communities and across the cultural landscape. Evidence of the manito presence was everywhere—except in the history books.

The migrations occurred as people left their villages in pursuit of employment. Some were permanent relocations and others were seasonal for labor in *el betabel, la papa, el algodón, el ferrocarril, la borrega, y en las minas.* Besides work in the sugar-beet, potato, and cotton fields, some people found jobs in sheepherding, ranching, agriculture, the railroad, mining, the service industries, and other types of employment that sustained them away from home. Although manitos established a new querencia away from their native homeland, they kept their Nuevomexicano identity, language, culture, and traditions intact. To call a new place home but continue to be emotionally and spiritually connected to one's place of origin is an interesting phenomenon. As Romero aptly states, it is a tale of two querencias.

These three chapters remind us how important stories and storytelling are in our lives and for our communities. It is important that we share them with our children and, in turn, their children. We know that many times, our stories are not told in the history books or in the classroom. We need to change that, too. But first, we need to sit at our kitchen tables, put away the distractions, break bread, and tell our stories. For it's the stories that anchor us to the ground of our beloved querencias.

CHAPTER THIRTEEN

La Llorona as Querencia
Shared Stories and Sense of Place

KELLY MEDINA-LÓPEZ

INTRODUCTION

Like many New Mexicans, I come from a family of storytellers. Stories framed my childhood and taught me to understand and make sense of the world. Whether they were individual family histories or classic, shared stories like *La Llorona* (The Wailing Woman), people, geographies, and important events were all contextualized through story. I couldn't meet someone new, pass by a specific location, or get through a family gathering without hearing someone start: "She's the one that . . ." or "Remember when . . . ?" As I grew older, these stories became mine; I went from hearing them to telling them, an important rite of passage. But when I sat down to write this essay, my stories didn't come. I stopped and started a million times. I came up against an adobe wall at every turn. In the back of my mind, I knew what the wall was, but I was too stubborn to admit it. I was eight pages through a shitty third draft when I finally gave in. My writing wasn't genuine. I was trying to make my "essay about the New Mexico homeland" an essay about someone else's "New Mexico homeland." The reason was simple: all my sources—the archival records, the books, the pictures, the internet searches, the articles, up to and including Juan Estevan Arellano himself—were not my recollection of homeland. For the first time in my life, I lost my sense of place. I was alienated from the land that meant so much to me. Why?

All good New Mexicans probably have the answer. Here I am, elbows-deep in beautiful writing about *querencia* (sense of place), and knowledge of the land passed through generations of farming families in Río Arriba, and *acequias* (irrigation canals) that have been flowing for hundreds of years, and *llanos* (open grasslands), pueblos, and centuries of unique language, fiestas, and traditions. I want so badly to try to make my story jibe with theirs because, let's be honest, those stories form the popular social imagination of what New Mexico is. But my story won't. My family doesn't farm. Although I grew up with tons of acequias to swim in, most of them came as part of Franklin Delano Roosevelt's New Deal programs.[1] I couldn't tell you where the llano is, and the only northern New Mexico towns I've been to are Albuquerque and Santa Fe. In my family, we trace our New Mexican roots as far back as my great-grandfather, Jesús Heredia Medina, but before that we're as Mexican as Guadalajara. Yes, I am a southern[2] New Mexican, and proud of it!

Southern New Mexico. Divide the state in half at Socorro, and there we are, down at the bottom, the land "New Mexico" forgot. But just because I don't know what *chicos* (dried ears of corn) are doesn't mean I am not New Mexican. I eat my green chile with the best of them, make no mistake. Like the northern New Mexicans who have farmed their ancestral land for centuries, my ancestral roots are as deep as they can be in the forgotten South. My great-grandfather settled in Las Cruces when New Mexico was only a US territory. After serving in the Spanish-American War, he built an adobe home on the corner of Bowman and San Pedro in the original Las Cruces townsite. The home, still occupied by my great-uncle, is one of the stops in *Las Cruces Magazine*'s online article "Walking Tour: Mesquite Historic District" by Bud Russo, and appears in other literature on early Las Cruces. Like the northern New Mexico families whose stories go back countless generations, the Medina family has a deep history in southern New Mexico. But the stigma remains: those histories include centuries of difference. There were hundreds of years for a distinct northern New Mexican culture to establish itself before my distinct southern New Mexican culture even began.[3]

I had to stop and start this essay so many times because the imaginary border between northern and southern New Mexico became a real wall in my writing. As a southern New Mexican, I couldn't claim the same querencia that my research found. My idea of New Mexico as a place was different. I had to come to recognize the divides. I remember years ago when I first realized how dissimilar my New Mexican culture was from northern New Mexican culture. I was teaching a university course for Spanish-heritage learners at New Mexico State University. We were reviewing New Mexican Spanish vocabulary words and, even though I grew up with Spanish, I was unfamiliar with half of them. We got to the word *mayordomo* and one of my students from the North laughed. "I didn't know that was a Spanish word," she blurted out, "We say that all the time! It's the person who controls the water." Other students from the North corroborated her story, but all I could do was smile, nod, and take their word for it. Those of us from southern New Mexico, Texas, and Mexico shyly exchanged puzzled looks.

Perhaps I was secretly jealous of these mayordomo-saying Northerners. All the history, literature, research, and media about New Mexico I had seen in my studies seemed to identify northern New Mexican culture as true New Mexican culture. But I also knew that my New Mexico—the land I grew up on and the ancestors who placed me there—was just as beautiful, magical, and rich with culture as its northern counterpart. To write this essay, I first had to acknowledge and set aside the cultural divides, and instead search for the essence of what brings us together: New Mexico. What makes us all New Mexican? What is New Mexico as a place? How do we make ourselves recognizable as New Mexicans, whether from Santa Fe or Las Cruces? How does the shared experience of being from the Land of Enchantment bring us together as a unified group?

As a rhetoric and composition scholar, I turned to language, words, and stories. Stories are one thing all New Mexicans have in common. In the May 2016 online issue of *New Mexico Magazine*, Elena Vicentita Valdez's article "Cuentos y Querencia" discusses the connection between stories and querencia for New Mexican people. Valdez argues, "New Mexicans have stories for everything, from the food we eat to the rock formations we see on the roadside. I often feel that there is something about the homeland, our Nuevo Mexico, that calls to us and demands our stories." I agree. Whether you're a *Manitx del norte* or a *Surumatx del sur*,[4] I am positive you have stories. While many of these are the colorful family histories that anchor us to the land, our culture, and our *antepasados* (ancestors), there are also stories that transcend familial boundaries. These shared stories weave us together across the real geography and imagined borders of our homeland and give us all a sense of place, a sense of belonging, a New Mexico querencia. One that touches all New Mexicans is the story of La Llorona. Although not particular to New Mexican culture or folklore, this character is an undeniable part of it. Popular New Mexican author Rudolfo Anaya published three books about her. On the back cover of *La Llorona: The Crying Woman* (2011), the book description reveals that "like other children who grow up in New Mexico, author Rudolfo Anaya heard stories of La Llorona when he was a boy. She was a kind of 'boogeyman,' looking for children who disobeyed their parents or stayed out late." La Llorona is a common part of New Mexico storytelling that unifies

New Mexicans in a shared experience, giving us all a sense of place and New Mexican querencia.

DAMMING WATERS

The La Llorona story I grew up with is grounded in the geography of Las Cruces. In the Medina family version of the tale, La Llorona's primary hangout was the Río Grande that ran just west of Las Cruces, but when my cousins or I were acting especially *malcriados* (bratty), she swooped through the network of Las Cruces acequias to end up right behind my grandparents' house, our church (Holy Cross), my grandma's favorite store (Montgomery Ward), or wherever else we were causing trouble. Understanding La Llorona meant knowing Las Cruces and the language and landmarks tied to it, highlighting a crucial link between La Llorona as story and La Llorona as epistemology of place. Valdez notes that New Mexicans use stories to make sense of geography. I agree, but must add that New Mexicans also use geography as pivotal to our linguistic and cultural understanding of our homeland. Often—as in my experience with learning Las Cruces geography through an approximation of which acequias La Llorona could grab me from given my current location—our landmarks and geographical knowledge come from water. Arellano (2014) confirms the link between New Mexican epistemologies of place and water. In *Enduring Acequias*, "the underlying theme is water, *agua*, that which sustains life" (15). Throughout the text, water defines querencia, or "love of place" and "sense of place." He argues that "acequias are what give us a sense of place, and the water becomes the blood that brings communities together" (5). Nevertheless, the water flow that is the "blood that brings communities together" reinforces the northern/southern New Mexico divide.

Eighty miles north of Las Cruces, there is a dam on the Río Grande at Elephant Butte. Sixty miles north of Las Cruces, there is another at Caballo. Although not the geographic center of the state, the dams mark a stark contrast between the ponderosa pines and cottonwoods of the North and the creosote and mesquite of the South. The landscape south of the dams yields to the dust and dirt of the Chihuahuan Desert, a change that further reifies the northern/southern divide. The United States Bureau of Reclamation uses the dams to regulate water flow from northern New Mexico into southern New Mexico.[5] Beginning in March, it releases water from the dams into the southern half of the Río Grande for irrigation season. This is when the Río Grande and its acequias in Las Cruces come to life, full of the "blood" that brings northern and southern New Mexico together. The season runs until late July or early August, depending on drought conditions. Then the Bureau stops the water and the Río Grande turns back into the "Río Seco." For most of the year, southern New Mexico's rivers and acequias are dry. The dams, physical structures underpinning our linguistic and cultural differences, cut southern New Mexico communities off from the "blood that brings [them] together."

Despite our dammed waters, La Llorona persists. Although anchored in geographic knowledge, La Llorona as New Mexican querencia transcends the geographies, structures, and waters that further divide the North and South. Her story remains a shared epistemology, even when our water, geography, language, and culture do not. In "La Querencia: La Raza Bioregionalism" (1997), Arellano argues, "Our memory has now assumed the form of the landscape itself. This is the essence of *Querencia*, if we lose either memory or landscape, we lose both" (32). Here, he worries that changes to our landscape will affect our epistemologies of place: querencia cannot survive if either geography or memory is threatened. However, the southern New Mexico landscape already assumes a contentious past that does not mirror the same ancient wisdom Arellano pulls from his own northern New Mexico land. We have dammed our culture and we have lost our landscape, but our sense of querencia remains constant, even if our geographies do not. La Llorona, geographic "memory" preserved through story, sustains our querencia even when we dam the uniting waters of our home state. La Llorona is a shared New Mexican epistemology of place that persists despite the regional, cultural, and physical barriers that displace us. There is something about her story that grounds us in our individual and shared understanding of New Mexico as place.

STORY AS PLACE

To consider how the story of La Llorona unites New Mexicans in a shared querencia despite real and imagined barriers, we should first examine story as a rhetorical practice. Many critical discourses document the value of story as resistance to various forms of oppression.[6] While this essay does not intend to engage with La Llorona politically to surface themes of sexism, racism, or other discrimination,[7] examining the significance of story within these frameworks can provide a more nuanced perspective of the dynamic role that it plays in our lives. Story intersects with academia as a pushback against the limitations of traditional scholarship. For example, *testimonio* (testimony)—a practice originating in Latin America in which marginalized speakers narrate their experiences of suffering and oppression—comes into academic contexts through the Chicanx and postcolonial movements that emerged in the 1970s.[8] Testimonio moves audiences to recognize wrongdoings by flipping typical discursive patterns, interpolating listeners from the subaltern (rather than vice versa, as is commonplace), and "summoning us to a new kind of relationship with others, a new kind of politics" (Beverley 2004, 2). Engaging audiences in a new political relationship with marginalized groups through story is the underlying goal of testimonio, and why it remains a popular rhetorical device.

Story is valued similarly by theorists who acknowledge the complexities of the human experience. Malea Powell (2002) asserts that story "is essential in the creation of all human realities," exposing it as not belonging to one specific group or school of thought (429). In her essay "When the First Voice You Hear Is Not Your Own," Jacqueline Jones Royster (1996) shows how story can shift in response to the nuance of hybrid identities (619). Thus, while still working from marginalized perspectives, the critical role of story is not as nexus of essentialization, but rather a reflection of the multiplicity of human life. This idea continues through Critical Race Theory (CRT), where story becomes one of the primary research methods. In CRT, story doesn't just represent a singular truth or reality; rather, stories born from marginalized subject positions express critical truths about structures of racism in society (Rollock and Gillborn 2011, 2). CRT intersects with another theoretical framework, Chicana Feminist Epistemic (CFE). CFE argues that stories are key to "Cultural Intuition" and "Community Knowledge," epistemologies born from the specific social, political, and cultural histories of marginalized groups (Delgado Bernal 1998, 556). Recognizing the academic sites where story is an essential rhetorical practice exposes it as more than just cultural decoration. Story reflects experience; it is a way to voice and bear witness to cultural epistemologies. La Llorona as a shared New Mexican story reveals a common experience and cultural epistemology of New Mexicans. However, as argued above, this experience also reveals knowledge of La Llorona as place through her ties to water and acequia epistemology.

Connecting the rhetorical practice of storytelling to the geographic epistemology of La Llorona provides a sense of how she is both grounded in singular experience and representative of a uniting New Mexican querencia.

Like those theories and methodologies that recognize story as witness to the complexities of the human experience and hybrid identities, we can anchor our individual La Llorona stories to the various New Mexican geographies we come from. For me, this means the streets, acequias, and river banks of Las Cruces. La Llorona's geography helps me map specific locations, such as Holy Cross or Montgomery Ward, that formed part of my unique New Mexican childhood. For each New Mexican, these geographies will shift and change to reflect his or her own sense of place. However, being conscious of how story is a tool that reflects the realities of a specific group, collective experiences, and community knowledge also allows La Llorona to unite New Mexicans in a collective epistemology. All New Mexicans share the La Llorona story as knowledge that grounds us in our individual "sense of place" across the state's diverse landscape. In other words, as a common experience, La Llorona shapes our sense of place, our New Mexican querencia, regardless of whether that place is Las Cruces or Los Lunas. To demonstrate this, the following section will use my family's version of the myth to reveal my particular New Mexican sense of place and comment on how this might relate to a larger, shared New Mexican querencia.

LA LLORONA: OUR STORY

As New Mexicans, we claim La Llorona as our story. She is part of the common experience of growing up New Mexican, and she shapes our understanding of what New Mexico means. Claiming her story is complicated because it is not only a shared story, but also an individual story. There are many versions of La Llorona. One of the more popular ones connects her directly to Hernán Cortés, La Malinche, and the Spanish conquest of Mexico.[9] In other versions, she haunts Arizona[10] Texas,[11] New Mexico[12] and other geographies. These popularized accounts don't consider the individual familial versions we all have. La Llorona is not a solid, monolithic character or story, but a fluid tale that responds to the multiple geographies, languages, and cultures of New Mexicans. Nevertheless, La Llorona is a story that unifies New Mexicans in a shared querencia. It is part of what CFE recognizes as "Community Knowledge," taught through "legends, corridos, [and] storytelling" (Delgado Bernal 1998, 564). So La Llorona as a rhetorical commonplace in the legends, corridos, and storytelling of New Mexico is part of the community knowledge that designates her as cultural epistemology. Her story, and the act of telling her story, reify our New Mexican epistemologies of culture and geography. These ground us in our "sense of place" and help create our New Mexican querencia.

Here, I will reproduce the Medina family version of the myth to surface New Mexican querencia as both an individual and shared epistemology of place. I specify that it is the Medina family story because, again, each family has their own version of the tale that reflects the history, language, and geopolitics of that group. Built into each telling of the myth is an oral history of family experience, so learning about La Llorona from an episode of the NBC series *Grimm*[13] differs from hearing it firsthand from your *gramita* (grandmother). La Llorona's particularity as passed down through regional varieties and familial difference goes deeper than a generic code for the story learned through popular culture or other formats. Experiencing La Llorona as connected to family, geography, and culture produces an authentic querencia, something that hearing the story secondhand can't provide. Thus, recognizing La Llorona as a specific embodied New Mexican epistemology helps us to appreciate how querencia is shaped through, and responds to our individual geographical experiences. Exposing the unique sense of place that attaches itself to our epistemology through the circulation of the story can help us see how La Llorona becomes New Mexican querencia, a complex reflection of both shared and individual experience.

La Llorona as a shared and individual New Mexican story adds a robustness to her cultural significance. For example, I connect more deeply to the version I present below because it incorporates the geography and language I am comfortable with and mirrors the oral history of my family. I have trouble connecting to the popular formats that place La Llorona in the Spanish conquest because that history and geography feel removed from my own. Although I recognize that the scars of Mexico's colonial past are a part of my family history and cultural ties, my family has been in or around southern New Mexico's Río Grande valley for generations and, as geography and time distanced them from the Valle de México, their oral histories evolved to reflect those changes. The version of La Llorona that I am familiar with and that I share here recognizes the evolving experience of growing up in New Mexico. Although my myth differs from that of someone who learned the more traditional version, or who places La Llorona in Albuquerque, Santa Fe, or Río Arriba, all versions weave together through the rhetorical commonplace of New Mexico and the language and geography of New Mexican querencia. What I will try to represent here is the Medina family version of

La Llorona.[14] To preface, unlike many other people, I don't remember being sat down and told the story in any official capacity. My version is a collage of the bits and pieces I picked up from my *abuelos* (grandparents), *tíos* (aunts and uncles), *primos* (cousins), and parents. It is underscored by the geographical location of my upbringing and the storytelling practices of my family:

La Llorona was a young and beautiful woman who married a *viejo rico* (rich old man). She was spoiled by his gifts and affection, and grew accustomed to being *mimada* (spoiled) and *mantenida* (supported). Shortly after their marriage, she became pregnant. Over the next several years, she gave birth to three children. With each child, it seemed that her husband gave less attention to her and the children and more to younger women he met at El Patio, the bar on the Mesilla Plaza. La Llorona grew extremely *celosa* (jealous). She couldn't handle seeing her husband direct his attention away from her. She warned him that if he didn't change his ways, he would be sorry. The viejo rico continued to see other women and ignore La Llorona. The longer this persisted, the more La Llorona recognized her husband in her children. One day, while the viejo rico was gone, La Llorona took the three kids to the Río Grande for a picnic. She convinced them to get into the water with her, but when they did she turned on them and drowned them. La Llorona immediately realized what she had done and was consumed by regret. She spent the rest of her life wandering the river bank crying out, "¡Mis hijos! ¡Mis hijos!" (My children! My children!), until she finally died of heartbreak and remorse. Unsettled, her ghost still haunts the river bank, crying, "¡Mis hijos! ¡Mis hijos!"

What does the Medina family version of La Llorona make visible about my New Mexico querencia, as both a shared and individual epistemology? The first notable pieces of the myth are the words that remain in Spanish. Words like "mimada," "mantenida," and "celosa" reveal the common vernacular of my southern New Mexican tongue. Rather than characterizing these shifts in language as codeswitching or code-meshing, I connect my shift in language to Arellano's use of linguistic variety as a purposeful way to mark specific epistemologies of place. Throughout *Enduring Acequias* (2014), he builds his definition of querencia around the importance of water, agriculture, and acequia culture through archival research and practical knowledge. As he does, another essential aspect of querencia surfaces: language. Arellano never compromises by substituting English to name a concept when a word in Spanish, Arabic, French, Quechua, Nahuatl, or whatever else already exists.

For example, he refers to his garden as an "almunyah," an Arabic word for a type of "experimental and recreation garden" (63). In fact, much of the archival work he does as he explains the history of acequia water systems and their connection to New Mexican culture is also etymological. In the first chapter of *Enduring Acequias*, "Sacred Water," Arellano traces the migration of Sabaean language from Yemen to the Iberian Peninsula and finally to New Mexico, listing a number of Sabaean words related to water that still appear in acequia culture today (29–30). Among these words he includes "as-sirr," which he links to the word "sierra," and "wad," which he names as the root of "Guadalupe," or the "lobos river" (30). Following Arellano, New Mexican querencia becomes not just "love of place," but love of place built through an understanding of acequia culture and the significance of water, and a knowledge of the language that names that culture and the places it defines.

Although my words differ from Arellano's in that they do not speak of agricultural practices or histories, they parallel his usage as descriptors for specific cultural logics. Returning to my language, mimada and mantenida not only describe La Llorona's character, but ultimately highlight dynamic cultural epistemologies about relationship roles, gender binaries, and family. The cultural epistemologies echoed through this language reflect an untranslatable understanding of the roots of family life in New Mexico, much as Arellano's purposeful linguistic shifts reveal the roots of agricultural knowledge. Even though, as a feminist scholar, the cultural logics the words of my story expose may irritate me, I must also acknowledge the cultural history that generates them. Thus, my usage and understanding of these terms reflects a complicated past underscored by the identity, gender, and geographic politics of New Mexico as place. The phrases such as "viejo rico" and "mis hijos" that name the characters in the story mirror these political intersections. Both phrases, the second one especially, reflect a knowledge of New Mexican culture, history, and people that would change significantly if replaced by "old rich man" or "my kids." The epistemologies exposed by considering my language shifts are both individual and shared; they highlight the linguistic practices of my family while also informing collective cultural epistemologies about gender roles and family relationships.

In addition to the language choices in my version of the La Llorona myth, the geography of the story also emphasizes New Mexican querencia. The story highlights two key places: El Patio and the Río Grande. El Patio is a historic bar in Mesilla that often surfaced in my family stories, earning it a reputation as the place where people met, fought, fell in love, made mistakes, and suffered consequences. More than just a location, El Patio itself was a mythic place that held family secrets in its adobe walls. When I was old enough to go there for myself, I added my own stories to those already there. The Río Grande was another location that marked my childhood. I grew up a block away from the river, on the border between Las Cruces and the *colonia* (community) of Fairacres. This area of the river is home to the aptly named La Llorona Park (only in NM!) where my family and I often walked, played, and picnicked together. Further east on the river is a popular teen hangout called "Thousand Poles," which witnessed many of my coming-of-age stories. Thus, like El Patio, the Río Grande is an important piece of Las Cruces geography that anchors my knowledge of what it means to grow up New Mexican and formed my sense of place. The Medina family version of La Llorona reflects this knowledge, also found in Arellano's tracing of his family history through his own land.

In the end of *Enduring Acequias*, Arellano describes his land, "La Junta," and its history, location, and features. He recounts the work he has done, such as installing gates and pipes, and describes how the physical labor of working the land reminds him how his ancestors must have done similar projects. Reflecting on the patterns of owning and working the land, he says, "once I realized that the land, like us, also has a memory and one probably that is longer than ours, I found there were several bancos, or step terraces, on my property" (2014, 190). For Arellano, this process of working and uncovering the geography of his family plot became a way for him to connect to his ancestors and understand their story. Similarly, with the Medina family's La Llorona story, I am reminded that I am not the only Medina to ground myself in my New Mexican identity through the geographies of El Patio or the Río Grande. Instead, like Arellano, I am building on a shared knowledge, adding my individual stories to the stories and histories that are already in place. The individual and shared epistemologies attached to the geographies found in the Medina family's La Llorona story reflect how New Mexican querencia is perpetuated through our stories, both shared and individual.

STORY: *NUESTRA QUERENCIA*

Unlike Arellano, I am not worried about the loss of New Mexican querencia. As a southern New Mexican, my New Mexico already assumes a different past and a different geography than those of my northern counterparts. Colonial histories, manmade barriers, and playful stereotypes separate us. We use alternative vocabularies to name these differences. Yet despite our differences in culture, geography, and language, story connects us. These stories endure even if the people, land, and language shift. There is a reason we continue to hold on to them. La Llorona is a shared New Mexican epistemology that grounds each of us in our individual sense of place. With stories like hers, we are not just expressing culture, but rather exposing our epistemologies of place, naming our community knowledges, and ensuring that these important pieces of our New Mexico querencia survive in future generations.

NOTES

1. See Wozniak 1998 for more history on Las Cruces *acequias*.

2. Labels are always problematic. In this essay, I follow Garland Bills and Neddy Vigil (2008), who distinguish between New Mexican groups with the labels of Northern and Southern, or Northerners and Southerners: per their definition, "(1) Northerners, for those associated with the Traditional Spanish heartland of Northern New Mexico and Southern Colorado, and (2) Southerners, for those associated with the Border Spanish of Southern New Mexico" (8).

3. As Bills and Vigil summarize, "It is also to be expected with two such sharply delineated groups that there exists a bit of competition. The Northerners tend to feel socially superior by virtue of their longer history of landownership and access to economic and political power. The Southerners, those representing more recent immigration, tend to have less tradition of such material status" (13).

4. Manitx and Surumatx are the "Spanish term[s], more or less private, more or less derogatory" used, respectively, by Southerners to refer to Northerners and Northerners to refer to Southerners (Bills and Vigil 13). Although Bills and Vigil designate these terms as "more or less derogatory," I use them here to be playful and to continue to contextualize our perceived differences. I also replace the feminine "o/a" endings with the more gender-neutral "x" in favor of inclusive language.

5. See "Rio Grande Project" at https://www.usbr.gov/uc/elpaso/water/Reservoirs/.

6. See, for example, Acevedo 2001.

7. This work is important and has been done in other places. See, for example, Perez 2008, Carbonell 1999, and Doyle 1996.

8. See Reyes and Rodríguez 2012.

9. See, for example, Janvier 1910 and Gónzalez Obregon 1944.

10. See, for example, Leddy 1948.

11. See, for example, Pérez 1951.

12. See, for example, Espinosa 1910, Trujillo 2006, and Anaya 2011.

13. The myth has made many pop culture appearances. This is just one. See also Perez 2012.

14. This is also one of those interesting gray areas of academia where my educational knowledge conflicts with my home knowledge. Academia would encourage me to find a "source" for the story. However, the collective cultural values of *chicanidad* encourage me to believe that I would somehow be damaging both my integrity and La Llorona's by doing so. In other words, my story may sound exactly the same as other stories out there, or it might sound completely different. That is part of the La Llorona experience.

WORKS CITED

Acevedo, Luz A. 2001. *Telling to Live: Latina Feminist Testimonios.* Durham, NC: Duke University Press.

Anaya, Rudolfo. 2011. *La Llorona: The Crying Woman.* Translated by Enrique Lamadrid. Albuquerque: University of New Mexico Press.

Arellano, Juan Estevan. 1997. "La Querencia: La Raza Bioregionalism." *New Mexico Historical Review* 72, no. 1: 31–37.

———. 2014. *Enduring Acequias: Wisdom of the Land, Knowledge of the Water.* Albuquerque: University of New Mexico Press.

Beverley, John. 2004. *Testimonio: On the Politics of Truth.* Minneapolis: University of Minnesota Press.

Bills, Garland D, and Neddy A. Vigil. 2008. *The Spanish Language of New Mexico and Southern Colorado: A Linguistic Atlas.* Albuquerque: University of New Mexico Press.

Carbonell, Ana María. 1999. "From La Llorona to Gritona: Coatlicue in Feminist Tales by Viramontes and Cisneros." *MELUS* 24, no. 2: 53–74.

Delgado Bernal, Dolores. 1998. "Using a Chicana Feminist Epistemology in Educational Research." *Harvard Educational Review* 68, no. 4: 555–83.

Doyle, Jacqueline. 1996. "Haunting the Borderlands: La Llorona in Sandra Cisneros's 'Woman Hollering Creek.'" *Frontiers: A Journal of Women Studies* 16, no. 1: 53–70.

Espinosa, Aurelio M. 1910. "New-Mexican Spanish Folk-Lore." *The Journal of American Folklore* 23, no. 90: 395–418.

González Obregón, Luis. 1944. "La Llorona." *Las Calles de México: Leyendas y Sucedidos, Vida y Costumbres de Otros Tiempos,* 9–10. Mexico DF: Ediciones Botas.

Janvier, Thomas. 1910. *Legends of the City of Mexico.* New York: Harper and Brothers.

Leddy, Betty. 1948. "La Llorona in Southern Arizona." *Western Folklore* 7, no. 3: 272–77.

Perez, Domino Renee. 2008. *There Was a Woman: La Llorona from Folklore to Popular Culture.* Austin: University of Texas Press.

————. 2012. "The Politics of Taking: La Llorona in the Cultural Mainstream." *Journal of Popular Culture* 45, no. 1: 153–72.

Pérez, Soledad. 1951. "Mexican Folklore from Austin, Texas." In *The Healer of Los Olmos and Other Mexican Lore*, edited by Wilson M. Hudson, 71–127. Dallas: Southern Methodist University Press.

Powell, Malea. "Rhetorics of Survivance: How American Indians Use Writing." *College Composition and Communication* 53, no. 3 (2002): 396–434. http://www.jstor. org/stable/1512132.

Reyes, Kathryn Blackmer, and Julia E. Curry Rodríguez. 2012. "Testimonio: Origins, Terms, and Resources." *Equity & Excellence in Education* 45, no. 3: 525–38.

"Rio Grande Project." us Bureau of Reclamation. https://www.usbr.gov/uc/elpaso/water/Reservoirs/.

Rollock, Nicola, and David Gillborn. 2011. *Critical Race Theory (CRT)*. British Educational Research Association online resource. www.bera.ac.uk/files/2011/10/Critical-Race-Theory.pdf.

Royster, Jacqueline Jones. 1996. "When the First Voice You Hear Is Not Your Own." *College Composition and Communication* 47, no. 1: 29–40.

Russo, Bud. N.d. "Walking Tour: Mesquite Historic District." *Las Cruces Magazine*. http://lascrucesmagazine.com/walking-tour-mesquite-historic-district/.

Trujillo, Patricia Marina. "Becoming La Llorona." 2006. *Chicana/Latina Studies* 6, no. 1: 96–104.

Valdez, Elena Vicentita. 2016. "Cuentos y Querencia." *New Mexico Magazine*, May 2016. https://www.newmexico.org/nmmagazine/articles/post/only-in-nm-96038/.

Wozniak, Frank E. 1998. *Irrigation in the Rio Grande Valley, New Mexico: A Study of the Development of Irrigation Systems before 1945*. Fort Collins: New Mexico Historic Preservation Division, Rocky Mountain Research Station.

CHAPTER FOURTEEN

The Revolution Begins at La Cocina!

PATRICIA MARINA TRUJILLO, CORRINE KAA PEDI
POVI SANCHEZ, AND SCOTT DAVIS

U vi a'gin di.
Buenos días le dé Dios. Estamos aquí con respeto y permiso.
Howdy y'all.

We begin this chapter with guiding words from our everyday work; we open this engagement with respect, in keeping with the teachings of our communities and ancestors, and with our open hearts. Who are we? Dr. Corrine Sanchez is the executive director of Tewa Women United (TWU). Dr. Patricia Trujillo is a board member of TWU and the director of equity and diversity and an associate professor at Northern New Mexico College. Scott Davis is the coordinator for Men for TWU and a builder. We have TWU in common, but really, it's much more. Much of the way we ended up on the same path finds connections in our shared love for critical theory, critical race practice, and social justice in general, but in northern New Mexico, in particular. We have all put in hours on the "front line" of anti-oppression, Indigenous-centered work through our various positions and projects. But mostly, we are friends. We have deep relationships where we've celebrated each other at our best, fought side by side for what is right, and held space for each other at our most vulnerable of times. We are three friends in the process of becoming more human. We support each other in that. We call each other out and we call each other in. We bask in the sacred and keep each other from drowning in the mundane, because that's what this word *querencia* means, ¿qué no?: the place where we feel most at home, most comfortable. That is what our shared friendship is, despite the fact that we have different perspectives. We have found a home between and among ourselves, our backgrounds, and our experiences.

The three of us often find ourselves discussing, grappling with, and laughing at the complexities of our shared home place. It doesn't escape our notice that we embody the classic tricultural mythology of New Mexico, except that instead of a Spaniard, an Indian, and a cowboy, we are a fierce Tewa woman activist scholar with Mickey Mouse ears; a *Manita* feminist scholar who likes to hunt for *capulín* (choke cherries) and sew aprons in her spare time; and a white rogue scholar who enjoys disrupting white supremacy or planting tomatoes, depending. We were inspired to write this as a conversation, rather than an essay, for many reasons. We are using story-sharing—which is active and ongoing—recognizing that we each hold pieces of the story. This signals how our communities privilege oral communication and interpersonal interactions: that is to say, relationships. This dialoguing on the page embodies a resistance to individual authorship and its relationship to authority.

Patricia remembered that a friend of hers once referred to our home as "a squatter town on Pueblo land." That's a short sentence that encompasses several big ideas, including the idea that, unlike many of the pueblos and villages that surround it, the Americanized town of Española, with its Main Street and replica plaza built in the 1990s, is a relatively young town, incorporated in 1925. In the last decades of the nineteenth century, the railroad and its constituent entrepreneurs raised the town as a stop on the now infamous Chile Line. The story goes that the stop was named for a well-known eatery where travelers could visit to eat the food prepared by *La Española*, or the Spanish woman [*sic*]. We situate ourselves here, in Española, which we also acknowledge is a conglomeration of surrounding pueblos and traditional villages, in this shared narrative of food and conversation. Many of the conversations that started this project were shared over food—green chile cheeseburgers at Sonic, corn dogs on Scott's porch, or cheesy, delicious red chile Frito pies at La Cocina. It's also fitting to share stories from this particular "front line" as Española chronically suffers a bad rap, often described in the third-person point of view by journalists and writers who represent it from a single story.

So here we are, three friends grappling with community-building, dismantling white supremacy, and decolonial work in northern New Mexico. In trying to create more nuanced representations, we will utilize "kitchen table organizing" as a praxis-oriented theory introduced by Joy Harjo and Gloria Bird in their groundbreaking collection *Reinventing the Enemy's Language* (1998). They write, "Many revolutions, ideas, songs, and stories have been born around the table of our talk made from grief, joy, sorrow, and happiness" (19). In the spirit of continuing the decolonial work that originates from around the kitchen table, we expand our organizing praxis to our front porches, the car at Sonic, or a table at La Cocina.

What we are collectively beginning to recognize, as we do our work and even as we dialogue and write, is that this work of querencia—of feeling at home, of creating a sense of belonging, of feeling safe—is a daily practice. The act of belonging and building safety is multidimensional and constantly shifting. It is permeated with the mundane and set within the ordinary. In this dialogue, we do not all have the shared connection to the particular word "querencia," but we do each have a connection to a shared home. The promise of querencia often occurs in spaces that are not our home, where we do not belong, where safety is in short supply. In this conversation, we hope to illuminate the complicating of querencia within spaces layered through centuries of colonialism, that position of each of us here, in Española, New Mexico, together in this moment. For querencia to be evoked in the present tense, we suggest that it requires an ability to sit down again and again at our respective kitchen tables.

TABLE ONE

The written dialogue we are sharing here is split between the various tables around which we had many of our conversations. The first conversation we are trying to re-create on the page occurred at the Sonic Drive-In in Fairview, Española, New Mexico. We had not seen each other in about a month, and we planned to go to Sonic specifically to start talking about how to approach this project. For the most part, with this dialogue as with the others represented here, we chose highlights from much longer recording transcripts. We tried to capture the spirit of the moment. On this day, we were excited to see each other and to check out Scott's new ride, a truck he named "Slate."

CORRINE: Oh my god! Isn't this truck amazing?
PATRICIA: Yes! Really.
SCOTT: You know; there's more room in the back seat than in the front.
CORRINE: Sounds like a line! [laughter]
PATRICIA: It's a luxury vehicle plus a truck in one! How's your summer been, Corrine?
CORRINE: It's been good. But it's been . . . well, my aunt passed, and that

was hard. But then I got to be in Baltimore with Nathana, and that was good. Got to kick back.

PATRICIA: So sorry about your aunt.

CORRINE: Thanks.

PATRICIA: I saw the picture of you and Nathana eating crabs!

CORRINE: Yeah, we had to have the girl show us how to eat them! [everyone laughs] It was soooo goooood! Oh my god it was soooo good!

PATRICIA: I was in Chicago for a month, and the food was so good, but then this one day I was like, "I just want a bowl of beans." [laughter]

CORRINE: Are we going to park in the shade?

SCOTT: Yeah, definitely. North Side Sonic. Yeah, I guess there's enough shade.

CORRINE: Is this your car wax back here?

SCOTT: That's for when I wash the truck! Check it out; in the first five weeks that I had the vehicle, I waxed it twice. [laughter] I haven't waxed a car since I was twelve! [laughter]

CORRINE: Oh, look over there! That guy got a sundae! Hey, Patricia, how's your brother?

PATRICIA: He's doing well. The baby! She's adorable. She just turned four and all of a sudden, her language is just on! She just figured out in her head that "*Tía*" means "Daddy's sister." You can see her thinking, "so he has a sister! He has two! Huh? And *Tío* . . . that's my mom's brother. She has a brother?" [laughter]

CORRINE: Oh, cuuuuuute!

SONIC SPEAKER: Hello this is Jeanie, welcome to Sonic. May I take your order, please?

✦ ✦ ✦

PATRICIA: What do we mean by "kitchen table" nowadays? In many ways, the kitchen table is still at the core of home, but there have been some changes to how we connect around food, don't you think? Part of being a community activist/organizer/educator is that we are always on the go, and eating at a kitchen table—let alone the act of making a healthy meal—can sometimes feel like a luxury. We are out fighting for food justice and *acequias* [waterways] and community and students, and in the process, we can forget to take care of ourselves. So Sonic becomes a kitchen table of sorts. [laughter]

SCOTT: I don't even try to order anything healthy from Sonic. If I'm eating here, I have already made my decision and may as well. That said, I don't always go deep into the grease, either. And what Patricia says reminds me how much I need to focus on taking care of myself. I have gotten way too far from my own kitchen table.

CORRINE: I know, right? I even have to be mindful at work to not eat at my desk, to be purposeful and walk out of my office to the dining area of our TWU home. I have friends—heck, even my mom, who works with us—who forget to eat. We get so caught up in the doing and responding that we literally look up and it's 4:00 p.m. and our last meal was at 8:30 a.m. We talk all the time about self-care for the women who come through our doors but the practice of it in our own lives is very difficult.

PATRICIA: Man. It's that theory/practice thing in our own lives. Who knew that one of the greatest reminders of it would be mindful eating? She said, popping a Tater Tot in her mouth! [laughter]

CORRINE: Though most nights I am eating at my sister's home or my parents' home, who definitely have kitchen tables and where great thought-provoking conversations and conspiracy theory goes on. And our [Scott and Patricia] conversations have been at tables in local restaurants with a family feel. And when we have been in a rush or in want of more privacy at Sonic in the comfort and roominess of "Slate" [Scott's new-used Tundra]. All I know is that my personal experience has been that great conversation, learning, and sharing happens over food, no matter where I find myself in the world! Be it a yurt in the middle of the steppes in Russia, outdoors at a camp in the Cordeleria of the Philippines, or as we prepare for ceremony at my Pueblo. Places that there was not per se kitchen tables as one might visualize but definitely peoples sharing food, thought, and cultural learnings.

SCOTT: Awww, the cultural learnings of Sonic.

PATRICIA: Not even joking, one of my grandma's signature meals when I was growing up was the Brown Bag Special.[1] This place, as much as any around here, is part of the culture. Española and Sonic, that's querencia! I love the concept of querencia; it really resonates with me. I also love to think of it as a neologism that connects the two Spanish words, *querer* [to love, to want] and *herencia* [heritage]. But it dawns on me that it might not feel as comfortable to you two. What do you think? Are there words that connect for you in different ways?

SCOTT: I have to say that I don't even really know what it means.

PATRICIA: Well, I think many people think of Juan Estevan Arellano when they think of querencia. He wrote of querencia as the relationship between place and identity. "*Querencia*," Arellano (2014, 50) writes, "is that which gives us a sense of place, that which anchors us to the land, that which makes us a unique people, for it implies a deeply rooted knowledge of place, and for that reason we respect it as our home. *Querencia* is a place where one feels safe, a place from which one's strength of character is drawn."

CORRINE: Yes, it's an interesting word and concept, one that was created to describe a new connection to a new place for peoples, right? It makes me think about place, connection, and formation of identity. Since in the context that Arellano describes is a peoples' claiming connection and fit and belonging to a place that was not theirs to begin with, but as connection is formed through intimate interaction with the land, one finds a sense of belonging and identity. My sense of belonging and identity, too, is connected to this place, which is longer than most here in northern New Mexico, since my ancestors have coevolved with these lands. Yet shorter than some, since my time in this dimensional plane has only been forty-five years. To some, I am nothing but a brown Native body, and to others, I am not Indian enough. I am *tewah towah*. To many, I am a strong, powerful, articulate Native woman, and to others, I am not the "right kind" of Native woman. Like many others, I feel deeply at home here, but safe? That has not always been the situation for me as a brown Native girl or young woman, and now as a woman here in the homelands of my Tewa peoples.

PATRICIA: Wow, you're right. We have to think about the privilege of safety and place. It's crazy how we can be a part of a place and apart from it at the same time. For me, querencia as a concept includes the contradictions and the pain we cause one another in this land base we call home. One moment I can be all about being *Manita*, and saying/feeling that I'm from here (and I am), but I have to then remember that I am the descendant of people who invaded the Tewa homelands.[2] It's funny to think about it, Corrine, about it being a new connection to a new place for peoples, because, on one hand, yes. But on the other hand, only in New

Mexico can over four hundred years be considered new. I'm not negating what you're saying, not at all: I think this is at the heart of thinking about belonging and earning relationships through place and time.

If querencia is about loving and wanting a home, it reminds me of a saying I heard once, "Love brings up everything unlike itself for the purpose of healing and release."[3] Being in the *Norte* now, living and working here, I feel that healing has to be part of querencia. Man, I've had elders call me out for not having a command of Spanish, or not having the same relationship to land that they may have. I realize that part of my querencia is about recuperating pieces that have been lost or changed, but what I am certain about is that my political consciousness is inextricable from my land-based identity.

CORRINE: That's the thing, right? Living in the community that you work or write about is that everybody, and we mean *everybody*, questions your authority or your truths. I think that is the power of story-sharing. Recognizing how this place we each call home can hold many stories and that all can be true at once. But people always want to be rigid about identity and history and whose version is the most accurate and has the most authority. Like, you are from this place and it means this or has to mean that, exactly.

PATRICIA: Right?! I've had all kinds of men—scholars, writers, educators— call me out on how I identify in regard to being Nuevomexicana. There's a professor who has singled me out when I say that I am from Española. Once, at a national conference, he corrected me while I was speaking and said, "Actually, aren't you from Arroyo Seco?" Actually, yes. And, actually, my parents' home, where I grew up, is literally, *literally*, about a quarter-mile from the Española city limits. If that. And, actually, my grandma lived in El Guache and my dad was from Taos and I went to school for thirteen years in Pojoaque. Actually, I can be from all of these places at once—they all formed me—and that can all mean I'm Manita.

SCOTT: Dang . . . it really resonates for you. The word "querencia" doesn't really impact me in any way. I like the sound of it . . . it sounds musical to me. It feels good in my mouth. But not in a familiar way. It tastes like something I want to have more of, but is still foreign to me. Reading the explanation, and Patricia's take/feelings/thoughts on it, I feel a little guilty for enjoying it so much! But the connection to the word itself is brand new and fresh. There are not the deep connections to place for me. It feels like something that I hope will be present for my grandkids. Or their kids. Somewhere out in the future. For me, it is exotic. And I understand how problematic that word is. But the truth is the truth. And that is how it feels. Despite my best efforts, I am, and will always be, a white male settler colonial.

PATRICIA: Wow, say that three times fast. [laughter from group] But I have to interject, the one place querencia is not exotic is the Norte! In fact, you are the one who is exotic here, Scott. [more laughter from group]

SCOTT: I am? Yup, I totally am. We white male settler colonials need to name it. I got called out at a training in Tucson last week. It sucked. The guy who did it was very compassionate and present and did his best to be gentle. But still, I knew better and was ashamed to be seen with my pants down. He did it off to the side. He was beautiful. One of the pieces he spoke with me about, by way of advice, was exploring my own roots. I am really struggling with this. And maybe in this, there is some affinity with what Patricia is expressing. It's not the same, but it feels like it is in the same conversation.

PATRICIA: What do you mean? What's the problem with exploring your roots?

SCOTT: My roots are a mixture of cultures and places across Europe. Describing my lineage is basically a math problem. Twenty-five percent Italian, twenty-five percent Swedish, twenty-five percent Norwegian, and twenty-five percent mixed (mostly German, I think). So, who am I? All that Euro-blood comes from cultures and places that are very different. Calling me European is as broad as calling someone Native American. What does that mean? Of course, I am white. That is the easiest and most accessible identity I have. To explore my "roots" would take at least three lifetimes. Even living in Austria for those six years did little to connect me with my roots. It did show me other things about European people in general. I witnessed and met Indigenous Euro culture.[4] Not my European culture, but part of where I come from.

PATRICIA: My roots are a mixture of cultures and places too, but they've been growing here for a while. This reminds me of something that my *comadre*, Ana X, says.[5] The two of us often find ourselves connected to sacred work around here (and she's taught me that it's all sacred). We've talked about how so many white people come to New Mexico to connect with the Indigenous practices of the region, but she always asks: Why don't these people seek out the Indigenous practices from their home-lands? There are Indigenous peoples all over the world, and what does it mean for people of European descent to find out more about their tradi-tional practices?

SCOTT: Maybe that's because of the cultures themselves. The Indigenous folks I met in Austria were incredibly impacted by colonialism. To such an extent that there was little, if any, awareness of how the colonization had taken place. The link back (over millennia?) to precolonial times was all but severed. It only showed itself in tiny sparks. But here, I can still access white supremacist culture. Indeed, it feels way too present for my tastes! And growing up embedded in white supremacy, that influence can feel comforting. How fucked up is that? To feel comfort in white supremacy.

CORRINE AND PATRICIA: Pretty fucked up!

PATRICIA: Jinx. You owe me a coke.

CORRINE: What does that mean? To feel comfort in white supremacy? You realize you're talking to two brown women who will never feel that?

PATRICIA: Yeah, can you say more? What I've witnessed about white priv-ilege in Española is that it's almost like white folks get a "Get out of privilege free" pass around here. Because we live in a minority majority (I hate that concept!) county, you have white folks saying that they are "The Minority" here, that they suffer "reverse racism" (I hate that concept even more), and what about all those terrible conquistadores? Rightfully, we have to challenge and contest Spanish colonialism and all constituent violence, I'm committed to that. But what I've seen happen is white privi-lege operates differently here because of the multiple foci we have to have on several colonial waves: Spanish, Mexican, and American, accomplished through the Culture of Violence, militarization, exploitation, and domi-nation. Because our history is complex, it oversimplifies how whiteness, power, and privilege operate here in the present moment.[6]

CORRINE: Yeah, because history says something ended. You can see aca-demia's influence here. This was colonial times, that was prehistory, and there's post-history, post-neoliberalism, and all that as opposed to saying the story is continuing to build and shift with no definitive ending.

SCOTT: To me, that all points to the insulating qualities of white privilege. Like the water the fish are swimming in. There are multiple layers op-erating simultaneously, most of which are not recognized by white folks coming to The Valley.[7] Language, right off the bat. Most people speak English here, so I don't have to struggle with that. Or I can ignore people who speak other languages. Economics, the rules of commerce and real estate, are pretty much the same here as anywhere else in the country. So I have as much opportunity in Española to leverage my financial power to buy land stolen from Indigenous people as anywhere else. And really, *more* opportunity due to the depressed economy of the valley. Woven through all of this is a "justice" system that I understand and was constructed for my benefit. So when I come here as a white person, I am swimming in the same language, economic, and legal waters as I would be in Boston.

PATRICIA: Wait, wait, wait! I was with you until Boston. It's not really the same, and I think that's why we are having the conversation about querencia. I acknowledge that the majority of places here can operate in this schema of white privilege, but what immediately comes to mind is how our place still holds multiple identities in the present moment, not just in the past. There are places here the whiteness cannot permeate. I'm thinking about languages, practices, land use, traditions. You know, all those living rooms where families gather and speak *manito* [New Mexican Spanish].

SCOTT: Certainly, with nuances. I am not saying that these are the *only* systems present here, rather the overarching principles, which could be framed as "national." That's what makes it hard for white folks to get along here. We often enter with entitlement from this privilege we carry, and are confronted with the *culture* and resistance in northern New Mexico that responds to that entitlement. So politically, we come here privileged, but culturally, we arrive challenged. As you both know, many white folks don't understand white privilege to begin with. The pushback we feel in the community gets easily translated to "reverse racism." Which I think we all can agree is a pile of horse shit anyway. That's the comfort of white supremacy. I am swimming in economic and legal waters that are familiar to me. I know that despite cultural pushback, the law will be on my side.

But when I focus on learning how I fit in this place, Española makes sense to me. This leaves me with a question: How much of querencia is about understanding how one "fits" in a place? With all my strange and convoluted lineages, with a legacy of colonial privilege, I still feel like I fit here. Not the same as you two. Not even close! But still somehow, I feel like I fit. It is often an uncomfortable fit. But it fits.

CORRINE: That's why writing this as a collective is so important. This conversation about race, place, land, and gender needs to be a collective; we need all the voices. It's when our relationships push against each other's that we actually figure things out. We figure out how we fit.

PATRICIA: And that's interesting to me, because querencia feels like never having to think about where you fit. You just do. But I can see how I think about that in other places in my life. I've really been thinking about fit as it pertains to academic writing a lot lately. It dawns on me that when I publish in local New Mexico periodicals, I get so much more feedback from the audience then I do when I'm working in academic publications. People go out of their way to send you a note or give you a call. People will call my mom and tell her that they cut out the article and mailed it to their family. Even if someone doesn't agree with me, we are engaged in discourse. Living and working in my community of origin, I feel a great deal of pressure to be responsive, reflective, and representative. Also, I do not write in isolation. I'll vet my essays for *Green Fire Times* with my family, people in my community, and other scholars.[8] Often, it's my family that offers the closest readings, but there is a certain kind of integrity that comes from being a voice from your family and community. You have to be communal about your process, and that's one of the reasons I think us writing in community with one another is important. Figuring out how to write with another is intimate. We get to see what's going on backstage, and then we realize it's all backstage.

CORRINE: As one who does *not* like to write, I think this is a great format; it feels more natural to me. Being in circle, having conversation over food, building thought and analysis happens in community or connection with others. Or at least this has been my experience. Whether that was as a young child playing in the library near where my mom was taking brain development class at the College of Santa Fe, running around the house as my dad was having meetings about tribal politics at my grandma's, sitting in circle with women from a diversity of cultures/races/professions/communities, and of course family and Pueblo community gatherings for various births, deaths, and ceremonies.

PATRICIA: Come to think of it, maybe that's why *Manitos* love bonfires so much! It's an insta-circle.

CORRINE: And, as I was going through the Pueblo PhD program, I was like, why can't I cite my grandma, my great-great grandma, or my dad? Or when I think about all the amazing people I've met—the women whose names I may not be able to remember because we were having a meal on the ground in the Cordillera. At that time, I was not thinking about documenting every conversation in a notebook that was annotated. But I can remember clearly where I was and I can describe the woman's face and what she was wearing and remember her words because they impacted my thoughts on family and community organizing.

SCOTT: Yeah. Credentials. That's a superefficient way that white supremacy reifies itself, and simultaneously erases Indigenous knowing. If you can't back it up with credible sources, if you can't show your credentials, then you just get ignored.

CORRINE: Exactly, and who gets to decide who or what a credible source is? It's also reality that my thoughts and analysis builds upon the cultural sharing passed onto me which is/has been accumulated throughout time in my community context and knowingness. And my continued evolution on race, place, and identity comes from my interactions and conversations with the two of you as well as many others. But our ability to go deeper and make mistakes with one another is very different than in other spaces I find myself having similar conversations. So the sense of vulnerability and truthfulness is more real here 'cause I know you will not disown me, shame me, or no longer love me for misstepping or if I don't have a fully formed response, thought, or analysis. Coauthorship matters for those particular reasons and many others. Not one of us is an expert on the area where we find our lives intertwined. This place we all call home.

PATRICIA: Yeah, like if we mess up, chances are that you'd call me or text me to talk to me about it, not banish me from the work. The word "mistake" is key. It loosens up ideas about how any one person or perspective can be definitive. Even when I think about this conversation becoming writing, I have to acknowledge that I'm struggling with my inner academic voice that keeps wanting to point to this theorist or that book. You know, we have to acknowledge that Corrine and I do have these "credentials," and that we're in a book filled with our friends who have them as well. We are women of color with PhDs. I am trained to think that to talk about my querencia I need to work in that academic structure, but then you're here living in the Norte and all of sudden the structures don't work or they shift. And, it's like Corrine is saying, it's because academia also has an accumulated knowledge of place, but that place doesn't necessarily allow for vulnerability, intimacy, and mistakes. Without those freedoms, how can it be our querencia? How can we feel at home there? And that's why we have to build new or different structures with our community—like this book—as well as acknowledge the ones that have always been there.

SCOTT: I see all the work the two of you have put into building your academic credentials, your lived experience, and *still* you get doubted and questioned on "how you know." Which keeps me interrogating how to be accountable to not only you, Patricia and Corrine, but also to the community I live in.

PATRICIA: Between us, we know the reality of that too well. And who gets listened to and in what contexts . . .

SCOTT: Totally. My formal education ends with my apprenticeship as a mason.[9] But people still listen to me on any fucking topic I choose to opine about! I can count on one hand the times people asked me to "prove" my authority on any subject.

PATRICIA: All I can say about that is, ¡*Ala*, I wish! One time I was in a meeting at work talking about teaching writing at Hispanic Serving Institutions and I was told by a white male colleague, "You should only speak when you are quoting someone else." How do you respond to that?

CORRINE: Okay, how about, "in the immortal words of my *tía*: Fuck off!" [laughter]

TABLE TWO

What can probably never be captured in a single essay is how we spent hours and hours challenging each other to think about querencia, racial justice, and our relationships to the issues and each other. We met often, recording our conversations, which usually spiraled out in many directions. The second table that we invite the reader to was at La Cocina, a New Mexican restaurant in Española. We live in a rural area, and our town is small. This is one of the restaurants where working meetings are hosted by the city's professionals; we all joke that if you can't find us in the office, you can probably find us at La Cocina. It is also a restaurant where many family meals are held for graduations, first holy communions, and even rehearsal dinners. It is a space where work and home collide. When you live in a town and become intimate with its spaces, querencia extends to public tables as well as the tables in kitchens.

SERVER: Are you guys ready?
PATRICIA: No, I think we need a couple minutes to read the menu.
CORRINE: Yeah, no. I need a sec.
[The server places chips and salsa in front of Scott.]
SERVER: Ok, I put these chips here . . . but that doesn't mean he *rules* them. [laughter]
SCOTT: Welcome to New Mexico, Scott! [laughter]
PATRICIA: Geez, they're gonna start charging us rent because we're here so often.
CORRINE: Right. Remember the time we were all here having meetings with other people but we were all talking across the restaurant?
SCOTT: Yeah, that was funny.
PATRICIA: I always see people here having all kinds of meetings from Tewa Women United, from the birth center, from the college, from the county. This is where it all gets done. If these walls could talk, huh?
CORRINE: Oh, the stories they would tell! I was here the other day and saw Nathana.[10] On her way out she said, "The revolution begins at La Cocina!" [laughter]

✿ ✿ ✿

CORRINE: I've been thinking about what you said last time we were together about how that guy said that you should only speak if you're quoting someone else and it made me think about the difference between story-telling and story-sharing. Story-sharing is interactive and communal, and in storytelling one voice commands attention to a particular experience or moment in time. It's usually someone telling someone else's story or [something] very universal in nature. For example, in the telling of the history of this place, women and Native voices have been left out or told through the interpretation of male colonizers' perspective. We [Native women] don't have that authority and power in the telling, but when we are part of story-sharing, we share our own story, our own truths, and recuperate that power. Even the story of this land isn't in the past: it is still happening. It's the collective pieces of past, present, and future. Why is there this resistance to the ongoing knowledge of multiple stories existing in one place, together, simultaneously?

Story-sharing is the continuation of breath. Like your house, Patricia, it's not just your mom's or your grandma's or your *gramita*'s (grandmother's), but also yours. How you are adding to the breath of that house is story-sharing, you are an active creator/ contributor to the continuation of story.

PATRICIA: Yeah, for sure. This reminds me of something one of my favorite writers says about people trying to define space: she says, "space is the simultaneity of stories told so far" (Massey 2005). But there is always a challenge to whose stories and why and which one is authoritative. I love the image of all the stories sitting together and holding each other, because that's really what we're grappling with here.

CORRINE: Why does there have to be one authority? Why does there have to be one god? Why does there have to be one leader? Story-sharing is where I can share my perspective, tell my story, but it is connected to and in conversation with other stories. Sharing doesn't have any rules. It continues to build. People are always asking me for my opinion about how to solve issues for Native America. I'm not an expert on all Native American peoples; I am an expert at my experience of being a Tewa woman, and I can share my story. And, for me, my story-sharing as a survivor of multiple violences has shifted and changed over time. If I just focus on or document the pain, that's not the whole story. It is part of it, but there is more because I am healing, reconciling, and continually evolving. It does not make any version of what I share any less true or one more correct than the other, either.

PATRICIA: Yeah, like when I've identified myself here at home as a Chicana feminist, people have told me, "There aren't any Chicanas here." They don't even include the word feminist. And I'm, like, well, there's at least one, and I'm standing right here in front of you. I'm telling you that this is who I am; believe me. My story doesn't do anything to you. And for the record, there are many Chicana feminists here.

CORRINE: Your perspective and your pieces should just be incorporated into the bigger story braid. But if you put it in black and white, written on paper, then the storytelling gets stunted. People then want to "prove" the authenticity of that version. Often, denying the breath in the story continues. What pisses me off is that part of the storytelling of this place is the declaration that the peoples of Chaco and Mesa Verde are dead, extinct. No, they are not, we are not. We are here. We [*Tewah Towah*] are a continuation of that story.

SCOTT: That's what I love about the *Querencia* piece. Actively bringing our three stories into a story-sharing. It reminds me of the *Opide* that Kathy and Corrine talk about.[11] That braiding. And how all our stories braid together into a larger story. The story of this place is a braiding of hundreds of thousands of stories, from Indigenous, Spanish, Hispanic, Latinx, Chicanx, Anglo, Mexican, and American people. No one of us has "the" story. Unlike those "definitive" perspectives of academia, the *Opide* is durable through space and time in a way that carries each strand with total validity.

PATRICIA: Yeah, and you can add so many more identities to that list, right? African, Black, Japanese, *Genízara/o*, lesbian, gay, bisexual, transgender, gender nonconforming, nonbinary, poor, rich, middle-class, middling-class, working-class, and on and on. When we share the stories, the braid gets thicker and stronger. It also makes me think how we also need to put stories to rest—like Oñate. That's a story that's been told enough; Oñate's a *chispa* (flyaway) that we just need to tuck into the back of the braid and hide for a while.

CORRINE: Yes, our breath and focus doesn't have to dwell there. We are not going to forget it, we must acknowledge it, and we must learn from it, but we also need to let it go. We are much more than just that particular time; we all can contribute to building and transforming the story. There is no way we can deny the history, but there are so many more stories and experiences to be shared.

PATRICIA: Yeah, I always say I don't want to live there, and by "there" I mean in that place of perpetual hurt. Several scholars have referred to or write about Nuevomexicanos as being in a perpetual state of loss and longing. We don't want to deny what we've lost or the pain, but you want to be able to acknowledge it and grow. It's that simultaneity of stories: those stories of loss and longing are layered and stacked and swirled with stories of love and belonging.

CORRINE: As my mom says, we should be comfortable with ambiguity, but most white folks are not; the white supremacist frame does not allow for it. Not all answers are known, nor should they be. And personally, as well as in communities, we should be able to decide for ourselves who we want to share with and/or what we want to share.

PATRICIA: Yeah, I think about that a lot when I write about New Mexican women's history. There's just these walls we hit when using dominant ways of sharing our ideas—the stories get disappeared in archives, in books and classrooms. There's the frustration of negotiating what is or is not legitimate. But then there are funny and clever ways those stories come out. Like, once I found a cache of old home goods in ruins of a *dispensa* [storage shed] in my backyard. Since three generations of women were the heads of household before me, the items definitely held the stories of women. Like this *jerga* [rag rug] that I found; it was made out of used panty hose! And it made me laugh, because they used what they had and I could hear their voices as I imagined the story of that rug.

TABLE THREE

The dialogues included here occurred over the course of a year. Incidentally, the first dialogue from Table 1 happened to coincide with National Corndog Day. We joked about it and our hopeless addiction to Sonic on that day, and in days to follow. The third table we gathered around was on Scott's porch. Scott lives "in town," as opposed to Corrine and Patricia, who live on the outskirts in San Ildefonso Pueblo and El Guache, respectively. Scott's porch is the easiest to commandeer for our thought projects. On the day that we met for this discussion, Scott and Corrine sat on the porch, in the warm afternoon, waiting on Patricia. Porches are still important sights of *plática* (talk) in Española, and we often take advantage of being able to sit outside and enjoy the sun and the birds. It is fun and powerful to imagine how many hours of laughter and story-sharing have occurred on New Mexico porches, how they are sites that hold memories of family and community.

CORRINE: Didn't we say we're meeting at 4:30? Are we on Chicano Time or Patricia Standard Time?
[In walks Patricia with a smile on her face and a bag from Sonic.]
SCOTT: What's in the bag?
PATRICIA: Sorry I'm late, but I brought us some corn dogs! It's National Corn Dog Day!

✹ ✹ ✹

PATRICIA: How did you land up here, Scott?

SCOTT: After my divorce and total financial collapse, I was in Chimayó visiting a friend. He needed a construction manager, and I needed to close my contracting business in Colorado. So I came down here to work at Corrine's sister's construction company, and just find a quiet corner to lay down and bleed for a while. It was 2007.[12]

CORRINE: Most people walk in with plans, maps, agendas. People could relate to you because you didn't.

SCOTT: Instead of bringing an agenda, Corrine's sister Liana gave me one. She would send me to TWU to fix a door or hang some shelves. Over time, Corrine and I began a conversation. Granted, much of that conversation was Corrine telling me, in not so subtle ways, to pull my white head out of my male ass!

CORRINE: Awww, the Scott of today is *not* the Scott of 2007. As I reflect on these past ten years, each of us has grown and transformed our thoughts, beliefs, and actions. Scott has helped me see and heal my perspectives on men and masculinity. Patricia has contributed to my views on Chicana/o [and] Nuevomexicano culture and Pueblo peoples' relationships. The recognition of the violence and violations and the communal and community-building. And our ability go deep with each other in grappling with white supremacy and its impact on all peoples. This is due in part to the personal healing and growth we have done and through our friendship and *love* for one another and this place we call home.

PATRICIA: Yeah, it's funny to think that while y'all were becoming friends, I was still in San Anto doing my grad school thing. But that was me getting some distance and perspective of my own on how I belong and understand my connection to home and home knowledges. But sitting here now, and thinking about all of this, querencia is unfolding for me. It is about understanding the deep roots of knowledge in a given place. It's about our connection and respect for our land base. But here in the Valley it's also how we all continue to grow and connect from this shared place.

CORRINE: The story-sharing of querencia is always to be continued, and with all these recordings and transcripts, I think we need to write a book. And with that, I got to go. So we're meeting at La Cocina for lunch next Tuesday?

When we met to discuss how to tie all this up, to address how difficult this writing of querencia actually is, we once again dove into dialogue. As any writer knows, there are always ways that a piece of writing comes to life and how place affects our ideas. As we sat down in Scott's dining room to get to work on our conclusion, we could never have understood the promise of querencia more than in the moment when Juan de Oñate came knocking at the door. We were reading from our computer screens, snacking on tortilla chips and TJ's mochi, when we heard *bam! bam! bam!* on Scott's screen door. We all jumped. Scott opened the door and said, "Heeeey, it's Oñate!" And then turned and explained to Corrine and Patricia, "I told him you guys would be here tonight. He's been wanting to meet you!"

"Well, he's got some 'splaining to do!"

Sound outlandish? Talk about challenging our own premises about belonging and safety, right? This Oñate happened to be Ralph Martínez, the man elected by the city fiesta council to portray the conquistador in the 2017 fiestas. He'd come over to talk about how he's trying to make the fiestas more inclusive and community-oriented, and to invite each of us to participate in different ways in a communitywide *matanza* (pig roast) he was hosting a month before the fiestas. He shared his plans and we all talked about how we need to come together more often, how we need to listen to artists and community members more, and how sometimes the best way to do this is over a pig that's been slow-roasted in the ground. We problem-solved issues together, like how the health department procedures do not allow for the *ceremonia* of a matanza to be public and how we could use technology (video projection) and our shared resources to bring the ceremonia to life in other ways. We joked and laughed about our unbelievable, beautiful, and complex home and how we all belong here. We explained our writing project to him, and we all laughed at the timing of it. To have our writing/dialoguing process end with this extraordinary, yet ordinary moment folded within a year of otherwise mundane meetings and discussions was a reminder of the power of querencia, about how our place and identity consciousness is deeply rooted and simultaneously emerging.

NOTES

1. The Brown Bag Special consisted of two hamburgers, two orders of Tater Tots, and two drinks. Fast food crept into households in northern New Mexico as a low-cost option for food. We understand that it is problematic and advocate for local, healthy eating, but the reality is that Sonic restaurants frame Española, and they are part of the culture of the place.

2. *Manita* and *Manito* are intimate monikers of inclusion for Indohispano people from northern New Mexico.

3. Other kitchen tables are present in this conversation: Patricia's friend Peter Snyder shared this quote with her over lunch when she was having a difficult time with her father's death. It is commonly associated with the spiritual program *A Course in Miracles: A Foundation to Inner Peace.*

4. The concept of "Indigenous Euro culture" is one that Scott has identified on his own while witnessing some of the traditions and rituals in the higher elevations of the Austrian Alps. It is not intended to define Indigeneity for any group of people. These words are the closest he can find to describe the land-based cultures he witnessed.

5. Dr. Ana X Gutiérrez Sisneros is an assistant professor of nursing at Northern New Mexico College, a longtime resident of the Española Valley, and a well-known healer in the region.

6. Kathy Wan Povi Sanchez has shared her conceptualization of the Culture of Violence with us through numerous talks and presentations.

7. "The Valley" is in reference to the Española Valley, where the authors all live.

8. *Green Fire Times* is a monthly thirty-thousand-copy, forty-page full-color newsprint publication distributed throughout north central New Mexico and on the web. Editor Seth Roffman seeks out the multiple voices of the community.

9. The apprenticeship referred to occurred in Austria between 1993 and 1996. The trade guilds of central Europe still operate there in some fashion. This was not a mason as we may imagine it, but specifically a *Hafner*, the title of one who builds masonry heaters.

10. Nathana Bird is from Ohkay Owingeh Pueblo. She is a longtime youth organizer and community-builder. She is currently the Program Manager of TWU's Women's Leadership and Economic Freedom Program.

11. Kathy Wan Povi Sanchez is the mother of Corrine and is from San Ildefonso Pueblo. She is one of the founders of Tewa Women United. For more on the Theory of Opide, see Sanchez 2016.

12. Avanyu General Contracting, LLC is a Native Woman Owned company on San Ildefonso Pueblo, co-owned and operated by Liana Sanchez and Mateo Piexihno.

Harjo, Joy, and Gloria Bird. 1998. *Reinventing the Enemy's Language: Contemporary Native Women's Writings of North America*. New York: W. W. Norton & Company.

Massey, Doreen. 2005. *For Space*. London: Sage.

Sanchez, Corrine. 2016. "Herstories and the Braiding of Environment and Reproductive Justice to Protect Those Most Vulnerable." *Journal of American Indian Education* 55, no. 3: 48–71.

CHAPTER FIFTEEN

Following the Manito Trail

A Tale of Two Querencias

LEVI ROMERO

*LOS MANITOS EN LA QUERENCIA DE LA NACIONCITA
DE LA SANGRE DE CRISTO* (THE MANITOS IN THE LITTLE
NATION OF LA SANGRE DE CRISTO HOMELAND)

"Those of us from northern New Mexico tend to look at the world in a different way," I once said to a university department administrator during a conversation we were having about differences in sociocultural perspectives. "I know you," she responded. "You're the *manito* people!" "You've heard of the Manitos?" I said, intrigued by her use of the term. "Where'd you hear about them?" She replied, "Well, when I was a young girl working in a law office in Long Beach, I would hear coworkers who had moved to California from New Mexico refer to each other as 'Mano so and so or 'Mana so and so. The rest of us called them *hermanitos* or *hermanitas* because that was how they referred to one another." I have heard that the term originated in the agricultural fields of Colorado's San Luis Valley and in the cotton fields of the Texas Panhandle where field workers from Mexico working alongside Nuevomexicanos began to refer to them as los manitos. My African American friend's description, placing Manitos that much farther from their native homeland, added further interest to my contemplations on the manito diaspora.

The word "manito" is a derivative of the word "hermanito," little brother. It is a term of endearment and it was common for people to refer to one another as *Mano* or *Mana*, short for *hermano* or *hermana*—*Mano Juan, Mano Fidel, Mana Bersabé, Mana Juanita*. Rubén Cobos's *A Dictionary of New Mexico and Southern Colorado Spanish* defines manito/ta (los Manitos) as a term applied by Mexican immigrants to New Mexican Hispanics. Some of the latter, however, found the term used with derogatory connotations. At times, they were ridiculed for speaking in the Spanish dialect of northern New Mexico and for carrying on with traditions and customs that seemed foreign to others. They were the Manitos, after all, different and unique in their culture.

Many Nuevomexicanos have long held an established belief that the manito homeland extends north of Socorro to the region along the border between New Mexico and Southern Colorado. Northern New Mexico is the geographical area so aptly referred to as *"La Querencia de La Nacioncita de La Sangre de Cristo"* by Cleofes Vigil, northern New Mexico cultural guru from San Cristobal. The Indio-Hispano people's language, foods, traditions, and social, religious, and spiritual customs are woven into a cultural blanket that envelops their identity. They have existed in this geographic area since the arrival of *los nuevos pobladores* (the new settlers) more than four hundred years ago, having first settled in San Gabriel del Yungue Owingeh, across the Río Grande from Ohkay Owingeh Pueblo, in 1585. They are *un mestizaje* (a mixed race) whose ethnicity was formed from interrelations with the Indigenous peoples, including the Comanche, Apache, Ute, Navajo, and, of course, *los vecinos* (the neighbors), the Pueblo.

New Mexico's cultural, political, and geographical isolation contributes to its keeping centuries-old traditions and customs intact. The decline in the use of the Spanish language and traditions linked with an agrarian way of life is a recent occurrence coinciding with the end of World War II. Recognizing northern New Mexico's cultural uniqueness has never been a difficult assertion for us. *Que digan lo que digan*, say what they may about our language, traditions, and customs, we maintain a strong allegiance to *nuestra querencia*, our beloved homeland. It is that proud affirmation and arrogant defiance that has enabled *norteños* (people from northern New Mexico) to keep their sense of identity, even as Western society's heavy-handed influence has permeated their towns and villages. Cultural traditions are sustained more easily when they remain undisturbed within their traditional contexts. The imposition of variables that may diminish or completely eradicate a culture when it is removed from its cultural environment undermines the sustainability of social constructs, language, spiritual and religious faith, and other customs and traditions.

When I was growing up in northern New Mexico, it was quite common to hear of relatives who had migrated outside of the state following employment opportunities. *Se fueron pa Guayma. Andan en Colo'. ¿Qué se oye decir de la parentela de Califa? Izque fue a dar en Utah* (They went to Wyoming. They are in Colorado. What have you heard from the relatives in California? It was said they went to work in Utah). As a *Nuevomexicano del norte de más allá* (New Mexican from the far northern frontier), those were but a few of the comments

I heard about relatives and neighbors who left the village for work throughout the Southwest. It is common to have uncles, aunts, or neighbors who moved to Wyoming, California, Colorado, Utah, Texas, Arizona, or Nevada, as well as other states, in search of a better livelihood for themselves and their families. The saying among the *plebe* in the 1950s and 1960s in my community of Dixon was *pa' Utah, Califa, o el Army* (to Utah, California, or the Army). Some were permanent relocations and others were seasonal migrations for employment in *el betabel, la papa, el algodón, el ferrocarril, la borrega, y en las minas*. Besides work in the sugar-beet, potato, and cotton fields, people found jobs sheepherding, ranching, in agriculture, on the railroad, and in mining and service industries. Others established businesses, offered taxi services, worked as healthcare providers, educators, and auto mechanics, went into construction, and found other types of employment that sustained them away from home.

Migration occurred on both sides of my family. My uncle Alfonso Romero earned his law degree from the University of New Mexico after returning from military duty in wwii. He moved to California and worked in the law profession until he retired as a judge in Palo Alto. Another uncle, Celestino Durán, moved to the fertile valleys of San José, California, working at odd jobs until he established his own landscaping business. My grandfather, Juan Andrés Romero, was working as a *borreguero* (sheepherder) in Monte Vista, Colorado when he received notice that World War II had come to an end. He threw his hat up in the air and exclaimed, "*¡Ay, ahora sí viene mi Elías!*" (Ay! Here comes my Elías!). By the time his hat hit the ground, my grandfather lay dead of a heart attack. Elías, the youngest of his three sons and the last to return from the war, was coming home. *Norteño* families like mine have their own personal stories of what has been gained and lost, and how they endured and persevered through the struggles and triumphs of life and living on the road in the quest to provide for family and home.

A BARRIO TESTAMENT

I first began to consider a project to document the manito diaspora from northern New Mexico to Wyoming (*Guayuma, Guayma* or *Guayomin* were the colloquial pronunciations) when my wife and I made our first trip to visit her relatives in Riverton, Wyoming—a small town in Fremont County— where she was born and raised. We had been married earlier that summer and decided to go on an extension of our honeymoon to meet her *tíos, tías, y primos* (uncles, aunts, and cousins). We spent almost a week amid her family and friends, who composed the manito community of Riverton in the area known to the locals as "The Barrio." While we were there, her aunt and uncle hosted a barbeque with many people from the barrio in attendance, all of whom had origins in New Mexico. As I sat enjoying the festive occasion, I was able to observe and note the conversations I was overhearing among the various guests. I was intrigued by the Spanish being spoken. It was the same dialect that we speak in northern New Mexico. I was particularly captivated by some of the words, which I had not heard since my childhood. The manito Spanish that I was hearing had remained intact and seemed even less bastardized than the Spanish spoken back home. Throughout our visit with my wife's relatives, it became evident that they and others in Riverton whose families had originated in New Mexico had sustained and nurtured a culture far removed from its ethnic homeland. From its querencia. *Hmmm,* I thought, *someone should do an oral history documentation project on New Mexico Manitos who now call Wyoming their home.*

My wife's parents' families both migrated to Riverton from Gascón, a small village outside of Las Vegas, New Mexico, during the Depression. Her grandfather, Valentín Rodarte, moved there to work in the sugar-beet fields and refinery. The company then transported Valentín back to Gascón to pick up his wife and children. Some of their neighbors decided to come along and loaded themselves and their meager belongings onto the company's flatbed truck. And thus, a *vecindad* (neighborhood) of people from Gascón and Rociada were transplanted to Riverton. Valentín and his family lived in a railroad car until they could save enough money to buy a house. The younger Rodarte siblings found picking betabel too laborious, but were eventually able to gain other forms of employment. It was not long after when they met and married their spouses. My wife's father, Margarito "Mike" Rodarte, married Clorinda Trammell. His brother Ben married Dorothy Apodaca. Their sister, Beatrice, married Jimmie Martínez. Their youngest sister, Helen, married Emilio Vigil.

The *gente* (people) in Riverton carried on with many of the New Mexico traditions they had left behind. They ate the same traditional New Mexican foods: *chile verde, chile molido, chile pequí, papas fritas, papas con spam, papas con weenies, papas con corned beef, papas con huevos, papas con de todo.* Or, as the old joke goes, "*Para el almuerzo, comíamos papas con huevos. Al medio día, huevos con papas. Y en la tarde, papas a huevo*" (For breakfast, we ate potatoes and eggs. At midday, eggs with potatoes. And in the evening, potatoes by force). The foods that Manitos were accustomed to—*frijoles, chicos, tortillas, macarones, arroz dulce, yela de capulín*—remained among their staples. Even potted meat, Vienna sausages, banana peppers in vinegar, and similar goods that stocked the *trasteros* (cabinets) of their *parientes'* kitchens in northern New Mexico continued to be part of their cuisine. Their homes were furnished and decorated with the same *santos* (saints) and religious iconography found in New Mexico homes. On Friday nights, in the early period of life in the Barrio, the young mothers and wives convened to pray the rosary at someone's home. The Barrio residents kept small backyard garden plots where they grew tomatoes, chili peppers, *calabazas, calabacitas, maíz, frijól, alverjón*, and other vegetables. And the Spanish music they listened to came from New Mexico. In the fall they sent requests to their New Mexico relatives for *chile, piñón*, and the latest village *mitote* (gossip).

As the years went by, I became more and more fond of our visits to Riverton. The feeling of *familia*. The fishing excursions that awaited. The laughter. The stories. Uncle Emilio's never-ending stories, full of humor and insight. They spoke of a time that evoked a strong sense of community among the Manitos living in the Barrio. Of all-night poker games, hunting trips, fishing outings, and camping excursions to the Sinks that included games such as the spoon-and-egg relay, the three-legged race, the egg toss, and bike races down the Switchbacks. They told stories of someone getting their lights knocked out at the local tavern and ending the night in a chorus of laughter. The names the family dropped during my visits over the years—Grandpa Pipes, Grandma Angélica, Bonay, Fishy, Chiefy, Grandma Cookie, Doña Franque, Uncle Jimmie, Moises—became familiar. It seemed as if I had even known them. They were more than just names remembered in conversations or faces captured in faded black-and-white pictures peering out of a dusty photo album. These were people who had formed a kinship among each other that was time everlasting. Their bonds had been cultivated and nurtured by the need to share of what everyone had in the best interest and well-being of their community. The Barrio.

SOUTH PARK ADDITION COMMUNITY DEVELOPMENT
PROJECT: SIDE BY SIDE, THEY WORKED TOGETHER

Perhaps no story in Riverton evokes the sense of community more than that of the South Park Addition Community Development Project, initiated by residents of the neighborhood known formally as the South Park Addition. In 1986, after many years of arduous obstacles and setbacks, the City of Riverton agreed to provide sewer, water, and street paving to the neighborhood. However, despite numerous requests by residents of the Barrio, it refused to provide sidewalks, curbs, and gutters. The residents sought out donations of materials from the local cement factory (which used the Barrio roads) and other local businesses. The residents agreed to provide their labor and skills. After coming home from long days at their jobs, the men worked on the construction crews that had been formed for the project, while the women cooked meals and provided assistance. Driving down any of those streets today, it is taken for granted that the Barrio community was responsible for the infrastructure that exists in South Park.

A thirty-year anniversary gathering was held on July 16, 2016 at Monroe Park in celebration of the South Park Addition Community Development Project. In attendance were men and women who had worked on or contributed to the project in various capacities. They were recognized and the names of those no longer present were acknowledged and fondly remembered. The South Park Addition Community Development Project endures as a testament to the strong work ethic and resiliency of Manitos working together, side by side, to create a home for their families and their community. Jimmie Martínez, my wife's uncle, who volunteered on the project, captured the spirit of unity in his poem "South Park Improvement" (1986).

SOUTH PARK IMPROVEMENT

Side by side we work together
On the streets of South and West
Until the work is finished
This crew will never rest

Hard work is all we met
People will tell you that
Annie is always with us
Ready for this and that

Keeping the gang together
Is Emilio's everyday chore
Making sure we get enough cement
Perhaps a little more

Remember we are doing this
Our way and without pay
Very little time is wasted
Everybody is there each day

My last favor I will ask you
Everybody please cooperate
Never try to overdo-it
Time can always wait.

FOLLOWING THE MANITO TRAIL:
A TALE OF TWO QUERENCIAS

Several years after I had been introduced to my wife's family, I met other Manitos at a literary presentation I did at the Laramie County Community College in Cheyenne, Wyoming. They had come to listen to me, a New Mexico author whose poetry and stories captured the New Mexico they remembered from their early childhood upbringing and from visits back to their family's querencia. After my reading, people shared stories and memories with me of their beloved New Mexico and how their families had arrived in Cheyenne and established and sustained themselves through various forms of employment. *Hmmm*, I thought again, *Someone really should do an oral history documentation project on New Mexico Manitos who now call Wyoming their home.*

Through annual family visits to Riverton and my literary presentations and travels through Wyoming for over two decades, I have met other Manitos whose family origins are in northern New Mexico. Their personal accounts of the new lives that were formed are oftentimes as impressive as the old lives they left behind. Neither time nor distance nor geographical separations has diminished their cultural identity. In addition to requests for chile, posole, piñón, and other Nuevomexicano delicacies, Rudolfo Anaya novels and copies of *La Herencia*, *New Mexico Magazine*, the local newspaper, and recordings of northern New Mexico music are always on the most-requested lists created by relatives living across state lines. Even holiday traditions such as posadas and many Lenten season and Holy Week observances are carried out in customs that are particular to northern New Mexico. To call a new place home but continue to be emotionally and spiritually connected to one's place of origin is an interesting phenomenon. It is a tale of two querencias.

AN UNDOCUMENTED HISTORY: *DESDE NUEVO MÉXICO HASTA GUAYOMIN* (FROM NEW MEXICO TO WYOMING)

The migration of people from northern New Mexico to Wyoming is an important history in the diaspora of northern Nuevomexicano culture. It remains, however, an undocumented account. Wyoming's rich and broad historical legacy has been affected by the contributions of this cultural group of people. Yet they have been left out of its history books.

Fremont County Wyoming: A Pictorial History, for example, fails to mention Nuevomexicanos who settled in Riverton's county and contributed to its history. The author states in the book's introduction that "the story of Fremont County, Wyoming is as fascinating as the story of the West. And because that story has been played out within the not-too-distant past, it remains accessible and believable. Many visual reminders remain and conversations with friends and neighbors provide living ties to people and events that shaped that past" (Loren 1996, 6). Those words could be just as applicable to the Manitos of Fremont County. The book chronicles Western explorers and Anglo settlers and the Shoshone and Arapaho tribes, and even provides a short section on immigrants from Scotland. Visibly missing, however, are the Mexican American people, most notably the Nuevomexicanos who made enormous contributions to Fremont County and the entire state of Wyoming. And yet, the visual reminders and conversations with Manitos can be found throughout Fremont County and they continue to provide a connection to people and events that shaped its past.

MANITOS Y SU POESÍA (MANITOS AND THEIR POETRY)

Even if the state of Wyoming hasn't recognized the contributions of Manitos to the state's cultural landscape, there is other documentation: a rich tradition of poetry written by Manitos during their travels further north. These testimonies were written by betabeleros, borregueros, and other Nuevomexicano migrant workers in the form of verses and song ballads. Their poems and *corridos* (folk songs) were published in New Mexico Spanish-language newspapers and literary publications of the era. Anselmo Arellano's book *Los Pobladores Nuevo Mexicanos y Su Poesía, 1880–1950* is an important collection of these writings. Various works in Arellano's anthology document *manito* experiences and struggles of life *en Guayma. Acequias*, traditional open-air irrigation systems common throughout New Mexico, even inspired a poem about an acequia in Wyoming. Daniel García, born around 1882 near Antón Chico, New Mexico, wrote "La Sequía en Wyoming," which poetically describes the conditions of a drought in the late 1930s. García, who worked primarily as a sheepherder, distinguishes himself as a poet in the following corrido:

LA SEQUÍA EN WYOMING

O, Santo Niño no nos castigues,
Por tu pureza y divinidad,
Retira Niño con tus poderes
Esta terrible calamidad.

Los vegetales están marchitos
A consecuencia de la sequía,
Y los pasteos agonizando
La madre tierra ya no los cría.

Endurecida la madre tierra
Y aletargada le falta vida
De su producto menoscabado
A las ovejas poco convida.

La madre tierra pierde las fibras
De las corrientes de flujo magno
Del corazón que salen sus venas
De blancas linfas, el gran océano.

Amarillentes se van secando
Plantas silvestres también alubia,
Porque ya mustias no han recibido
Los dulces toques de fresca lluvia.

Las nubecillas suben volando
Y en las regiones quedan íntegras,
Pero la lluvia que tanto amamos
No la derraman las nubes negras.

Dos fuertes ríos y manantiales
Las claras aguas disminuendo,
Y los pastores de varios puntos
De los tormentos se van huyendo.

Ya los pastores todos en grupos
Crueles afanes van lamentando,
También el poeta que aproxima
Grande rebaño va apocentando.

Escuchen todos este corrido
Tanto presente como vosotros,
Es de un castigo que cae severo
De lo celeste sobre nosotros.

La lluvia venga por gracia Santa
Se lo suplico a mi Diós Divino
Este corrido verbal se canta
Por una copa de dulce vino.

14 de septiembre, 1939

Many of the corridos and poems in Arellano's book, usually following a quatrain and ABAB rhyme scheme, dispel the misconception that Manitos were primarily an illiterate people. Poems like "La Sequía en Wyoming" exhibit the same concerns that Manitos had for water in their native New Mexico villages, including a regard for patron saints such as El Santo Niño de Atocha (The Holy Child of Atocha). Their eloquent and passionate verses often express the challenges of life away from home and not only chronicle life in Wyoming, but in other states like Colorado where they found similar types of employment, as is evident in the following poem by Maggie Sánchez (1931) from Holman, New Mexico, about life for a sugar-beet worker:

LAS PENAS DE LOS BETABELEROS

Para empesar estos versos,
Pongo mi atención primero
Para contarles amigos
La vida de un betabelero.

Nos levantamos muy tempranito
Nos empezamos a estirar
Cuando salemos al frío
Empezamos a temblar.

Cuando llegamos al "fild"
Agarramos los machetes,
Con la única esperanza
De alcanzarnos buen cheque.

El betabel es penoso
No se le puede negar,
Llegamos en la tarde
No podemos ni cenar.

Los que salen cansados
Y son debiles de mente
Parece que se han de echado
Sus tragos de aguardiente.

El que no lo quiera creer
Que pase a Colorado,
Aquí no es Nuevo México
Para andar de enamorado.

Les digo a los muchachos
Los que nunca han trabajado;
Si quieren saber de penas
Que pasen pa Colorado.

En Nuevo México no trabajan duro
Ni andan a pantalones,
En Colorodo ni se polvean
Ni andan de vacilones.

Les encargo a los viejitos
No vendan sus ranchitos,
Pa venirse a Colorado
A rodar como palitos.

El que compuso estos versos
Su nombre les va a dar:
Es Maggie Sánchez de Holman
Lo deben de dispensar.

15 de octubre, 1931

The poems and corridos depict life away from the manito homeland and indicate a longing for home. Manitos, after all, did not leave their querencias to go on vacation, but as a necessary act of survival. When they left home, they left behind their *ranchitos* and entrusted them to the care of their wives and children. Arellano (1976) writes:

> Por muchos años desde los fines del siglo pasado, los nativos de Nuevo México han salido a otros estados buscando empleo en ranchos de ganado, la agricultura y el ferrocarril. Entre esta gente labradora había muchos que cuidaban borregas en los campos verdes de las montañas. Algunos borregueros dedicaban mucho de su tiempo a las letras y pasaban su tiempo en los campos de la soledad escribiendo poesía. Algunas veces enviaban sus composiciones a Nuevo México para que fueran publicadas en los periódicos españoles de sus pueblos natales. La poesía de la gente trabajadora deja un reflejo de los pensamientos de esos que salen de los pueblitos nuevo mexicanos para supervivir la pobreza que afectó a muchas familias que fueron despoblados de sus tierras (149).[1]

Many borregueros dedicated their free time to writing poetry while in the solitude of their camps, finding consolation in the songs they wrote but never quite being able to find a sense of home. Felipe Pacheco's verses in this excerpt from "Lamentos de un Pastor" (1898) express the duality of a poet who worked as a sheepherder while also tending to his literary craft:

A tal grado, los pastores,
Llegan a ser unos poetas,
Cantando dos mil poesías
A las bragadas y broquetas,

Todos a su diligencia
Cantan para su consuelo,
Pero no todos se aquerencian
Mas que le paguen sueldo.

Writers like Pacheco understood that they were not only *labradores* (workers), but also men of letters whose writings could convey to their families back in New Mexico the harsh realities of life *en la cuacha* (sheepherding), *en los traques* (railroad), *en la pisca* (agriculture) *y en las minas* (mining). Their writings went beyond personal journal entries and became historical accounts in the form of poems and songs published in newspapers and shared around the kitchen table or in the *resolana* among family and friends. They endure to the present day, giving us an insight into life of Manitos on the trail.

FOLLOWING THE MANITO TRAIL: PROJECT ORIGINS

Inspired by my encounters with Manitos living in Wyoming and the exclusion of their contributions to its history in *Fremont County Wyoming: A Pictorial History*, I decided to take a group of students from the University of New Mexico to Wyoming and conduct interviews for an oral history documentation project I entitled "Following the Manito Trail." In preparation for the spring 2007 intersession class, ethnologist, folklorist, and documentarian Enrique Lamadrid facilitated a workshop on oral history documentation techniques. On the day of our departure for Cheyenne, where we were scheduled to do the interviews, we met with writer, historian, and cultural activist Juan Estevan Arellano in Dixon, who spoke to the class on manito identity and northern New Mexico culture. The students sat attentively under a crabapple tree at my grandmother's residence listening to Estevan's informative and inspiring *plática* (talk). Later that evening at New Mexico Highlands University, Anselmo Arellano and Julián Josué Vigil, historians and retired instructors from Las Vegas, did a semester-long presentation on Nuevomexicano history and cultural identity in three hours for our group. Eric Romero from NMHU acquired accommodations for us at the campus dormitories for our first night on the manito trail. The following day, we were hosted by an *Hermano* and his family at La Morada de San José in Trinidad, Colorado. It was an interesting and insightful experience that magnified the Hispano spiritual and religious customs of northern New Mexico and southern Colorado.

Once in Cheyenne, through the help of Ann Redman—a Manita from LeDoux, New Mexico who founded the Wyoming Latina Youth Conference—we were able to stay at the Laramie County Community College's dormitories free of charge and use the school's facilities to conduct a dozen interviews. The interviews were informative, insightful, and inspiring. The oral history documentation project fulfilled the mission proposed in the course description. The Jesse Anaya family, whose origins are in New Mexico, even hosted a barbeque at their compound in celebration of our project the evening before we departed. It was a beautiful act of manito hospitality considering that my students and I had never met Jesse or her family before.

In 2014, Vanessa Fonseca, who had recently been hired as an assistant professor at the University of Wyoming, contacted me and asked if I would be interested in working with her on a collaboration and resurrected version of *Following the Manito Trail.* Vanessa and I, with the assistance of Trisha Martínez, Adam Herrera, and Robert Perea (most of whom are Manitos and have experienced life on the trail themselves) and contributions from Troy Lovata, whose grandfather traveled along the manito trail to Wyoming, have continued the documentation project I had envisioned at a backyard family gathering in Riverton more than two decades before.

In the fall of 2017, the University of Wyoming's American Heritage Center (AHC) worked with our project team to curate a gallery exhibit titled *Following the Manito Trail.* It included photographs, videos, and a panel discussion by the project's team members, "Following the Manito Trail: A Conversation with the Researchers" (Siguiendo el camino de los Manitos: una conversación con los investigadores). The AHC described our effort as "an interdisciplinary ethnographic project that documents the Hispanic New Mexican, or Manito, migration from New Mexico to different parts of the United States during the last century. The project consists of a collection of oral histories, photographs, and artifacts that document, for the first time, the many contributions that Manitos have had on the Western United States." In addition, they wrote, "The Following the Manito Trail exhibition focuses on Manito migration into Wyoming. It looks at the many sociocultural facets that have allowed Manito culture to endure beyond geographic restraints. The exhibit contextualizes the many aspects of Wyoming life and culture that Manitos have shaped, contributed to, and influenced."

The exhibit and panel discussion exceeded our highest expectations. People from Wyoming and neighboring states attended the premiere, and many were able to view photos of themselves and family members in the exhibit's materials. Adam produced several videos, including one that used original footage from 1986 provided to the project by Annie Mejorado and Susana Lawson Vigil of the South Park Addition Community Development Project. Also included were photographs, interviews, and a section on the arborglyph work done by Vanessa, Troy, and Adam when they traveled to northeastern Wyoming in the summer of 2016 to document trees carved with names, dates, and New Mexico place names by Manito borregueros. Since Vanessa and I began our collaborative work on *Following the Manito Trail* in 2014, our project team has conducted more than forty oral history interviews, taken hundreds of photos, produced three documentaries, received four grants, published three articles, and done numerous panel presentations at conferences and for communities. The exhibit concluded in November 2017 but is now available as a traveling gallery exhibit. We view this as an important endeavor to share the work with the communities we have visited.

AFTERWORD

Manitos from the Las Vegas and Taos regions tended to migrate to northern states such as Wyoming or Nevada. The ones from eastern New Mexico made their way to pick algodón and other crops in Texas. Western New Mexico Manitos often left to work the mines in Arizona. Many of my vecinos and parientes from Dixon made their way to California, Utah, and Colorado (and, yes, some signed up for the Army). Manitos, of course, went everywhere—anywhere they could find employment. They didn't leave on vacation. They went to work! Such were the values and ethics of our gente.

Throughout the Southwest, just as in Wyoming, Manitos have established their querencias and contributed to the social, economic, and overall well-being of their communities. Yet their cultural presence and contributions to the places where they migrated goes unrecognized. The *Following the Manito Trail* project collects, documents, and shares stories and memories that reflect a people's uprooting of themselves in search of work and opportunity. We collect *testimonios* directly from persons who experienced the migration and include their children's and grandchildren's accounts of growing up Manito away from their ancestral homeland. In doing so, the project addresses issues of identity, migration, and the preservation of cultural traditions. Discussions and dialogues with people whose families originated in New Mexico help to compose a narrative that evokes the resiliency and determination required to establish and sustain querencia, both in New Mexico and beyond the borders of the state. As the great Manito scholar Sabine Ulibarrí (1995, 239) reminds us, to know where you are going, you need to know where you are at—and ultimately, to remember where you came from.

¿Quién Eres?	Who Are You?
Si olvidas de donde vienes,	If you forget where you come from,
¿sabes, tú, a donde vas?	do you know where you are going?
Si has perdido tu pasado,	If you have lost your past,
¿dónde está tu porvenir?	where is your future?
Si eres hombre sin historia,	If you are a person without a history
serás hombre sin futuro.	you will be a person without a future.
Si reniegas de tus padres,	If you deny your parents,
¿qué esperarás de tus hijos?	what will you expect of your children?
Si no tienes parentesco	If you have no relationship
con tu familia y tu pueblo	with your family or your community
cuando ríes, ríes solo,	when you laugh, you laugh alone,
cuando lloras, lloras solo.	when you cry, you cry alone.
Un presente solitario,	A lonely present,
sin ayer y sin mañana,	without yesterday and without tomorrow,
sin parientes, sin compadres,	without relatives, without comrades,
sin amigos, sin hermanos.	without friends, without brothers.
Qué solo estás en el mundo,	How alone you are in the world,
perdido en la niebla blanca.	lost in the haze.
Solo, con tu culpa a cuestas	Alone, you carry your guilt,
y tu soledad a solas.	and alone you remain.

NOTE

1. For many years since the end of the last century, New Mexico natives have gone out to other states seeking employment with cattle ranches, agriculture, and railroads. Among these laborers were many who cared for sheep in the mountains' green fields. Some sheepherders devoted much of their time to composing lyrics and spent their time in the solitude of the fields writing poetry. Sometimes they sent their compositions to New Mexico for publication in the Spanish language periodicals of their native communities. The poetry of working people leaves a reflection of the thoughts of those who come out of the New Mexican towns to survive the poverty that affected many families who were depopulated from their lands. (Author's translation.)

Arellano, Anselmo F. 1976. *Los pobladores nuevo mexicanos y su poesía, 1889–1950*. Albuquerque: Pajarito Publications.

Cobos, Rubén. 2003. *A Dictionary of New Mexico and Southern Colorado Spanish*, Revised and Expanded Edition. Santa Fe: Museum of New Mexico Press.

García, Daniel. 1939. "La Sequía en Wyoming." In Arellano, *Los pobladores nuevo mexicanos y su poesía*, n.p.

Jost, Loren. 1996. *Fremont County Wyoming: A Pictorial History*. Virginia Beach, VA: Donning Company.

Lamadrid, Enrique. 1994. *Tesoros del espíritu: A Portrait in Sound of Hispanic New Mexico*. With Jack Loeffler, recordist, and Miguel Gandert, photographer. Albuquerque: Academia/El Norte Publications.

Martínez, Jimmie. 1986. "South Park Improvement." In *South Park Improvement Project* by Susan M. Lawson. Independent Study. n.p. Author's collection.

Pacheco, Felipe. 1898. "Lamentos de un Pastor." In Arellano, *Los pobladores nuevo mexicanos y su poesía*, n.p.

Sánchez, Maggie. 1931. "Las penas de los betabeleros." In Arellano, *Los pobladores nuevo mexicanos y su poesía*, n.p.

Ulibarrí, Sabine. 1995. "¿Quién Eres?" In *Sabine R. Ulibarrí: Critical Essays*, edited by Maria I. Duke Dos Santos and Patricia De La Fuente, 239. Albuquerque: University of New Mexico Press.

RUDOLFO ANAYA was born in 1937 in the small town of Pastura in the llano of eastern New Mexico, to Martín and Rafaelita (Mares) Anaya. His formative years were spent in Santa Rosa and Albuquerque. He graduated from the University of New Mexico in 1963 with a BA in English. In 1966 he married Patricia Lawless, who supported her husband's desire to write and served as his editor. He went on to complete two master's degrees at the University of New Mexico, one in 1968 in English and another in 1972 in Guidance and Counseling. He is best known for his award-winning novel *Bless Me, Ultima* (Quinto Sol Publications, 1972), which has sold nearly half a million copies and was made into a movie. He has written and edited over forty books in diverse genres, including fiction, poetry, essays, plays, and children's literature. Due to his prolific career, he has been unofficially designated as the "Godfather of Chicano Letters." On September 22, 2015, President Barack Obama awarded him a National Humanities Medal. He is a Professor Emeritus of Creative Writing in the Department of English at the University of New Mexico. He continues to write every day and is working to publish new material.

KEVIN BROWN is a member of the Navajo Nation. He joined the University of New Mexico University Libraries in March 2016 as the Program Administrator of the Indigenous Nations Library Program. Kevin has two BAs, one in Museum Studies from the Institute of American Indian Arts and the other in anthropology from the University of Arizona. He also has an MA in public archaeology from the University of New Mexico and is currently working toward his MBA in Educational Leadership at UNM. Through his work with New Mexico Native American youth, he gained a wealth of experience in student engagement and retention. He is also an artist and photographer.

C. MAURUS CHINO is from the Acoma Tribe in northwest New Mexico. He belongs to the Eagle Clan and is a child of the Sun Clan. He earned a BFA from New Mexico State University. Before attending NMSU, he worked for the US Forest Service fighting wildfires and in the underground uranium mines. In 1992, Maurus decided to divide his time between life as an artist, an activist, and, more recently, a writer. In 2007, his work protesting conquistador monuments in New Mexico and El Paso, Texas became part of the PBS documentary *The Last Conquistador* (2008). He lives in Albuquerque, where he continues to paint and to make jewelry. He has one child, a daughter, Anathea.

SCOTT DAVIS is from Los Osos, California. His primary experience has been as a mason, contractor, and project manager in the construction industry. In 2007, he moved to Española, New Mexico. At this time, he came into conversation with Dr. Corrine Kaa Pedi Povi Sanchez and Dr. Patricia Marina Trujillo, which began (and continues to inspire) his path toward social justice. He engages in transformative conversations that have resulted in a recalibration of his goals to pivot from the construction industry toward full-time work engaged with social justice. He has worked locally with Tewa Women United, as well as with the national organization A CALL TO MEN. Recently, he completed a residency at the Santa Fe Art Institute, under the theme of "Equal Justice." There, he began a book focusing on white men's role in working toward collective liberation.

VANESSA FONSECA-CHÁVEZ is from Grants, New Mexico. She received her BA in Spanish and her MA in Southwest Hispanic Studies from the University of New Mexico. Her PhD from Arizona State University is in Spanish Cultural Studies, with an emphasis in Chicana/o literature. Her writings have appeared in *Chicana/Latina Studies: The Journal of Mujeres Activas en Letras y Cambio Social* and *Chiricú Journal: Latina/o Literatures, Arts, and Cultures*, among others. Her coedited book (with Jesús Rosales), *Spanish Perspectives on Chicano Literature: Literary and Cultural Essays* was published by Ohio State University Press in 2017. Her book, *Colonial Legacies in Chicana/o Literature and Culture: Looking through the Kaleidoscope*, is forthcoming from the University of Arizona Press. She is an Assistant Professor of English at Arizona State University.

MYRRIAH GÓMEZ is from El Rancho, New Mexico, in the Pojoaque Valley. She is a graduate of New Mexico Highlands University (BA) and the University of New Mexico (MA). She earned her PhD in English with an emphasis in US Latina/o Literature and Theory from the University of Texas at San Antonio. Her book *Nuclear Nuevo México: Identity, Ethnicity, and Resistance in Atomic Third Spaces* is forthcoming from the University of Arizona Press. She is an Assistant Professor in the Honors College at the University of New Mexico.

MOISES GONZALES is a Genízaro heir of both the Cañón de Carnué Land Grant and the San Antonio de Las Huertas Land Grant. He is a danzante of the Matachín and Comanche traditions of the Sandía Mountain communities. He serves on the Board of Trustees of the Carnué Land Grant and has written various academic articles on the history and culture of Genízaro settlements of New Mexico. He is coeditor, with Enrique Lamadrid, of *Nación Genízara: Ethnogenesis, Place, and Identity in New Mexico*, published by the University of New Mexico Press in 2019. He is an Associate Professor of Urban Design in Community and Regional Planning at the School of Architecture and Planning at the University of New Mexico.

LILLIAN GORMAN is a Chicana from Albuquerque, New Mexico. She grew up between the city's west side and her maternal grandparents' home in the South Valley. Her grandparents are natives of Belen, Santa Fe, and Taos. She graduated with a BA in Spanish and an MA in Southwest Hispanic Studies from the University of New Mexico and was part of its first class of McNair scholars. Her PhD in Hispanic Studies with concentrations in Latina/o cultural studies and sociolinguistics is from the University of Illinois at Chicago. Her essays have appeared in the edited volumes *Transnational Encounters: Music and Performance at the U.S.–Mexico Border* and *Bilingual Youth: Spanish in English-Speaking Societies*. She is the Director of the Spanish as a Heritage Language Program and an Assistant Professor in the Department of Spanish and Portuguese at the University of Arizona.

BERNADINE HERNÁNDEZ is from the South Valley in Albuquerque, New Mexico. She received her BA in English and Spanish and her MA in English Language Literatures from the University of New Mexico. Her PhD is in Literatures in English and Cultural Studies from the University of California, San Diego. Her writings have appeared in *Comparative Literature and Culture*, *Women's Studies Quarterly*, and *Transgender Studies Quarterly*, among others. She specializes in transnational feminism and sexual economies of the US borderlands, along with American Literary Studies/Empire from the mid-nineteenth to early twentieth centuries, borderlands theory, and Chicana/Latina literature and sexualities. She is an Assistant Professor in the Department of English at the University of New Mexico and a research professor at the Institute of American Cultures at the University of California, Los Angeles, where she is finishing her book manuscript titled *Border Bodies:*

Racialized Sexuality, Sexual Capital, and Violence in the Nineteenth-Century Borderlands.

SPENCER R. HERRERA was born and raised in Houston, Texas, but has enjoyed living in Nuevo México with his wife, Jessica, and their two daughters, Sofía and Emiliana, for twenty years. He is the coauthor of *Sagrado: A Photopoetics across the Chicano Homeland* (UNM Press, 2013), winner of a Border Regional Library Association Southwest Book Award, a New Mexico–Arizona Book award, and a Pima County Public Library Southwest Book of the Year award. He is the coauthor of *Tertulia: La escritura como acto público, social y cultural* (Kendall Hunt, 2014) and author/editor of *Before/Beyond Borders: An Anthology of Chicano/a Literature* (Kendall Hunt, 2010). He also guest-edited a special issue on Chicano/a literature for *Revista Casa de las Américas,* a premier Latin American literary journal published in Havana, Cuba. He completed his PhD in Spanish with a minor in film at the University of New Mexico. He is an Associate Professor of Spanish at New Mexico State University in Las Cruces, where he teaches Chicano/a Studies.

KELLY MEDINA-LÓPEZ is from Las Cruces, New Mexico. She received her BA in Spanish and English and her MA in Spanish from New Mexico State University. Her PhD, also from New Mexico State University, is in Rhetoric and Professional Communication with an emphasis in Cultural Rhetorics and Composition Studies. Her work explores research methodologies, composition pedagogy, and Chicanx/Latinx rhetoric and composition. Her writing appears in *Constellations: A Cultural Rhetorics Publishing Space.* She is proud to be a fourth-generation New Mexican, and to represent southern New Mexico. She is an Assistant Professor of Composition Studies at California State University, Monterey Bay.

TEY MARIANNA NUNN is the Director and Chief Curator of the Art Museum at the National Hispanic Cultural Center in Albuquerque, New Mexico. Prior to that, she spent nine years as the Curator of Contemporary Hispano and Latino collections at the Museum of International Folk Art in Santa Fe. She received her MA and PhD in Latin American Studies from the University of New Mexico, where her research focused on Spanish Colonial, contemporary Latin American, and Chicana/o and Latina/o history and art history. She is the author of *Sin Nombre: Hispana and Hispano Artists of the*

New Deal Era (University of New Mexico Press, 2001). Nunn has curated such acclaimed exhibits as *Sin Nombre: Hispana and Hispano Artists of the New Deal Era, Cyber Arte: Tradition Meets Technology, Flor y Canto: Reflections from Nuevo México, Meso-Americhanics (Maneuvering Mestizaje): de la Torre Brothers and Border Baroque, Stitching Resistance: The History of Chilean Arpilleras, PAPEL! Pico, Rico y Chico, El Retrato Nuevomexicano Ahora/New Mexican Portraiture Now,* and *The Piñata Exhibit (Sure to Be a Smash Hit!)*. She recently curated *Luis Tapia: Sculpture as Sanctuary,* the first solo exhibition of a New Mexican artist at the National Museum of Mexican Art in Chicago. An ardent advocate for artists, Nunn is active in issues concerning Latinos and museums. She has served as a two-term director/trustee for the boards of the American Alliance of Museums, the Western States Arts Federation (WESTAF), and El Rancho de las Golondrinas, a living history museum. A recipient of numerous research fellowships from the Smithsonian Institution and the Bogliasco Foundation, Nunn was voted "Santa Fe Arts Person and Woman of the Year" in 2001. She received the 2008 President's Award from the Women's Caucus for the Arts of the College Art Association and in 2014 she was honored by Los Amigos de Arte Popular with the Van Deren Coke award for outstanding contributions to expanding the knowledge of Mexican, Mexican American, and Latin American folk art. In November 2016, President Barack Obama appointed Dr. Nunn to the National Museum and Library Services Board.

LEVI ROMERO, the inaugural Poet Laureate of New Mexico, is from the Embudo Valley of northern New Mexico. His most recent book is *Sagrado: A Photopoetics across the Chicano Homeland* (coauthored with Spencer R. Herrera and Robert Kaiser). His two collections of poetry are *A Poetry of Remembrance: New and Rejected Works* and *In the Gathering of Silence.* His publications have received numerous awards, including two 2017 Society for Humanistic Anthropology Ethnographic Poetry Honorable Mention Awards, a 2015 International Latino Book Award Honorable Mention, a 2014–2015 Southwest Book Award, a New Mexico Arizona Book Award, a Writers' League of Texas Book Award Finalist, and a Best Books of the Southwest. He is also the recipient of several NEA and NEH grants. He was awarded the post of New Mexico Centennial Poet in 2012. His work has been featured in numerous anthologies and online publications. He has codirected two films on acequia culture: *Bendición del agua,* which premiered at the 2017 National Cowboy

Poetry Gathering in Elko, Nevada, and *Going Home Homeless*, which won a People's Choice Award at the Taos Shortz Film Festival. He is an Assistant Professor in the Department of Chicana and Chicano Studies at the University of New Mexico and Director of the New Mexico Cultural Landscapes Certificate Program.

KAREN R. ROYBAL is from Pecos, New Mexico. She received her PhD in American Studies (with an emphasis in Southwest Studies) from the University of New Mexico. Her writings have appeared in *Aztlán: A Journal of Chicano Studies*; *Western American Literature*; *Culture, Theory and Critique*; *Chicana/Latina Studies*; and *Teaching Western American Literature*. Her book, *Archives of Dispossession: Recovering the Testimonios of Mexican American Herederas, 1848–1960*, was published in 2017 by the University of North Carolina Press. She is an Assistant Professor of Southwest Studies at Colorado College.

CORRINE KAA PEDI POVI SANCHEZ is from San Ildefonso Pueblo in northern New Mexico. She received her BA in Environment, Technology and Society from Clark University. She earned her MA in American Studies with a minor in Health Education from the University of New Mexico and completed her PhD in Justice Studies at Arizona State University. She has been part of the cocreation process of building Indigenous Knowledge through the contribution of Tewa Women United's Research Methodology and Theory of Opide, a braiding of practice to action. She was one of sixteen visionary leaders across the country selected as the first cohort of Move to End Violence. She was selected in 2016 for the Stepping into Power Fellowship of Forward Together, a movement building fellowship for reproductive justice. She is the Executive Director of Tewa Women United.

PATRICIA MARINA TRUJILLO is a proud Manita, born and raised in the Española Valley. She received her BA in English and Law & Society from New Mexico State University. Her MA in English is from the University of Nebraska, and she received her PhD in US Latina/o Studies from the University of Texas at San Antonio. She practices community-based research methodology in her work; she is the faculty adviser for the ¡Sostenga! Farm and serves on the boards of the Northern Río Grande National Heritage Area, NewMexicoWomen.org, and Tewa Women United. She is the creative writing editor of *Chicana/Latina Studies: The Journal of Mujeres Activas en Letras y Cambio Social*. She is the Director of Equity and Diversity and an Associate Professor of English and Chicana/o Studies at Northern New Mexico College.

SIMÓN VENTURA TRUJILLO was born and raised in Albuquerque, New Mexico. He earned his BA in English and Philosophy from the University of New Mexico and his PhD in English Language and Literature from the University of Washington. He teaches and researches on Chicanx and Latinx literature, borderland methodologies, decolonial social movements, and comparative racialization in the Americas. His current book project is *Land Uprising: Native Story Power and the Insurgent Horizons of Latinx Indigeneity*. He is an Assistant Professor of Latinx Studies in the English Department at New York University.

NORMA A. VALENZUELA was born in Torreón, Coahuila, México, and arrived in Albuquerque, New Mexico in 1979. She earned an AA in Business Technology and a BUS with an emphasis in Spanish and Bilingual Education from the University of New Mexico. Her MA in Spanish Language and Culture and PhD in Spanish Cultural Studies, with an emphasis in Chicano/Latino and Latin American Cultural Studies, are from Arizona State University. Her writings appear in *Chicana/Latina Studies: The Journal of Mujeres Activas en Letras y Cambio Social*, *Chican@: Critical Perspectives and Praxis at the Turn of the 21st Century*, and the *International Journal of Curriculum and Social Justice*. Her book *Lourdes Portillo: Luchas feministas barriales y transnacionales en Después del terremoto, Las Madres y Señorita extraviada* is the first single-authored text that positions Portillo as a Chicana transnational filmmaker. She is working on a chapter for the first volume in the "MLA Options for Teaching" series, *Teaching the Narrative of Mexicana and Chicana Writers*. She is an Assistant Professor of Spanish at New Mexico Highlands University.

IRENE VÁSQUEZ specializes in the intersectional histories and politics of Mexican-descent populations in the Americas. Her research and teaching interests include US and transnational social and political movements. She coauthored *Making Aztlán: Ideology and Culture of the Chicana and Chicano Movement: Ideology, 1966–1977*, published by the University of New Mexico Press in 2014. She has written several essays in English and Spanish on the historical and contemporary relations between African Americans and people of Latin American descent in the Americas. Her current project is a history survey of Chicana women in the United States. She is the Chair of the Chicana and Chicano Studies Department at the University of New Mexico and serves as the Director of the Southwest Hispanic Research Institute. Under her leadership, from 2013–2018, UNM established a Department of Chicana and Chicano Studies and bachelor's, Master's, and doctoral programs in Chicana and Chicano Studies.

MYLA VICENTI CARPIO is a citizen of the Jicarilla Apache Nation and also of Laguna and Isleta Pueblo heritage. She is the author of *Indigenous Albuquerque* (2011). Vicenti Carpio is a coeditor with Jeffrey Shepherd (UTEP) of the "Critical Issues in Indigenous Studies" book series through the University of Arizona Press. She is an Associate Professor of American Indian Studies at Arizona State University.

JONATHAN WILSON is from Artesia, New Mexico. His BA and MA degrees in English are from Eastern New Mexico University. He holds a PhD in English from University of Texas at Arlington. He has published articles in *Studies in American Indian Literatures* (*SAIL*) and given numerous academic presentations, ranging in subject matter from Early American literature to twentieth-century American fiction to rhetorical theory. He specializes in Native American literature(s) and nineteenth- and twentieth-century American fiction, and also teaches technical/professional writing, argumentative strategies, literary theory, literary research and methods, and American, Transatlantic, Chicano, and women's literatures. He is currently an Associate Professor II of Humanities and English at Odessa College.

Page numbers in *italic* text indicate illustrations.

grounded regionality, 35, 45, 47–49. *See also* identity
Gutiérrez, Ernesto, 122
Gutiérrez Family (Cañón de Carnué Land Grant), 255
Gutiérrez Sisneros, Dr. Ana X, 294, 306

"Happily Ever After" (Ortiz), 227
HCPL (New Mexico Hispanic Culture Preservation League), 82–86
healing: and catharsis, 220–41; collective power of, 72, 87, 304; from colonial trauma, 71, 84, 94; and la cultura cura, xix, xx, xxi, 131; and curanderismo, 181, 183, 185, 248, 251; and decolonization, 59, 87; and narrative, 227; and place, 236; and querencia, 293; and self-care, 291. *See also* trauma; violence
herederos (heirs), *249*
la Hermandad, 261–62, 265, 266. *See also* Hermanos de La Fraternidad Piadosa de Nuestro Padre Jesús Nazareno
Hermanos de La Fraternidad Piadosa de Nuestro Padre Jesús Nazareno (The Brothers of the Pious Fraternity of Our Father Jesus the Nazarene), 248, *249*, 250, 261–62. *See also* la Hermandad
Hernández de Pulido, Doña Fidencia, 182, 185, 191, 192
Herrera, Adam, 321
"Hiding, West of Here" (Ortiz), 225–26
hierarchy, 66, 71, 103, 178
hills (lomas/lomitas), xiii, 246, *249*
Hispanism, 80
Hispanophiles, 79, 81, 85, 91, 96
Hispanos/Hispanics: and conquistador glory, 215–18; diasporic, 14, 43–44; diverse perspectives, 84; elite, 144, 157, 159; and *The Last Conquistador*

(2008), 86–87, 89; and New Mexico ethnic identity, 35–36; New Mexico Hispanic Culture Preservation League (HCPL), 82–86; and race, 22; terminology, 96, 219
Historia de la Nueva México (Villagrá), 79, 89, 91, 95–96
histories: acknowledgement of, 61; complex, 66; (mis)constructed, 146; decolonization of, 72; environmental, 161–62; and erasure, 58, 161, 164, 168–69, 173, 315; family, 273, 275; and film, 77; "Following the Manito Trail," 320–22; imposition of, 15, 64; Indigenous, 58, 59, 64, 65–66, 215–16; local, 39, 45; and memory, 58, 86, 92, 146; multiple, 54, 55, 60, 70, 274; New Western, 222–23; oral, 7; and poems and corridos, 319–20; shared, 215, 218, 223, 241; and storytelling, 278, 280, 283; Texas and New Mexico, 114–15
Hollywood Ten, 99–101
home (homeland): and Acoma Pueblo, 197–98; competing claims to, 86; homeplaces, 49, 53; and multiple histories, 55; and Ortiz, 221; and Plaza de Las Vegas, 14; and querencia, 33; and relationships, 297–99; (re) remembering and (re)imagining, 220–39, 241
"Home Country" (Ortiz), 228–29
house lots (solares), xiii, 246, 249
Houser, John S., 89–91
House Un-American Activities Committee (HUAC), 100–101, 113

iconography, 47, 312
identidad, grounded, 35, 44–45. *See also* identity
identity: Americanness, 32, 48;

identity (*continued*)

"American Way of Life," 123–24; artificially dichotomous notions of, 33; and citizenship, 23, 33–35, 47–48; and colonialism, 87; and community, 67; (re)defining, 222, 241; and food, 186–90; genízaro, 216–17; grounded identidad, 35, 44–45; grounded regionality, 35, 45, 47–49; imposition of, 15; Indigenous, 216–17; Indo-Hispano, 13, 21–23, 29, 306, 309; influence of film and media on, 77; and language, 184–85; and Las Vegas 4th of July Fiestas, 40–41; and mestiza consciousness, 180, 181, 183, 194; and patriotism, 32; and politics, 293; and querencia, 92, 292; scholarship, 222–24; social, 183; Spanish-American, 26–27; and story-sharing, 302; and storytelling, 269–70, 273–84; and terminology, 35–36, 113, 177, 244, 275, 301–2, 308–9. *See also* culture

Ideological State Apparatuses (ISAs), 104, 113

ideologies, 57, 104, 110, 113, 221, 224

Idle No More, 69

immigration, 100–101. *See also* migration

imperialism, 23, 66, 72, 81, 86, 98, 157. *See also* colonialism; government

incarceration, xix, 23

inclusion, 55, 71

Independence Day, 38–39, 42

Indian Pueblo Cultural Center, 69, 216

Indigenous Nations Library Program (UNM), 56

Indigenous peoples: activism, 69, 72, 210–13, 217–18; architecture, 203–5; ceremony, 174, 203–5, 214; and community, 70–71; and education, 69, 71–73, 192; histories, 58, 59, 64, 65–66,

215–16; identity, 216–17; knowing, 298; the Land and the People, 201; and land grants, 18, 19, 26–27, 29; language, 202, 204–5; and *The Last Conquistador* (2008), 86–87, 89; and mestizaje, 184–85; names, 215; in New Mexico, 54–55, 58–59, 61, 63; and place, 56–59; and querencia, 81, 174–75, 189; and racial discourse, 165, 168; and resistance, 210–13, 215–16; and slavery, 63, 149, 160, 252–53, 256; in the Southwest, 215–16; as sovereign nations, 65; and spirituality, 214; and tourism, 61; women, 140; in World War II, 20. *See also* American Indians; colonialism; genízaras/os; Native Americans; Pueblo Indians

Indo-Hispanos, 13, 21–23, 29, 199–200, 243–67, 306, 309. *See also* genízaras/os

inflation, 125

institutions, 104

Interstate 40, 18

ISAs (Ideological State Apparatuses), 104, 113

Isleta Pueblo, 263

"It Was That Indian" (Ortiz), 235–36

Jaremillo, Mariana, 151–52

Jarrico, Paul, 99

Jicarilla Apaches, 58, 70

Juárez, Benito, 85

K'a aimais'iwa, 207

Kat'ishtya (San Felipe), 202

Kawaika (Laguna), 202

Kaweshdima (Mount Taylor), 208

Kearny, Gen. Stephen Watts, 28, 36

Keresan People, 202

Kewa (Santo Domingo), 202

Kiowa, 251, 253, 256, 265

kitchen table organizing, 270–71, 288–91, 306

mercedes (land grants). *See* land grants
mestizaje, 181, 184–85, 309
mestizas/os, 26–27, 109, 152, 156–57, 160
Mestizx, 19–20
MeXicana identity, 140, 180, 182, 189,
    193–94
Mexican Americans: and colonialism,
    68; cultural identity, 115; elite, 157;
    and Eurocentric ideas, 66, 71; and
    land grants, 24–26; in *Salt of the Earth*
    (1954), 101, 102, 110, 113; in World
    War II, 20
Mexican-American War, 26, 54
Mexicanidad, 32, 52
Mexicans, 149–50
Mexico, 136, 160
"The Mexico-Texan" (Paredes), 115
migration: and colonialism, 66–67; and
    employment, 11, 43, 120, 269, 271,
    309–10, 322, 324; and querencia, 311,
    315, 319, 322–23. *See also* geography;
    immigration; labor
military service, 8, 28, 119, 120, 122, 310.
    See also World War II
miners, 76, 101–11, 236, 237, 242
molino (mill), 133–34, 137
"Molino abandonado" (Romero), 76–77,
    118, 131–34
Momaday, N. Scott, 222
montes (mountains), 246, *249*
moradas (prayer chapels), 248, *249*, 250,
    255, 261–62
mountain ranges (sierras), 246, *249*
mountains (montes), 246, *249*
Mount Taylor (Kaweshdima), 208
mulattos, 152
music, 39, 132–33, 314, 315
musicians (músicos), 248
mutualismo (mutualism), 7
"My Father's Song" (Ortiz), 233

nacimiento, 252
Naranjo, Cristina, 169
narratives: (re)appropriation of, 37–38;
    collective, 66; complex, 121; control
    of, 66; incomplete, 117–18, 124–31; and
    lived experiences, 68; and memory,
    145; nuanced, 94; (re)remembering
    and (re)imagining, 220–39, 241; in *Salt
    of the Earth* (1954), 110; settler, 64, 65;
    and social sciences, 241; what is false?
    129–31
nation, 33, 75
National Anthem, 32
National Hispanic Cultural Center Art
    Museum, 55
nationalism, 23, 26. *See also* patriotrism
native, 3, 136
Native Americans, 161–71, 174–75, 222,
    224, 242, 301. *See also* American
    Indians; Indigenous peoples; Pueblo
    Indians
Natural System (querencia model), 199,
    246, 249, 251, 259
Navajos, 26, 54, 187, 253, 255, 309. *See also*
    Diné
nepantilism, 141, 180, 181
Nepantla, 184, 187
New Deal, 67, 144. *See also* Works Proj-
    ects Administration (*la diabla a pie*)
New Mexico: El norte, xvi, xvii, 180,
    183, 185, 273–75, 293, 294, 298; ethnic
    identity, 35–36; as Indigenous space,
    58–59; myth of triracial harmony,
    26–27, 288; norteños, 183, 193, 309,
    310; points of arrival, 61; popular
    social imagination, 273–74; Southern,
    274–86; statehood, 149–50; Territorial
    Supreme Court, 143, 151–52. *See also*
    fiestas
New Mexico Cucui, xx

"New Mexico True" (NM Dept. of Tourism), 76–77, 117–18, 124–31, *127*, *128*, 134, 137

"New Mexico Truth" (CHI-St. Joseph's Children), 130–31, *131*

New World Cobalt/Comexico LLC, 111

norteños, 183, 193, 309, 310. *See also* Nuevomexicanas/os

Northern New Mexico College, 69

Northern Río Grande National Heritage Center, 93. *See also* Oñate Monument Resource and Visitors Center

nostalgia, 41, 43–45. *See also* memory

And Now, Miguel (1953), 76–77, 118–24, 134

"Nuestro Himno" (Our Anthem), 32

Nuevomexicanas/os: and *Agueda Martínez: Our People, Our Country* (1977), 187; fictional representations of in *Manhattan* (TV series), 161–65, 175; historical body, 144–57; and identity, 113, 293; in Los Alamos, NM, 140, 169, 171–75; in *Salt of the Earth* (1954), 99, 101–11; in the Sangre de Cristo Mountains, 118–24; and Spanish colonialism, 64; terminology, 177, 308–9. *See also* Manitas/os; norteños

Occom, Samson, 226–27

Ohkay Owingeh, 171, 307, 309

ojitos (springs), *249*, 250

Oñate, Juan de: and Acoma Pueblo, 65, 75–76, 79, 81, 88, 96, 206–7, 210–11, 218; controversies, 75–76, 79–94, 96, 218, 302; and Española Fiestas, 305; statue in Alcalde, NM, 64–65, 81–82, 210–11. *See also* colonialism; conquistadors

Oñate Monument Resource and Visitors Center, 81, 92–93

Opide, 302

oppression, 55, 57, 69, 94, 105–6, 165, 168

oral histories, 7

Ortiz, Simon, 198–99

Otero, Miguel A., 150

Our Lady of Sorrows, 36, 38

Oventic Zapatista camp, 212–14

Pablo Montoya Land Grant, 19, 29

Pacheco, Felipe, 319

Paloma (*Manhattan*), 165–68, 174, 178

"The Panic of 1862" (WPA), 153–54

"The Panther Waits" (Ortiz), 230–32

Paquimé, Chihuahua, Mexico, 203

parciantes (irrigators), *xviii*, 248, *249*, 250, 260

Paredes, Américo, 115

la patria chica, xv, xx

patriarchy, 23, 66, 71, 72, 99, 106

patriotrism, 14, 33, 38, 48. *See also* nationalism

Pecos River, 111

Pedro Sánchez Land Grant, 173

"Las Penas de los betabeleros" (Sánchez), 317–18

Penitentes, 248, 261–62

peons, 148, 149, 150–57, 253. *See also* debt peonage

Perea, Don José Leander, 153–57

Perea, Robert, 321

Physical System (querencia model), 199, 246, 248, 249–50, 259

pig roast (matanza), 305

place: belonging to, 2–3; and healing, 236; in Indigenous lands, 56–57; and Las Vegas 4th of July Fiestas, 40–41; placemaking, 15, 55, 57–58, 60; and querencia, xvi, 33; sense of place, 55–59, 181–82, 184–85, 186–87; and storytelling, 198–99, 277–79, 284. *See also* geography; querencia; space

race: and antiblackness, 23; and class,
23; Critical Race Theory, 278; and
Indigenous sovereign nations, 65; and
labor rights, 104; legal categories of,
160; in Los Alamos, NM, 170–71; in
Manhattan (TV series), 164, 165–68,
173; and New Mexico statehood,
149–50; and the Nuevomexicana
body, 143–57; and regional contexts,
69; "reverse" racism, 295, 296; and
sexuality, 145, 146, 156. *See also* debt
peonage; privilege; slavery; white
supremacy
The Radiation Exposure Compensation
Act, 242
radicalism, 18, 23, 24–25, 26. *See also*
activism; resistance
Ranchos de Taos, NM, 249
Recopilación de las leyes de los reinos de
las Indias (Laws of the Indies), 246
Redman, Ann, 320
The Red Nation, 63. *See also* activism
regionality, grounded, 35, 45, 47–49. *See*
also identity
relationships, 288, 293, 297
religion: Catholic Church, 207, 252, 262,
265; and ceremony, 174, 203–5, 214,
248, 250, 305; Christianity, 149, 204,
205, 215; iconography, 312; saints, 250,
262, 263, 312, 317; societies, 250, *259,*
261–65; and spirituality, 184–86, 214;
traditions, 314
repartimiento, 149, 151, 159
resiliency, 7, 197, 243–44, 246, 248, 251,
258–60, 265–66, 313, 322
resistance, 36–37, 71, 106–11, 184, 210–13,
215–16, 234, 277. *See also* activism;
radicalism
resolana, xiii–xv
Revueltas, Rosaura, 100–101

riítos (streams), 246, 250. *See also* ritos
(streams)
Río Bravo, 187
Río Grande, 187, 276–77, 281, 283
ríos (rivers), 246, *249,* 250
Río San José (Chuna), 208
riparian zones (bosques), 246, *249*
ritos (streams), *249. See also* riítos
(streams)
ritual societies, 250, *259,* 261–65
Rivera, Dr. José, 266
rivers (ríos), 246, 250
Riverton, WY, 312–14, 321
Robinson, Cedric, 23
Rodarte family, 311
Romero, Alfonso, 310
Romero, Elías, 310
Romero, Eric, 320
Romero, José de la Cruz, 151–52
Romero, Juan Andrés, 310
Romero, Levi, 76–77, 118, 131–34, 136
Romo, David, 88
rutas de ceremonía (ceremonial routes),
248, 250

sacred space, 80, 132, 168, 174, 294
salas (community halls), 248, 249, *249*
Salt of the Earth (1954), 76, 98–111
San Antonio settlement, 249, 253, 255–56.
See also Cañón de Carnué Land
Grant (Carnué)
Sánchez, Alfonso, 20
Sanchez, Dr. Corrine Kaa Pedi Povi, 287
Sanchez, Kathy Wan Povi, 306
Sánchez, Maggie, 317–18
Sánchez, Mayor Henry, 43
Sánchez, Mayor Javier, 219
Sandia Pueblo, 263
San Felipe (Kat'ishtya), 202
sangrías (lateral ditches), 246

spirituality, 184–86, 214
springs (ojitos), *249*, 250
State Apparatus, 104, 113
stereotypes, 61–63, 67–68, 164, 222, 242
"A Story of How a Wall Stands" (Ortiz),
   234–35
story-sharing, 288, 293, 300–304
storytelling: and authority, 288;
   challenging stereotypes, 222;
   and connection to place, 198–99,
   277–79; and identity, 269–70, 273–84;
   importance of, 269, 271; and land, 13–
   14, 220–39; and organic radicalism, 18;
   and power, 61; and querencia, 188–89,
   192–93; rebellious, 28; and story-
   sharing, 300–304. *See also* testimonio
streams (riítos), 246, 250
Strottman, Theresa, 173
subject positions, 106
suertes (farm plots), 246, 248, *249*, 253–54,
   256, 260. *See also* agrarian life
Surumatx del sur, 275, 286
survivance, 234
sustainability, 243–48
SWIA (Southwest Indigenous Alliance),
   211

Talweg Creative, 137
T'amaya (Santa Ana), 202
tanques (water reservoirs), 250
tareas de obligación (obligatory
   community work contribution), 248,
   249–52
Taylor, Carl, 261–62
technology of democratics, 110
Tejanos, 114–15, 136
Tererro Mine, 111
terminology: according to Chino, 219;
   according to Fonseca-Chávez, 96;
   according to Gómez, 177; according

to Gonzales, 244; according to
Gorman, 35–36; according to
Hernández, 159; according to
Medina-López, 275, 285, 286;
according to Roybal, 113; according
to Trujillo, Sanchez, and Davis, 306;
according to Wilson, 242; Chávez,
13, 21–23, 29; "forefathers," 42; and
identity, 301–2, 308–9
testimonio, 140–41, 187, 278, 322. *See also*
   storytelling
Tewa, 292, 301
Tewah Towah, 292, 302
Tewa Women United, 287, 307
Texas, 114–15, 136, 153–54, 173
Thanksgiving, 58
"That's the Place Indians Talk About"
   (Ortiz), 236
Thorp, Annette Hesch, 159
The Three Peoples mural (UNM), 15,
   62–63, 67–68. *See also* colonialism
Tierra Amarilla courthouse raid, 20–21,
   24–25. *See also* La Alianza Federal de
   Mercedes (The Federal Alliance of
   Land Grants)
Tiguex Park (Albuquerque, NM), 65
Tijeras, NM, 256
Tijerina, Reies López, 7, 13, 19–20, 24–25
Torreón, Coahuila, Mexico, 180, 183, 184,
   190, 191, 192
Torres, Miguel, 216
tourism: and economy, 137; in El Paso,
   TX, 96; and Indigenous peoples, 61;
   and modern-day colonial violence,
   88, 89; and "New Mexico True" (NM
   Dept. of Tourism), 76–77, 117–18, 124–
   31, *127*, *128*, 134, 137. *See also* capitalism;
   economy
tradiciones (traditions), 7–8. *See also*
   tradition

tradition: and community, 39–46; as contestatory practice, 14, 42–46; and culture, 296; in Embudo Valley, 7–8; and food, 41, 311–12, 314; and Las Vegas 4th of July Fiestas, 39–41; and migrations, 311–12, 314, 317, 322; in *And Now, Miguel* (1953), 118

Trammell, Clorinda, 311

transculturation, 39, 42

transference, 223, 224, 230, 235, 238. *See also* catharsis

trauma: acknowledgement of, 66, 86, 87–89; and the Acoma People, 206–7; and catharsis, 220–41; healing from, 71–73, 84, 94; legacy of historical, 88, 89, 206, 220, 224, 230, 235; Native accounts of, 220–39; and unresolved grief, 230. *See also* colonialism; healing; violence

treaties, 227, 242

Treaty of Guadalupe Hidalgo, 13, 24–26, 28, 29, 113, 177

triptych, 75–77, 116–18

Trujillo, Dr. Patricia, 70, 287

Trujillo, Modesto, 262

Tsé Bit' a' í (Rock That Has Wings), 56

T'siya (Zia), 202

umbilical cord burial, 56, 141, 185–86

United States Forest Service, 7, 20, 257

United States Government: American narrative, 121–22; Americanness, 32, 48; "American Way of Life," 123–24; and antiblackness, 23; and anticommunist movement, 100–101, 117, 119–24; Bureau of Land Management (BLM), 7, 10; Census Bureau, 21–23, 52; El Morro National Monument, 75, 83; and Indigenous sovereign nations, 65, 222; and

institutions, 104; and Kearny, 28, 36; and land grants, 30, 256–58, 257; and land theft, 20, 37, 162–63, 174, 226–27; military service, 8, 28, 119, 120, 122, 310; and privilege, 296; The Radiation Exposure Compensation Act, 242; and soft power, 122–23; State Department, 117, 118–24; stories of mestizx, 19–20; Supreme Court, 242, 256–57; Territorial Supreme Court, 143, 151–52; Thirteenth Amendment, 150, 152; treaties, 227, 242; and US Information Service narrative, 121–22; view of Mexicans in nineteenth century, 149–50. *See also* Anglos; colonialism; white supremacy

University of New Mexico, 15, 56, 62–64, 67–68

University of Wyoming, 321

uplands (altitos), 246, 249

Utes, 26, 251, 252, 253, 255, 256, 265, 309

Valadez, John J., 82, 84

Valdez, Dr. Facundo B., 265, 267

Valdez, Lina and Chemo, 42

Valencia settlement, 253

Valenzuela López, José Tobías, 182, 191

Vásquez, Esperanza, 187

vecinos, xv–xvi, xvii, xviii

Vidal, Teresa (*Salt of the Earth*), 108, 109

Vigil, Cleofes, xv, xvii

Vigil, Emilio, 311, 312–13

Vigil, Julián Josué, 320

Villa de Nuestra Señora de los Dolores de Las Vegas Grandes, 36. *See also* Las Vegas, NM

violence, 27, 63, 88–89, 104, 113, 147–48, 154, 159. *See also* colonialism; healing; trauma

Virgen de Guadalupe, 185

Washbushuka (Chaco Canyon), 202
water, 33, 186–87, 208, 246, *249*, 250,
    276–77. *See also* acequias
Water is Life, 69
"The Way You See Horses" (Ortiz), 226
wetlands (ciénegas), 246, *249*
white supremacy, 66, 71, 96–97, 288,
    294, 296, 298, 302, 304. *See also*
    Anglos; Europeans; United States
    Government
Wilson, Michael, 99
Winters, Frank (*Manhattan*), 165–68, 174
women: at Acoma Pueblo, 201; of Cañón
    de Carnué Land Grant, 261, 262;
    Chicanas, 110, 194, 301; and cultural
    capital, 193; and debt peonage,
    139–40, 143–57; desert, 187–9; and
    the domestic sphere, 107–11, 143–57;
    elite, 157; feminists, 98, 143, 147, 301;
    genízaras, 31; Hispanas, 144, 157, 159;
    in Los Alamos, NM, 169–75; and
    Matachines (Matachín Dancers),
    263; mestizas, 109, 156–57; MeXicana
    identity, 140, 180, 182, 189, 193–94;
    Native, 292; Nuevomexicanas, 140,

144–57, 187, 293; and safe space, 270; in
    Salt of the Earth (1954), 76, 99, 106–11;
    and slavery, 147–48; and story-sharing,
    300–304; Women's Guild, 261, 262.
    See also gender; sexuality
*Women's Tales from the New Mexico WPA:
    La Diabla a Pie*, 144–45, 153–57
Works Projects Administration (*la
    diabla a pie*), 144–45, 153–57. *See also*
    New Deal
World War II, 19–20, 29, 30, 43–44, 261,
    263, 265. *See also* military service
Woven Stone (Ortiz), 234–35
Wyoming, 310–22

Yermo, Durango, Mexico, 182, 183, 184,
    186
youth, 15, 60, 62, 63, 69, 260, 265. *See also*
    children

Zapata, Carmen, 187
Zapatista Movement, 211–14
Zia (T'siya), 202
Zimmerman, James, 62
zoquete, *xiv*

CPSIA information can be obtained
at www.ICGtesting.com
Printed in the USA
LVHW041631130223
739371LV00003B/78